Gladness Their Escort

D1453553

Gladness Their Escort

Homiletic Reflections For Sundays and Feastdays

Years A, B and C

by

Monika K. Hellwig

A Michael Glazier Book
THE LITURGICAL PRESS
Collegeville, Minnesota

ABOUT THE AUTHOR

Monika K. Hellwig is Professor of Theology at Georgetown University. Among her many publications are *Jesus, The Compassion of God; The Eucharist and The Hunger of the World; Understanding Catholicism;* and *Sign of Reconciliation and Conversion: The Sacrament of Penance for Our Times,* which is published in The Message of the Sacraments series of which she is the Editor.

A Michael Glazier Book
published by
THE LITURGICAL PRESS

Typography by Connie Runkel.
Cover art by Erica Hellwig.

*To my colleagues of the
Tuesday Eucharist Group
at Georgetown University,
this book is dedicated
with gratitude and affection.*

Contents

Year A

Year B

Year C

Year A

First Sunday of Advent

READINGS: Is 2:1-5; Rom 13:11-14; Mt 24:37-44.

Remember how critical the moment is. It is time for you to wake out of sleep, for deliverance is nearer to us now than it was when we first believed. It is far on in the night; day is near. Rom 13:11.

It is the beginning of Advent again, and once more the readings challenge us to realize that we are not simply marking time with our lives. Scripture is always reminding us that history, our history, has a goal that is not distant but can be attained in various ways in our own time, our own lives and our own decisions and actions. Redemption is now, and not a thousand or a hundred years from now, yet this is not an altogether welcome message. In our own times, no less than in Isaiah's or Paul's, people are curiously anxious to cling to the old order they know, with all its acknowledged injustices, fears, bullying and hatreds. Advent comes to us, therefore, as a yearly challenge to rise out of such lethargy and small-mindedness into the great hopes which our faith offers us.

Isaiah, the poet, is at the same time an eminently practical person. Surrounded by great conquering forces, by voices willing to compromise morality for the sake of the balance of power, and by all manner of political intrigue and dishonesty, Isaiah proclaims international peace and well-being as the fruit of loyalty to God's covenant. Mount Zion, the mountain of the Lord's house, is the center of that peace because it is the symbol and focal point of the divine covenant. The mountain of the Lord is to be raised above all other mountains not in conquest but in peace. That is to say, the peoples will climb God's mountain of their own accord, attracted by the instruction of the Law and the vision of the prophets. Yet Isaiah is not speaking of some airy fantasy; the world for which he promises a lasting peace is the real world of his day and ours. If peace with justice has not succeeded in the world, that is because it has not yet really been tried, at least not in terms of the divine covenant of universal respect and concern. It is clear that in our local and national and international affairs we are really in the same position as the people to whom Isaiah prophesied in his own days. We still choose to seek security in our power to kill or subdue others, in our cunning in balancing the opposing forces in a stalemate, and in the skillfulness of our deceptions and intrigues. The reading from Isaiah asks us to have more faith in God and more hope in the divine promises.

Paul, in the second reading, addresses a community which though residing at the center of the Roman Empire does not seem to include those who wield power of a dominating kind in the society at large. Yet he sees them as people who can have a significant impact by the way they shape their own communities from within, so as to become a leavening force in society. While Isaiah envisions the transformed society on a grand scale, Paul looks at it microscopically. But his message is the same: redemption is at hand; in the grace of God life can be profoundly changed; the old order is already overcome in principle just as the night is ended and the day at hand when the light begins to dawn. But as much as Paul insists in all his writings on divine grace, there is no mistaking his insistence that it is also necessary for people to shake off their lethargy, to wake from their sleep and live in the realization that the day of salvation is dawning now, and that it makes demands on the way we live our lives and make our decisions.

As so often happens in the liturgy, the Gospel reading gives us in story and image what the second reading has presented in the form of exhortation of an immediately practical kind. The story of Noah and the flood is an obvious prototype of situations calling for attentive discernment of what God is doing in history, or of God's judgment on what people are doing with their history. Perhaps the suggestion in the allusion that Jesus makes to the story of Noah is that we are always in a time of ultimate decisions and ultimate consequences. The time of redemption is at hand but we must recognize it and acknowledge it if we are not to be overtaken by worldwide disaster. Hence the image of the men in the field and the women at the mill, overtaken by the decisive moment of the coming of the Son of Man.

But perhaps the more interesting image is that of the burglar breaking into the house during the night. That appears to have been a favorite image of that time, representing significant but unpredictable events. At first sight this seems a strange image for the coming of salvation, yet there is one aspect of it that is most apt. To prevent a burglary it is necessary to be prepared at all times. It is wise not to postpone safety measures to some later, more convenient time, as though burglary were a possibility remote in time and not of present interest or concern. The burglar, of course, comes precisely at the unexpected time, before the householder has made adequate preparation. The point is not that the Lord wants to catch us by surprise in a state of unpreparedness. Rather, it keeps happening that way because we do not expect the hour of grace to be here and now, but are quite content to envision it as somewhere in the far distant future making no demands on our present.

The liturgy of Advent keeps telling us: salvation is near.

Second Sunday of Advent

READINGS: Is 11:1-10; Rom 15:4-9; Mt 3:1-12.

Repent, for the kingdom of heaven is upon you! . . . Prepare a way for the Lord; clear a straight path for him. Mt 3:2, 3.

Lest we should lose ourselves in visionary dreams and romantic imaginings of a far off ultimate consummation, the liturgy stations the practical figure of the Baptist across the middle of Advent, on the second and third Sundays. Earnest longing and starry eyed expectation are not enough; Advent is a call to maintain our hope with fortitude, as the excerpt from Romans reminds us.

Once again Isaiah insists that the hope we have is of one who is to bring justice and vindication to the poor and the helpless. In its original context this passage promises a new king in the Davidic line—one who will be a perfect ruler and through whom there will come a great peace, a great reconciliation. But the price of this peace is made quite clear: ruthless oppressors will be struck down, wickedness will be punished and avarice restrained. It is quite clear that God is on the side of the poor and the oppressed, not because of any special merit of theirs, but because of their suffering and their need. Isaiah's language is poetic, but his concerns are practical in the economic and political realm.

It is not immediately obvious that the passage from Romans pursues a similar thought, but in its context it is also concerned with community and reconciliation and with the price that must be paid. It is part of a plea to followers of Jesus to do the things that make for peace and for the building up of community life, even though this will involve certain renunciations. The price of peace is always some kind of renunciation, because true peace is only made by righting injustices by which some of us profit, and by extending genuine compassion beyond our own interest groups. When Paul writes that the ancient scriptures are for our instruction, encouraging us to maintain our hope with fortitude, it is clear that he sees the fulfillment of the promises as something that must come about within the community by the free cooperation of the community, completing what Jesus has begun. In fact, Paul frequently seems concerned about people who seem to expect salvation to come from heaven without any real need for conversion of human persons and human society in the process.

Such also is the preoccupation of John the Baptist, who comes in the garb and spirit of Elijah. The gospels identify John with the message of consolation and encouragement of Isaiah 40, in which God's own voice goes out over the waste land calling the people to prepare themselves for the coming salvation of God. It is the advent message that has meaning as long as human history lasts. We always find ourselves to greater or lesser extent in situations that seem like wilderness or waste land left by human devastation. Matthew tells us that the rugged figure of the Baptist comes upon the scene with a simple message: preparing the way of the Lord involves radical repentance. The Hebrew word implies turning around, retracing one's steps, changing direction. The Greek word of the New Testament text implies a changing of one's mind, one's outlook, one's horizons and expectations. In the English translation we seem to miss the radical demands implied in the message. It is much more than being sorry about a particular action and resolving not to repeat it. Rather, it is a matter of a kind of death and rebirth, of a profound transformation. It is this that is signified by the immersion in the waters of the Jordan.

It is not only the figure of John that is symbolic in this passage, but also the Jordan river. In the history of Israel, the Jordan river represented the last step, the last crossing, into the Promised Land. To pass through the waters of the Jordan in baptism is to recapitulate a moment of hope and of commitment. It is a renewed acceptance of the vocation of God's Chosen People. It is an acknowledgement of a new realization of the meaning of that calling—a fresh beginning, and an openness to divine grace. But John is adamant that this does not remain in the realm of ritual and of feelings of elation and consolation. It is a practical matter. John demands fruits of repentance, and insists that promises of salvation are also warnings of a judgment to come. The savior is coming, but he comes as to a threshing floor with a winnowing fan to separate the good seed from the chaff. There is to be no deception and no escape from that judgement. He comes with a baptism of spirit and fire which will be decisive.

The liturgy lifts this proclamation out of pre-Christian time, and sets it before us again as a message about our present and our future. It is a message about the seriousness of decisions that we make in our own society in our own times—decisions for peace or conflict, for justice or privilege, for community or partisan interest. The savior is before us in our future with a winnowing fan that will sift it all, with a baptism of spirit and fire that will reveal it all in its true value. It is set before us again so that we may maintain our hope with fortitude.

Third Sunday of Advent (Gaudete)

READINGS: Is 35:1-6, 10; Jas 5:7-10; Mt 11:2-11.

The Lord's redeemed come home; they shall enter Zion with shouts of triumph, crowned with everlasting gladness. Gladness and joy shall be their escort, and suffering and weariness shall flee away.   Is 35:10.

The Advent scripture readings present a curious mixture. They exhort us so to live and act as to be ready for the Lord's coming, but they also promise fulfillment far beyond our deserts and even our dreams. They offer promises but also warnings. They counsel patience but also a kind of passionate impatience. Isaiah's comfort to an exiled people gives us the poetic and visionary aspect of advent: the weary refugees return home shouting in triumph, crowned with joy, escorted by gladness. It is made to sound like the end of a fairy tale, and so it must have seemed to the exiles returning to their own land.

In case the fairy tale quality of it might make it seem unreal, unpractical, or impossibly distant, the second reading is from James who is always practical and well aware of human limitations and foibles. Having set out in his letter to provide a kind of manual for proper Christian behavior, in which everyone comes in for some scolding about one thing or another, James comes finally, in the passage read for this day, to counsel patience. Such counsels of patience are all too easily misunderstood. They are not intended as encouragement in inactivity. James refers to the farmer waiting for the precious crop, knowing that the crop needs the autumn and spring rains. But it is clear that the farmer who is passive in waiting for rain must be active and diligent in tilling and planting and harvesting. James also refers to the prophets who are passive in expectation of the salvation of God but intensely and obstinately active in speaking both welcome and unwelcome words in the name of God. This is the kind of patience that James recommends—a patient perseverance in acting according to our hope when there seems to be no change brought about by it. And this is the kind of patience appropriate to any time in history and to any human society.

The Gospel reading reintroduces John the Baptist—the great model combining patience and passionate impatience. John, who once long ago sent his disciples to Jesus, sends us today with the same questions, so that we may learn to see the same signs. Is Jesus the one that is to come? We too are blessed if we do not find the concerns and priorities of Jesus a stumbling block. We are blessed if we can acknowledge that the one who is to come in judgement is the one who was concerned to give sight to the blind, agility to the lame, a clean bill of health to outcast lepers, hearing to the deaf, life to the dead and good news to the poor.

This point about good news to the poor appears as a very significant messianic sign. It is not only a matter of good news, but of good news to those who most need it. That means that the Gospel can be in some ways threatening to the powerful and privileged. Whether we can hear it as good news depends on the degree of our solidarity with the poor and suffering of all kinds. We are blessed if we can recognize messengers like John as true prophets. Then we also shall have gladness as our escort.

Fourth Sunday of Advent

READINGS: Is 7:10-14; Rom 1:1-7; Mt 1:18-24.

Ask the Lord your God for a sign, from lowest Sheol or from highest heaven . . . the Lord himself shall give you a sign: a young woman is with child, and she will bear a son, and will call him Immanuel.   Is 7:11, 14.

The message is discernment, attention, willingness to see. There is something pathetic and of universal significance in the dialogue between God's prophet and Ahaz. The prophet has tried to persuade Ahaz not to ally himself with ruthless and unscrupulous powers, but to follow the way of the Lord. To back up his exhortation, Isaiah invites Ahaz to seek a sign from God. Ahaz does not want to see a sign because he has no intention of following the good advice. That is where this dialogue begins, and that may be where many of us stand much of the time—not anxious to see any signs from God because of the change in our lives which such signs might signal. But the outcome has a universal significance also: God sends signs all the time, is self-revealing all the time, in spite of human unwillingness to look.

Yet, as the letter of Paul to the Romans points out, the revelation that is made is grace and peace. The good news brought by the prophets of old is manifest in the new sign, the great sign, of Jesus, Son of David and Son of God. Paul, who was himself so reluctant to open his eyes to the sign, has become the herald to proclaim that sign to others far and wide, even in Rome, that they may believe and become truly the people of God. The appeal to the Romans is an appeal to all of us. The Sign of Jesus is as new and surprising in our own days as it has ever been. But is is also a challenge to see in a new way and to act on what we see. And that is the Advent theme.

The Gospel reading for the day gives us the story of the birth of the Messiah, citing the Isaian text and highlighting the allusions that show this birth as the great sign. Every birth is a sign of love and reconciliation and of the forgiveness of old infidelities, but this birth is the great reconciliation. Matthew tells of Jesus of the house of David, born by the power of the Holy Spirit, named both savior and Emmanuel (God with us), reconciling the new and the old, the wonderful and the ordinary, bringing new hope. The familiarity of the story should not dull our perception to its ever new meaning.

The question to us is whether we are willing to seek the sign that is offered to us, even thrust before us, or whether we will say with Ahaz that we are not interested in asking for a sign, that we do not care for God's communication to us because we have our own alliances with power and influence and wealth as provision for our security. When we recall what manner of man Jesus was, and what his concerns and interests were, it may take a certain kind of courage to ask for the sign to be made clear to us in our times.

Christmas

READINGS:

At Midnight:	Is 9:1-6; Tit 2:11-14; Lk 2:1-14
At Dawn:	Is 62:11-12; Tit 3:4-7; Lk 2:15-20
During the Day:	Is 52:7-10; Heb 1:1-6;
	Jn 1:1-18 (or 1-5, 9-14).

So the Word became flesh; he came to dwell among us, and we saw his glory, such glory as befits the Father's only Son, full of grace and truth.

Jn 1:14.

In spite of all commercial efforts to trivialize and foreshorten our hope and our celebration of Christmas, the liturgy for this feast opens up each year great vistas into promised future redemption—vistas that transform the possibilities of our present. The very first reading at the Midnight Eucharist which opens the celebration is the declaration that light has dawned for people who have been walking in darkness. One might be tempted to stop there and build an entire Christmas meditation around this image. If Isaiah can so celebrate the ordinary birth of a new prince of the Davidic line after a period of foreign domination and oppression, we certainly have greater cause to rejoice with new hope. If Isaiah so readily expresses new hope in this prince as a savior figure and a future prince of peace, we have far more reason to apply these titles to Jesus and to look to him for a peace based on justice and right-eousness.

The second reading at midnight, from the letter to Titus, takes up the same image of dawn: God's grace has dawned on the human race with the appearance of Jesus in the midst of our troubled history, promising a future fulfillment full of healing and splendor, a future that quite changes the interpretation and possibilities of our present. It is a fitting introduction to the Gospel reading chosen for this Eucharist, poised between a timeless fairy-tale quality and the dogged ordinary reality of taxation and of the all too common ruthless disregard of officials for the human dilemmas caused by public edicts.

The brutal taxing of the poor, the awkward journey from the far north to the southern province for registration, the lodging pro-blem—all these are the stuff of everyday life for many ordinary people in our own times. The vision of light and splendor and healing to come refers not to some mythic time but to this historical time in which such things as these happen.

Those who celebrate the Eucharist at dawn hear first the proclamation of the third Isaiah collection: the Lord comes to ransom and deliver his long sought people, to reward their per-severing hope and fidelity. But the passage from Titus, still presenting the coming of Jesus into our history as a new dawn for the whole world, stresses the utter generosity and gratuity of it; the mercy and kindness by which God offers new possibilities to a broken world goes measurably beyond anything that good deeds and faithful lives have earned. The new birth that we share and the renewing power of the Holy Spirit shed abroad through Jesus Christ should set us beyond all discouragement concerning the affairs of the human race.

It is in this context, in the dawn Mass, that the Lukan infancy narrative offers us the revelation to the poor, the marginated, the unimportant, as represented by the shepherds. There is something very moving in the story of the shepherds. They are so greatly consoled by a discovery which makes no immediate or practical change in their lives of extreme hardship and poverty. Their joy is in the proclamation of the messianic birth that promises future happiness for all the people and the dawning of a great peace. It is a selfless joy over the future salvation of the whole people, and it speaks of a kind of solidarity in human community which is itself a sign of redemption.

At the Eucharist celebrated during the day, Second Isaiah introduces the theme—the feet hastening over the mountains bearing the good news, the watchmen raising the cry as they see the Lord returning to the rescue, and the people shouting together as the redeeming power of God is revealed to the whole world and all the nations. In this Eucharist also the proclamation from Isaiah is followed immediately by a New Testament passage identifying the moment of the great triumphal breakthrough with the appearance of Jesus in human history. Hebrews opens with a comprehensive theological statement about the person of Jesus and his redeeming role: he is the shining forth of divine splendor, the image, the creative and sustaining word, the redeemer of a world gone astray, the authentic son. It is his very existence that entirely changes the possible outcome of human history.

When all this has already been said, the prologue of John's Gospel serves to draw these themes and images together in its powerfully symbolic narrative. It is the Divine Word by which God creates and which God is speaking into our history which is embodied in the human Jesus; in his whole being he is that very word. In him there echoes through history unmistakably what God is saying to us. In him the light of God's splendor has become visible to human eyes, and the very life of God becomes our life, a life of undreamed-of intensity and of healing, transcending power. Revelation is become very clear and concrete in the historical event of

Jesus. The Christmas question is how seriously we believe that in Jesus the Word that God speaks to us is made human so that we might more easily listen.

Feast of the Holy Family

READINGS: Sir 3:2-6, 12-14; Col 3:12-21; Mt 2:13-15, 19-23.

Respect for a father atones for sins, and to honor your mother is to lay up a fortune. A son who respects his father will be made happy by his own children; when he prays he will be heard.   Sir 3:6-7.

The liturgy of this feast is troublesome because it is being made to say many things all at once. It continues the story of Jesus from the infancy narrative as the Gospel of Matthew relates it. It also offers general words of wisdom about human existence as shaped by family life. At the same time it presents exhortations about Christian community life as distinctively redeemed and redemptive.

The lesson from the wisdom literature offers reflections upon universal patterns of human life—reflections which, upon quiet consideration, turn out to be self-evident. Each generation shapes the conditions in which life will be lived in the future. This happens in the family circle and also in the larger society. It means that we are responsible in our decisions and actions not only for the making of our own lives and personalities, but in large measure also for the making of the lives and personalities of others. This is certainly the sense of the doctrine of original sin: each and every life is burdened by the consequences of prior destructive deeds. But the heritage of Hebrew wisdom also insists upon the acknowledgment of the "merits of the ancestors", that is to say upon the recognition that we are deeply indebted to those who have gone before us for all that they have done to build a good and cohesive society, and to prepare healthy and helpful conditions of human life in the world in our times. To acknowledge both the heritage of sin and the merits of the ancestors implies in turn a sense of responsibility for the shaping of the future.

When we turn to the second reading we seem to move to the more particular. The passage from Colossians is addressed to a Christian community and is concerned with the manner of life that is characteristically Christian. What seems to be particular, and goes to some extent beyond the advice in the Wisdom literature of the Hebrew Scriptures, is the emphasis on forbearance, compassion, patience and forgiveness—all redemptive virtues, that is, virtues needed in a situation that is not perfect. These Christians are not only exhorted to be good people, truthful, honest and caring for one another, but they are being asked to be in some measure heroic in situations which are often unjust. Paul's specific advice for personal relationships is obviously not a timeless Christian order for society, because it includes, for instance, (just beyond today's excerpt) an admonition to slaves to accept their condition. We should reflect therefore not on the latter but on the spirit of the admonition, because that is relevant to all times and situations.

The third reading continues the infancy narrative with the flight into Egypt and the return to settle in Nazareth, drawing a parallel with Israel's origins; the patriarchs had fled to Egypt for survival from famine and had left Egypt to become God's people and heirs of the promises. In this broad symbolic sense also, the story of exile and return is a model for Christian life.

In a narrower sense it is not helpful to take the Holy Family as the model for Christian family life because the circumstances were unique and because we know almost nothing about their life together, except that Scripture insists that they were bent upon discerning and doing the will of God. The feast of the Holy Family is a celebration of our human bonds with Jesus of Nazareth, and therefore of our redeeming bonds of grace with all the human family, but particularly the poor, the distressed and the despised.

Solemnity of Mary, the Mother of God, and Giving of the Name Jesus

READINGS: Num 6:22-27; Gal 4:4-7; Lk 2:16-21.

Eight days later the time came to circumcise him, and he was given the name Jesus, the name given by the angel before he was conceived.   Lk 2:21.

Like the Sunday within the octave of Christmas, this feast blends together several different themes. As the feast of the circumcision of Jesus, it celebrates the bond we Christians have in the person of Jesus with our Jewish antecedents and with our Jewish brethren in the contemporary world. As the octave of Christmas it echoes the Christmas theme of gratitude and expectation, looking back with thanksgiving for the event of Jesus in the midst of our human history, and looking forward with attentive discernment to the completion of that event in a fulness of salvation yet to come for the whole world.

At the same time this feast, standing at the entrance to the calendar year, commemorates and celebrates the naming of Jesus: *yeshua*, God saves. And the tradition of the Church identifies this day of the savior's naming as the solemnity of Mary, symbol and representative of the Church, the community of believers and disciples. It is certainly this interweaving of the themes which explains the choice of the readings. The theme of the name is presented first. In the reading from Numbers it is the name of the transcendent God that is invoked upon Israel in blessing. The liturgy suggests a parallel in the invoking of the name of Jesus, because Scripture prompts us to say that the name of Jesus is "Lord", hinting at divinity, suggesting the point of encounter with God in creation and history.

The reading from Galatians gives us the Christmas echo: the redeeming birth; God's own Son born of woman under the law; the wonderful exchange in which the divine Word becomes human that we might become in some sense divinized; the Son's acceptance of slave conditions so that the slaves might enter into the condition of sins. The theme links the Christian experience with the liberation feast of Israel—a coming out of subjection into freedom and responsible peoplehood in the moment of Exodus, celebrated in Passover. Indeed Paul's vision links the birth with the Resurrection.

The Gospel reading continues the infancy narrative in Luke's version, which gives us the adoration of the shepherds and the naming of Jesus. In effect the adoration of the shepherds is also a story in which Jesus is named or proclaimed as savior, deliverer, the one looked for, because the shepherds come to see for themselves and to acknowledge the angelic revelation made to them. And these shepherds are the poor, the despised, the people who do not count.

Here especially, Mary emerges quietly as the representative and symbol of the community of believing disciples; she treasures the revelatory experiences and ponders over the testimonies as foundation for discerning the way of salvation. This certainly continues to be our task as church. Here and elsewhere the New Testament points to the figure of Mary as representative and exemplary, and Christian iconography has shown her most usually as the one who presents Jesus to the world, as the Church is called to do. This is the fuller meaning of celebrating the name of Jesus.

Feast of the Epiphany

READINGS: Is 60:1-6; Eph 3:2-3, 5-6; Mt 2:1-12.

Though darkness covers the earth and dark night the nations, the Lord shall shine upon you...the nations shall march towards your light, and their kings to your sunrise.   Is 60:2-3.

Today we celebrate the first of the three feasts of the manifestation of the Lord: the adoration of the magi, the baptism of Jesus by John, and the marriage feast at Cana. The emphasis in this first celebration is certainly on the gathering of the Gentiles to witness the self-revelation of God, and all three readings are concerned with journeys from afar to share in the joy and transforming power of the revelation.

As so often happens, the Isaian passage is one that originally referred to a particular rebuilding and repopulation of Jerusalem in ancient times. It depicts pilgrim throngs on their journey back to the city, and seems to promise also that peoples led by their kings shall come to pay tribute, so that untold wealth will pour into the new Jerusalem. But this is all because it is the city of God, fashioned by the divine rule and by the temple in its midst. It is not surprising that the poetry and visual imagery of Isaiah's prophetic utterance should provide the backdrop for the Gospel narrative of the adoration of the magi.

It is fitting also that there should be in the second reading an autobiographical note from the Apostle of the Gentiles. Paul himself expresses surprise and wonder that a long-kept secret is now made plain to all: the Gentiles are joint heirs with the Jews of God's promises. From far and near they shall come, for there is no constraint on God's saving generosity. This Paul is called to proclaim and to bring nearer to its realization.

What the first two readings proclaim, the Gospel passage narrates in powerfully symbolic fashion. The story is full of allusion and also of gentle irony. He who is born to be King of the Jews is recognized not by his own people but by strangers from a distant land. The place and time of his birth are identified by Herod's advisors, but Jesus is rejected by Herod. He is proclaimed by a star but it seems to be visible only those who come from far away.

This text, of course, is enshrined in our Scriptures and in our liturgy, not to tell us something about the Jews but to suggest something about ourselves. The members of the household are inclined to miss the splendor of a revelation that takes place close by, while strangers may well catch the radiance of it. The story should challenge all of us to reflect whether we have become so familiar with the mysteries of the church year that we miss the splendor and the revelatory impact and return to our lives quite unchanged by the celebrations. There is a metaphorical sense in which we are all called to make a journey from afar.

The Baptism of the Lord

READINGS: Is 42:1-4, 6-7; Acts 10:34-38; Mt 3:13-17.

After baptism Jesus came up out of the water at once, and at that moment heaven opened.   Mt 3:16.

The theme of the day is that of special vocation and of the gift of Spirit and power. The passage from the second Isaian collection, the first "servant song", did not originally refer to Jesus, but it did refer to the special vocation of Israel and of certain divinely chosen prophetic figures within Israel. The privilege is also a burden, and sometimes a heavy one, though this first servant song does not speak of persecution and suffering as distinctly as the later ones. The liturgy applies the text to the election and calling of Jesus for a healing and redemptive ministry in the world.

This is the point made precisely and explicitly by Peter's sermon in the house of Cornelius—the content of the second reading. Peter sets out to tell the story beginning with the baptism proclaimed by John. He speaks of Jesus, anointed with the Holy Spirit and with power, going about healing and doing good. This, Peter maintains, is the Good News to be proclaimed to the Gentiles as well as the Jews—the manifestation of God's compassionate power extended to all. The excerpt is short, and serves to make the transition from the Isaian prophetic utterance to the Matthean story.

The story of the baptism is familiar and we might easily miss its many layers of meaning. In the first place, a baptism of repentance in the Jordan has a special vocational connotation. To enter the Jordan in this ritual is also to leave one's past life behind and enter anew into the Promised Land as Israel had done long before. It implies therefore the beginning of a new life in response to a new divine call. Secondly, the friendly argument between Jesus and John about who should be baptized by whom serves to establish the relationship between the two men and the movements of their followers: John's ministry leads up to that of Jesus and gives place to it, but the ministry of Jesus is in continuity, not in contradiction of John. Thirdly, it is not a show for other people to see but a genuine moment of vocation for Jesus—a crossing over from the ordinariness of his life in Nazareth to his very extraordinary mission and ministry. It is not simply a show for others because the text reads that *he* saw the Spirit of God descending like a dove to alight upon him, and then the voice was heard (apparently by all present) declaring his unique sonship of God.

So striking is the transition that is made in the life of Jesus at this point that an early tradition seems to have seen this as the moment of the Incarnation. In any case, the three points just indicated above, which seem to have been the points which the evangelist wanted to make, certainly offer very helpful guidance for our own vocational discernments, and a better approach to understanding the claim that Jesus was anointed with Spirit and power.

Ash Wednesday

READINGS: Joel 2:12-18; 2 Cor 5:20-6:2; Mt 6:1-6, 16-18.

And yet, the Lord says, even now turn back to me with your whole heart, fast, weep, and beat your breasts. Rend your hearts and not your garments;

turn back to the Lord your God; for he is gracious and compassionate.

Joel 2:12-13.

Among younger Catholics the pace of life in our pluralistic society threatens to eliminate any real experience of Ash Wednesday. Yet among older Catholics there are many who cling to this weekday observance even when they are not regular Sunday Eucharist participants. The reason may be that it is not really a day of gloom but a celebration of great hope, and recollection of creation, re-creation and redemption to new fullness of life and community.

This celebration of hope in spite of all evidence to the contrary seems to be the theme of the reading from Joel. The original context of the passage is the movement of a plague of locusts towards the land of Israel, so wholly dependent upon grazing and agriculture. The great black cloud that has been sighted is portrayed in apocalyptic terms as turning sun and moon to darkness. The prophet rallies the community to prayer and repentance before it is too late and all is devastated; the latter part of the prophecy acknowledges the unsurpassable compassion of God who has given deliverance and even new fertility to the land.

Paul's word in the excerpt from 2 Corinthians is that such a time of deliverance and compassion has dawned for us all in the person and death of Jesus Christ. Jesus, the innocent, aligning himself with sinners, accomplished a turning back to God at the very heart of the human community. We stand already in the time of the second grace, the time of deliverance from evil.

Nevertheless, the Gospel reading spells out the terms of our expectation and welcoming of the kingdom of God which is that new creation. There is no circumventing of the traditional ways of refocussing or rebuilding: prayer, fasting and almsdeeds. Put in the broader context of attention to God in all aspects of one's life, reaching out to the needs of others, and self-restraint, these Gospel admonitions are clearly indispensable elements of the realization of God's reign in human society with the peace and harmony which that reign brings.

Lent is both the invitation to a profound renewal and the

guarantee that such a renewal is possible and is offered to us. For a renewal of personal attitudes, expectations and relationships, and of community values and structures and policies, this is the acceptable time.

First Sunday of Lent

READINGS: Gen 2:7-9; 3:1-7; Rom 5:12-19 (or 5:12, 17-19); Mt 4:1-11.

Sin was already in the world before there was law, though in the absence of law no reckoning is kept of sin. But death held sway from Adam to Moses... And Adam foreshadows the Man who was to come.

Rom 5:13-14.

For many people in the pews, the first Sunday of Lent is really the beginning of Lent because they do not participate in the Ash Wednesday liturgy. This beginning then immediately proposes an inclusive frame of reference for the interpretation of the human situation and of the whole of human history. The three readings link together the story of creation and Adam's sin with the story of the "temptations" of Christ, and the redemptive death that reverses the fall from grace.

The simple graphic account of creation and sin excerpted from the second and third chapters of Genesis is so rich in symbolism that it takes a lifetime to assimilate all the allusions and implications. But the issue brought into focus by the juxtaposition of readings for today's liturgy is the issue of what is truly life-giving. God gives life by breathing the divine breath into the person in the act of creation and setting a tree of life in the center of a place of harmony that is to be the human habitation. But there are conditions of restraint for the enjoyment of fulness of life. The story pits the wisdom of the creature against the wisdom of God. The tempter's claim is that a fuller life is to be had by throwing off the creaturely restraints. It will be a life informed by divine knowledge, and therefore a life of unconditioned freedom. It is an experience and a temptation we all know—the sense that greater freedom can be had by throwing off the constraints of concern for others and responsibility for the consequences of our own actions. In fact, however, when liberty becomes license, people discover again and again that it leads not to fulness of life, but to death.

For Paul, in this rather difficult passage in Romans, the story of Adam's disobedience in Eden becomes the foil for an exposition of the redeeming act of Jesus Christ. The solidarity of the human community in a history of sin and sinfulness is the counterfoil for Christian confidence in the solidarity of human redemption in Christ. The action of one man, Jesus, may seem insignificant compared with the larger miseries of the human race, but the Man and the action are inclusive, countering the destructive force behind all the dislocation of values and relationships.

It is in this context that the liturgy presents us with another graphic story: the confrontation between Jesus the Savior and the great tempter personifying the rebellion of creatures against God. The scene recapitulates the temptations of the people of Israel throughout their history: to trust the power of domination; to see salvation in material wealth; to look for divine intervention in extraordinary ways that do not involve human conversion. The Temptations are universal and perennial. They are facets of the human situation as we know it. The story is packed with allusion and symbolism, but the central issue is clear: there is no restoration to fulness of life by the worldly wisdom emerging from a history of sinfulness and distortion. It is only by the word of God that there is fulness of life for all.

Second Sunday of Lent

READINGS: Gen 12:1-4; 2 Tim 1:8-10; Mt 17:1-9.

He was transfigured; his face shone like the sun, and his clothes became white as the light. And they saw Moses and Elijah appear, conversing with him.   Mt 17:2-3.

It is more difficult than usual to discern a common theme in today's readings. The Abraham story speaks of vocation and of setting out on a long journey in trust. The passage from 2 Timothy speaks of fidelity in discipleship and in witness while the gospel passage describes the transformed perception of three disciples of Jesus which called them to a new level of intimacy and understanding in their discipleship. Perhaps all three are to be read as a call to a new beginning and a long journey whose destination must be accepted in trust. In that sense, then, all three are representations of the meaning of Lent for us in our own times.

The story of the calling of Abraham is familiar, and we easily fail to notice how stark it is. We learn little other than that Abram's family had already been on the move, migrating, and that after his father's death Abram discerned a divine call to move again with his wife and his dead brother's son whom he had adopted. Precisely because the narrative is so sparse, it offers a prototypical story of the quest in each human life and family for the fulfillment of what we discern to be the divine promise in our lives and situation. We are told that Abram obeyed what he discerned to be the call of God, and set forth in trust.

The passage from 2 Timothy which is chosen for the day might be addressed to any one of us, exhorting us to fidelity under difficult circumstances, and then setting out the reasons on which such fidelity is founded. This text, like all the Pauline and sub-Pauline writings, rests on the assumption that true and faithful discipleship is going to be very costly—an assumption that might give most of us in our time and our society pause for thought. We do not generally expect our faith to make extraordinary demands, yet for those early

Christians who did have that expectation, the call to a dedicated life is presented as a special favor, earned not by their own merit but by the life, death and resurrection of Jesus. It is he who has broken the power of death and sin, and has made a wholly new and different life possible. The task for the earliest Christians was to trust that the power of the resurrection would sustain them in that wholly different life. The task for us may begin with the effort to discern a real newness and difference.

The text from Matthew, like the Abraham story, describes a prototypical experience. Perhaps it is not so much that something changes in Jesus which transfigures him, but rather that something changes in the disciples' relationship to him which enables them to see him quite differently, more in perspective, more truly. What we are privileged to witness is a crossing over or transformation from the Jesus of history, seen within a rather small and inadequate frame of reference, to the Christ of faith, seen in relation to God's plan of salvation and in relation to the whole history of expectation represented by Moses and Elijah. In juxtaposition with Moses as representing the Law and with Elijah as representing the prophets, the life and person of Jesus, and even more particularly his death, take on a clearer and more far-reaching meaning. As Jesus now appears to his disciples, he is radiant as the sun with its life-giving beams, and even his clothing (as often in the biblical accounts of revelatory visions) reflects pure white light. He is engulfed in a bright cloud, such as the cloud that heralds God's presence among human persons in the Exodus desert story. And a voice calls out from that bright cloud like the voice that called from the burning bush—a voice with a declaration and a command. This is the Beloved Son of God, and all attention is to be turned to him.

No doubt this text of the transfiguration is set before us in Bible and liturgy so that we might look attentively for an experience like that in our own lives—an experience in which the meaning of Jesus and the meaning of our own discipleship are transfigured, appearing with greater clarity and broader scope, and giving a new and sharpened focus to everything in our world.

Third Sunday of Lent

READINGS: Ex 17:3-7; Rom 5:1-2, 5-8; Jn 4:5-42.

Whoever drinks the water that I shall give him will never suffer thirst any more. The water that I shall give him will be an inner spring always welling up for eternal life. Jn 4:14-15.

Today's Gospel reading intertwines many themes, images and allusions, but the liturgy focuses on one, which is that of the living water. In the first reading Moses is confronted with the frightened and angry people demanding drinking water. In the course of their desert wanderings they have had to camp in a place where there was no water, and their trust in God was strained to the breaking point. Yet not far ahead of them, at their destination in Horeb, running water was waiting for them by the gift of God. This story is one of many texts about water and wells in the desert, all of which set the stage for the story of the Samaritan woman.

Living, that is running, not stagnant, water readily becomes a symbol, for Isaiah, Jeremiah and Psalms, of the divine wisdom graciously bestowed upon the human community in the form of the Torah and of a gift for discernment. Paul in today's passage from Romans suggests an analogy with grace, the love of God, and the Holy Spirit (all different ways of looking at the same reality). These, writes Paul, have flooded our inmost heart—the verb evoking an image of flowing waters. Moreover, for Christians such imagery would also carry an allusion to baptism and its effects.

With this preparation the liturgy takes us to the story of the Samaritan woman at Jacob's well. If the original hearers of John's Gospel were well versed in the Hebrew Scriptures, the encounter of Jesus with the woman would have wakened memories—the meeting of Abraham's servant with Rebecca at a well, ending his quest for a wife for Isaac; Jacob's first meeting with Rachel at a well (not this one); and the first meeting of Moses with his future wife, Zipporah, at a well. In the first case the man, the stranger is asking the woman for a drink as she comes to draw water at the well, and considers it a propitious sign for his role in the history of salvation when she willingly draws water for him. In the other two cases the stranger intervenes to draw water for the woman. They are symbolic scenes in which the women represent the collaboration of a whole people and a whole tradition. As John tells it, the story of the meeting of Jesus with the Samaritan woman seems to allude to these other stories and to exceed them with its claims.

But the Christians who first heard John's Gospel proclaimed may have had another memory in mind also—that of a vigorous and fruitful early preaching of the gospel among the Samaritans. Even though Samaria in its history had had affairs with strange gods— and to Jewish eyes Samaria even in Jesus' time was not properly wedded to the true God—this apparently unfaithful Samaria, positioned somewhere between authentic Judaism and total pagan- ism, was responsive to the gospel of Jesus Christ. Some Judaic Christians may even have wondered whether it was appropriate to address the Samaritans, just as the disciples in the story wonder why Jesus was talking to a Samaritan woman.

There seems to be a prophetic and feminist element at another level of this story. Jesus asks for a drink of water from a Samaritan who is at the well with a pitcher, whereas Jews and Samaritans were not supposed to share drinking vessels or eating utensils. He then engages in a long conversation with her, whereas an observant Jew was not supposed to speak familiarly with strange women— least of all Samaritan women of whom very harsh things were written. The concern of Jesus with worshipping the Father in spirit and truth, however, sweeps away all such humanly contrived and discriminatory ritual distinctions, and sees the ultimate irrelevance even of the great dispute about the true place for worship. All that Jesus sees is the readiness of the Samaritans to hear the good news and be converted. The fields white for the harvest.

There is much to think about in the symbolism of the water. Jesus comes seeking water from Jacob's well—the tradition to which both Jews and Samaritans look for spiritual sustenance. Instead of receiving fresh water from this source, he discovers the impotence of the tradition in the squabbles over interpretation of ritual obligations. He turns the situation around and offers fresh running water from his own new source. In the course of John's Gospel it is a theme that echoes the offer of a new birth from water and the Holy Spirit to Nicodemus, and which anticipates the Temple sermon on the last and greatest day of the feast of Tabernacles. This theme applies as much to us as to those who met Jesus in Samaria, Judea and Galilee during his preaching tours. To accept the message of Jesus in a radical way appropriate to the baptized is to receive an inner source bubbling inexhaustibly with the water of life.

Fourth Sunday of Lent (Laetare)

READINGS: 1 Sam 16:1, 6-7, 10-13; Eph 5:8-14; Jn 9:1-41 (or 1, 6-9, 13-17, 34-38).

To open the eyes of a man born blind—it is unheard of since time began. If that man had not come from God he could have done nothing. Jn 9:32-33.

It should perhaps be a consolation to all of us that even Jesus had difficulty fulfilling his mission because he seemed to be too insignificant, too ordinary, to be God's representative in the salvation of the world. Indeed, he seemed to be too ordinary even to have cured a blind man in God's name. The leaders of his society were so affronted by it that they found it more reasonable to attribute the cure to diabolic forces.

The first reading prepares us to see this in the wider context of the whole broad sweep of salvation history. The anointing of David as king stands forever as the great prototype of the election of the weak and unlikely. The story is that of a liberating revolution against an erratic and unjust ruler who has disobeyed God's commands. There is a secret plot endorsed by God, by which Samuel believes he is risking his own life. But the focus of the story is on the search to discern who it is that God has chosen. The search ends with the youngest (and therefore least important) son of a large farming family in Bethlehem. Saul's reign was an experiment in strength; David's reign is to be an experiment in trust. No matter what sins David committed later, today's reading leaves him the symbol of innocence and powerlessness, the unlikely chosen one.

The other two readings carry on the theme of the unlikely chosen but intertwine it with the theme of light—the light of God's truth shining through the person of Jesus Christ into the affairs of the human race and its history. It is the great theme of the all-engulfing struggle of the darkness and the light within creation and within human minds and hearts. The story from John's Gospel has many levels. There is first the simple story of the curing of a blind man—one understood to be incurably blind because he has been so from birth. At this level the story begins with a discussion about whose fault it is that this man and others like him have been born blind. Jesus answers that the link between sin and suffering cannot be made in this simplistic way; the suffering is to be understood as a call for redemption. The man receives his sight, but this becomes an occasion of scandal: one who heals in the name of God should not be doing it on the sabbath. The outcome is that the man born blind and now able to see is expelled from the synagogue.

There is a second level to this story. As so often in John's Gospel, there is a certain irony in the implied question as to who it is in the story who is really blind. In face of the clear evidence, the religious leaders would not believe at first that the man had really ever been blind: the whole thing must have been a deliberate deception through faked identity. When this becomes untenable, they call the formerly blind man again, trying to establish that it could not have been Jesus who effected the cure because Jesus is undistinguished and scandalous. Finally, when it is unavoidably clear that it was Jesus who effected the cure, this nevertheless is not accepted as evidence of his divine calling. At the end of the story we have to acknowledge that it is the devout religious leaders who are blinded by their own obstinacy and exclusivity.

But there is yet a third level of the story. It also refers to the opening of the eyes of the spirit in baptism, the receiving of the new light of Christ. The whole argument with the religious leaders, and the banning of the one who has received the light and the sight to see the light, describes the experience of the Christian community at the end of the first century when Jewish Christians were being expelled from the synagogues. The first hearers of John's Gospel were no doubt intended to see their own story in this account, and their own position in this argument. For us it may be important at a fourth level, within the Christian community itself. The prophetic opening of eyes and gift of the light of God's truth through the person of Jesus Christ really never ends. It does not come to a moment of definitive codification beyond which there is no more to learn. It may yet come from the unlikely, the unimportant, the ones we would not expect to be God's chosen.

The excerpt from the letter to the Ephesians seems to be concerned with the implications of baptism as an invitation to remain in the light. The possibility of the encroaching of darkness even into the community of believers is always there. To be within the Church does not guarantee life in the light; it guarantees only the possibility and the invitation. As Christians we have had our eyes opened, we have been brought out of the prevailing darkness, but we must live as people who are at home in the light. We must act as those who are chosen.

Fifth Sunday of Lent

READINGS: Ezek 37:12-14; Rom 8:8-11; Jn 11:1-45.

You shall know that I am the Lord when I open your graves and bring you up from them, O my people. Then I will put my spirit into you and you shall live...and you shall know that I the Lord have spoken and will act.
Ezek 37:13-14

The liturgical readings for the Fifth Sunday of Lent focus on the Resurrection. The message is to trust that we are being led to the fulness of life, though all appearances may be to the contrary. The conclusion of Jesus' own life is exemplary, and we are bidden to look at it in retrospect by the light of the Resurrection in order to see the total meaning of that life.

The first reading is brief, consisting of a proclamation of God as the life-giver to whom even the dead may look with hope. In its setting in the Book of Ezekiel, this proclamation follows the story of the valley or plain full of dry bones left unburied as after a huge battle. The prophet has been commanded to call upon the wind, the breath or Spirit of God, to come and breathe new life into the dead bones. And these bones, he has been told, are the people of Israel who have lost hope and vision and identity. This new creation, like the first creation as told in Genesis 2, constitutes human beings in two phases: first the material is gathered and drawn from the earth so that the bones are knit together into whole skeletons, subsequently enfleshed, and then the divine breath is put into them so that they become living beings again. But the bones are not only Israel; they are all of us, and the story has something to say to all of us. The redemptive recreation typified by the Resurrection also involves two phases: that gathering of the earthly, indeed earthy, material or resources in response to God's enabling call, and the advent of the divine Spirit breathing a new and more intense sharing of divine life into all that has been assembled.

That certainly is the sense of Paul's argument about the lower nature and the level of the Spirit. Paul's understanding of the lower nature seems to be concerned not so much with the material or corporeal as with the demonstrable inability of human beings to complete the human project in good lives and good communities by their own efforts alone. It is the gift of the Spirit that lifts believers beyond the obstacles and restraints into the realm of fulness of life, of immeasurably enhanced life. And this gift of the Spirit is the new creation that bursts forth in the Resurrection of Jesus which we share.

All this is told us in story form in the Gospel account of the raising of Lazarus. This highly stylized story, packed with allusion and symbol, is a story about us all. Lazarus, the friend of Jesus with whom Jesus liked to stay when in the Jerusalem area, is a representative figure. The Hebrew form of his name, Eleazar, could be translated "God to the rescue". He dwells in Bethany, the original form of which seems to have meant "house of affliction". In the composite picture that we get from the several Gospel references, this man is flanked by two sisters. These again are very stylized figures and, like many of the female figures in the Scriptures, seem to be representative of traditions, communities, attitudes, virtues, rather than descriptive of individual persons. In this account they are made to represent two different ways of looking to the messianic time, the time of salvation, in Israel. One is the busy activity of conscientious and elaborately detailed observation of the Mosaic Law and all the minute accretions it had acquired in the course of time. The other way is that of the *anawim*, the poor in spirit, living in humility and trust, waiting for God's intervention at the divinely chosen moment.

John's Gospel suggests that the raising of Lazarus to life, when all hope of resuscitation had long been abandoned, had a direct connection with the execution of Jesus in his prime. It is readily apparent that the people of Israel, the unlearned poor and ordinary people, were just like Lazarus in John's account. They certainly lived in the "house of affliction," and they had languished and perhaps given up hope so that once again, as in Ezekiel's time, they were like a plain full of dry bones, long dead. And they were indeed accompanied by the two traditions, among others, which stressed in one case the rigorous and elaborate observance of the Law and in the other case total trust in God and humility before the inscrutable divine wisdom. To such a people Jesus came. With them he chose to consort, and them he raised from the stupor and hopelessness of death.

Like the dry bones on the plain, Lazarus in his tomb is not only an image of Israel. He depicts all of us; he shows the human situation and the impact that Jesus has upon it. They refer to our public affairs as well as our private lives. If it were not so, the raising of Lazarus would not have such a direct connection with the death of Jesus. But it is in the values and expectations and structures of our public affairs that we are like the bones already dried out, and like the man dead four days and already decomposing. Among ourselves also there is the Martha voice that says it is too late and nothing can be done about it now. But among ourselves, at the same time, we must be able to find the Mary silence that says nothing is ever too late for God who says, "You shall live".

Passion Sunday

READINGS: Mt 21:1-11; Is 50:4-7; Phil 2:6-11; Mt 26:14–27:66 (or Mt 27:11-54).

Then they led him away to be crucified.   Mt 27:31.

For those who are able to maintain their attention over the the time span of all four readings, the sequence of the texts and their context in the liturgical actions carries a powerful interpretation of the human situation and human history. The leap from "Palm Sunday" to "Good Friday" is in itself theologically important, and certainly preserves the intent of Matthew's Gospel. We have the sequence: Jesus performs a symbolic pageant in the entry into Jerusalem, in which he both makes the messianic claim and cautions against any military understanding of his saving role, being understood by the crowds perhaps in the messianic claim but not in the caution; we, the liturgical worshippers, are reminded of the third Suffering Servant Song of Isaiah, and guided into seeing Jesus in this role; the hymn from Philippians 2 interprets what is about to be read from the Gospel as the reversal of the drama of Adam in the garden of Eden; finally, now that we have been prepared to interpret it, we hear the story of the death of Jesus.

The meaning of the palm procession is, of course, the welcoming of the saving king who comes to fulfill his appointed role as champion of the people to set them free from tyranny—a welcome conqueror, a prince of peace. But then and now there is ambiguity in the promise and quest of liberation. The waving palms and the garments strewn on the street can be the acceptance of a true and very exigent liberation from all the inauthentic relationships and values that oppress us. They can also, however, be a kind of shallow partisan triumphalism that entirely misses the meaning of true liberation. Hence the very real importance of the donkeys, whose symbolism modern listeners do not know without being told. To Hebrews of Jesus' time the she-ass and her foal were a direct allusion to the prophecy of Zechariah 9:9, where the king is to come in humility, peacefully, mounted on these animals in token of the banishment of war, speaking peaceably and setting prisoners free. It is in this context that the liturgy invites us to take up our welcoming palms, understanding that it is not in any triumphalist spirit that we are called to join that procession.

The text from Isaiah speaks of the mission of God's servant. The mission is not to suffer, though it is fulfilled at the cost of extreme suffering. The mission is to receive the revelatory word of God, to assimilate it in all its depth, and out of that depth to teach and console, standing firm in face of all resistance and persecution. The assumption underlying this, with which Israel was all too familiar, is that a truly redemptive expression of God's revelation will challenge power and privilege and greed in ways that will provide the bitterest persecution.

The ultimate reason for that is set out in the hymn from Philippians. Adam is made in the likeness of God and yields to the temptation to snatch equality with God by asserting independence from God. Jesus, made in the likeness of the fallen Adam, acknowledges total dependence even to the point of death—death in a form that is consequent upon a history of sin, and which is the punishment of earthly rebellion against forces that have usurped authority. It is this which reverses the whole fallen human situation as God raises Jesus to Lordship, naming him above all in creation.

Thus we have the interpretation before the story, perhaps because those things in human experience which are stunningly painful and bewildering to acknowledge can best be faced through ritual and symbol. The Gospel account itself, while calling for an identification with Jesus in empathy does not elaborate Jesus' own experience of his sufferings but stays with a very restrained account of events, selecting always those details that interpret the meaning for us. However, thinking about the great themes of the Passion presented here must become very practical for us in our times when outrageous accounts of torture of prisoners, and particularly of prisoners of conscience, come to us daily from so many parts of the world. Our reflection must become practical because in Matthew 25, just before the Passion accounts, Jesus warns that what we do to or for the least of our fellow human beings we do to him, and also because it becomes daily more inescapably apparent that many of these tortures are intended to protect unjust systems from which we ourselves profit in some way.

The choice, whether to read the entire selection or the shorter version, is a difficult one. There is an inexorable progression in the chain of events: the betrayal, the farewell Passover supper, the Gethsemani vigil, the arrest, the night-time meeting to frame charges against him, Peter's denial, Judas' suicide, the trial before the governor, the crowd's choice of Bar-Abbas, the condemnation, the mocking by the soldiers and the swift and cruel public execution, followed by a hasty private burial and the sealing and guarding of the tomb. If we take the whole sequence, moving through it quickly and picking up the main points, the account also describes many martyrs to conscience in our own times. We may call ourselves the Christian West, but we have not stopped doing this kind of thing. There is a perennial temptation to suppose that people who receive this kind of treatment must certainly have done something that deserved it—meddled foolishly in politics, made seditious speeches, and so forth—but the Passion of Jesus stands before us forever, challenging the assumptions that people who are punished are guilty, that the law of the land expresses true justice, that authority whether of a religious or a secular character is rightly exercised and not to be questioned. The crucifixion of Jesus warns us that we cannot make any of these assumptions.

However, most of us are not used to listening to long texts read aloud, and it may be easier for most people to focus if the shorter version is read. That also has its advantages because the shorter version offers a series of vivid tableaux filled with symbolically representative figures. Each of those tableaux is a challenge to the listeners to consider where they themselves stand in that scene, and whether they can really accept it as the message, "your King comes."

Easter Sunday

READINGS:
>   At the Vigil: Rom 6:3-11; Mt 28:1-10
>   During the day: Acts 10:34, 37-43; Col 3:1-4; Jn 20:1-9.

You have nothing to fear. I know you are looking for Jesus who was crucified. . . He has been raised from the dead and is going on before you into Galilee; there you will see him.   Mt 28:5, 7.

Because most Christians celebrate only one Eucharist on Easter Sunday, either the vigil or the one during the day, it seems as though the liturgy gives a choice of two very different ways of entering into the Paschal Mystery. Either one can arrive, like Mary of Magdala and the other disciples, when the Resurrection of Jesus has already happened, and the worshipper comes upon the scene to contemplate the empty tomb. Or else one can relive the whole history of salvation with the neophytes, experiencing once again what it means to die to the old life and to be reborn into the new creation. But even for those who come only to the daytime Eucharist, the readings are chosen to evoke the memory and imagination of the personal passage from death to life in Christ.

What the reading from Romans says succinctly and rather abstractly to those who have already experienced all the symbolism of the vigil, the lesson from Acts spells out in story form. Briefly it sketches the apostolate of Jesus, beginning from the baptism proclaimed by John, from which Jesus, anointed with the Holy Spirit and power, went forth doing good in the name of God all about the countryside from Galilee to Jerusalem and Judea. Relating how this ministry led to his death, Peter's sermon comes to its climax: God raised Jesus to life in fulfillment of the prophecies of salvation and reconciliation, sending forth witnesses of this event to announce that all human history is to be judged by Jesus, the crucified and the Risen. With this announcement, Peter's sermon draws us also into the drama of forgiveness and transformation.

Lest we should miss the realization that this lesson is about the present—our present—the reading from Colossians is explicit: were we ourselves not raised to a new life in Christ? It behooves us to be where Christ is. The rhetoric of the passage is interesting; Paul reminds us so forcefully that we have already died in Christ precisely because he suspects that in practical ways this is not entirely accurate. He suspects that we cling to the old ways of a world that is out of focus, distorted, disoriented so that there can be no peace, no reconciliation, no personal or social harmony except on terms of a further death to the old ways. Christ has passed through death to the new life, but Paul suspects that the rest of us may have done so ritually without actually having passed through to where Christ is in the daily reality of our lives. The purpose of the liturgy seems to be to offer at least an annual reminder and invitation to set out again on that passage which our baptism ought to have been.

Both the Gospel readings could be interpreted in the same sense: Jesus has passed through but the vowed followers of Jesus have to be urged to move on from the tomb and from the past. It was, after all, a past in which they could always depend on him and leave everything to him to do. It seemed a safe past; they may have resented the way he moved on to death and beyond to new life. His moving on presented them with a crisis, a call for commitment in a much deeper way, a call for their death to their old life, even of dependence on Jesus to handle every situation.

The two Gospel readings tell the same story in slightly different ways. The Matthean account takes place at daybreak, when Mary of Magdala and another Mary come to the grave to be greeted by an earthquake and a heavenly messenger who rolls away the stone sealing the tomb to convince them that Jesus is not to be found there but has already gone ahead of his disciples to meet them in Galilee. According to Matthew, they accept the message with awe and joy and set out to tell other disciples as they have been bidden. On their way Jesus himself greets them, encourages them and repeats the message that the disciples are to meet him in Galilee.

John gives a different account, in which Mary of Magdala comes to the tomb while it is yet dark, and is horrified to find the tomb empty. Having summoned Peter and another disciple, she remains outside weeping while they go in, see the linen wrappings from the body still lying there, and understand that he has risen according to the Scriptures. Today's selection does not complete the story, so we do not hear John's version of Mary's encounter, first with two angels and then with Jesus himself.

What is clear about both versions of the story is the insistence of the evangelists that the followers of Jesus must not cling to the tomb, but must find Resurrection faith. That faith requires them to go forth, to move on, to accept their task in the world, in order to be where Christ is. He is not among the dead; he does not belong to the past; he is risen to a new life in and among his disciples. He beckons them forward into a mission to Galilee and to the whole world, calling them to meet him in the continuing task of redemption and reconciliation. The message of the day's liturgy is that we are challenged really to pass through death to the old life into rebirth in the new, not ritually only but in reality. We are called to be where Christ is.

Second Sunday of Easter

READINGS: Acts 2:42-47; I Pet 1:3-9; Jn 20:19-31.

Praised be the God and Father of our Lord Jesus Christ, who in his great
mercy gave us new birth into a living hope by the resurrection of Jesus Christ
from the dead! The inheritance to which we are born is one which nothing
can destroy or spoil or wither.   I Pet 1:3-4.

The reminder of that living hope and its endurance in spite of all
setbacks, troubles and persecution, comes most appropriately on this
octave day of Easter. In the early centuries it was the Sunday of the
laying down of the white garments of the newly baptized. It was the
end of that time of intense liturgical celebration which was designed
to heighten experience and sensitivity to the saving grace of God.
Therefore it marked a transition into apparent ordinariness again,
and that made it particularly important to remind not only the
newcomers but the whole community of believers that for them
nothing will ever be quite ordinary again because they have crossed
over with Christ into a new life.

It is true, of course, that the mode in which we enjoy the new life
most of the time is that of a living hope, not of a total realization.
Community life, prayer and encouragement are needed to keep the
hope alive and visible. The first reading, from Acts, describes a
situation like that in rather idealistic terms. The community is the
first one we read about, when the number of the disciples has been
greatly increased in response to Peter's post-Resurrection preaching.
They shared a common life, we are told, sharing their resources,
pursuing a deeper understanding and experience of the good news of
salvation, meeting in one another's houses for meals and Eucharist in
simple, joyful enthusiasm, and presenting a very attractive style of
life to people around them who came in contact with them. Their
numbers grew because their way of life was so obviously deeply
fulfilling.

Luke, as the author of Acts, is suspect of drawing a picture that is
more an ideal to be sought than a straightforward description of an

historical fact. Peter's exhortation, on the gift and responsibility of the new life in Christ, introduces a note of realism. This text acknowledges that the response of outsiders is not always enthusiastic praise and conversion, but may often be persecution. It allows that the life of a Christian community is not usually one of uninterrupted joyful celebration, but is full of trials of many kinds. This letter emphasizes the paradox that profound peace and joy can be experienced in the midst of persecution and of internal difficulties of the community. What is important is not to lose sight of the new birth that has really been granted to us, the new and living hope that it offers, and the utter fidelity of God who holds out salvation to us.

The final reading is the passage which seems to have been the original ending of the Gospel of John, condensing into a single story the mysteries of Resurrection, Ascension and Pentecost, and closing a book of "seven signs" with an invitation to deeper and persevering faith. The story is set on the evening of Easter day, among the gathered disciples huddled together in fear behind locked doors. But the power of the risen Christ can penetrate the defenses of the fearful in their hiding. Jesus is among them with a message of peace and a gift of new joy exploding into a situation that had seemed past all redemption. The new joy is also a new mission: as the Father has sent him, he now sends his friends and followers on the task of reconciliation and redemption of the world.

The company that is gathered there is described simply as the disciples, not the Twelve (though Thomas is described as one of the Twelve) nor the Apostles. It is to this company of his various followers that the risen Jesus gives his mandate. He breathes on them, a symbolic action bestowing the Holy Spirit. It parallels the first creation, in which God's breath brings the living human being into existence, with a new creation which restores and enhances the life of the human community. It is the gift that shapes the people of God anew, and contains the imperative to share that new life and peoplehood with all who will respond and hear the good news. That is perhaps the main point in the saying of Jesus about the disciples' forgiving or pronouncing unforgiven. Only God forgives sin, and it is clear that Jesus does not intend to place an arbitrary power in the discretion of human beings. But the role of the community of believers is decisive in another sense. The task of presenting the good news and eliciting the response of faith is now theirs, which means ours. There is a sense in which God has entrusted the reconciliation of the world to all of us who are reborn in Christ—entrusted it to the whole Christ in all his members. It is our responsibility to make the good news credible and faith in Christ possible. It is also true that the offer of faith and salvation presents those to whom it is made with a choice laden with consequences. But the offer of faith and salvation is not made by words alone. Jesus makes that offer to his disciples by the sign of his death and resurrection. The community portrayed in the reading from Acts makes the offer to its neighbors and acquaintances by the self-surrender of its life style. It is experience, not hearsay, which is decisive.

The story of Thomas seems to reflect on this. Thomas as a representative figure has appeared in John's Gospel twice before this, once when he said "Let us go and die with him" (Jn 11:16), and once when he said to Jesus "We don't know where you are going, so how can we know the way there?" (Jn 14:15). On that latter occasion Jesus had said that he himself was the way, and the truth that they needed to guide them, and the life that they were invited to live. On this occasion Thomas again insists on an experiential basis for faith, and it is not denied to him. Yet the emphasis of the narrative is on the concluding remark of Jesus; it consoles and reassures those of us who were not present in those ecstatic first moments of the community's resurrection experience, and who have not known Jesus in the flesh. To us the text says that we are not thereby deprived of a firm foundation for faith. We are invited to reflect on the book of the seven signs, seeking their relevance in our own lives, in order to hold on to the faith, remembering our new birth into a living hope.

Third Sunday of Easter

READINGS: Acts 2:14, 22-28; I Pet 1:17-21; Lk 24:13-35.

When he had sat down with them at table, he took bread and said the blessing; he broke the bread and offered it to them. Then their eyes were opened, and they recognized him; and he vanished from their sight.

Lk 24:30-31

The Emmaus story, like most of the stories in Scripture, is a story about us. It is an account of the whole history of the followers of Jesus from the beginning to the present day, and it is also a story of the spiritual pilgrimage of individual Christians. The subject matter of the story, as of the other two readings, is the interpretation of the life, death and resurrection of Jesus in the focus of salvation history. All three readings deal with the scandal of the cross and the hard task of coming to terms with it, claiming that this is at the heart of Easter faith, for neither empty tomb nor apparitions suffice to sustain faith if the disciples have not dealt with that central scandal about God's care for Jesus and for us.

The passage from Acts gives us once again a synopsis of an early sermon of Peter. Once again this sermon rehearses the public life of Jesus, his good deeds and his death, asserting the resurrection as liberation from death, and indeed conquest of death. But the main emphasis of the speech seems to be that reflection on the Scriptures of Israel will help us to understand God's wisdom and God's ways. The particular reference is to Psalm 16, which proclaims unshakable faith in God in face of threat and suffering, and declares "the gods whom earth holds sacred" to be worthless. The citation of this Psalm suggests an invitation to a reversal of the usual worldly values by which we assess people and events and promises. It suggests a new humility in trying to understand the ways of God in our own lives and in the whole of human history.

The second text, though following its separate sequence of continuous readings, addresses the scandal of the cross from a slightly different angle. To pray the Lord's Prayer, to call God Father, has practical implications for our new way of life. "It was no perishable stuff, like gold or silver, that bought (our) freedom from the empty folly of (our) traditional ways". The price was paid in the blood of Christ. That metaphor of buying freedom with the blood of Christ is one that we accept readily enough when it refers to the distant past and when we do not think too much about what it means. But the evident intent of the inclusion of this passage in the New Testament is that it does not pertain only to the past but also to our continuing present. Moreover, the passage is explicit that the blood of Christ does not purchase freedom in some abstract or ethereal sense, but freedom from the empty folly of our traditional ways. The continuing present relevance of that is obvious, because the folly of traditional ways is still with us in matters private and public, in the way we evaluate ourselves and others, in the economic structures of our society that place profit before relationships and community, in the arms build-up in which we look for security in the power to kill rather than in the power of friendship. The sense of Peter's letter is that the resurrection of the crucified is our warrant that it can all be very different, and that the process of redemption is a continuing agenda in the present.

Yet there is a sense in which, again and again, we are in the position of the disciples who are yet on the way to Emmaus—puzzled, discouraged, unable to see any liberation in the death, the empty tomb, the messages about appearances. One is tempted to wonder why these two disciples were going away from Jerusalem to a village perhaps seven miles away. Had they concluded that the action was over, the feast finished, the tragedy ended? The narrative has them moving away just when they have heard that heavenly messengers have assured their friends that Jesus was alive. Were they simply going home? The story tells us there were two disciples, and that their journey's end was a house in which they were staying in Emmaus. It seems unlikely (though modern commentators have assumed it) that they were two men; they may well have been a married couple returning to their own home. Only two factors are quite clear: they did not believe the message of the resurrection, and that was because of the scandal of the cross. In their eyes either the mission of Jesus had entirely failed, or else they themselves had been badly deceived in their expectation of Jesus.

The narrative as it reaches us in Luke's Gospel is still a very human story, full of pathos, but it is also stylized in pattern. There is a strong suggestion of Eucharistic celebration: disciples come with their questions and their worries and doubts; the Scriptures are recited; there is a homily in which the Scriptures are explained so as to meet the questions, difficulties and doubts of the disciples here and now; and finally there is a Eucharist in the context of a fellowship meal. All this seems to invite us quite urgently to see their story as our story, to see ourselves as similarly inclined to move away from the heart of the mystery, not really having faith that it has changed everything and bought our freedom from the empty folly of our traditional ways. The text also seems to say that even as we move away Christ seeks us out in ways we do not at first recognize, that it is in the Scriptures that we can begin to understand the events of our own lives and the testimony of those who have been there before us, that we must allow Christ to open the Scriptures for us (probably through the mediation of the community of believers), and that it is in the Eucharist that we shall know that we have really met Jesus himself.

There is a spiritual and a liturgical pattern to the journey that these two disciples make. Spiritually, they are moving away from the promise and testimony of the resurrection because of the scandal of the cross; Jesus finds them in spite of themselves; they are drawn into a deeper understanding by means of Scripture and commentary; they arrive at the celebration of the mystery in the company of Jesus; and they turn around and go back to Jerusalem. Liturgically, they bring their quest as disciples to the Eucharistic celebration, and they take from that celebration a new sense of direction and a task in the world. That is the journey to Emmaus and back.

Fourth Sunday of Easter

READINGS: Acts 2:14, 36–41; I Pet 2:20–25; Jn 10:1–10.

God has made this Jesus, whom you crucified, both Lord and Messiah.
Acts 2:36.

We cannot celebrate the season of the Resurrection without remembering constantly who it was that was raised from the dead to become spirit and life among us in a new and transcending way. The liturgical readings for the Easter season are still full of references to the passion and death of Jesus. Indeed, they present a continuing struggle to understand the meaning of such a death for the history of redemption.

The interpretation of the death and Resurrection of Jesus as Paschal Mystery is one that does not come easily. If it seems easy to accept, that is only because we tend to mistake familiarity for understanding, and frequent repetition for acceptance. In reality we are dealing with an overwhelming scandal, with a stumbling block of massive proportions. Perhaps that is why we are returning Sunday after Sunday to Peter's sermon in Acts. Today's reading brings the sermon to a climax: the recital and interpretation of the life, death and Resurrection of Jesus was followed by a demonstration from the Hebrew Scriptures of the significance of the events, and is now brought to the conclusion that in the unfolding of these events God has made Jesus Lord and Messiah (Christ).

This is an unusual way for contemporary Christians to think about Jesus—as growing into this role of divine mediator and chosen savior, to come to the fulness of his task and being in the Resurrection. But this notion, that the Incarnation is a moment co-extensive with the entire event of Jesus in history, is not strange or unusual in the New Testament. Many passages, such as today's readings, become startlingly clear when we come to them with this understanding of the events that make Jesus Lord and Messiah for us. The reading from I Peter invites us to see the innocent suffering of Jesus as radically changing human relationships. It is the non-violent appeal to God's vindication that changes the possibilities of history in all its dimensions. Peter does not present God as ordaining or requiring the suffering but as redeeming from the suffering and death inflicted by sin and evil. It is the trust and non-violence of Jesus that mediates the very possibility of redemption, and it is in this that Jesus emerges as the Divine Word spoken to us in our history, and as the savior who opens up the access to God's mercy.

The passage from John's Gospel deals with the same theme in the guise of two images, that of the faithful shepherd and that of the gate. Though taken from Chapter 10 of John's Gospel, the passage is obviously intended to be read in the light of the whole Paschal Mystery, looking back through the experience of the Resurrecton. This invitation to see Jesus as the tried and trustworthy shepherd and as the only way into the community of salvation, certainly refers to the complete, mature Jesus who has gone ahead of us through every challenge, including persecution, torture, death and abandonment.

The imagery of the shepherd is so rich with biblical allusions that it is difficult for us to catch the full intellectual and affective content of it. The patriarchal heritage was one of nomadic herders, so that family and social structures were built around the shepherd's tasks, thus the comparison of leaders in society with shepherds readily suggested itself. David, the national hero of legendary exploits, is a shepherd-king. Occasionally, as in Psalm 23, God is seen as the shepherd of those who place their trust in divine providence. Here in the shepherd passages of John 10, there is clearly an allusion to Ezekiel 34, in which God takes the evil and unfaithful shepherds of Israel to task and promises to send the one true shepherd.

The biblical shepherd, of course, does not drive the sheep before him, but leads the flock, staff in hand, ready to fight to the death to defend the sheep of his flock from marauding wild animals. He is their champion, who risks being seriously wounded, perhaps even killed, so that his charges may live. He walks ahead to show the sheep the way to refreshing water and sustaining pastures in a land of sparse vegetation. He brings them to life and safety. These Johannine passages seem particularly to rest upon the shepherd's role as champion and pathfinder, in offering images by which to understand the part that Jesus plays in the redemption. The reference to "leading out" seems to link the shepherd theme to that of Exodus. As Moses was a true shepherd leading the people out of the place of captivity, so in a more profound way is Jesus the true shepherd to lead those who will follow out of the state of captivity to sin. As in the case of Moses, when Jesus has led his flock out of captivity, there is still a long journey ahead. That is why, even after baptism and a first serious conversion, there is continuing need for real trust that Jesus knows the way to full redemption and ultimate happiness, that Jesus is the gateway by which one may safely go in and out. There is a continuing need to follow along the paths that he has taken.

This is all so easy to say and so demanding to do. The poetry of it is inviting; the day by day prose is so contrary to our accustomed ways that it is bewildering. Non-violent response to threat and attack is not the normal mode of the "star wars" generation. Defense of the weak at the risk of one's own economic, social, physical or ecclesiastical security runs counter to a culture based on universal competition. Entrusting one's cause to divine vindication is not easily compatible with the Enlightenment motto of ultimate self-reliance and self-assertion. In practice it is a difficult and far-reaching question whether we really believe that Jesus is the gateway to life.

Fifth Sunday of Easter

READINGS: Acts 6:1-7; 1 Pet 2:4-9; Jn 14:1-12.

You are a chosen race, a royal priesthood, a dedicated nation, and a people claimed by God for his own, to proclaim the triumphs of him who has called you out of darkness into his marvelous light.   1 Pet 2:9.

The readings for this Sunday address the question of Christian vocation and of the hope that makes perseverance possible. With blunt realism the text from Acts admits what life in the community of believers is really like from day to day; it is fraught with internal as well as external difficulties. Even in this first golden moment of the Church's existence, human rivalries and prejudices, that are supposed to be left behind with entry into the community of the Resurrection, crop up again in virulent forms. Typically, the passage relates, when the numbers increase, problems emerge.

It would appear that these communities are still composed entirely of Jews, so that the tension between Jew and Gentile is not directly in question. But among the Jewish followers of Jesus there are the Hellenists, who favor greater assimilation in language and culture, and the Hebraists, who favor sharper separation and national identity. Consciousness of the distinction leads to suspicions of discrimination and unfairness. It is a situation we all know from experience in many forms. The solution here is interesting: the Twelve, acting collegially, appoint as ministers to the community seven people of such radiant and evident goodness and integrity, exemplars of Spirit and wisdom, that there can be no doubt about trusting them, so that the apostolic task of the community will not be hindered by internal dissension.

Because the problems of that first expanded community are perennial for us all, the passage from 1 Peter 2 is apt. Addressed to a Gentile community, reminding them of their baptism and its implications, the text is concerned with restoring the harmony and integration of the human community, intended by God as creator and now made possible by Jesus Christ. Baptism is entry to a community with a vocation for the world at large. To make Gentile Christians aware of this, the writer uses a set of metaphors drawn from Israel's sense of vocation: temple and priesthood, a chosen race which constitutes a royal priesthood, a dedicated nation, a people who are God's own, heralds of a triumphant exodus from darkness to light. Some of these images do not appeal spontaneously to modern readers and listeners. Priesthood is not greatly respected or well understood in our times. Temples suggest Reformed Judaism, Free Masonry or Hinduism. Royalty is not an American experience, and reference to a chosen race has all the negative connotations of racial prejudice and discrimination in the contemporary world. It is necessary, therefore, to explore the imagery used in its own historical and cultural context.

Jesus, as cornerstone or foundation stone, either determines the shape of that which is built upon him, or serves as a stumblingblock to those who would see their place in the construction of human society quite differently. Jesus is a new beginning, calling for a new design in human history and society. It is the design of a spiritual temple, that is to say, of a place of worship, of encounter with the divine, of the presence of the divine. It is the community as community that is to mediate the possibility of worship in spirit and truth, because it is the community by its way of life that must provide the experience of encounter with the divine presence. That same community, built upon the relationship of its members with Christ, must have that sense of dedicated solidarity which was and is the hallmark of faithful Israel. Most demanding of all, it is a solidarity that must not be self-absorbed but must look outward to the task in the world. And that is why the community must be a royal priesthood—the mediators and reconcilers who are the intimates of the divine monarch, having only the divine cause at heart in their impact on the world. As in the first Exodus, the emerging peoplehood of the followers of Jesus will be a proclamation to other peoples to lead them triumphantly out of darkness to light.

The lyricism of this passage begs the question whether it is descriptive of the real world and its real possibilities. To this the passage from John 14 replies with a word of encouragement: Jesus would surely not have set out upon the arduous path that he took if it were all doomed to be in vain. He would not have issued the invitations to faith and trust that he broadcast, if salvation were not possible for all the human race. In retrospect the invitation to trust God and to trust Jesus is much easier to understand. So is the imagery of "the way": Jesus leads the way; Jesus is the way; those who follow him will enter into his own task of making the Father known, will do what he has done, and even more, because it is in his name that the work of redemption goes forward among the peoples of the earth.

We in our own times might well say with the reluctant disciples that we are not all sure of the way, that it would be easier to trust that Jesus went ahead to prepare a place for all of us in the Father's house, in the restored, redeemed creation, if we could really see what God is like. Long before the time of Jesus, the Hebrews had realized that there was an answer to this: it was useless and counterproductive to make images of God, because the only way we can see God is in the creation, and more especially in the human person fully alive, fully responsive to what a human person is created to be. The answer Jesus gives his hesitant disciples is really the old Hebrew answer: he can show us the face of God only by the way he reflects God in his own humanity. He can show us the face of God only by showing us his own face. We can know where God has passed by looking into history and into our own lives to see where Jesus has passed.

As Christians we see Jesus as the unique image of God in humanity. But we also see Jesus as prototypical and inclusive of us all, drawing us into his witness and his ministry of reconciliation and reconstruction, making us in union with himself a kind of temple where God is to be encountered, experienced, and brought to others by a royal priesthood.

Sixth Sunday of Easter

READINGS: Acts 8:5-8, 14-17; I Pet 3:15-18; Jn 14:15-21.

I will ask the Father, and he will give you another to be your Advocate, who will be with you forever—the Spirit of truth.   Jn 14:16-17.

With this Sixth Sunday of Easter, the liturgy directs our attention to the Holy Spirit as the parting gift of the risen Jesus. The first reading is a story, the second an exhortation and the third a promise. The story in Acts takes place after the first intensive persecution of the young Christian community in Jerusalem. Everyone was much saddened by the death of the greatly loved deacon, Stephen, who had been stoned. Now members of the church were being arrested in their houses and dragged off to prison, so the Apostles were encouraging the believers to flee from Jerusalem into country districts of Judea and Samaria.

It is in this context that Philip, another of the seven deacons, finds himself in Samaria, proclaiming there that Jesus is the expected Messiah. The schismatic and proverbially half-pagan Samaritans seem to have been very receptive to the message, and Philip's preaching was attested by many wonderful works of God performed through a ministry of healing and exorcisms. The narrator of this account evidently intends it as exemplary, and explains how a new local church is to be set up. First the Good News is proclaimed, then when there is a response of faith from the people they are baptized (apparently by Philip), then the news is sent to the apostles in Jerusalem who send two from among themselves to lay hands on the new converts and pray that they may receive the Holy Spirit. Perhaps even the choice of Peter and John is intended to tell us of the importance of unity and continuity for the expanding church.

It is clear that the followers of Jesus in the apostolic generation placed great importance upon the receiving of the Holy Spirit, and considered it an event accessible to observation, as charismatic communities do today. In this passage what is evident to observation is that the new community, though living in some way by faith, has not yet received the Spirit which marks the maturity of the followers of Jesus. We are not told how this was evident, but many passages in the Pauline letters give indications of a certain joy, courage, vision and depth and sureness of self-dedication in those for whom the Spirit of Jesus has become the Spirit by which they live spontaneously.

I Peter 3, fitting into a separate continuous sequence of readings, is nevertheless related to this, as all parts of Scripture are in some way related to all others. In particular, this passage warns and acknowledges that most of us most of the time are not living or experiencing life at the level of spontaneity in the Spirit. On the one hand we have received the Spirit through our baptism into, and confirmation in, the community of the Risen Jesus, who in that passing through death to life breathed forth the Spirit to us. Yet on the other hand we are never beyond praying for the Spirit to come upon us and take possession of us, as we do especially in this season, because there are all too many aspects of the lives of good Christians that are not marked with evident signs of the empowering and motivating Spirit of Jesus.

Peter, therefore, does not find it inappropriate to instruct fellow Christians in some very basic attitudes of Christian life and apostolate. In a context of persecution he reminds them that suffering for doing good places one in the company of Jesus whose suffering was redemptive. Indeed, the text urges Christians to be watchful of their own behavior so that when they are accused or attacked their innocent behavior may testify to the real reason for the persecution and their Christian witness may therefore be quite clear. It is all a matter, so the passage maintains, of truly reverencing Christ as Lord, of acknowledging his lordship in the manner of one's life, modeled upon his. And this includes modest, respectful but persistent readiness to give an account of one's hope. For most of us today persecution is not open or violent. Yet the advice is appropriate, for those who really live and act in the Spirit of Jesus are certainly taking many counter-cultural positions which invite ridicule, discrimination, opposition and various subtle kinds of persecution.

In fact, Peter's advice and warning becomes more daunting the more one reflects on its appropriateness for our own times. Christian life as envisaged in this text is so daunting that it is difficult not to be thoroughly discouraged or conveniently to turn a deaf ear to it. That is perhaps the reason for the liturgy's insistence in bringing us back again and again to the promise of Jesus expressed in today's Gospel reading. Taking us back into the pre-Resurrection part of the Gospel narrative, the farewell address at the Last Supper shows again and again that the disciples are all too dependent on the personal presence and intervention of Jesus. They cling to his human presence because they expect him to do everything for them, to protect them from enemies, doubt, uncertainty, risk. Their faith is portrayed for us as the faith of children which depends upon the continuous presence of one who personally sustains that faith for them. Their love for Jesus is also portrayed as a childish love that consists of a clinging dependence and of a sense of panic at the very suggestion of his leaving them to face their own responsibilities.

The promise of Jesus is that with his necessary departure the Father will give another to stand beside them—using a term that has always been difficult to translate. The promise is identified with the commitment of Jesus to return to them and be with them again in a new way—a way that is internal to their own being, to their experience, to their freedom. The new presence of Jesus and the indwelling of the Spirit of truth are mentioned interchangeably in this text, and that should give us food for thought. It suggests new insights as we pray during this season for the sending of the Spirit of God to be our Advocate.

Ascension Thursday

READINGS: Acts 1:1-11; Eph 1:17-23; Mt 28:16-20.

This Jesus who has been taken away from you up to heaven, will come in the same way as you have seen him go.　Acts 1:11.

All three readings for this day are concerned with the relationship of the Church to Jesus. The story as told in the Gospel of Matthew is the simplest and shortest version of this. Following the story of the women's encounter with the risen Christ, and an argument about the value of the resurrection testimonies, we are told that in obedience to the message from the risen Jesus, the eleven who have been his closest male associates also set out to meet him. Arriving at the designated mountain in Galilee, they saw him and worshipped him, and received from him the charge to extend his mission, making disciples everywhere until the end of time—disciples that would know their lives to be the gift of God the Creator, and Jesus the Redeemer, and the Spirit that had been breathed forth by Jesus into the world.

In the first reading of the day the story is given more detail. All that is to be told in this book of the Acts of the Apostles of those earliest times is first linked with what has already been told of the story of the ministry, death and resurrection of Jesus in the Gospel according to Luke. We are told that Jesus gave ample proof that he was alive, and that over a period of forty days he completed his teaching about the Reign of God. These forty days echo the forty years of Israel's apprenticeship in the desert wanderings. We are also told that the disciples were instructed to remain in Jerusalem for the fulfillment of the promise of baptism in the Holy Spirit. Literally, they were to wait to be "immersed" in the Holy Spirit which was the breath of God by which Jesus himself had lived all along, and now lived in a new and intensified way.

As we ourselves might well have done, the disciples asked whether this would be the end-time in which foreign domination and all other injustices and deprivations would be ended. They seem to hope that it could all be done for them without too much of their own collaboration being required for the project. It is a very common human response to hope that difficult matters can be settled by others or by divine intervention that saves us from having to become involved. The answer of Jesus is direct and plain: the timing of the outcome is not given to us to see in advance, but the Holy Spirit will empower us to continue the mission in all parts of the world.

It is only when all the foregoing has been made clear that the author of the Acts is willing to let us witness in imagination the Ascension of Jesus to take his place with God the Father. The cloud in this tableau recalls the cloud in the story of Israel's desert wandering; it is the representation in visual form of the dwelling of God with the faithful community. In this story it is Jesus who is taken into the cloud; he becomes part of the divine realm. But what is even more interesting and pertinent is the challenge and declaration of the two heavenly messengers in white garments. The disciples' gazing into the sky where Jesus has been swept out of sight is like looking backward in history, but they are told to look forward to a new coming, and that means that they must apply themselves to the task of witness that has been entrusted to them.

The text from Ephesians is a prayer that we may understand the power and wisdom and hope that are bequeathed to us, and that we may realize that nothing is beyond the power of God, for Jesus is now enthroned at God's right hand. The power of Jesus is now invincible, and his way will transform everything no matter what governments, authorities and powers may oppose him.

Seventh Sunday of Easter

READINGS: Acts 1:12-14; I Pet 4:13-16; Jn 17:1-11.

I have glorified thee on earth by completing the work which thou gavest me to do; and now, Father, glorify me in thy own presence with the glory which I had with thee before the world began. Jn 17:4-5.

John's Gospel recounts the priestly prayer of Jesus at the farewell supper in imagery that anticipates the theme of the Ascension. In fact John seems to blend crucifixion and glorification/ascension together in a rather disconcerting way. It should startle us into deeper awareness because we do not usually think of the crucifixion as being in itself an ascent to the Father and a glorification. The glory of which this text speaks is the weight of God's presence and power manifest in human context, and the glorification of Jesus is the realization of that divine presence and power in him. The prayer of Jesus for glorification, therefore, is a prayer for the fulfillment of his mission.

Fittingly, the introductory reading from the Acts of the Apostles picks up the story of the disciples when they have just been witnesses to the Ascension of Jesus. The tableau of the Ascension is powerfully symbolic. Jesus, who has come as the gift of heaven has returned whence he came. He has been lifted up out of the sight of his disciples; until the end-time his palpable human presence has been withdrawn from them, but they are to continue in hope because he will return and the promises will be fulfilled. Meanwhile, he has been lifted up to where a cloud received him out of their sight—a cloud reminiscent of the presence of God that accompanied the Exodus pilgrims as a pillar of cloud by day and a pillar of fire by night. They are both symbols of the presence and power of God— the cloud and the fire. And, finally, there are heavenly messengers in white garments, as there were at the tomb. Moreover they bear the same message as the angels by the tomb; the disciples are to seek Jesus not in the past but in the future, no longer in mortal form but in immortality.

The disciples have been left, but they have been left with a mission to accomplish: they are to entrust the outcome of their hope to God, to dispose themselves to receive the Holy Spirit, and to go forth and bear witness even to the ends of the earth. In today's reading, therefore, they return to Jerusalem, the center of the great drama of the redemption, traveling the short distance over the steep descent and equally steep ascent of the road from Mount Olivet into the city. The text says only that they repaired to an upper room where they were lodging, but Christian piety has wanted to identify that room with the place of the farewell supper. Certainly there is a continuity of theme and connotations. The narrative enumerates the eleven as lodging there, and further tells us that they gathered regularly in prayer with Mary the mother of Jesus and some of his relatives and a group of women disciples. Evidently it is the nucleus of the church that is to come into being with the descent of the Holy Spirit.

Like so much else in the Acts, this scene is exemplary for the founding of churches: people are gathered into the apostolic fellowship in faith and prayer, and they are to pray and wait in confident expectation for the descent of the Spirit among them, empowering them to become witnesses in their turn. There is a liturgical resonance to the recital, which leads immediately to the choice of Mathias to replace Judas, and subsequently to the descent of the Spirit.

Though from a separate sequence, the exhortation for I Peter seems to fit well enough into the theme of the day. The struggle of the redemptive restoration of God's rule in human society is such that it almost inevitably brings persecution upon those who engage in it as followers of Jesus. But this kind of suffering is a share in the sufferings of Christ which lead to the revelation of the divine glory in him and therefore also in his followers, as God's pervasive presence in the world is once more realized. Paradoxically Peter insists that suffering not for wrongdoing but for Christian life and testimony is to be seen as privilege and as the anticipation of glorification. Such suffering is the sign of the Spirit at work in the world which is being challenged and reshaped.

That reflection brings us to the third reading with a new perspective. As John sees it, the prayer of Jesus for the fulfillment of the Father's will and for the completion of his own mission is a prayer that hastens the execution of Jesus, not for its own sake but for the sake of what will be accomplished through it. It is a priestly prayer of mediation, and it is also a kingly prayer claiming a kind of jurisdiction. Jesus acknowledges that he has received sovereignty over the whole human race, to give them eternal life. But the gift does not reach all immediately: it reaches them through the ministry of the disciples of Jesus. It is for these disciples, that is for all of us who are claimed as Christians, that Jesus especially prays, because the presence and power of God must be realized in them, in us, so that the mission may be completed.

The Ascension leaves us with a challenge and with a certain ambivalence, for it leaves us with the promise of the Spirit but it also leaves us with the task of completing the mission.

Pentecost

READINGS: Acts 2:1-11; 1 Cor 12:3-7, 12-13; Jn 20:19-23.

Jesus repeated, 'Peace be with you!', and said, 'As the Father has sent me, so I send you.' Then he breathed on them, saying, 'Receive the Holy Spirit!' Jn 20:21-22.

Today's readings begin with a brief and apparently simple account of the Pentecost story. It is simple on one level because it tells a story that is easily grasped: it is fifty days after Passover, and the disciples are gathered together in one place where they are suddenly engulfed in mighty wind and startled by flames of fire resting on each of them, filling them with Spirit and power to speak and be heard by many pilgrims in their own various tongues. Though startling, it is a story that is easy to follow and also to visualize.

There is, however, much greater complexity in the story because of its allusions. Both wind and fire are symbols for the divine presence. The previous chapter of Acts has told us that the more intimate disciples of Jesus, including Mary and a group of women, had gathered in an upper room. From this upper room, apparently, they emerge later, able to speak to Passover pilgrims from many lands in their local languages. This sequence begs to be compared with the story of the tower of Babel. In that story men are climbing and building together in defiance of God, to usurp God's power, and have their language confused so that they can no longer communicate—a significant representation of deep alienation. In this story, on the other hand, people are gathered, aware of their alienation and their helplessness in face of evil, praying in acknowledgement of their total dependence on God. In that context the divine presence "descends" to them, empowering them, and restoring their ability to communicate across all the barriers that have been created by a sinful history.

Yet even this does not exhaust the allusions that make the story significant for subsequent Christians. The fire that descends upon the disciples individually is reminiscent of the pillar of fire that led the

Israelites in the desert, of the flaming bush that Moses had seen on the mountain, of the fiery chariot that carried Elijah to heaven, of the burning coal that purified the lips of Isaiah that he might prophesy, and so forth. This recurrent theme of God as fire has two aspects: the fire can either purify and enhance, or it can destroy. It represents both redemptive mercy and inescapable judgment. In this passage, the symbol of the fire is complemented by that of the mighty rushing wind recalling the theme of creation by the breath of God that gives life which is in some way similar to God's life, and the theme of inspiration to give utterance to God's word and judgment in the world, and the theme of recreation even of dead and scattered bones. In this passage, therefore, the mighty rushing wind is certainly intended to say that something new and wonderful is coming to pass by the power of God, newly quickening human persons who had been, as it were, dead.

The reading from Corinthians emphasizes the consequences of empowerment by the Spirit. It is the Spirit that enables otherwise timid and evasive people to acknowledge wholeheartedly the paradox that the crucified Jesus is Lord. It is the Spirit, consequently, that so relativizes personal ambitions and insecurities, that believers are able to recognize and call forth one another's gifts, recognizing their complementarity without envy or anxiety. And it is the Spirit, therefore, that unifies the followers of Jesus into a single presence, a single embodiment of the risen Christ redemptively at work in the world.

Appropriately, the reading from John's Gospel presents the risen Jesus as a bringer of peace—of his own characteristic peace. He has brought this peace not for his immediate disciples only but so that he may send them as the Father has sent him, to bring that peace to the whole world. In John's Gospel this short narrative seems to refer to the same reality of the founding of the Church as the Pentecost story presents in Acts. John places it on the great Lord's day, the Sunday of the Resurrection, and adds that the reason the disciples were gathered so secretly behind closed doors was that they feared further persecution. Indeed in this passage the scene is depicted as the first appearance of the risen Jesus to the assembled disciples, so that the moment of the Resurrection and that of Pentecost are brought together.

In this account it is not the mighty rushing wind that comes like a mysterious force from the transcendent holiness of God, to be manifest in human beings in the everyday conduct of human affairs. Here it is rather the personal and intimate breath of Jesus in which the Spirit of God is communicated to them, recreating, inspiring and empowering them for the great mission of reconciliation. How fully they are entrusted with that mission is emphasized in the narrative by the words of Jesus which point out the positive and negative aspects of their mission. The word that they are to preach will either heal or condemn; the word of the gospel itself will be a judgment according to the way the world and its individual inhabitants respond. Those whom they are able to reach will be reconciled, but those who reject the good news will be the more bitterly alienated and lost.

The difference between the two accounts of the descent of the Spirit and the empowerment and commissioning of the Church is a paradox rather than a contradiction. Both versions are demonstrably true: the Spirit comes to us most intimately from the mediation and self-gift of the human Jesus, but it is the powerful Spirit of the transcendent God which comes, as it were, from nowhere and lifts human endeavors beyond their utmost bounds to undreamed of possibilities. And this is the message that comes to us in our own times and situations: to receive the Spirit.

Trinity Sunday

READINGS: Ex 34:4-6, 8-9; 2 Cor 13:11-14; Jn 3:16-18.

The grace of the Lord Jesus Christ, and the love of God, and fellowship in the Holy Spirit, be with you all.   2 Cor 13:14.

As the liturgical cycle brings us to the conclusion of the mysteries of the life of Christ and back to the passage of "ordinary time", the theme for the Sunday is the covenant fidelity of God. We know and experience that covenant fidelity in the triune pattern of our encounter with God, and the three readings for the day's Eucharist open vistas of insight and further reflection on the life experiences in which the triune character of God is expressed.

The first reading is concerned with Israel's covenant relationship with God as mediated by Moses—a relationship that Christian tradition has seen as the prototype of the covenant of the nations with God mediated by Jesus. In the sequence in which the events appear in Exodus, these verses come after the incident of the golden calf. They represent a second redemptive outreach to the people who have been so unresponsive. Our excerpt begins when God has summoned Moses to come up into the mountain again with a second set of freshly cut tablets to await the encounter with God. When Moses arrives as instructed, God descends to take a place beside him to proclaim to him again the divine attributes of compassion, graciousness, longsuffering, constancy and truth. Moses then begs for the favor of God's dwelling in a permanent way in the midst of the people.

The placement of this reading in its liturgical context suggests to us a reflection on the paradoxically triune character of our experience of God. We know God as the transcendent one who calls us to an encounter in prayer and in conscience, but we also meet God taking a place beside us in history, and we know God as immanent within us and within our community. The selection of such a text from the Hebrew Scriptures serves as a warning against the tendency to see somehow three gods; we know God as triune in the paradoxical aspects of the divine in our experience.

The second selection, from 2 Corinthians, links two ideas that may have been more or less accidentally linked in Paul's letter. He sums up his letter with farewell greetings and admonitions, followed by a concluding benediction. Yet there is a connection: the greetings and good wishes are expressions of the fellowship that exists and of the need to maintain and foster it so that the God of love and peace may dwell with them, and the concluding blessing spells out what the dwelling of God among them means. It means that by the grace of Jesus Christ they will know the love of the transcendent creator god, and will have true fellowship with one another in the Holy Spirit which Jesus has breathed into them. In this way the greeting is most apt for the Sunday that follows Pentecost and celebrates the mystery of the triune God.

It is with the Gospel reading that we are brought more intimately into the significance that the mystery has in our lives. The text is taken from the conclusion of the meeting and conversation of Jesus with Nicodemus. The conversation has revolved around the question whether a rebirth in the Spirit is really possible, whether people can really change their ways, whether there is a new entry into the reign of God. There is something old and tired and discouraged about the question—perhaps even something of defensive cynicism. And it is a question that is widely shared in all societies, even the most pious. As the wind seems to blow from nowhere, Jesus answers, so the power of the Spirit is beyond our calculations and our scrutiny.

We can confidently expect the Spirit to be an empowering force within and among us because we learn our true relationship with God through Jesus himself. In our acquaintance with Jesus we recognize the parental disposition of God whose response to human alienation is not condemnation but rescue. What is expressed in Jesus, in whom God comes to take a place beside us in our history, is an invitation to rebirth, a new creation, an entry into the reign of God. The intent of the invitation is not to judge but to save, yet inevitably the rejection of such an invitation is in itself a judgment against those who do not trust and will not take the risk of faith. The human judgment that God does not have power to save us from our own confusion—from our prejudices, injustices, wars, cupidity and anxiety—becomes a judgment against ourselves that leaves us in this darkness. It is a darkness of quiet despair that claims there is no possibility of truly redemptive change, of new beginnings, of being born again when we have grown old with discouragement and cynicism.

The answer of Jesus is that it is our experience of God as triune that should illuminate beyond all possibility of doubt the all-encompassing recreative power of God. It is in Jesus that we come to know with certainty that God's response to the troubled world is saving love and empowering Spirit; when Jesus takes his place beside us in history we also hear the proclamation once more of the divine attributes of compassion, graciousness, longsuffering, constancy and truth.

Solemnity of Corpus Christi

READINGS: Deut 8:2-3, 14:16; 1 Cor 10:16-17; Jn 6:51-58.

He fed you on manna which neither you nor your fathers had known before, to teach you that man cannot live on bread alone but lives by every word that comes from the mouth of the Lord.   Deut 8:3.

The celebration of the Lord's Supper on Holy Thursday is so totally overshadowed by the commemoration of the passion and death in Holy Week, that there is certainly good reason for a separate feast to dwell upon the gift that has been entrusted to us in the Eucharist. As the readings imply, the Eucharist is deeply rooted in the long history of salvation as the Scriptures present it to us.

In the selection of these reading much is already taken for granted: the shape of the ritual based in the Hebrew table grace over the breaking and sharing of bread; the understanding that all food is the gift of the creator; the heightening of the awareness in the Passover seder celebration; and the new meaning with which Jesus invests that age old ritual on the eve of his death. With all this as a background, we have a first reading from Deuteronomy, which calls for our awareness of being guests of God's hospitality. Quite specifically the text claims that God first humbled the people by letting them experience hunger and need in the wilderness, and letting them realize their own helplessness and utter dependence on God as creator. Only then was the mysterious manna given—something new and unexpected, coming as it were from heaven, which neither that generation nor any of their ancestors had experienced before.

So they were brought to realize that both life and livelihood come from God, who does not cease to create but brings forth new possibilities and new gifts at all times in human history, even in those times that seem most hopeless and frightening. This text, therefore, concludes with an exhortation not to forget in the good times what has been learned in those times of desperation, not to become proud and ungrateful, forgetting past mercies and deliverance. This is certainly a text and an exhortation apt for any time and particularly for a time like our own in which many of us in our own society take prosperity for granted and even tend to think we deserve it.

Liturgical custom requires the Gospel selection to be the last reading, but for reflection it may in this case be more helpful to turn to it as the second text. The context of the passage is that very complex chapter 6 of John's Gospel which opens with the miracle of the feeding of the five thousand, and then moves into a discussion of the real reason why anyone should put faith in Jesus. The dialogue has juxtaposed Jesus with Moses, claiming that Moses gave the people manna from heaven. To this Jesus has replied that then as now it is not Moses but God who gives bread from heaven. Moreover, the bread that the Father gives is Jesus in person; to put one's faith in him is to receive the sustenance of eternal life.

It may be a mistake to leap too quickly to the eucharistic equation without first asking what it means to be sustenance for another person. It is an idea that is not altogether alien to our own everyday experience; by their work, their companionship, their caring, people sustain one another. By his self-gift, in his presence, his preaching, his friendship, Jesus is certainly nourishment for others, especially for their growth in graced humanity, in love and dedication. But there seems to be little doubt that there is special reference here to what we can see in retrospect, namely his self-gift for others in his death. In a Hebrew context the parallel reference to flesh and blood would tend to be seen as an allusion to the death of something to be sacrificed, and the mention of eating and drinking would bear further allusion to a sacrificial meal signifying communion with God.

The answer that Jesus gives to the objections raised in this passage does indeed emphasize communion: he links his own communion of life with the Father and the communion of life which his followers will have with him if they accept him as the bread given them from heaven. It is a communion of life that transcends death and is forever. It may be helpful to recall the sentence from Deuteronomy in today's reading: "he fed you on manna . . . to teach you that man cannot live on bread alone but lives by every word that comes from the mouth of the Lord." It is a text that Jesus quoted (according to Matthew 4:4 and Luke 4:4), and Christians know Jesus not only as the bread of life, but also as the Word of God.

The passage from 1 Corinthians concerns the eucharistic celebration of this communion with Jesus and in Jesus with the Father, and carries the imagery to practical conclusions. On the one hand Paul is concerned to warn people against idolatry: it is not possible to have communion with destructive powers and also maintain communion with Christ. On the other hand, Paul is concerned with the implications of the communion in Christ for the relationships that we should maintain among ourselves. The sharing in Christ makes us one body. Members of one body live and function for one another. To share in the eucharistic celebration must be in some measure to do for one another what Jesus did and does for us, namely to be nourishment for one another's lives and being, to care for one another as for oneself, and indeed to be for one another manna in the wilderness.

Second Sunday of the Year

READINGS: Is 49:3,5-6; I Cor 1:1-3; Jn 1:29-34.

I will make you a light to the nations, to be my salvation to earth's farthest bounds.   Is 49:6.

The theme is still the manifestation of Jesus as the one who brings salvation, but now there is a clear link made between the vocation of the Savior and the call to his followers. The radiance of the Christmas season leaves its after glow with the poetry of Second Isaiah, the "Book of Consolation" which sees the salvation of God reaching out to all peoples. The particular verses chosen are from the second servant song, an important vocational text. The Servant is destined from birth, summoned from his mother's womb, for a prophetic task that is to concern not Israel only but all the nations even to the farthest bounds of the earth. The role of this Servant in the original context is to gather and restore Israel to its God-given destiny which is that of witness to the nations, and then to expand and complete the task by drawing the Gentiles to the God of Israel. In the Christian context we see this calling truly fulfilled in the person of Jesus.

It may be for this reason that the second reading gives us merely the official greeting at the beginning of Paul's first letter to the Corinthians. That brief greeting speaks of the calling of Jesus as Savior, the calling of Paul as apostle of Jesus, the calling of the people of Corinth to God through Christ, and the calling of all people everywhere to invoke the name of Jesus as their way to God. When the greeting concludes by wishing us all grace and peace from God our Father and from the Lord Jesus Christ, it is in a context which has made us aware of the links established among us by our giftedness and by our mission. But the greeting also identifies what that gift and that mission is, namely grace and peace—the kind of grace and peace that we can know more concretely because it is given human shape in the person of Jesus. This introductory greeting says a good deal.

The Gospel reading for the day captures what has become Christian tradition's favorite ikon of John the Baptist: the rugged ascetic stands in clear view of all, pointing away from himself towards Jesus. He stands there like a road sign, "this way to salvation, this way to the One you seek whether or not you know it." In these verses John sees Jesus coming towards him where he stands by the Jordan baptizing, and John responds with words which are so familiar to us from our liturgy that we may forget to ask what they mean. Apparently the text intends an allusion to the fourth Isaian servant song in which the Servant is led like a sheep to slaughter, making himself a sacrifice for sin, vindicating many by taking upon himself the burden of their sins (Is 53:7-12). It is in this context that the Baptist says, "Look, there is the Lamb of God; it is he who takes away the sin of the world." Moreover, the Christian community that recorded this remembrance of John's words had already begun to think of Jesus as the lamb of the Passover sacrifice, as Paul testifies (I Cor 5:7).

The discourse of the Baptist in this text continues with the linking of John's own mission with that of Jesus in terms of forerunner and fulfilment. John presents himself as a witness to the person and mission of Jesus in a particularly striking way. He says that he preached of one who would come (as long expected in Israel) but that it was only in retrospect that he recognized who this was and only in retrospect that he realized fully the meaning of his own mission of preparation. The goal of John's mission was the manifestation of Jesus to Israel, and John claims to have been a witness to the initial phase of this, saying that he saw the Spirit descend on Jesus under the image of a dove hovering over him,—a sign that gave John assurance of the special mission of Jesus. Accordingly he presents his witness: this is God's Chosen One. In its Hebrew context this is probably a reference to the first servant song, where the Servant is called the Chosen One of God's delight, who is going to make justice shine on every race while coasts and islands wait for his teaching (Is 42:1-4).

The excerpt chosen for the liturgy stops short of the narrative of the calling of particular disciples which follows in John's Gospel.

Yet the message is already clear: follow him; it is the way of God's salvation; he it is whom we have all been awaiting. God's gift to us in Christ is also a demand, an exigence, a calling to discipleship. Salvation does not come by some magic trick, but by the transformation of human lives and of human society, and if we ask how we are to find the way to such a transformation, Scripture answers in the Baptist's words, "Follow him; this is God's Chosen One".

Third Sunday of the Year

READINGS: Is 8:23-9:3; I Cor 1:10-13, 17; Mt 4:12-23 (or Mt 4:12-17).

The people who walked in darkness have seen a great light: light has dawned upon them, dwellers in a land as dark as death...They rejoice in thy presence as men rejoice at harvest..."   Is 9:2, 3.

The texts chosen for this Sunday link together the nativity celebration with the initiation of Christ's manifestation of divine power and compassion through his ministry. Understood in its original context, the Isaian text is particularly apt for this. When it speaks of the birth of a new prince as a new light shed over a people in darkness, there seems to be an ambiguous reference. It may indeed refer in the first place to the birth of a crown prince to continue the line of David now that the yoke of the foreign oppressor has been broken and the wars are finally over. The verses immediately following today's excerpt have become for Christians a favorite nativity text. On the other hand, the reference in the original may be a different one. Isaiah may have incorporated a liturgical text recited at the installation of a king and celebrating that new king's adoption as a son of God—a kind of divine birth therefore. In that case Isaiah may have in mind not a particular historical king but the perfect descendant of David's line who would come in the future and whose administration of God's justice and righteousness would bring light to a darkened history.

In this case, therefore, the manifestation of divine light is seen not in the birth of Jesus but in the initiation of his ministry of preaching, teaching and healing—a more practical approach that is much easier to understand.

That is certainly the connection suggested in the present reading from Matthew. Matthew's narrative has move from a description of the Baptist and his mission to the baptism of Jesus by John, and from there to the temptations in the wilderness, followed by the news that John has been arrested and that this has apparently brought John's ministry to an end. In today's reading, Jesus sees this as the sign to begin his own ministry. Returning to Galilee, he moves his residence from Nazareth to the larger, busier town of Capernaum on the Sea of Galilee. He opens his mission in the long troubled, racially mixed region of which the Isaian prophecy spoke. The shorter version of today's excerpt ends with the succinct statement of Jesus' mission: he proclaimed a message of repentance and the presence of God's reign.

The longer version of the day's Gospel reading, after relating the rather abrupt calling of four fishermen to be the first disciples, gives one of the more interesting accounts of the way Jesus went about his ministry. According to this text, he went around the whole of Galilee, teaching in the local synagogues, always preaching the good news of the reign of God present, and healing all manner of affliction. Matthew claims that in this first period of his Galilean ministry the fame of Jesus had already spread through the whole of Syria well to the north, and that crowds were following him not only from Galilee, but from the region of the Ten Towns that spread into the hills on the other side of Jordan, from land east of the Jordan stretching further south, and from Judaea lying west of the Jordan further south. This is rather a large area, and suggests that Jesus had become, in his own characteristic way, a powerful and magnetic figure, a sign of liberation unleashing forgotten and discarded hopes.

Because we have heard it all so often for so long, we may not be hearing this startling good news at all any more, relegating it to the status of background music dulled by our own interpretations of what Jesus was about. But the reading from Corinthians reminds us what it was about Jesus that made him such a dazzling light in a darkened history. What Paul asks for in the name of Jesus is dedicated community, concern for others, disregard for status and precedence, ministry not dominance, focus on the person of Jesus not on the factions that so easily arise among his followers, pursuit of the wisdom of the cross and not of worldly wisdom. Paul expresses a certain impatience with the unnecessary complications being introduced into the essential simplicity and integrity of the good news. As long as we are entangled in such unnecessary complications, it will be difficult to hear the gospel as good news, and it will be difficult really to see the startling figure of Jesus entering his ministry as Matthew paints it. To accept the teaching in its integrity is also to see Jesus as the great light in the darkening world.

Fourth Sunday of the Year

READINGS: Zeph 2:3; 3:12-13; I Cor 1:26-31; Mt 5:1-12.

How blest are they who know their need of God; the kingdom of heaven is theirs.   Mt 5:3.

This is not the translation of the opening beatitude that is most familiar to most of us, but it is one (in the New English Bible) which fully catches the theme of the day's readings. The theme is announced in the liturgy by Zephaniah's proclamation of a kind of liberation theology: the structures of oppression, cruelty and deceit will be broken; there will be no more corruption; the poor and powerless and unassuming will be left in possession. It is the kind of proclamation that has always been greeted with raucous derision— something generally assumed to belong in the realm of pure fantasy. Somehow we persist in thinking that the real world is necessarily one of power plays, ruthless competition, bullying, and compromises with truth and justice. A wholly communal or familial concern that begins with the poor and oppressed is a situation that we tend to place outside history and outside the world we know, in some quite other realm of existence.

Paul's letter to the Corinthians, however, points to inescapable evidence that such hope is practical. His evidence is the life of the community of believers as it has already taken root in Corinth and elsewhere. The foundations of the church are established in the poor and despised, yet among themselves they have already begun to subvert the established worldly order of society. As Paul sees it, the existing order is even then being overthrown. Of course, that is an argument which is most persuasive to those who have had the authentic experience of such a subversive community of Christians. Most of us, most of the time, are rather confused by the fact that our whole culture with its economy and its politics is inaccurately and indiscriminately known as Christian. Such lack of discrimination weakens the force of Paul's argument for us because it does not look as though the present order is being overthrown; in fact it does not seem that Christian life and faith make any difference in the structures of human society.

Yet it is clear that the preaching of Jesus, as his first followers understood it, was profoundly subversive of accepted patterns of domination. This is clear in today's excerpt from Matthew's Gospel. The sermon on the mount, which is a little like a campaign speech setting a program for the public ministry of Jesus, begins with the Beatitudes which call for a radical reversal in the way we look at the human situation. Familiarity has robbed this text of much of its power to shock or startle. If we were to take the eight proclamations of blessedness quite seriously, they would all seem highly unlikely.

By the values and perceptions operative in most of our activities, even those which are apostolically motivated, we look for change towards a more godly order in society through power to legislate, to compel observance, to persuade through the force of the communication media of the modern world, to threaten with military intervention, to bargain with material resources, and to lobby on the strength of money and connections. It is a startling reversal to say that the restoration of God's rule in creation is in the hands of the poor in spirit—of those who have the spirit of the poor, unassuming, undemanding, aware of their dependence on others and fundamentally on God.

It seems equally contrary to maintain that consolation is primarily for those who experience tragedy, that the possession of the earth is for those who do not fight for it, and that those who strive totally to see right prevail will themselves find fulfillment. By our operative values we suggest that it is better to distance oneself from tragedy in the world, to fight lustily for dominion over the world in the name of God, and to prefer what seems comfortably doable over what seems inconveniently right. We are not sure that mercy really begets mercy; it may be too much of a risk. Investing too much purity of heart or singlemindedness for the sake of seeing God carries the danger of missing some more immediate practical advantage. We profess to be scandalized at peacemakers because they condone evil, and we tend to the opinion that it is far better to compromise on thorny issues than to become involved in real persecution.

Year by year, however, the liturgy coaxes us to listen to the beatitudes again and try genuinely to hear them because, as the text of Zephaniah has it, God is waiting to bestow the divine reign upon a holy and humble people.

Fifth Sunday of the Year

READINGS: Is 58:7-10; I Cor 2:1-5; Mt 5:13-16.

If you cease to pervert justice, to point the accusing finger and lay false charges, if you feed the hungry from your own plenty and satisfy the needs of the wretched, then your light will rise like dawn out of darkness and your dusk will be like noonday. Is 58:9-10.

For some weeks we have been hearing of the great light that shall shine, and that that light is Jesus Christ whose radiance fills the whole human race through all its history. The theme of this week is that as Jesus is the shining of the Father's light, so are we called to be the shining of Christ's light in the world. If we had only today's gospel text, we might enjoy the metaphors of light and salt, and think no more about it, but the Isaian passage is inescapable in explaining what the metaphor of the light means in terms of practical everyday affairs.

The passage from Isaiah is actually taken from the third and last collection of Isaian writings which are concerned with the community that has returned from exile and is wrestling with the fact that life in Israel falls far short of all the wonderful promises that brought them back. Commitment to strict observance of ritual obligations has not been enough to constitute or reconstitute the returned exiles as the people of promise giving radiant testimony to the Gentiles of the power of Israel's God. The excerpt we hear in this liturgy is, in the original context, part of an argument about a solemn national fast. The question arises as to what use such a fast is, as it does not seem to change anything. The prophet's answer is that a ritual observance alone can hardly be expected to change anything. Even a solemn national fast is useless if all the injustices and oppressions of the society go on as usual—violence and quarrels, day laborers worked to exhaustion, ruthless pursuit of self-interest by the powerful, and such dealings.

Vehemently the prophet proclaims that God does not favor such fasts. The fast that God wants is the liberation of the burdened and the oppressed, the feeding of the hungry and taking the homeless into one's own house, the clothing of the inadequately clad and readiness to accept responsibility for others' need, most particularly that of the wretched. Then, says the prophet, speaking audaciously in the person of God, the people's light will indeed shine forth like a new dawn rising out of the prevailing darkness.

By the fortuitous concurrence of this theme with the continuous reading from I Corinthians, this shining of the divine light in human compassion is linked to the paradox of the Cross of Christ. Paul declares that it is not in any display of power or conquest, but in the weakness, poverty and suffering of the Cross that he expects the good news of salvation to shine through for his converts and all to whom he preaches. This Pauline theme of the divine folly is a further illumination of the theme that it is not a triumphant and powerful nor yet a ritually pure and conscientiously observant Church that can truly be a light to the nations, but one that does justice and practices authentic compassion.

In this context the Gospel reading comes to life. In its setting in Matthew's Gospel, this text comes after the Beatitudes and introduces with a global image some very demanding statements in which Jesus interprets what the true fulfillment of the law means. Salt, to be any use at all, must retain the intensity of its saltiness. Light, to be any use at all, must shine so that it can really be seen by others. It is easy to see that for faith and love to shine they must be expressed in genuine good deeds—redemptive deeds, compassionate deeds, deeds of practical justice and peace. That is the only way others can see the shining of the divine light in the community; ritual alone does not impress outsiders nor even our own young poeple. They want to see the world changing for the better, moving towards peace, structuring our society more justly, expressing practical concern for the outcast and marginated and unfortunate. Then it will be true that we have become the shining of the light of Jesus, as Jesus is the shining of the Father's light, and people will see it as though it were mounted on a lampstand.

Sixth Sunday of the Year

READINGS: Sir 15:15-20; I Cor 2:6-10; Mt 5:17-37.

Yet I do speak words of wisdom . . . not a wisdom belonging to this passing age, nor to any of its governing powers, which are declining to their end; I speak God's hidden wisdom, his secret purpose framed from the very beginning to bring us to our full glory. I Cor 2:6-7.

The thrust of all three readings today is that there is nothing arbitrary about God's Law, and therefore it is not a transient set of rules but the inherent wisdom of creation. The passage from the Wisdom of Sirach argues that within the great wisdom of God's creation human persons have freedom of choice in shaping their lives and their society, but that this does not make God responsible for human sin and destruction, nor does it constitute a license to sin and destroy. Life and death are before us. God sees all, God guides us, but we are responsible for our own actions. Though the larger context in the Book of Sirach allows for redemptive interventions, this passage, which we acknowledge as authentic biblical word of God, is stark in its insistence on human responsibility for the consequences of one's own actions and decisions.

Moving from this reading directly to that from I Corinthians, it would be easy to assume that Paul's attitude and understanding are simply the same. He also writes of God's wisdom. This passage, however, responds to closer attention. Unlike the author of Ecclesiasticus, who maintains that the wisdom of God is plainly in view for all who care to see, Paul speaks of a hidden wisdom, a secret purpose, which will after all bring the human story to its full realization. That hidden wisdom and secret purpose are fulfilled in redemption through the Cross of Christ, in which it becomes possible, after all, to bring the human community to "full glory." Revealed by the Spirit, this wisdom of the Cross offers a fulfillment beyond all experience and all imagining to those who love God.

This rather lyrical passage assumes the teaching of Jesus as he himself propounded it, and today's Gospel reading brings us face to face with that teaching in a rather ruthless way. The secret purpose of redemption in Christ clearly does not mean that the Law is abrogated in favor of license. God's Law is from the beginning and it will last to the end because it is not arbitrary but the very wisdom of creation. But there is clearly a question of the true understanding of the Law. We know from many Gospel stories that Jesus himself could be very free in his attitude to ritual obligations when these did not serve human life and compassion. When the Law touches the substance of human life and relationships, however, Jesus interprets the traditional prescriptions far more demandingly than most of us would have expected. He does not reduce the Law but brings it to its fulness and completion.

There is nothing arbitrary about the interpretation of the Law of the kingdom of God as it is presented here. The beginning of violence and destruction is not murder but all the many ways of putting another down, of hurting, excluding or despising another, of holding grudges and unwillingness to discuss problems. Likewise, personal insecurity and the breakdown of families come about not only through sensational adulteries but through every lack of serious commitment and enduring fidelity in personal relationships. The lustful eye that sees another as less than person, as instrument for pleasure, profit or one's own advancement, is at odds with the reality of the Reign of God. Again, the breaking of oaths is only the extreme form of the many lies, deceits and evasions that make oaths necessary in human society.

What Jesus suggests is an entirely new and different way of thinking about morality, not in terms of what has been explicitly commanded or forbidden, but in terms of the fullest and most creative response to the real needs of human life and community. He sketches some examples of a way of living shaped by radical respect for others and full solidarity with others without exception and at all times. It is easy to agree in theory that this is the wisdom of God's creation from the beginning, but in practice it is surely easier to see that only the special, redemptive intervention of God in Jesus Christ enables us to live by such wisdom in the world as we know it. The wisdom of God's Law is at the same time clear for all to read and yet a secret hidden from the ages and revealed by the Spirit in the Cross of Christ.

Seventh Sunday of the Year

READINGS: Lev 19:1-2, 17-18; I Cor 3:16-23; Mt 5:38-48.

There must be no limit to your goodness, as your heavenly Father's goodness knows no bounds.   Mt 5:48.

The demands of today's readings seem to be impossible to fulfill, yet reflection shows that they are indispensable to the realization of the Reign of God in the human situation. The readings present us with an overwhelming paradox: the necessary is the impossible.

As it is formulated in Leviticus, the message is not yet quite so stark. As Moses reports it, God demands that all the community of Israel shall be holy because God who is their Lord is holy. Further specification of what this holiness means includes some cultic regulations but comes quickly to focus on relationships with other people. Compassion for the poor, honesty in paying wages due for work, abstention from any kind of oppression, deceit, revenge, injustice or complicity in the sin of another, are capped in the original context by the injunction to love the neighbor as a person just like oneself. The excerpt used in today's liturgy omits the list of particulars and moves directly to the general principle. The idea seems to be that if everyone would have the same concern for the needs of others as for one's own, the whole society would reflect the holiness and integrity of God by realizing the intrinisic wisdom of creation.

The New Testament readings seem to challenge any easy assumption that this can be done as a matter of course and by ordinary human endeavors. The passage from I Corinthians reminds us again that the wisdom of God is an inversion of the wisdom of this world and commonly looks more like sheer folly to anyone who is not totally caught up in the redemption. In its original context this is part of an argument against factions in the community based on preferences for various ministers of the gospel. But the admonition fits well enough into the theme of the day: the individuals and the community are temples of God where the Spirit of God dwells, and as such are worthy of deepest respect. All creation exists for God's people, but they in turn belong to Christ who is dedicated whole-heartedly to God. There is a totality and integrity to this vision of the human project that has a certain correspondence to the depiction of the good life that is expected of the Chosen People in Leviticus. In both cases the texts are not moralizing but explaining how the plan of God fits together for the fullness of personal and community life. Paul, however, insists that it is only possible in the power of the Spirit and in communion with Christ.

This serves as a helpful transition to the gospel reading, because the command to offer no resistance to evil really does sound like folly to human common sense. That command is repeated in many very concrete and picturesque examples in this passage. But again there is an implacable logic in the discourse. If we were only to support those who reciprocate, and to act fairly with those who do likewise, we should be doing what worldly people do without further reflection. But this leaves all the usual factions, oppressions, class distinctions, national hostilities, and so forth in place as before. Indeed, by these means hostilities and suspicion and exclusions seem to intensify and proliferate. To realize God's Reign among us, with all that that means, obviously requires something more. It requires gestures of reconciliation that seem to run counter to common sense and prudence. It requires the overcoming of anger, hostility and suspicion in others not by retaliation and restraint of their power to act, but by a kind of de-escalation or defusion. Actual historical experience suggests that people who are violent and abusive act out of grievances, real or imagined, and never really think the score has been evened when their violence has been reciprocated. Therefore violence tends to spiral indefinitely, and to escalate.

Difficult as it is in practice, the wisdom that Jesus offers is a human sharing in the wisdom of God whose goodness is healing and redemptive in broken and hostile relationships, ever recreating and making something new and fresh out of the old and spoiled situation. To act like this even occasionally, even in some of our situations and relationships, is to be momentarily good as God is good.

Eighth Sunday of the Year

READINGS: Is 49:14-15; I Cor 4:1-5; Mt 6:24-34.

Set your mind on God's kingdom and his justice before everything else, and all the rest will come to you as well. So do not be anxious about tomorrow; tomorrow will look after itself. Each day has troubles enough of its own. Mt 6:33-34.

The theme of the day is the caring watchfulness of God, and it is a theme which appears in all three readings. Though the perspective in each is slightly different from the others, the practical advice is the same in all three: do not worry and do not attempt to calculate what is in the hands of a compassionate and all-powerful God.

The first reading is from that second part of the Isaian collection of prophecies, known as the book of the consolation of Israel, which anticipates the return from exile—which the Church has seen as symbolic of the redemption. The brief excerpt chosen here is probably one of the most poignant texts in all the Scriptures: God is likened to a mother with an infant child; God is less able to forget the chosen ones, than a mother is able to put her newborn infant out of her mind and out of her concerns. This sense of being immeasurably precious and constantly present to God is a vital and enduring heritage that we Christians have received from the people of Israel. The relationship that we have with God is essentially this: that God has first loved us with a love that enables us in turn to have the basic self-confidence and self-esteem that can overflow in genuine love of others.

The second reading, though part of a separate sequence in the liturgical cycle, deals with a closely related set of admonitions. The secrets of God have been entrusted to us by Christ, and we are called upon to be trustworthy with those secrets. However, we do need to have a certain freedom of spirit before the judgement of human courts, because it is only the judgement of God that matters. Indeed, it is vain to judge our own lives and achievements. The time for judgement will be the Lord's coming when hidden things and inner motives will be brought to light out of darkness in which we now try to see human reality. In this passage, however, when Paul speaks of hidden things coming to light it is not a threat but a promise—a promise that the judgement of God is likely to be far kinder than the judgement of human persons.

The Gospel reading speaks of trust in God not only for the realization of the promised Reign of God but also for ordinary temporal necessities. As happens throughout the Sermon on the Mount (from which the passage is taken) the advice of Jesus is frighteningly radical in its attitude to human needs and expectations, but it is argued with ruthless logic. With the analogy that one cannot serve two masters each of whom can make a total claim, Jesus comes to the question of the goals and objectives which shape our lives. It is simply impossible, he insists, to gear one's life wholly to the profit motive and also to put God first. To make food and clothing and other personal needs the sole measure of identity and success is to lose touch with the providence and call of God. Reversed, this is not true. On the contrary; to be wholly dedicated to the coming of the Reign of God is to find one's personal temporal needs fulfilled beyond expectations. Jesus invites us to consider carefully the hierarchy of importance between life and food, body and clothing, and to ask ourselves whether that hierarchy is really operative in our values and choices. With the comment that we cannot increase our own height, he hints at the need for trust that is inherent in the limits of our power and our ultimate total dependence on God. But in directing our attention to nature all about us, Jesus also invokes very tangible reasons for deep trust in God.

The burden of the day's readings is that God knows better than we do what we need, and cares better than we can that our authentic needs will be met. It is clear that we should concern ourselves first and foremost with the coming of the Reign of God because where God reigns human needs are satisfied. God will not forget.

Ninth Sunday of the Year

READINGS: Deut 11:18, 26-28; Rom 3:21-25, 28; Mt 7:21-27.

Understand that this day I offer you the choice of a blessing and a curse. The blessing will come if you listen to the commandments of the Lord your God which I give you this day, and the curse if you do not listen to the commandments of the Lord your God.   Deut 11:27-28.

At first reading the texts selected for this Sunday seem to contradict one another. The first and third readings sound the theme that all things will work together in harmony as long as we do them in God's way, which has been shown to us. But the second reading insists that we are justified (that is to say brought into the friendship of God) by faith alone quite apart from any success in keeping the law of God. Because all these texts are from the Canon of Scripture, and because the liturgy deliberately sets them side by side on this occasion, there must surely be a way to reconcile them.

The text from Deuteronomy is as simple as any text we shall find in that book. Bidden to take the words of God's law and covenant to heart, and to bind them as a sign on the hand and wear them as a band on the forehead, Jews through the ages have taken this rather literally and have donned phylacteries containing scrolls of the sacred words at times of prayer. It is done in the same spirit in which Christians might bless themselves with holy water to renew their baptism. But when this text of Deuteronomy is read to Christians who do not follow the instructions literally, the metaphorical sense remains just as strong; the law of God should be in our minds and our hearts and part of us in all we do. The other verses of the selection explain why: to live by God's law is a blessing, for all will go well, and to ignore God's law is a curse by which all will go ill—not because God is vindictive but because the law of God is written into the very pattern of creation.

The passage from the Sermon on the Mount in Matthew's Gospel is on much the same theme, but seems to be far more radical. There is no room for division or confusion of values; the heart is directed to the object of its desire, and that is its chosen home. Unless one has eyes to see the divine revelation, one remains wholly in the dark, stumbling. And it is a matter of frightening simplicity, where in the last analysis the choice is between God and money. Truly to live by the law and revelation of God means to trust wholly, to keep one's eyes on the true goal, and to trust that intermediate needs will be met. It is very easy to assent to this theoretically, in the abstract, but the practical demands of living like this are far-reaching and diametrically opposed to the values of the culture in which we live. The choice is drastic.

It is the second reading for the day, from the letter to the Romans, that tends to mediate between those demands and the apparent impossibility of fulfilling them. Into the impossibility of it, God sends redemption, that is liberation, in the person of Jesus Christ. It is not the keeping of the law that re-establishes us in the friendship, that is the empowering grace, of God. It is the person and the death of Christ that makes the complete breakthrough into a new era of grace, and we share in that empowering grace by faith in Christ. This does not imply that we can therefore forget about the law of

God and live licentiously, careless of the needs and sufferings of others. Such would be no liberation at all. It would be destruction and chaos. To have faith in Christ is to trust his message, to believe in his teaching and his way, and to accept the simplicity of the greatest commandment: the love of God which is inseparable from the love of neighbor.

If this is what it means to have faith in Christ as savior, that is indeed another way of listening to the word of God and taking the law of God to heart.

Tenth Sunday of the Year

READINGS: Hos 6:3-6; Rom 4:18-25; Mt 9:9-13.

Go and learn what that text means, "I require mercy, not sacrifice."
Mt 9:13.

It seems that one of the favorite themes of the preaching of Jesus was that the relationship with God does not consist in ritual observances but in the whole substance of human life, and in a special way in relationships with others who are in need. It is a theme that appears not only in today's Gospel but also in slightly different forms in the other two readings.

In the reading from Hosea, there are references which may be rather obscure to a modern listener. There were wars going on in which Israel itself was divided and at times shamefully treacherous to those on the other side of the dividing line. But the poem which is chosen for today's reading suggests hope in the midst of treachery and suffering. It is the nation and the country that has been torn by the fighting, which God for his own good reasons has permitted. But the prophet assures his listeners that the God who could allow this will also see to it that the wounds of the country are bound up again and healed. Then the prophet turns in God's name to the southern kingdom which has been the aggressor, claiming that its loyalty to God is as frail and fleeting as a morning mist. What God asks is loyalty and compassion, not ritual sacrifices, a true knowledge and appreciation of God's ways and not the destruction of animals in burnt offerings.

The reading from Romans chimes in with this theme by insisting that true salvation is not by meticulous observance of the ritual code but by faith in Christ and in his way. And Abraham is offered as the example of this because Abraham became the recipient of the promises long before the Law in its explicit form existed. It was by faith that Abraham left everything and set out to follow where God beckoned, both geographically and in the manner of his life. And we too have a promise and a hope that we are to follow in faith. It is the goal and the pursuit of that goal which shapes the meaning and the direction of our lives, not the implementation of a code in painstaking detail.

These readings form an interesting prelude to the story of the calling of Matthew the tax collector. Matthew is an exceptional model of faith in Jesus Christ; in this story, Jesus says "Follow me!", and Matthew rose up, left everything behind, so it seems, and followed Jesus, apparently not knowing where that might lead. Moreover, the response of the learned and devoutly respectable is one of horror that Jesus should mingle with people not too fastidious in their religious observances. It would seem to be their position that such people should not even be summoned into the friendship of Jesus and of God; it is assumed that anyone must earn such an invitation by observances of the ritual code. The attitude of Jesus is a round rejection of such a thesis, and it is expressed with a certain irony when he says that just as the sick and not the healthy need the physician, so he is come to call sinners to repentance and not the virtuous.

The story is so remote from our experience that it may have lost some of its shock value. Perhaps we need to substitute the unchurched, the disreputable, the throughly secularized as those to whom Jesus is above all attracted. And perhaps we should ask how much our own idea of our relationship with God is tied up with religious observances rather than with the substance of our lives and of all our relationships.

Eleventh Sunday of the Year

READINGS: Ex 19:2-6; Rom 5:6-11; Mt 9:36–10:8.

I have carried you on eagles wings and brought you here to me. If only you will now listen to me and keep my covenant, then out of all peoples you shall become my special possession. Exod 19:4-5.

The theme for this Sunday is God's covenant with us and strong appeal to respond to the call to enter into that covenant whole-heartedly and with great confidence. As Israel knew long ago and Christians have also realized, there is really only one covenant with God into which all peoples are called at different times and in different ways to enter. It is the covenant of creation and of the wisdom for living a good life and of redemption from the consequences of bad choices.

The passage selected from Exodus is concerned with a moment of transition in the history of the Hebrew people. They have escaped the slavery of Egypt and have witnessed many times the wonderful and compassionate intervention of God, saving them from disasters often of their own making. As they camp in the wilderness, Moses again turns to God for guidance, climbing up into the mountain in solitude. The word of God that comes to him is that the people are to hold themselves in readiness to hear the terms of the covenant, the great alliance, and to learn what it is to be called into special intimacy with God. They are to be a nation of holy life and holy patterns of society and government, reflecting the holiness of God in a world in which there has been much destruction and disruption. And they are to be a people of priests, that is to say a people of mediators between God and a disoriented world, witnessing to that world the saving grace of God.

The passage from Romans, of course, emphasizes that the role of mediation and redemption has been fulfilled in Christ. It is he who truly proved God's love when people were still wildly astray and at enmity with God and with one another. That death of Christ for us, when we were still as it were his enemies, is the pledge and assurance of salvation now that we have entered into friendship with him, and through him into the covenant with God. Our invitation is to enter into the covenant by entering both into the death and into the resurrection of Jesus. In those first days of enthusiasm and gratitude in which Paul wrote, it must have been very evident that once the death of Jesus had accomplished a radical reconciliation, those who joined themselves to him by faith were also living the new life of his resurrection. This is not so clear to us after all these centuries of taking Christianity for granted, but sometimes we receive testimonies of an experience similar to that of the first Christians when we hear testimony of people in our own times who have lived under harsh persecution or oppression, and who have experienced the life of some fervent Christian community as a life of resurrection in the midst of death and suffering.

The passage from Matthew's Gospel parallels the one from Exodus. It is also a transition. In this case it is a transition from a series of miracles, wonderful and compassionate works of God, to a call to the disciples to come into partnership with Jesus in his mission. Matthew tells us that Jesus went around to all the synagogues in the towns and villages of Galilee, teaching and announcing the good news of the Kingdom. The evangelist does not record what it was that Jesus was teaching at this time, so we must assume that it is the same understanding of the people's covenant with God which is presented elsewhere in the Gospel. It concerns gratitude and trust and a willing partnership in the wonderful hospitality of God to all human beings. And we are told that while Jesus gave this message to all, illustrating and substantiating it with works of healing and compassion, he could also see how great was the number and the need of those who had not really heard this message. Then, as now, he called some into closer partnership with him to bring the good news among the people.

Twelfth Sunday of the Year

READINGS: Jer 20:10-13; Rom 5:12-15; Mt 26–33.

Sing to the Lord, praise the Lord; for he rescues the poor from those who would do them wrong.   Jer 20:13.

In a world distorted and disoriented by the consequences of sin, violence and injustice are inevitable. But the word of the Scriptures for today is that whoever follows God's call has no reason to fear that violence. This is the conclusion of Jeremiah's prayer in the first reading. Jeremiah, proverbially the much-abused and persecuted prophet, begins with a bitter complaint to God. He cannot stop himself from proclaiming the word of God which burns within him, in spite of the painful consequences to himself from those who have no wish to hear that word. But in the second part of the prayer, there is a holy defiance of all persecution, based on unshakeable trust in God's protection.

The kind of persecution that Jeremiah describes here is common enough in our own times. People are spying on him and starting whispering campaigns, conspiring to trip him up somehow by tricking him into an indiscretion, luring him into taking a false step, so that they can pounce on him. But Jeremiah knows that the ultimate outcome must be the triumph of God's word, and the powerlessness of the persecutors. So he concludes, reminding himself that he has committed his cause to God and cannot fail, and reminding us that it is always so because God has not lost control of creation and history, even when the divine patience seems to us to last too long.

The letter to the Romans sets all this in its broadest frame of reference. The sin of Adam—that cumulative heritage of the consequences and distortions of sin in the world—has engulfed everything and everyone in a context of lawlessness and violence. But the rescue that Christ has brought into that situation far exceeds the original damage. The grace of reconciliation and restoration also reaches out to all and to everything in human history. We are invited to believe in that saving grace and to respond to it with our own cooperation in the work of restoration. That is the meaning of redemption in Christ, and that is the justification of the kind of hope that is expressed in the passage from Jeremiah.

The advice offered to apostles and missionaries in the reading from Matthew's Gospel makes this theme of trust and confidence in the midst of all kinds of difficulties and persecutions very practical. There is no need to fear for those doing God's will, because God is immediately aware of all that is going on, and God cares passionately and individually about what happens to each of us. Even in face of death there is reason to trust God who transcends all that can happen to anyone in this world, and who raises those who trust in divine love above all that can be done to them by the hands of the powerful and unscrupulous. The same God who provides for such numerous and insignificant creatures as sparrows, surely cares so much more for human beings. And Jesus, who calls his friends to follow him and to share in his own ministry, will surely introduce them as his special friends to the heavenly Father. Such friends can be confident of divine vindication.

Thirteenth Sunday of the Year

READINGS: 2 Kgs 4:8-11, 14-16; Rom 6:3-4, 8-11; Mt 10:37-42.

By gaining his life a man will lose it; by losing his life for my sake, he will gain it.　Mt 10:39.

The readings of the day revolve around two overlapping themes, that of new life as the gift of God, and that of the virtue of hospitality. The first reading takes us once more to the story of Elisha who, because of the many miracles told of him , is seen by Christians as a kind of foreshadowing of Jesus. Certainly the stories told about him served as literary prototypes of some of the stories about Jesus as they were formulated by the earliest Christians. In this case, a well endowed but childless woman offers most generous hospitality to the prophet; she persuades her husband to have a small apartment built onto the house and reserved for Elisha, so that he may have a place to rest whenever he comes that way. The prophet will not be outdone, and promises her the one thing that her wealth and connections cannot obtain, but which God alone can grant—a child. New life is God's own gift, and God rewards with divine hospitality the human hospitality offered to the prophet who is God's servant.

The second reading forms a kind of counter-point theme to this: Paul begs the community in Rome to recognize the gift of new life which God's hospitality has bestowed on them, and really to live that new life. In the resurrection of Jesus we have a new birth—not a biological birth as in the Elisha story but a rebirth into the life of the Spirit. But this also calls for a kind of hospitality to God's grace, to Jesus and the Spirit of Jesus. Paul writes of it as death to an old way of life, spelled out in baptism as burial with Christ, to be reborn from the tomb so that our feet are set upon the new path of life. The imagery here is rather alien to the imagination formed by our culture, but we need to reflect upon it and ease our way into it.

The Gospel text returns to the dominant theme of hospitality, but it includes two rather disparate sets of sayings of Jesus, of which the first ends again with the notion of losing and gaining life. The passage forms part of the larger collection of sayings gathered together by Matthew as instructions with which Jesus sends out the Twelve on a preaching mission. Today's excerpt begins with a ruthless statement of the kind of detachment necessary for an apostle, but balances that with the observation that what must look like death is in fact new life. From that point, the narrator turns to sayings of Jesus about those who offer hospitality to the disciples. No slightest act of hospitality is to go unrewarded; as the reward for entertaining a prophet is a prophet's reward, or of entertaining a good man is a good man's reward, so the reward for entertaining a disciple of Jesus is such as only Jesus himself can give.

The context which the liturgy provides is suggestive because we have just been reminded that the reward of the prophet Elisha was new life. And so the two themes intertwine; God's hospitality always outdoes ours, because God gives life itself, and when we think what is asked of us is sheer death we may find that it is a breakthrough to new life.

Fourteenth Sunday of the Year

READINGS: Zech 9:9-10; Rom 8:9, 11-13; Mt 11:25-30.

Your king is coming to you, his cause won, his victory gained, humble and mounted on an ass . . . he shall speak peaceably to every nation, and his rule shall extend from sea to sea.   Zech 9:9, 10.

The theme for this Sunday seems to be the coming of the King of Peace, and with him of a new order in human affairs. That is certainly a theme that is as relevant to our own times as it has ever been at any time in history. The short excerpt from Zechariah is set within a return from exile and a liberation from oppression by alien powers. In language full of messianic allusions, a king is promised who does not need pomp and circumstance and who signals his peaceful intent by the mount on which he enters the city. The messianic expectation is a promise of a new, divinely sanctioned order which offers peace and well-being.

The text from Romans fits unexpectedly well into this theme because in it Paul maintains that Jesus has accomplished what the Law could never do. Jesus has come with the gift of the Spirit to make possible a new order that fulfills all that the Law claimed and commanded. Because of the new life of the resurrection, our "lower nature" need have no claim on us; we are set free. The modern temptation is to interpret "lower nature" as the more material side of life: food and sex, sleep and comfort. Yet the context within the Pauline letters suggests a broader equation with self-centeredness, factions and prejudice, greed for possessions and power, and every kind of behavior that is contrary to community and charity. In this broader sense, Paul is making a very large claim when he insists that in Christ a new order has become possible in human society, an order that overcomes all of these destructive attitudes and actions.

The background formed by both these readings gives depth to the Gospel text. Here Jesus is saying that the new order that he has come to bring is more readily received and appreciated by the simple and unpretentious than by those who are taken to be wise and learned in the world. It is clear that the new order will not appeal as directly and spontaneously to those who have too great a stake in an old false order. The assurance of Jesus is that his "yoke", which is his Law, is not onerous or complicated or difficult to understand and observe; it is a discipline of simplicity yielding harmony and joy. That is the source of the new order and the widespread peace. If we can believe this and accept his "yoke" there is plentiful redemption for our tortured world. If we begin to live and relate to one another like this, we shall experience the coming of the reign of God, the peaceable kingdom.

Fifteenth Sunday of the Year

READINGS: Is 55:10-11; Rom 8:18-23; Mt 13:1-23.

Why do you speak to them in parables?   Mt 13:10.

Somehow, at this time of year, reflection on rain and seed, growth and yield, tilling and sowing and harvesting, is more than usually appropriate. We plan vacations and travel across the country, and briefly in the summer months we come closer to nature, remembering in our bones the rhythm of a world long since lost to most of us.

Not only Jesus, but all of Scripture and indeed all of nature, speaks to us in parables when we can make time and space to look and listen. The passage from Isaiah invites us to stop and notice the magic of rain and snow watering and fertilizing fields for blossom and fruit and the grain of daily bread. Isaiah beckons us further, to reflect on the fruitfulness of God's word accomplishing its purpose in our lives and in our world. In the dreamy haze of summer's heat and leisure there may yet be an important time of growth, moving from the outward world of nature to the inward world of spirit and out again in a redemptive participation in human history.

For this redemption of human history, Paul writes in Romans, the whole world groans. The world is so full of possibilities, many of them unrealized. Living on a continent among vast fields of golden grain, enormous fertile plains, orchards and vineyards, as Christians we must ask why from all this wealth the hungry of the world are not fed. The sad truth of the matter is that all of nature is in servitude to human greed and fear and rivalry, waiting to be set free to serve God's purpose in creation. The patterns of that servitude to greed are complicated. Individuals acting alone cannot reverse them. But those patterns express sin and call for redemption.

In the midst of summer vacation and fertile fields it is not difficult to tune in to the farming parables of Jesus and to begin to see something of what he saw, though his land by contrast was rocky and barren and hard to till. One may look at the parable from two quite different perspctives. One may be saddened at all the sowing that yields so little fruit. On the other hand, one may be amazed that in the inhospitable environment some seed yields so bountifully both in nature and in grace. The parable seems to suggest that Jesus takest the latter view. It is a matter of a certain poverty of spirit in the evangelical sense to be grateful and delighted with any fruitful outcome of one's own or others' efforts, knowing that it is always the gift of God that crowns our efforts with success. Knowing this experientially is the joy of the poor.

Sixteenth Sunday of the Year

READINGS: Wis 12:13, 16-19; Rom 8: 26-27; Mt 13:24-43.

The Kingdom of Heaven is like this.   Mt 13:24.

We would all, of course, very much like to know what the Kingdom of Heaven is really like. But the parables of Jesus never tell us what the Kingdom is like; they tell only how to look for its coming. The passage from the Wisdom of Solomon seems to say that this does not matter. All that it concerns us to know is that God is all-powerful, that there is no God besides the one God, and that this one God's justice is at the same time mercy. In fact it is the unmatched and unlimited power of God that makes all-encompassing mercy possible. Moreover, we have all around us in nature and history the testimonies of such benign power.

Paul, in the passage from Romans, seems to underscore this by saying that we do not even know how to pray, what to ask, what to yearn for. The Spirit has to come to our aid, to ask for us, to move us in the right direction for our own good and ultimate happiness. For many of us these are not favorite readings, with all this emphasis on not knowing. But what they stress is prayerful discernment of the way of the Creator and the way of the Spirit in human affairs.

A second look at the gospel reading for the day seems to offer more hope and more content. Jesus, it is true, spoke in parables about the kingdom coming, but parables unfold in our imagination and in our lives. These three parables about growing things - the grain with the weed, the tiny mustard seed and the leaven in the dough—seem to say something very hopeful and very helpful about the justice of God that is also mercy. They seem to say that we can learn something about the nature of the Kingdom by watching the way God allows what is already in process to come to maturity. They seem to say precisely that we *can* know something of the Kingdom of Heaven because we are part of its becoming—a becoming that is full of second chances. They also seem to say that it is always too soon for discouragement.

The world we live in is very much like the field that Jesus describes. We make progress in history in some ways, and yet evil grows also. We develop diplomatic channels, the United Nations, the Red Cross, rules for treatment of prisoners, but we also develop more terrible weapons of war. We raise the standard of living, but we also exclude so many people, pushing them into conditions just as dehumanizing. And so on . . . And yet the parable of Jesus assures us the wheat is growing, and we can see it and have a share in it. But it is not an excuse for inaction. It is rather an encouragement to act, knowing that the grace of Christ empowers our freedom in the justice of God.

Seventeenth Sunday of the Year

READINGS: I Kgs 3:5, 7-12; Rom 8:28-30; Mt 13:44-52.

Give thy servant, therefore, a heart with skill to listen, so that he may govern thy people justly and distinguish good from evil. For who is equal to the task of governing this great people of thine? I Kgs 3:9.

This Sunday's readings are curiously apt and incisive for our own times in their comments on the tasks of government and the nature of true wisdom. We are all agreed on the need for profound wisdom in the public decisions made on our behalf because there is little agreement on the nature and source of that wisdom that is needed for the governance of political affairs. Solomon's prayer is appropriate for our times and for all times.

In the history of the United States and in current affairs there is a rhetoric that has been named "civil religion." This discourse claims continuity with the biblical vision and hope, and acknowledges a covenant with God, shaping one nation under God. Yet the practical expectations of public policy are generally based on a far narrower vision, far lesser hope, and a considerably more restricted sense of responsibility. Christians in a representative democracy share Solomon's burden of discernment.

The passage from Romans today is blunt: the Spirit works for good in everything for the covenanted people. But the covenanted people are those whose lives and communities are being shaped in the likeness of God's Son. In the readings from Kings, Solomon is free to ask for long life or wealth for himself or for victory over his enemies. True wisdom for government can be had only by those who do not seek first and foremost a long political life by re-election, who do not hope to profit in the private sector by the influence and contacts of public office, and who do not see their security in crushing others. But there is a correlation with what the electors seek. The challenge concerning goals and values is addressed to the society at large, to all of us. The fate of the poor, the disadvantaged, the future, depends on the priorities really expressed in our public and private lives.

Today's Gospel reading points to the conditions for that, which never change because they are so basic to the human situation. The treasure in the field and the pearl of great price are bought by selling everything. God's rule among us is not attained by compromises or by double standards with regard to private and public life. We cannot be the people described in the rhetoric of covenant and biblical faith, nor can we expect to see peace and justice, if we do not act justly and compassionately at all costs in all aspects of life. A public policy for peace requires Solomon's renunciation from all of us.

Eighteenth Sunday of the Year

READINGS: Is 55:1-3; Rom 8:35, 37-39; Mt 14:13-21.

Why spend money and get what is not bread, why give the price of your labor and go unsatisfied? Only listen to me and you will have good food to eat, and you will enjoy the fat of the land.   Is 55:2.

This text from the conclusion of the Isaian "Book of Consolation" puts in a nutshell the substance of human history. Because of the heritage of sin and the distorting consequences of sin, we all seem to spend much of our lives exhausting ourselves in pursuit of goals that will never truly satisfy. And all the time God holds out to us the most lavish hospitality in those things that sustain a life of real happiness. The theme of water in a thirsty land and of bread in the wilderness is not new; it is a very strong theme in the story of Israel's sojourn in the Sinai desert on the way to the Promised Land. And it became a favorite theme in the preaching of Jesus as that preaching is passed on to us in the Gospel according to John.

The passage from Romans is like a commentary on that theme. Jesus has said that he would give living water to all who came to him seeking it—that he would give water welling up to life everlasting, so that those who drank of it would never thirst again, but would be truly satisfied. Likewise he had said that he was the living bread come down from heaven to satisfy the ultimate human hunger; the manna in the wilderness had only prefigured this true bread from heaven; the manna itself had never lasted for more than a day, but had been a pledge of hope for the future. Paul expresses it more plainly by saying that nothing can separate the believer from the love of Christ; no matter what hardships must be endured it is in the intimate relationship with Christ that the deepest human longing is satisfied and all else is overshadowed. In that relationship the full consummation of all human desire is already in some way anticipated, giving unshakeable assurance of what is yet to come.

The Gospel story for the day gives a vivid representation of the same theme. In spite of the need that Jesus felt to be alone and at rest for a while with some of his close friends, there were crowds that had begun to realize that Jesus could offer them a kind of nourishment that truly satisfied. They followed him until he turned around and met them again, healing the sick and giving hope and consolation to all. In response to the disciples' anxiety that the people should go away and find their own food, Jesus insists that he can feed them until they are satisfied. And he does it by what seems like a reckless gesture of sharing the slender available resources with as many as are in need. Moreover, his action proves that there is far more than enough.

There are many ways of reading that story. One can quickly decide that it was a miracle performed by Jesus in virtue of his divinity, and that it shows both how different he is from ourselves and how clearly God's revelation and redemption comes through him. But Jesus seems never to have made idle gestures, and in this story we are told in the plainest language that he involved his disciples in the action, and that it was a kind of challenge to them about the way they regarded the situation. Therefore we might rather look at the whole not only as a figure of the Eucharist, which it certainly is, but also as a challenge to us concerning the way we regard and use the resources of the earth which God has offered to all. And that is a point of convergence with the question of the day's first reading: what is it that we are pursuing for ourselves in our own lives; is it something that will never satisfy—possessions beyond the ordinary to show we are better or to feel we are more secure than others, power or fame to set us above others—or is it the will of God that Jesus spoke of as his food—the will of God which is community among human beings, generous response to those in need, acknowledgement of our interdependence?

Nineteenth Sunday of the Year

READINGS: I Kgs 19:9, 11-13; Rom 9:1-5; Mt 14:22-33.

Take heart! It is I; do not be afraid.   Mt 14:27.

It is really very easy to identify with the Peter stories of the New
Testament. There is the spontaneous, generous, sometimes bragging
and always extremely self-confident, response to Christ's inviting
presence. Then there is the situation that turns out to be far more
complicated, difficult and frightening than anticipated. By that time,
however, Peter is well into the situation, and the result is undisguised,
total panic. At that point, the Scriptures always invite us to look
through the eyes of Peter and evaluate the whole situation from a
different perspective—that of God's undeserved and unstinting
redemptive grace.

There is something divinely compassionate about the pattern of
this story that appears in several guises. In this Sunday's Gospel
reading we meet the same kind of challenge as in that other story of
Peter's confession of faith followed by the reluctance to go to
Jerusalem. It also follows the same pattern as his bragging affirmation
of Jesus in Jerusalem, followed by the triple denial after the arrest of
Jesus. But today's story is so concrete and picturesque that it lends
itself readily to situations we are all involved in in our own context.

The sense of drowning is not unfamiliar to those who conscientiously read our daily papers and ask themselves how they as
Christians can act redemptively in matters of world famine,
ecological irresponsibility, violence at home and abroad, corruption
and deception at many levels, and the ever present threat of nuclear
disaster that looms over us and even more desperately over our
children. The sense of drowning is perhaps most familiar to parents,
especially those with teenage youngsters. Peer group pressure and
advertising, producing cancerous growth of artificial wants and
artificial discontents, with possible extremes of chemical elation and
of suicidal despair; a general adult loss of confidence in holding the
values and standards of the society; the colossal risk of drugs, alcohol

and reckless driving—all these are very well represented by a story of waters threatening to drown us. We make confident professions of faith and commitment in our liturgy, but go out to face difficulties that seem to make redemptive living and action impossible.

Where is God in all this? What all three readings for today seem to say in their own dramatic ways is that God is where we least expect to find healing grace—in the still eye of the storm. The story of Elijah is concrete and dramatic. Things have become hopeless, and Elijah is fleeing for his life. Roused out of his despair by a heavenly messenger, Elijah is brought to the holy mountain to confront God. God is not found in storm or earthquake or fire, but in the stillness at the center of it all.

Similarly in the passage from Romans, Paul experiences rejection and persecution but finds the redemptive grace of God at the heart of it all. In the Gospel reading all this is depicted in physical, cosmic symbolism. God, these readings tell us, is always present, even when we appear most threatened and abandoned.

Twentieth Sunday of the Year

READINGS: Is 56:1, 6-7; Rom 11:13-15, 29-32; Mt 15:21-28.

For the gracious gifts of God's calling are irrevocable.   Rom 11:29.

Paul is writing this about the vocation of his fellow Jews who, to his own great distress, do not accept Jesus as the fulfillment of the hopes of Israel as Paul himself does. The Church, in presenting us with three texts about relationships between Jews and Gentiles in the history of salvation, seems to demand that we reflect on the continuing challenge of our attitudes as Christians to the Jews.

The text from Isaiah combines an exhortation to live justly in faith with the promise that all who do so from among the nations will enjoy God's favor and blessing. Not only in the preachings of Jesus but also long before that in the utterances of the great prophets, there were many warnings against the partisan assumption that God takes sides against other peoples. God is on the side of all people against whatever sufferings and burdens oppress them. Election to a more intimate relationship is always for the benefit of others rather than to their exclusion.

In the passage from Romans, Paul carries this to its logical conclusion: God who would not on Israel's account shut out the Gentiles from salvation, surely will not shut out the Jews on account of the newcomers to faith in God through Jesus. For God does not abandon people or forget promises. There is such a yearning for special status, special privilege, in human history, that there is always the temptation to define others as outsiders, as less worthy or significant. Israel was not exempt from this temptation, nor are Christians.

The Gospel reading stands oddly in relation to these two texts. Jesus, who has just argued with his fellow Jews over their too narrow interpretation of the response due to God, at first fails to answer the Canaanite mother and seems to ignore her. No matter how we read this passage, it is puzzling. However, the most important part of it is certainly the conclusion. Jesus sees salvation as coming to the Jews and shared with the rest of us from their tables. And Jesus responds to faith even when it comes from unlikely people in unlikely situations. His first answer to the Canaanite woman expresses the accepted pattern of values and expectations. Perhaps the story is in the Gospel because that pattern so often emerges in our own values. But it is the final answer of Jesus to the Canaanite woman that we are expected to take to heart as the Christian transcendence of racial, cultural and other barriers between people.

There is therefore a contemporary meaning in the three readings. That same temptation to exclusion of others which influenced Jews in relation to Gentiles and early Christians in relation to Jews, continues to affect our attitudes to all whom we consider "outsiders", whether to our faith, or our culture or our political and economic structures. It is difficult to remember that God does not take sides against the people whom we see as our enemies.

Twenty-first Sunday of the Year

READINGS: Is 22:15-23; Rom 11:33-36; Mt 16:13-20.

I will give you the keys of the Kingdom of heaven.   Mt 16:19.

We met the story of Peter and the keys earlier in the summer on the feast of Saints Peter and Paul. The focus then was on the person of Peter. Now it seems to be on the symbolism of the keys. The first reading also holds a divine promise of keys—that is, of the key of the house of David.

The symbolism of keys is quite common in our lives. We speak of the key to a problem or situation, the key of a musical composition, the key which holds the proper answers to a set of academic exercises, and so forth. An ancient custom honors a favored stranger by giving that person the key of the city. In all of these cases the symbolism of the keys is that of access to what is hidden, secret, mysterious, protected. But people tend to interpret the symbolism according to different expectations and dispositions. To some it means primarily power *over* others—power to lock up, withhold, forbid, deprive, judge worthiness. To others it means primarily responsibility *for* others—freedom, trust, the opportunity to open doors to adventure, happiness, wisdom and knowledge, beauty and love. Those of us who have teenage children know much about the allure and promise of keys. They mean a new freedom, a coming into one's own, an entrance into adulthood, though in this generation we associate all this more with the car keys than with the key of the house.

The Bible uses the symbolism of keys, and of opening and closing, a number of times. In today's first reading God will lay the key of the house of David on Eliakim's shoulder, and in the Gospel Jesus says in response to Peter's declaration of faith in him that he will give him the keys of the Kingdom of Heaven. The book of Revelation says that the Risen Christ, living forever, holds the keys of death and death's domain (Rev 1:18), and speaks of an angel who carries the key to the abyss where the ancient dragon is chained and kept from harming the nations.

In rabbinic tradition it seems that the keys are often the symbol of access to God's Law and wisdom, the interpretation of God's will in the world. Jesus warns that those who seem to hold those keys sometimes betray their trust, shutting the door in people's faces, neither entering themselves nor allowing others to do so (Mt 23:13), and he speaks angrily of those who have taken away the key (Lk 11:52). The Peter story of today's liturgy promises genuine possession of the keys in response to faith in Jesus. An Advent antiphon for December 20th explains why this is possible: Jesus himself is that promised key of David which can open and shut everything and liberate the captive from prison and darkness and the shadow of death.

Catholic theology has in past centuries linked the story of Peter and the keys to the authority of the Pope. Scripture seems to have a broader intent. All believers hold keys to the Kingdom of Heaven because of their faith, and all are challenged concerning their use of the keys, both for themselves and for others.

Twenty-second Sunday of the Year

READINGS: Jer 20:7-9; Rom 12:1-2; Mt 16:21-27.

What will a man gain by winning the whole world at the cost of his true self? Or what can he give that will buy that self back?   Mt 16:26.

Most of us are very familiar with this quotation in an older translation which speaks of losing one's soul. That older translation made the matter sound more remote than the Gospel seems to intend, the more so as we often met the quotation in the past as an admonition to fulfill churchly obligations. But in today's gospel reading Jesus does not seem to be admonishing other people, not even Peter who has tried to deflect him from his path. Rather, Jesus seems to be explaining himself and his deliberate choice to pursue the course that is bound to lead to his arrest and criminal execution. He seems to be giving his own *apologia* or defense before us who are his disciples and who (like Peter) may well think the way of Jesus foolish and unreasonable.

In these verses, Jesus summarizes what is at stake in the redemption. It is a distorted human self-centeredness that puts personal safety and well-being before all else, and therefore loses meaning and purpose, identity and community. This is the heritage and distortion of sin. In spite of its seductive promises, it never leads to true personhood or authentic fulfillment. Only an utter trust in God, a subordination of oneself and one's life to the divine will, expresses authentic human personhood and gives ultimate fulfillment. In a sinful world the divine will is redemptive, but subordination of oneself and one's life to the divine will is bound to involve some sort of death to apparent self-interest. Jesus appears in this reading not so much to be giving us stern warnings about how we should conduct ourselves, but rather to be pleading with us to understand why it is that he must go about his work in this very peculiar way. It is the only possible authentic expression of what he is and what he is called to be in a sinful world.

Jeremiah's text illuminates this in some measure when he explains that, in spite of the persecution and ridicule which it brings him, he finds he cannot repress the word of God for it is a fire blazing in his heart—a fire to which he must be true. Paul helps us to understand this by imploring Christians to offer themselves to God as a living sacrifice, to be remade, transformed, able to discern the will of God, getting things in focus so as to know what is truly good. Jesus had fire in his heart and offered himself, a living sacrifice, to be transformed. Losing his life, he became the living one who holds the key to death. Paul sees this as the prototype for the followers of Jesus who must pass through death in baptism to the new life of the resurrection. And indeed Jeremiah's expression describes the early Christians very well when he writes that in spite of persecution and setbacks he must continue because God is a fire in his heart.

Twenty-third Sunday of the Year

READINGS: Ezek 33:7-9; Rom 13:8-10; Mt 18:15-20.

If you do not warn him to give up his ways, the guilt is his and because of his wickedness he shall die, but I will hold you answerable for his death.   Ezek 33:8.

The responsibility of the prophet is evidently very great and also very dangerous. Warning one's friends and fellow countrymen about their sins does not endear the prophet to them. Warning one's own community or society about the godlessness of its assumptions, values and policies is not the path to popularity and promotion. Almost daily our more critical newspapers relate the fate of "whistleblowers," reporting it with helpless indignation. But the word of the Lord to the prophet is that he must accept the task of calling a warning when all is not well in Israel.

Scripture is, of course, written and preserved for all of us, and in the history of the redemption none of us can entirely escape that difficult task of warning. The redemption is necessarily a community affair. No one errs without in some measure confusing others; no one falls without upsetting the balance of those around. Our culture, however, does not favor the acceptance of such responsibility. The prevailing ethos is one of permissiveness to the limit of endurance. The assumption is that if others wish to ruin themselves that is their own affair. Like Cain we are inclined to object that we are not our brother's keeper, and have more than enough to do managing our own affairs.

Yet warning or admonition is certainly an aspect of that debt of love that we owe one another, of which Paul writes in today's excerpt from Romans. It is not because we hate others that we are likely to be willing to warn them of danger, but rather because we accept them as members of a common fellowship, bound together in a common destiny. It is, of course, always easier, at least in the short run, to evade and smooth over. But that is treatment which in the long run rejects the other; it is not acceptance. True challenge to values and behavior becomes possible only in a context of solid concern for others and strong bonds of fellowship.

The Gospel reading adds to this a wise way of going about the task of admonition—a way that is not original to the Gospel but is shared by many communities who have been in quest of community harmony. The advice here is directed to Christians among themselves. They should first admonish a wrongdoer quietly and discreetly in private, and only move step by step to broader community involvement if the first moves are not successful. Yet there is never any question that all share the prophetic task, and that what is sinful cannot go unchallenged in the community, both for the common good and for the good of the individuals involved.

In our world today, this says much not only to individuals and church bodies, but also to so-called Christian nations, and especially to reflective Christians about their prophetic task within their own nations. The challenge that has been expressed by the U.S. bishops' statements, and by Church leaders in other parts of the world, is most appropriate. So are the movements within the local churches for peace, for sanctuary for those fleeing persecution, for racial and economic justice, and so forth. They are admonitions to one's own people in accord with the biblical command, "Carry my warnings!"

Twenty-fourth Sunday of the Year

READINGS: Sir 27:30–28:7; Rom 14:7-9; Mt 21–35.

Were you not bound to show your fellow servant the same pity as I showed you?   Mt 18:33.

There is a strong parallel between the first reading for today and the Gospel excerpt. They seem to say that God cannot forgive us if we do not forgive. They seem to imply that this is not a limit of God's omnipotence but is in the very nature of the case. There is an existential logic that requires this rule. It is, however, very difficult for most of us to understand forgiveness. The passage from Paul in today's readings, just like that from the Book of Sirach, suggests that anything other than forgiveness is quite out of place because judgment can safely be left to God. But there is more to it than that.

We have difficulty in understanding forgiveness because we tend to identify it with permissiveness. Few of us in practice want to let anyone injure us unchallenged seventy times seven times while we pretend to like it. But this is not what is commanded by the Gospel reading. The saying and the story about forgiveness must be read in sequence with last Sunday's readings which stressed the obligation in love to challenge evil doing and admonish sinners. To let evil go unchallenged is in fact unforgiving because such permissiveness does not heal or restore but allows destructive forces to gather momentum, rushing persons and societies to their doom.

Poets, such as Gerard Manley Hopkins, have long noted that in creation itself God teaches us what forgiveness really is. The forgiving earth swallows up again and again the filth and pollution of our industries and our carelessness and our greed and brings forth fresh vegetation, regenerating the air and the landscape. Streams and rivers cleanse themselves of our wastes, and rains continually wash our world clean again. It is not because our mess is left to lie there that we know the creator's forgiveness, but precisely because nature challenges our destruction and our wasteful ways, and constantly strains to repair the consequences.

Something similar may be said of the course of human history. We know from the Exodus theme that it is not when the oppressed of the world are quiescent and cowed under their oppressors that the redemptive, forgiving, healing spirit of God is abroad among us. It is when the oppressed stand up and challenge their oppressors and demand liberation that we know there can be forgiveness even of the sins of oppression of the powerless. It may be a painful forgiveness, but it effectively heals and restores. God's forgiveness is the model for human forgiveness. It involves challenge of evil, restoration, healing.

It is in this context that we hear the Gospel passage read. This parable links our attitude to God with our practical behavior towards other people. In the story of the unforgiving servant, what is stressed most is the fantastic disproportion between the debt we owe God and the debts that others owe us. If God is willing to heal and redeem all that human persons have destroyed and distorted in creation, it is clearly important that we help to repair those particular distortions of relationship that others inflict on us. The issue is not blame but reconstruction.

Twenty-fifth Sunday of the Year

READINGS: Is 55:6-9; Phil 1:20-24, 27; Mt 20:1-16.

Why be jealous because I am kind? Thus will the last be first and the first last. Mt 20:16.

Many times in Sacred Scripture God is self-defined as generosity—boundless creative love and relentless redemptive compassion. But we are fools reading with one eye, listening with one ear, if we do not realize the tremendous exigency that this revelation carries with it.

Strange as it may at first seem, in our sinful condition we do not really want God to be indiscriminately compassionate. It offends our sense of law and order. Our notions of justice are petty and self-serving when compared with divine justice. The second Isaiah is sadly right in our days as in his own when he heard God saying to the people, "Your thoughts are not my thoughts . . . as the heavens are higher than the earth, so are my ways higher than your ways" (Is 55:8-9). In its original context, it is a word of promise and of peace, a word of encouragement and affection. Why, then, do we tend to hear it as a word of reproof and condemnation? The passage promises that God will freely forgive. It offers universal compassionate welcome to those who will abandon evil and return to God. It tells us that we can hope for more than our own hearts would offer.

The parable that Jesus tells in today's Gospel illuminated the matter so well that it is rather embarrassing. I suppose that most of us, if we are honest with ourselves, must admit to a strong reaction to the story. It simply does not seem fair. In the original context of Matthew's Gospel, the workers in the vineyard, hired at various hours of the day as day laborers, must have brought to mind the situation of Jews confronted with Jesus. Persecuted for centuries in the observance of a law full of onerous ritual obligations, they were now confronted with the claim that Gentiles were welcome into God's covenant of salvation on much easier terms.

However, the parable also suggests many situations in which we ourselves are far more intimately involved. It suggests many secular situations having to do with community and compassionate use of resources. It suggests some comparison with affirmative action policies and welfare programs. Is it not true that in such matters our thoughts are not God's thoughts; that we may be willing to help the unfortunate, but we do not want the unsuccessful put on equal terms with ourselves; that we tend to see an ungodly hint of Marxist socialism in the very suggestion of such a thing? It also suggests comparison with our less reflective attitudes to the poorer countries of the world. Our past success in war and trade, our good fortune in natural resources and industrialization are taken for granted, as we see ourselves somehow more worthy because of our success. It seems only right that we are rich and they are poor and often starving.

What I find particularly disconcerting in the parable of Jesus is the fact that it mirrors our own social life so accurately. It is true that the first worked all day in the heat of the sun, but we are told that the last are standing idle all day in the market place because no one hired them. That is the daily experience of many in our own time, but we consider ourselves better than they are and therefore more worthy of consideration in economic and social policies. After all, we tend to think, we are where we are because we worked so hard.

Perhaps it is most of all in the matters spiritual and ecclesial that we feel the proper distinctions between various degrees of merit should be made. Sad to say, our history as a church is full of examples of judgmental attitudes and thinly disguised vindictive sanctions and threats in the name of Christ. Even today statements are made, for instance in relation to the Presidential election campaigns, expressing condemnations in the name of Christ that would be very hard to reconcile with this Sunday's Gospel. The need to be approved and rewarded by being preferred to others seems never far from any of us, and the inclination to see Christian life as a competition for higher places in heaven has, so it seems, never quite left us. As a child I used to think it quite unfair that the conditions for attaining sanctity were so much easier for penitents and for some martyrs (the ones who were dispatched swiftly and not too painfully) than for ordinary good folk who plodded along all their lives. The Gospel reading is unsettling even now, because I'm not sure I have entirely shifted from that view.

If Paul really meant what he wrote to the Philippians in the passage excerpted for today, he must indeed have shifted his position quite drastically from the stance that he attributed to himself in his days as a Pharisee. But perhaps it is only something that he prays for and aspires to: that the greatness of Christ should shine out in his person, whether in a laborious life or an early death, because in any case life to him is Christ with all the implications which that holds.

Twenty-sixth Sunday of the Year

READINGS: Ezek 18:25-28; Phil 2:1-11 (or 2:1-5); Mt 21:28-32.

Again, if a wicked man turns from his wicked ways and does what is just and right, he will save his life. If he sees his offences as they are and turns his back on them all, then he shall live; he shall not die. Ezek 18:27-28.

This Sunday's readings give the lie to that cherished bookkeeping analogy for the life of grace which we all find so hard to abandon. Ezekiel tells us that the people of Israel consider God's attitudes unprincipled, because God so readily forgives the repentant sinner but does not turn a blind eye to the misdeeds of those whose established righteousness is well documented. Patiently Ezekiel goes over the old argument again: it is rather that these human expectations of established credit are perverse. God is constant, not vindictive; it is in the nature of human freedom that sin destroys and conversion saves.

Both Scripture and liturgy return to this theme so often that we can assume it is central to the redemption. We demand that God conform to our "principles", and are scandalized again and again to find God demanding that we conform to a higher wisdom, a more sublime justice. Yet Jesus, whose parables often invite conventional wisdom to turn several somersaults, offers the parable of the two sons as an appeal to good common sense. The situation is a familiar one—the courteous, suave reply of the son who manages the appearance without the substance of obedience, and the rough rudeness of his brother who expresses all the resentment he feels but nevertheless does what is asked. In daily life, we find it so much more pleasant to deal with the former and yet we are betrayed by this response. It eats away at the whole fabric of human society and human relationships. We meet this stance in the respectable good citizen who cheats on income tax, in the merchant with slick advertising for profitable but health-destroying products, in the "generous" person who always manages to put others at a disadvantage, in those whose "friendships" are leverage for self-promotion at the expense of others. In other words, we constantly meet this stance in ourselves.

Jesus invites reflection on this. We may be angered by the crude expression of hostile feelings, but it is the substance of the response or the relationship which counts. In our human relationships we are often deceived by fair manners and smooth talk. God, as Jesus implies, is never fooled. God sees right through the massive edifice of human respectability, righteousness and merit-banking, and looks at the outcome of it all. That is why Jesus seems to have had such easy relationships with the disreputable. That is why in him such discouraged and abandoned people found hope and affirmation; conversion is always possible to those who know they are astray. God's will is salvation and not the wreaking of vengeance.

It is small wonder that Paul writes, even to the Philippians whom we see as a rather model Christian community, that they should leave no room for rivalry or personal vanity. The life of grace is not a banking account and it is not a competition. Out of the consolation of life in Christ, and out of the warmth and affection that comes from the sharing of the Spirit, life should overflow in gratitude with love and concern for others' salvation. The salvation of others is our gain, not our loss. Therefore there is no need to keep an account of our relative standing in the sight of God. It is meaningless. It is like those drivers on the highway who cannot afford to let anyone pass them, even to get into a "turn lane", as though a car that overtakes them somehow prevents them from getting to their destination. In fact those who so desperately need to get ahead of others in the traffic may be hurrying to an untimely death, and those who desperately need to be better than others may be betrayed by their own need to establish righteousness.

The liturgy offers us a choice. We may stop there, or we may follow Paul's thought further into the ancient Christian hymn about the humility and exaltation of Jesus. We usually read this text about Jesus being in the image of God and emptying himself, taking it as referring to the divinity. But perhaps that is not what Paul had in mind. Perhaps Paul thought of Adam in the image of God and asserting his excellence and freedom in independence, and then of Jesus in the image of God accepting total dependence, not ashamed or afraid to be identified with sinners and criminals on the cross, not asserting his own righteousness. Perhaps that is why Paul quotes this hymn in the midst of his exhortation to the Philippians. Perhaps that is why the liturgy wants us to reflect on this hymn in the context of Ezekiel's warning and of the story of the two sons.

Twenty-seventh Sunday of the Year

READINGS: Is 5:1-7; Phil 4:6-9; Mt 21:33-43.

The vineyard of the Lord of hosts is Israel, and the men of Judah are the plant he cherished. He looked for justice but found it denied, for righteousness, but heard cries of distress.   Is 5:7.

This week's readings are certainly not easy to apply. There is always the temptation to see the parable of Isaiah about the vineyard, and the parable of Jesus about the vine-growers, as referring to the people of Israel and the leaders of Israel who did not recognize Jesus as the Christ. That way it all works out neatly: the vineyard which is Israel is left unprotected and the nation is dispersed, as happened historically; and the vine-growers who are Israel's chief priests and pharisees have no office in the "new dispensation" which is the Church. There is no doubt that this was originally intended, and indeed Matthew's Gospel assures us that the chief priests and pharisees well knew the reference was to them and wanted to arrest Jesus.

However, the Canon of Scripture and the lectionary for the liturgy do not incorporate texts unless they have a meaning for Christians of every age. So we must reflect further about what these parables mean in relation to our own lives, although the imagery tends to be remote for most of us. But, as it happens, I planted a grapevine three years ago in our back yard. I put it by a fence it might like to climb and crawl on, and I fed it plenty of cow manure, catering to the strange taste of grapevines. It grew and spread and asserted itself, even putting out long tentacles to attack my apple tree. But never a blossom, never a grape appeared. My disappointment was bitter but I persevered two more years. A few blossoms came but no fruit. Next year I'll move it and put it against the south wall of the house. Of course, I could buy grapes at the store when there is no boycott on, probably better ones than I could ever grow. But this is my grapevine and I really care about it. No matter how much I care and toil, this living growing thing cannot be compelled, but I will continue to coax it.

This experience has somehow brought the parables of Isaiah and of Jesus much closer. It suggests that God really cares and will not be thwarted. It suggests something about the indefatigable fidelity of God. It also seems to suggest that the difference between the two parables is important. Isaiah writes of the vineyard itself and the bitter disappointment of the owner of the vineyard who has tended it. Though Isaiah speaks of justice and righteousness denied and of cries of distress, he does not actually distinguish between the people at large and the responsible leaders. Jesus does. His parable refers to the vine-dressers, to those responsible for the state of the vineyard and the rendering of its fruits.

The parable of Jesus is a kind of projection test. One can read his account and his judgment as sad, or as angry, or even as coaxing. One can read it as a judgment upon church authorities in our own times, along the lines of Dostoievsky's story of the Grand Inquisitor. Or one can read it as a challenge and a cautionary tale about one's own responsibilities. One can even read it as an explanation of the social character of human freedom and the consequent social devastation of sin in human history. But it also suggests the death of Jesus as a turning point in human history. History does not in all respects repeat itself; the change brought about by the son's death in the parable is final and, strangely enough, in the parable of Jesus, redemptive.

As though anticipating that all of this would not make sense by our accustomed logic, the liturgy gives us a reading from Paul which speaks of the peace of God which is beyond the utmost understanding. Assured of the intimate presence of the Risen Lord, Paul is convinced that there is no ground for anxiety, but only for hopeful petitions in prayer, springing from overflowing gratitude. Paul, who has been intimately aligned with the killing of the son, and intimately affected by the vineyard owner's transfer of authority to other vine-dressers, is full of hope. Everything has changed by the death, not vindictively but redemptively—not for the worse, but immeasurably for the better. That is why Paul has no hesitation in counseling a certain serenity, bidding his friends focus their attention on what is noble, just, pure, lovable, gracious, excellent and admirable. With Christ's final coming hovering near before his eyes, Paul seems carried away with the possibilities that this offers. His advice is confident: follow the teaching and the tradition passed on, and the God of peace will be with you.

Twenty-eighth Sunday of the Year

READINGS: Is 25:6-10; Phil 4:12-14, 19-20; Mt 22:1-14 (or 1-10).

. . . The Lord of Hosts will prepare a banquet of rich fare for all the peoples . . . the Lord God will wipe away the tears from every face and remove the reproach of his people from the whole earth. The Lord has spoken.   Is 25:6,8.

Most of us love a party. There is magic in the very word. When people have worked hard in a political campaign, or in putting on a play or concert, or preparing for a competition or examination, or in redecorating the house or cleaning up the yard, the thought springs to mind spontaneously: let's celebrate; let's have a party. When people are born, or married, when they return from a trip or graduate or are promoted, there is a party. Even a wake for the dead is a party, though in a more solemn mode.

Because Scripture and liturgy love to use the symbolism of a party to express what God offers to the human race, it is worth asking what makes parties so appealing. Usually the host, out of sheer joy, wants to make others happy too. Or, in difficult moments like a funeral or a farewell, the host gathers friends to share the experience and help one another to come to terms with the grief and loss.It is this sharing and sense of solidarity and belonging, and of security in friendship with others, that attracts. Even those of us who can afford to eat adequately and well at home find a sense of cheer and heightened experience in a party that has less to do with the food than with the fellowship that shares the food. For those who are poor, lonely, deprived, the joy of a party is even greater.

The passage from Isaiah in this Sunday's readings jubilantly proclaims the advent of a universal party that will cancel all grief and want and will even do away with death. It is a feast that God as host offers all peoples—a triumphant overflow of divine joy and goodness. In strange contrast, the gospel gives a parable of Jesus lamenting that, invited to this feast, people are unwilling or reluctant to come. In fact, in the parable they respond with hatred and terrible violence against the messengers who bring the invitation. Of course, in its original context the story has something to do with his own people as those first invited and with the Gentiles as the rag-tag crowd drawn in from the lanes and alleys. But the story is there in Bible and liturgy because it means something for us now.

Perhaps we restrict the meaning in ways Jesus did not intend if we think of this banquet that God offers as only beyond death and outside history, or if we think of it in "churchy" terms of some rather elusive spiritual salvation. Jesus, as we know from his many references to the bounty of nature and the interdependence of creatures, saw all creation as the joyful hospitality of God, inviting everyone to feast and to share the fellowship of God's hospitality. Perhaps we should hear his lament over the rejected invitation in that context. The way we respond to the invitation to ultimate happiness, the consummation God offers, the "heavenly feast", is expressed in terms of the lives we live here and now.

If we think of the whole world and all its resources and opportunities as divine hospitality, as a feast, a party, even a wedding feast of the divine Word with free human response, the meaning of history and of our lives in it is startlingly transformed. It becomes an invitation to share the gifts and the fellowship, to rejoice in the joy of others and to take on the burden of their grief. And then, perhaps, it becomes clearer why the anguish of Jesus over the rejecting of the invitation is a matter for all of us to reflect upon at all times. It is a rejection evident in every injustice, oppression, exclusion, and failure to care. It is a refusal of the divine invitation expressed whenever a blind eye is turned to the sufferings of the poor, or a deaf ear to the cries of the hungry and homeless. In that light one can begin to guess at the meaning of that strange ending which does not really fit, that ending about the man without the wedding garment which seems to have been added on to the original parable.

The touching passage of Paul in these readings is curiously apt. On the one hand he expresses his deep contentment with his life as it is, with all that it has held of joy and of grief, and on the other hand he responds to the sharing of the Philippians with a keen sense that his labors are rewarded because they have understood the gospel that he brought them, the invitation to God's feast.

This reflection on the invitation to be guests of God's hospitality, and to behave as guests together at a wedding feast, is not confined to the readings for this particular Sunday. The celebration of Eucharist suggests it to us every Sunday and every time we celebrate. What we enact in the Eucharist is an interpretation of the whole reality of our lives.

Twenty-ninth Sunday of the Year

READINGS: Is 45:1, 4-6; I Thess 1:1-5; Mt 22:15-21.

I have called you by name and given you your title, though you have not known me. I am the Lord, there is no other; there is no God besides me.
                                                                                                    Is 45:4-5.

One might almost imagine that the texts for this Sunday had been chosen for our reflection on our own public and political responsibilities in the U.S., though they are in fact simply part of the three year cycle of readings for the universal Church. In light of the continuing heated debates over the role of religious and ethical values in public policy and administration and in the election of candidates, Isaiah's pronouncement, though couched in royal terms, is directly to the point: political power is given for the sake of the people, but the authority it carries comes from God, and is conferred so that the divine purpose in the world may be realized. Whether a ruler or government acknowledges or even knows this or not, and whether the people appreciate this or not, the matter stands thus. Political power is not personal property of those who wield it, but a mandate from God for the implementing of the divine purpose for the whole people.

According to the Gospels, Jesus had occasion to comment on this a number of times, notably in his conversation with Pilate in the Passion narrative (Jn 19:11). But in the Gospel reading for this Sunday, the issue is discussed in a particularly interesting way. His political enemies "went away and agreed on a plan to trap him in his own words", we are told (Mt 22:15). How familiar this scene is in our own days requires no comment. However, it may be worth noting that we take this manner of proceeding for granted in politics as in much else, and fail to see its essentially sinful, destructive and non-human character. The purpose of any debate or discussion, much more so of one in political or church affairs, which has important practical consequences "for the sake of the people", ought to be the quest for truth, not the quest for victory. Yet arguing and setting the stage so as to trap the rival in his own words is accepted as a more realistic and practical way of going about things—though perhaps it is now even more popular to make a plan to trap the rival in his financial disclosures or tax forms.

The society in which Jesus moved and the situations with which he had to deal were really not so very different from our own. The substance of the trap was the unpopular tax imposed by the pagan emperor in violation of stricter interpretations of the ritual law of Israel. The answer of Jesus, which we are told took his interlocutors completely by surprise, puts the matter on an entirely different footing, more closely akin to the utterance of Isaiah. But it was not only a brilliant escape from the trap. It is an answer that holds a challenge for us all at all times. It proposes the need to discern from a believer's point of view how the actual use of present political power relates to the sovereign command and authority of God in creation and history. In our days that is a challenge not only for those in power and for those seeking offices of power but for us all as responsible members of a democracy.

There is something haunting about the Isaian passage, with its reiteration that God is Lord, that there is no other, that there is and can be no god besides the One God. Most of us today seldom feel the urge to sneak off to "high places" to pour secret libations to strange local deities at their private shrines. It is in our political and economic lives that modern idolatries threaten. It would be so convenient to suppose that in political affairs and in the economic structures and interests which our political actions protect or challenge, God is essentially a stranger, with no interests to protect. But the whole prophetic tradition of Israel insists that there is but one God, one Lord of all, to whom all powers in heaven and earth are answerable—a God of the orphaned and widowed and the stranger, a God of the poor, the enslaved and the oppressed, a God of all peoples and of all times.

The consequences of this assertion, which Jesus endorses with his preaching, his relationships, his life and his death, are so far-reaching and so exigent, that it is small wonder that the other reading chosen for this Sunday is one containing a quiet, sober reminder by Paul to his friends in Thessalonica, that faith shows itself in action, love in labor, and the hope that is focused on Jesus Christ in fortitude.

Thirtieth Sunday of the Year

READINGS: Ex 22:20-27; I Thess 5:5-10; Mt 22:34-40.

We, who belong to daylight, must keep sober, armed with faith and love for coat of mail, and the hope of salvation for helmet. For God has not destined us to the terrors of judgment, but to the full attainment of salvation through our Lord Jesus Christ.   I Thess 5:8-9.

Today's Gospel reading carries a story that is very familiar because we meet it in different guises in three Gospels. As a matter of fact, it is so familiar that one is inclined to be really bored at hearing it once again in church this Sunday. It is so fatally easy to mistake familiarity for understanding or even for assimilation and implementation of the message, and to assume that there is nothing new to learn by reflecting on it. As we hear it from Matthew this Sunday, the story is

very brief: Jesus has silenced the Sadducees, and the Pharisees take
their turn to test him; someone comes up with the question about the
greatest commandent. Like so much else in the story of Jesus, this
question has a long Jewish history. It had long been a concern to
reduce the 613 commandments found in the Pentateuch to a small
and manageable number that would capture the essence of obedience
to God's Law. Obviously, any teacher in Israel might rightly be
called upon to comment, and would reveal what he thought
important by doing so. The advantage is that it gives focus to
spiritual life and religious commitment, The disadvantage is that by
being condensed into such a short statement, the law of God can
sound rather general and vague.

However, in giving us Matthew's short account of the exchange,
the liturgy provides against that danger by supplying a reading from
Exodus which is anything but vague. Worship of anything but God is
punishable by death and, without finding any need to explain the
connection, the text goes directly to some very practical matters.
"You shall not wrong an alien, or be hard upon him; you were
yourselves aliens in Egypt." (Ex 22:21). How can we read or hear a
text like this without thinking of the fate of illegal immigrants who
go to their death if returned to their country of origin and who are
prey to the worst elements of our society while trying to avoid
detection? Can we read it or hear it without thinking of the
American military impact on those aliens who are the poor of the
Third World? Or hear it without remembering that we are
historically a nation of refugees from oppression? But the text does
not leave us in blissful heedlessness even then, for it speaks of harsh
conditions for widows and orphans, high interest rates for poor
borrowers, and expropriation of necessities of life among those
clinging to precarious survival. The text declares that God will hear
their appeal with compassion, and will in anger turn the tables
against their oppressors.

If the simple commandment to love God above everything and
one's neighbor as oneself sounds vague out of context, it is not so
within its proper context of the teaching of the Pentateuch which is
being summarized. Paul, who had grasped that message in depth is

often brutally concrete about its application, listing actions and attitudes which he considers a travesty of Christian life and juxtaposing them with a description of relationships and responses that do indeed fulfill the greatest commandment and its inseparable second. His reflections in this passage from I Thessalonians is interesting in the context of the other two readings. The situation suggested by the Exodus passage is that of a people in the dark, a people asleep and unaware of the reckoning that must come upon them. But believers, writes Paul, are not, after all, in the dark; they know the situation. Paul's idea of sober, practical response to that situation is to make faith and love and the hope of salvation one's protective armor, and his reason for that is that God does not intend to destroy but to save.

One might be tempted to assume that this advice was given to the Christians of Thessalonica for that early Christian generation only, while the Church was young and fervent, martyrdom the order of the day, and the situation quite different from ours. But in that case it is difficult to understand why the liturgy for today should have skipped over several chapters since last week to be sure to present us with this passage in this context. One might also suppose that protective armor of faith and love and hope of salvation is intended in a purely metaphorical sense to parry the blows of temptation. But in that case, why should the passage be matched with that very specific list of prohibitions from Exodus, so clearly concerned with social conditions and social justice of the powerless? It would seem that the theological and anthropological virtues of faith and hope and love are expected to serve in quite practical ways in the ordering of society and its public affairs.

But of course Jesus makes it even simpler. By quoting the "sh'ma" or basic profession of faith of Israel (Deut 6:5) and linking it with a summing up of the social obligations of the law (Lev 19:18), he makes all depend simply on life lived out of love. That is his answer to a question that can be asked for various reasons and with various motivations. Matthew's Pharisee asks this question as part of a group strategy to trap Jesus. Mark's scribe, on the other hand, asks because he sees that Jesus is very wise and because he really wants to learn from the answer Jesus might give (Mk 12:28-34). Luke's lawyer knows the answer well enough himself, but wants to excuse himself by complicating the matter with subtle distinctions (Lk 10:25-28). It does make one wonder: "Do I ask the question, what is it really all about, and if so for what reasons, with what motivations.?"

Thirty-first Sunday of the Year

READINGS: Mal 1:14-2:2, 8-10; I Thess 2:7-9, 13; Mt 23:1-12.

Have we not all one father? Did not one God create us? Why do we violate the covenant of our forefathers by being faithless to one another? Mal 2:10.

All of the readings for this Sunday seem to be concerned with good news and with proper and improper ways of passing on good news. Malachi accuses the leaders of his people in his own time of making people stumble with their instruction, tripping people by the way they pass on the good news of God. The basis of his accusations appears to be not so much the spoken words as the actions of the priests of his time. They have been accessories to dishonest and hypocritical conduct among the people they were supposed to guide in the ways of God. Malachi sees it as faithlessness in the covenant of intimacy with God.

Paul, writing of the positive and cheerful side of the question, rejoices because he is assured that what the Thessalonians received from him and from his companions really was "the good news of God". He thinks it is because of the affectionate concern he had for them, and because of the example he gave when he worked hard to support himself. He has conducted himself in a fatherly way, genuinely reflecting the parental solicitude of God. That is why the Thessalonians have been able to receive the gospel preached to them, knowing it in their experience as good news.

Jesus, in reading from Matthew's Gospel, addresses a situation all too familiar to believers both Jewish and Christian in any age of history. He takes up the question of authorized teachers who do not practice what they preach. Sadly, Jesus gives the advice that we ourselves should *be* good news to others (along the lines that Paul described) but that we must make constant efforts to discern and receive the teaching of God's word even in the human words of those who, in their persons, are not good news to us. In fact, he goes on to point out that any claim to be a teacher of spirituality to others—any claim to special status in relation to God's word and authority—is perilous. In truth we are all learners, all receivers , from God alone. Only God really has a parental role and only his Christ has the credentials to teach.

There has been much discussion in our own times about "evangelization", and much concern about reaching out to the "unchurched". The most important question in this discussion is the question of what *is* good news, and *how* good news is communicated and understood. Many of the unchurched, after all, are our own relatives and friends, our own children perhaps, who were raised in the Catholic (or another Christian) community and given a good deal of instruction about its beliefs, worship and way of life. The spoken and written words are not missing. The comment on that situation from today's readings appears to be, in the much-worn phrase of Marshall McLuhan, that "the medium is the message". The words we speak are hollow if the experience that accompanies those words is not one of a community of fellow learners, fellow pilgrims, whose lives and persons speak the warmth and exigence of God's parental concern.

According to Jesus, greatness consists of being in quest of fuller understanding in the posture of a learner, thereby "humbling oneself", not in claiming to dispense wisdom, thereby "exalting oneself". That raises the question whether testimony in words, teaching in the usual sense of that term, has any place at all in Christian life. But, of course, it must have, if only because verbal communication is such an important and inescapable part of human existence. Because we must speak words, and because we must communicate our hope and our faith and our concerns in words, we must look to the quality of our words in terms of the way they relate to our lives. There are really two kinds of testimony: one which comes directly out of one's own experience, shaped as that experience is bound to have been by our tradition and all we have learned; and another which comes directly out of book-learning or hearsay, shaped as that bookish knowledge is bound to be by our life-experiences and expectations. If we insisted on speaking from our own immediate experience alone, we would lose much of the wisdom of the tradition, and that may be why Jesus advised his listeners to follow the teaching of official teachers even when the lives of those teachers betrayed the teaching. On the other hand, if we were to insist that the truth of the faith we have to hand on is only what is in the books, or even that the primary way of handing on the faith is to hand on the formulations, we would have lost the existential grounds of credibility.

When I reflect, sadly, on my many friends and relatives who have apparently abandoned the faith, and who seem to experience little or no loss in that abandonment, I realize that it is not for want of solid information or systematic explanations of beliefs that they have gone their own way. I think they found the situation against which Malachi so harshly prophesies: compromises and accommodations by those who should have been leaders and teachers by their lives. I think they found the situation which Jesus so sadly acknowledges: that those who dispense the official teachings often do not present in themselves an example which can be followed; that those who ought to incarnate the parental solicitude of God are too busy bundling up those heavy back-packs to load onto frail shoulders, and expecting to be honored for doing it while standing aloof from the portage. The situation which the "unchurched" people have *not* found is the one that Paul describes.

We could simply blame the clergy and stand back. We could shift the blame out of the parish and into the diocese, or out of the diocese and over to Rome. Or, though it seems less entertaining, we could reflect on the ways we are called to be the good news of God to one another within the circles of the faith, and to those outside.

Thirty-second Sunday of the Year

READINGS: Wis 6:12-16; I Thess 4:13-18 (or 13-14); Mt 25:1-13.

We believe that Jesus died and rose again; and so it shall be for those who died as Christians; God will bring them to life with Jesus.   I Thess 4:14.

At first sight the three readings for this Sunday seem oddly assembled—a passage in praise of wisdom, an assurance concerning the resurrection and the final coming of Christ, and the parable of the wise and foolish bridesmaids. In the light of what those passages probably meant to their original listeners or readers, however, there is a common theme. It is the theme of covenant fidelity—the unshakable fidelity of the creating and redeeming God and the persistent, coaxing, cajoling exigence that God's unwearying fidelity places on our hesitant and rather inattentive response.

The parable of the wise and foolish bridesmaids seems to spring from a rather realistic illustration of fidelity that Jesus took from daily life. Girls chosen as bridesmaids were to be in attendance for a night-time procession with the bridegroom to the house of the bride, to meet her and escort her to her new home, where a feast was held for the bridal party. But the oil in the lamps was not only a detail to make the story realistic; oil had a rainbow aura of symbolic meanings shading into one another. Oil was connected with covenant-making and covenant fidelity. It also referred to the Spirit of God coming upon people. And to the wisdom which the Holy Spirit confers, and to the fruits of the Spirit which are joy and peace and charity expressing itself in good deeds and a good life.

With all of those connotations, the parable becomes much clearer.

It seems from the context that both Jesus in his preaching and Matthew in editing and compiling the Gospel were concerned with preparing the followers of Jesus for times of great crises—times of judgment, testing, and radical decisions. It becomes easier, then, to see that everything depends upon having oil in the lamps. One can confidently meet sudden crisis if one is living by the Spirit of God, in covenant fidelity, by wisdom and the fruits of the Spirit. It also becomes easier to see why the teller of the parable does not expect the wise bridesmaids to share their oil with the foolish. In terms of what the oil means, that would not be possible.

The passage from the book of Wisdom is set, by a literary device, in the mouth of Solomon addressing the kings of the world. Solomon represents wisdom because of him it is told that on assuming power and responsibility as king, he sought from God neither wealth nor fame but only the wisdom by which he might govern justly according to God's will. Having things in this true order of priorities, he was blessed by God and flourished. That certainly is intended as acknowledgement and praise of the unfailing covenant fidelity of God. God shares the wisdom of the covenant of creation with all who seek, holds it back from none and meets docility half-way. Indeed there is a further, surprising promise: to live by wisdom is a guarantee of immortality.

For Christians, of course, the wisdom of God is closely identified with Jesus. Paul, in the letter to the Thessalonians, is also writing of the covenant fidelity of God. It seems that the Thessalonians were concerned about those who had died before the final coming of Christ and the fulfillment of all the promises. Paul assures them, on the Lord's own authority, that all who have died and all who yet live shall meet Christ when he comes in the final fulfillment. Paul refers to those who have died as Christians rather similarly to the way in which the parable refers to those who have oil in their lamps. No sudden disaster or crisis can destroy them; for them and in them Christ has conquered death and they shall live with Christ.

There is an interweaving in these readings of the immortality theme with that of the readiness for a harsh crisis, a time of testing. That intertwining of themes is deeply touching when we remember that originally the parable was part of the teaching by which Jesus tried to prepare his followers for the monstrous crisis which his own arrest and execution would be for them. The promise that wisdom and covenant fidelity offer immortality, seems to mean so much more than continued existence beyond death. It seems to mean an entirely new quality of life, because what is so destructive is not the moment of death at the end of life, but the shadow of fear which it casts before itself through the reaches of the years. It is all too easy to be enslaved by fear all one's life, subtly, imperceptibly, devastatingly. It is too easy to build one's existence around the project of staving off various aspects of death by insuring oneself against catastrophe, accumulating wealth, status , job-security, weapons for personal defense, weapons for national defense, uneasy personal alliances, uneasy national alliances. It is both easy and tragic to define one's existence by these.

The true wisdom of God, the wisdom that is incarnate in Jesus Christ, has conquered both death and the fear of death that enslaves. To live by the Spirit of that wisdom, knowing that the time of testing is always at hand and can happen at any moment in ways we could not predict, is to have oil in the lamps and to be ready to meet the bridegroom at any time of the night.

Thirty-third Sunday of the Year

READINGS: Prov 31:10-13, 19-20, 30-31; I Thess 5:1-6; Mt 25:14-30.

A long time afterwards their master returned and proceeded to settle accounts with them.   Mt 25:19.

God always surprises us in the end with something far beyond our expectations or imaginings. But then it is also true that God often seems just like the master of the household who has gone on a long journey and left us in charge. Jesus and his earliest followers seem to have found this parable particularly incisive; we meet it in many forms in the Gospels. Perhaps it originally bore reference to the differences in attitude among Jesus' fellow Jews.

There were those who lived with a passionate longing and expectation of God's visitation of Israel in vindication. "That day" of the future coming of God's rule and kingdom cast a shadow of expectation before, which some saw as an invitation to covenant fidelity and zeal. But it seems that most of them were more like most of us, interpreting their calling as a kind of "holding pattern." The precious treasure of divine friendship and wisdom was lodged with them useless, reduced apparently to routine observances performed for their personal salvation.

The attitude of Jesus and his early disciples was that of accepting priceless treasure in trust, with a sense of urgency about making it productive, making it increase. There are not many parables of Jesus that depict mercantile analogies and are concerned with investment, but the recurrence of this particular parable in different forms suggests that it was recognized from the first as especially apt. Across centuries and cultures, it still challenges us with the same question: is the grace of God given to us in Christ something to be wrapped up safely and kept untarnished, or is it something to be made productive, active, transforming the world, a "seed of unity and hope and salvation for all the human race" (*Lumen gentium)?*

It seems to me that the most important part of this parable of the three men with the sums of money (better known to most of us as the parable of the talents) is the point that the householder apparently went far away and stayed for a long time. That seems to be such a good analogy for the way most of us experience our situation in the world as Christians. For us the householder seems to be Jesus, whom a cloud caught up out of our sight long ago, as the Ascension story has it, and who is to return in judgment and glory one day that seems impossibly distant. We are left holding onto a hope that is a faint memory passed on by hearsay, and we wrap that memory in a napkin, laying it reverently to rest against the time of that far-off coming.

But the parable speaks of the reckoning in terms that do not accept such an attitude to the grace of God in history and human society. It also stirs memories of some of the extraordinary things certain Christians have done to make the grace given to them productive in the world—memories of apostles and martyrs of the early centuries, memories of people who brought about great transformations in human society from apparently unfavorable positions—Francis of Assisi, Catherine of Sienna, Bridget of Sweden, Ignatius of Loyola, George Fox, John Wesley, Florence Nightingale, Dorothy Day, Mother Teresa, Martin Luther King . . . And the parable anticipates our objection. Perhaps these are special people to whom special tasks were entrusted, but the question is what we are doing with the tasks entrusted to us in our own situations. The question is whether we see our role as Christians only in terms of preservation or in terms of redemptive transformation.

One almost wonders whether it is with a little humor that the liturgy sets the stage for this gospel reading with the concluding passage from the Book of Proverbs. That passage describes an immensely creative, inventive, industrious housewife who sounds just like some of the American pioneer women of whom we read. She juggles a hundred and one domestic chores and activities and finds time for some business enterprises of her own on the side. The juxtaposition of the readings seems to suggest that this kind of enthusiasm and verve and creativity ought to characterize Christians in the redemption of the world.

Paul, in the passage from I Thessalonians, strikes a contrasting somber note with the comment that the day of the Lord comes as unexpectedly as a thief in the night, and as suddenly and inescapably as labor pains, but that this should not catch us unawares for we belong to the light. Once we untangle Paul's mixed metaphors, a message emerges: there is no ordinary time for Christians, in which they can settle down and take things for granted. Every time is a time for special vigilance. The moment of opportunity and the moment of judgment can come at any time in history. We are not living in a long time of suspended activity between initial and final times of redemptive crises. We must think of ourselves as living in the midst of the action, in the heart of the crisis, in perpetual readiness. To suppose that we are not involved in the great struggle of the redemption is to court disaster. Those to whom Paul alludes as assuming untroubled security seem to be closely akin to that servant of the parable who thought he had nothing to do but keep the treasure wrapped up safely and hidden.

The Last Sunday of the Year: The Feast of Christ the King

READINGS: Ezek 34:11-12, 15-17; I Cor 15:20-26, 28; Mt 25:31-46.

And the King will answer, "I tell you this: anything you did for one of my brothers here, however humble, you did for me!" ... "Anything you did not do for one of these, however humble, you did not do for me."   Mt 25:40,45.

We end the Church's year by celebrating the feast of Christ the King. This remains something of a problem for Christians of the United States, who tend to associate kingship with tyranny. We have to remember an older way of thinking in which kingship means protection, inspirational leadership, the harmonizing of disparate interests, the guarantee of peoplehood and of representation among the nations. The king represents the whole people, and has the welfare of the whole people at heart. The king always wants what is best for the people; indeed what is best for the people is best for the king.

This is, of course, an idealized picture. Kings in history have never quite matched it, though some came closer than others to realizing a relationship that could arouse passionate loyalty and enthusiasm from their people. The history of Israel as presented in the Hebrew Scriptures is full of ambivalence about the role of kings. Ultimately only God can exercise true kingship in Israel; all vice-regents or representatives do it more or less inadequately. However, this is at least in part because the people do not really want the Kingship of God exercised in their midst; they do not want to relinquish certain unfair advantages and certain unjust relationships. Their own hearts are divided in their perception of the social order and the accepted values of their society.

Ezekiel's warning, as we meet it in today's reading, goes first to the leaders of Israel and then to their following. It is a warning which is at the same time a promise, and which perhaps carries an ambivalent note for many of its hearers. God will take over in person. God will intervene so that all leadership in God's name will be judged most exigently. But the behavior of the people towards one another will be judged also. This warning of Ezekiel is relevant not only to the age of kings but to our own. In fact, the interdependence between rulers and ruled, between popular values and expectations and governmental action, is even more evident in our democratic situation.

When we celebrate the feast of Christ the King we proclaim our faith that God's rule will prevail through the impact of Jesus on human history and society. The first letter of Paul to the Corinthians offers us a passage today in which this confident expectation is expressed pictorially. In Christ all are brought back to life; all are restored to their proper place in the harmony of God's rule. All is gathered up in Christ and put back in focus, and when Christ's work is complete, he will have ended all wrongful power, including that ultimate power which is the terror of death. Having accomplished all that a true vice-regent ought to have done, Christ will turn over the restored creation to the eternal Father. This is true kingship—the realization of that long cherished dream of what kings should be and should mean for their people. It is no less relevant to our own times, though we deal with representative, elected governments rather than kings.

In today's readings it is the gospel which gives the truly practical content to the imagery of God as shepherd king, ruling through the vice-regency of Jesus who brings all back into focus. This passage states very concretely the criteria of the restoration by which Jesus is to make the kingly judgment that includes in or excludes from the kingdom. The right order which Jesus establishes is not based on deserts or schemes of justice but on need. He ushers in God's reign by introducing a reign of compassion—an order of things that gives food to the hungry, drink to the thirsty, homes to refugees and street people, clothes to those who need them, a healing presence to the sick, and practical friendship and encouragement to prisoners. In this parable Jesus invokes the old sense of kingship when he gives the king's judgment: what is done for any, even the poorest, of the realm is accounted as done for the king, and what is refused to the poorest of the realm is refused to the king.

It seems to me that none of us can listen to that parable with total complacency. If we ask what motivated our vote in the last elections, it becomes clear that even for the most enlightened and generous among us it might have been difficult to vote for Jesus had he chosen to run as an independent presidential candidate. I suspect we would have concluded that in matters of public affairs in which the fate of the world is at risk, his standards are naive, his policies would not work, he has a facile view of human nature, and one could not risk entrusting the future of the country and of the world to him. Of course, this is wild fantasy because in his own time Jesus did not seek the power to govern but the freedom to inspire.

And yet we celebrate the feast of Christ the King, and that celebration seems to pose rather relentlessly the question under whose banner we really stand in the choices we make about the shape of human life and human society.

Year B

First Sunday of Advent

READINGS: Is 63:16-17, 19; 64:2-7; I Cor 1:3-9; Mk 13:33-37.

Evening or midnight, cock-crow or early dawn—if he comes suddenly, he must not find you asleep. And what I say to you, I say to everyone: Keep awake.   Mk 13:35-37.

Advent brings us shortening days and a sense of darkness closing in around us. Comfort draws into smaller circles behind closed doors, in the lamplight and around the hearth. It is the dying of the year but also its turning—the eternal return of the seasons that echoes the fidelity of God who creates and sustains. Some deep, vague stirrings of an hibernating instinct may suggest that it is a time to care less and sleep more—a time of somnolence, a time of withdrawal.

But Advent itself, approaching the Christmas and Epiphany festivities, gives a different interpretation to the same experiences. It expresses the excitement of intense expectation. It bids us await a great breakthrough that is always at hand though yet beckoning far forward—new light, new life, new hope. But this depends upon a true vision of our present situation, a real sense of our great need. Isaiah, in today's reading, calls on God as from a distance, across a barrier. He speaks of wandering away with hearts preoccupied with other things, and asks how this is even possible. God is, after all, Father and rescuer; we claim close kinship with God, but this is poorly expressed in the fabric of our lives. If there is to be a return, a rescue, it must come from God.

Indeed it has come from God, and is forever still coming. Such is Paul's message in the reading from the First Letter to the Corinthians. We are not yearning for the impossible, but responding all too reluctantly to the insistent urgency of the divine invitation. We might, Paul suggests be much bolder in our hope and in our response. So much has already been given to us. So much has been put into our power, brought within our reach. But we are like dreamers dozing by our own fireside, not presuming to make a great impact on the world and its ways. Paul's message here seems to be exactly the message of Advent; we must rouse ourselves and reawaken our hope. The grace of radical transformation of human life and possibilities is a gift that has already been put into our possession. We are called to be alert at all times, to welcome its fulfillment knowing that God keeps faith with us.

The Gospel reading presents the same message. The time of God's coming is not something for us to determine; it can be at any time and we must be ready at any time. We know that the earliest followers of Jesus were keenly aware of this and lived in a condition of "eschatological tension," a sense of suspense and expectation between the "already" of the Resurrection and the "not yet" of the final coming of Christ, the "parousia." With the passage of centuries we seem to have lost much of that eagerness of expectation. At least since the time of the Emperor Constantine, who ended persecution and made Christianity respectable, there has been a persistent temptation to settle down in history as though God's Reign had already been fully established among us, and we had no need to look to another Coming of Christ. We have even tended to look to Advent as a time commemorating the ancient past before Christ's first coming, leading to a commemoration of the birth of Jesus long ago.

But the liturgy keeps nudging us into a fuller sense of the meaning of Advent. It recalls that first coming because it foreshadows or projects that great and final coming in which all creation will finally fulfill its purpose. But we might wonder what is the value of our contemplating that final Coming each year in this season. It seems to be twofold. Only if we have a vision of the end and destiny of the world, can we focus our activity in the world appropriately. And if we do keep that vision of the end and destiny in focus, we are more apt to recognize those many intermediate "comings" of Christ in our lives and in our history. Christian hagiography and fiction is full of stories of the comings of Christ in disguise. We have the legend of St. Martin who gave half his cloak to the poor man in the cold and was rewarded by the dream in which Christ wore the half cloak. There is also the legend of St. Francis with the leper, and there are many others of the same type.

What this folklore suggests is what the liturgy is saying so insistently at this time of year. Not only do we tend to weary of living in expectation of the final Coming of Christ in setting the world to right and drawing all back into harmony in worship of the Father. But, for this very reason, we tend not to live in expectation of those other visitations of Christ that are in the form of the poor and needy and suffering of all kinds. We tend not to live in expectation of them and, therefore, we tend not to recognize them when they come. To live in eager expectation of the final Coming of Christ is to welcome every coming of his in whatever disguise, and to read aright the signs of the times. Again and again the liturgy tries to point the way for this in the course of the Church's year. But Advent, more than any other time, tries to set this focus by reminding us of the promises and reminding us that God keeps faith with us in sending Christ the Savior.

Second Sunday of Advent

READINGS: Is 40:1-5, 9-11; 2 Pet 3:8-14; Mk 1-8.

And here is one point, my friends, which you must not lose sight of: with the Lord one day is like a thousand years and a thousand years one day. It is not that the Lord is slow in fulfilling his promise, as some suppose, but that he is very patient with you, because it is not his will for anyone to be lost but for all to come to repentance.   2 Pet 3:8-9.

On this Sunday the liturgy marshals the second Isaiah, John the Baptist and Peter the Apostle as witnesses to the firm grounds of hope that the Lord is coming and salvation is at hand. The unknown writer who speaks in Peter's name after Peter's death, is already aware that we tend to relegate this message to the dim margins of consciousness as background music to the practical affairs that really hold our attention. Israel's hope was thousands of years old. Nothing seemed to change much. Now the generations of the followers of Jesus were growing in numbers and it often seemed still that nothing had changed much. What might be said then is of course even more compelling in our days as the centuries stretch on and we are more inclined to look backwards in faith than forwards in hope of real change.

The message of the second Isaiah, to prepare a way for the Lord through the wilderness, a highway across the desert, has the solidity of the event that fulfilled it, for indeed the exiles returned to the promised land and took up their lives as the covenant people again. But when we hear that message applied to our own times, we tend to give it a meaning so ethereal that it is no meaning anymore. Yet there is clearly a reason to draw this particular text into the prayer and consciousness of Christians, generation after generation, and century after century. And this began in the Apostolic period, for the Gospel writers invoke the text to explain the ministry and significance of John the Baptist.

When Mark, in today's reading, begins the good news of Jesus Christ the Son of God by quoting the Isaian text and referring it to the proclamation of the Baptist, he does more than quote a short section of the passage. He evokes the hopeful expectation and immediacy of the whole prophecy. John's baptism of repentance appears as a new passage through the waters of the Jordan into the Promised Land, just as the exiles were recalled to the land in the time of the second Isaiah. It meant repentance and forgiveness and covenant renewal in both cases. It meant God's coming to the people in a saving event.

As we prepare to celebrate the Christmas and Epiphany mystery, these liturgical texts recall to our minds the saving events in our history, more particularly the coming of Jesus in the midst of human history as an event that profoundly transforms all human possibilities, bringing hope alive again. But the whole gospel of Christian faith is constructed to direct our attention forward. We are not supposed to look upon the historical event of Christ as though the action were complete. We are not marking time endlessly, expecting no further change in history. The hour of God's grace is at all times. The moment of salvation is now, not only for individuals in some isolated sense, but for the world with all its troubles and its wars and injustices. The figure of John the Baptist stands tall in Advent, talking about real conversion in the affairs of the real world.

Somehow in every age, in every generation, we tend to take the "bite" out of the message by the way we relegate this hope of salvation to a state entirely outside history, entirely outside the world and our responsibilities to one another in the world. In the passage of the Second Letter of Peter which we read today, there is a wonderfully imaginative use of cosmic symbols for the Lord's coming. It speaks of the heavens ablaze, disappearing with a great rushing sound, melting the elements in the flames, so that the whole universe breaks up. It is, of course, this passage along with others like it, also using apocalyptic imagery to express the mysterious and ineffable, that has given rise to some foolish fundamentalist speculations. It is not altogether surprising that in a time of nuclear threat and continuing armaments race between great earthly powers, the speculation about a nuclear realization of "Armageddon" should have invaded our public discourse. It is not surprising, but it is entirely inappropriate, for it belies the author's intent in this passage as in those other similar ones.

The intent here is to rekindle practical and effective hope in believers. Quite explicitly, the author corrects our perception about the apparent delay of God in completing the redemption. God has, so to speak, all the time that there is and more. It is a matter of indifference whether the time is long or short; what is crucial is the opportunity for genuine repentance for all. The tension between the certainty that the promises will be fulfilled and the lengthening of the time of expectation, is not a reason for apathy or despair. It is proposed rather as a reason for rededication, more radical conversion, convenant renewal. Our times are unstable and unpredictable, but the time of the Lord transcends time. The time of the Lord is every time, and it does not make much difference whether we are speaking of a thousand years or of a single day. He comes.

Third Sunday of Advent (Gaudete)

READINGS: Is 61:1-2, 10-11; I Thess 5:16-24; Jn 1:6-8, 19-28.

As the earth puts forth her blossoms or bushes in the garden burst into flower, so shall the Lord God make righteousness and praise blossom before all the nations.   Is 61:11.

Isaiah's blossoms do not fall onto the earth from heaven; they are brought forth out of the earth by God's power. The garden bushes burst into flower from what is already growing within them, by the marvelous providence of God. This "third" Isaiah of these final chapters is insistent that in spite of hardships and discouragement, God's bringing the people back into the Promised Land is not in vain. What God has planted will flourish and bear fruit, and there is reason to rejoice in hope. The justice of God will be reestablished and the mercy of God will be evident to all. So it is a different, better, more just society that is to emerge.

The well-known verses at the beginning of this reading inevitably stir the Christian memory with the synagogue sermon of Jesus in Luke 4 which formally inaugurates his public ministry. To us the one anointed to preach good news to the poor, the humble, the prisoners and the broken victims, will always be in the first place Jesus himself. Yet today's readings refer this vocation of bearing (and being) good news, to Isaiah, to John the Baptist, and to Christians. The essential task is to dare to hope and to spark hope in others—hope that the Reign of God can be restored in human affairs, hope that the vision of Jesus can be realized, and hope that it can begin now, in this year, in our society, that there can always be a new beginning.

What is to be restored is the justice of God's reign in human society. That means good news for the poor and the oppressed. It means practical consolation to those who had given up all hope. It means freedom to prisoners of every kind, and most of all it means justice and a decent way of life for all. Therefore, it envisages a re-structuring of society according to the will of God—a re-structuring in which no one is excluded and held of less account. And this is certainly cause for rejoicing and wonder.

That is the burden of Paul's injunction to the Thessalonians to be joyful always, praying continually, giving thanks, not stifling inspiration nor despising prophetic utterances, but trying them in faith and hope because the power of God encompasses all. God will fulfill the promises in us and among us. Paul writes of something that is already happening among believers.

This seems to be the reason for which the Baptist continues to accompany us in the liturgy. John continues to point to the coming Savior and to invite to a baptism of repentance that allows people really to see Christ coming. For the problem is not that he does not come, but that year after year we do not see him coming. For us, as for Israel in third Isaiah's time, there is a certain sense that so many centuries have gone by with so little change. There is an inclination to weariness, to settling down to compromises. But the message of Advent is to look forward in hope and confidence in the saving power of God and to be always joyful.

Fourth Sunday of Advent

READINGS: 2 Sam 7:1-5, 8-11, 16; Rom 16:25-27; Lk 1:26-38.

The Holy Spirit will come upon you and the power of the Most High will overshadow you; and for that reason the Holy Child to be born of you will be called 'Son of God.'   Lk 1:35.

If the liturgy invites us on this Sunday to keep Mary company and to look at the mystery of the Lord's coming through her eyes, it is not because we actually know much about her as an individual. It is on account of the role that she plays as a model for the Church and for all followers of Jesus, who are called in various ways to bring Christ forth to the world—in most cases under apparently inauspicious circumstances.

The passage from 2 Samuel gives some sense of the way God

chooses to enter into human history. Wherever God journeyed with Israel it was "in a tent and a tabernacle." God did not ask that the divine presence among them be relocated in a house of fine cedar. God was not asking David to build him a house. On the contrary it was God who would build King David a house, a dynasty, a succession that would ultimately fulfill all the promises of salvation. This story in 2 Samuel gives us an important insight into the meaning of the angelic message in the Lucan scene of the annunciation of the birth of Jesus. Jesus, the pure gift of God to the virgin Mary and the virgin Church, is the one in whom the promises of salvation are really to be fulfilled in a definitive way. The throne is to be his; here is the true vice-regent of the transcendent God, in whom the rule of God in all human affairs is to be restored, though that restoration is to be very different and far more extensive than anything that has been expected.

The circumstances, as Mary's answer implies, are not auspicious; it would seem that the moment is not ripe. Certainly this is not the way any of us would have planned it. And in this, the scene is typical of human experience. God so frequently works from below in human society, like leaven working through the dough. God works from unlikely and marginal situations in history, through the poor and the despised and those who are apparently incompetent.

The passage from Romans speaks of the divine secret, long kept hidden in silence, and now revealed—the secret of the overthrow of the principalities and powers which hold the human race captive and enslaved. That overthrow is sure and decisive because it does not come with the decrees of mighty conquerors but with the conversion and transformation and deepening fellowship of the powerless. And we may also ask ourselves what these principalities and powers are that hold the human race captive. They are perhaps prejudice, lust for domination of others, competition for unnecessary wealth, suspicion, wars and provocation of wars.

Perhaps, we have not yet realized the breadth and depth of what the promised transformation means in human society. Perhaps it is still in some sense a secret hidden through the ages—a secret which each Advent and Christmas bids us discover, so that we may learn the extent to which God has been gracious, and may have courage to live and act accordingly.

Christmas

READINGS: At Midnight: Is 9:1-6; Tit 2:11-14; Lk 2:1-14.

At Dawn: Is 62:11-12; Tit 3:4-7; Lk 2:15-20.

A boy has been born for us, a son given to us to bear the symbol of dominion on his shoulder; and he shall be called in purpose wonderful, in battle God-like, Father for all time, Prince of peace."   Is 9:6.

Not many of us will celebrate the three Masses of Christmas this year. Our renewed understanding of the Eucharist is not easily compatible with such repetitions. Yet from the point of view of the readings this is unfortunate, for they form a tightly knit sequence. Perhaps, no matter which Mass one celebrates, it will be helpful to read all the Scripture selections meditatively in the sequence in which they are assigned.

Like fanfare of trumpets proclaiming a royal birth, the first Isaian passage sets the theme: darkness and gloom are shattered; God's gift to us is a new beginning that makes everything different, everything possible. We are offered new leadership, new direction, the genuine possibility of true peace. This, Paul writes in the letter to Titus, is the dawn of God's grace in the world, healing human tragedies and making a changed way of life possible by a magnetic pull towards a future yet to be. The birth related in the Lukan passage puts the new beginning squarely in the context of a history of oppression and injustice, a history of cruelty and poverty, a story of homelessness and insecurity. That is the place in human society where we are invited to recognize and welcome God's visitation—a new birth, a new beginning, a new initiative for community and peace among the poor, the despised, the excluded. The scene is a prototype of what we have in our own time, in our world, in our country, in our city. Today also God's coming to us is hard to recognize, hard to accept, because it is poised between the wonderful and the desperate, the heavenly and the wretched. Today we could too easily miss the moment of such great grace.

The dawn reading from Isaiah calls on us to recognize our own moment of liberation. Again Paul responds, coaxing us to believe that we are not abandoned to our own deserts, but enabled to transcend the self-centeredness that causes all human oppression— enabled to transcend a history misshapen by the consequences of selfish deeds and desires. We are not abandoned to increasing enmities and injustices because the mercy of God has sprung up within human freedom in the person of Jesus Christ and in the Spirit he has breathed into us, which is a new power in the world, a power for restoration of the world in justice and peace.

That is why Luke's narrative finds the response of the poor and despised shepherds so significant. The great renewal of the earth can come from the poorest, from the marginated, because the power is not that of wealth or earthly dominion, but the divine power of compassion and community.

Christmas Day

READINGS: Is 52:7-10; Heb 1:1-6; Jn 1:1-18.

In this the final age he has spoken to us in the Son whom he has made heir to the whole universe and through whom he created all orders of existence: the Son who is the effulgence of God's splendor and the stamp of God's very being, and sustains the universe by his word of power.   Heb 1:2-3.

Even those of us who celebrate Christmas Mass solemnly in the daytime cannot but be touched by the symbolism of the light that breaks through the darkness. Cumulative memories since childhood of Christmas trees, lamps in windows, light streaming from open church doors into the crisp, dark night, all carry forever the symbolism of word and welcome, of light and life, of mystery and merriment. The brightness of high noon bursting upon the world at midnight is an apt figure of all that Christmas means. Isaiah speaks of good news from swift messengers, of watchmen shouting in triumph among the ruins, of the whole world witnessing God's merciful power. And we witness it too, for Christmas touches even the least religious with a moment of fellowship and peace, and moves many a Scrooge to a moment of truth, a moment of genuine generosity and fellow feeling.

That moment of breakthrough, as the letter to the Hebrews suggests, is because God who speaks in many and unexpected ways elsewhere, here speaks with inescapable clarity and finality in the Son who comes to us as the shining comes from the light—the Son who is heir to the universe because he is the design and pattern of it all, the one who gives it meaning and integrity. And so, at the end of the Christmas readings, the liturgy brings us to the classic statement of the Incarnation, the Prologue to the Gospel of John. The divine light is enkindled among us and shines through the darkness of bullying and greed, of prejudice and oppression. But all the horrors of human history cannot obscure the light, or snuff out the glory, or cancel the power of new life that is the shining of divine splendor in the person of Jesus Christ.

Feast of the Holy Family

READINGS: Sir 3:2-6, 12-14; Col 3:12-21; Lk 2:22-40.

To crown all, there must be love, to bind all together and complete the whole. Let Christ's peace be arbiter in your hearts; to this peace you were called as members of a single body. Col 3:14-15.

This feast of the Holy Family is evidently intended to provide a model for Christian families and therefore for Christian community. Broadly speaking, that is what these readings offer. Paul gives authority to his advice in the second reading by saying that it is the Christian way, the Christian duty. When we reflect on his advice carefully, it becomes evident that he is concerned with a community built upon mutual respect, service arising out of personal dignity and vocation, a way of life arising from lively gratitude and enthusiasm, and resulting in peace—the true peace of Christ.

A reading of this Pauline text which takes it in a fundamentalist sense, could be very upsetting. Such a fundamentalist reading might suggest a God-ordained bullying system with mandatory permanent subjection of women and heavy-handed patriarchal authority over grown children. This, however, is obviously not intended. We know from parallel texts in pagan and Jewish literature that Paul is writing about the relationships taken for granted in his society, and that the point of his remarks is precisely the changed focus he gives to established patterns—namely that life in Christ gives a community new possibilities of mutual respect and affection.

The first reading, from the Wisdom of Ben Sirach, suggests a foundation for this in the order of creation and the structure of human life in inter-dependent generations, in which responsibilities and relationships are clustered in family units. The emphasis is not on the nuclear family with growing children, but on the extended family and respect for the aged. The admonitions of this text are peculiarly apt for our own times and for our highly mobile, fast-moving society.

In the Gospel reading it is the parents of Jesus, with their child, who are held up as the model for the Christian family. Many of us are uncomfortable with that. First of all, we actually know very little about them—about their lives and character, their thoughts and feelings, their daily doings and the impact they had on their neighbors and the society about them. Secondly, some of us have a surreptitious sense of unfair competition; of course one can have an ideal family life with a saintly and dedicated spouse and one perfect child! Actually, all we are told of them here is that they were observers of the Law of Moses, unpretentious in their making the offering of the poor for such an occasion, and prepared by the prophecies of Simeon and Anna for great demands to be made upon them. Perhaps that is not such a bad model for Christian family life after all.

But the Gospel text was not originally intended to provide a model for Christian family life. It was intended to give a vivid image of the role of Jesus in relation to the tradition of Israel and to the saving will of God. Jesus is brought to the Temple in observance of the Law, as one subject to the Law. An elderly devout man, representing the long traditions and observance of Israel, testifies that this is the Savior for whom Israel has watched and waited, and that he, Simeon, can now die in peace. Then a prophetess, a very old woman, representative it seems of the whole prophetic tradition, recognizes Jesus with gratitude and talks of him to those who look for liberation. This scene is a family scene on a much larger scale.

Solemnity of Mary, the Mother of God and the Giving of the Name Jesus

READINGS: Num 6:22-27; Gal 4:4-7; Lk 2:16-21.

God sent his own Son, born of a woman, born under the law, to purchase freedom for the subjects of the law, in order that we might attain the status of sons.   Gal 4:4-5.

On this octave day of Christmas, historical circumstances have led the Church to combine two celebrations: the outcome of the Council of Ephesus in 431 A.D. which named Mary, Mother of God; and the mystery of God's intervention in human affairs, which names her son Jesus, that is "savior," or "God saves." Both celebrate the mystery of our redemption and both speak hope and commitment as well as memory. The first reading, from Numbers, links the two celebrations. It gives us as God's message to the Chosen People that triple blessing which in later centuries we came to remember as the blessing of St. Francis of Assisi, and it culminates in the promise that the proclamation of the divine name over the people shall be a blessing to them. The blessing of protection, divine favor and peace, is linked to the "shining of God's face" upon the people. For Christians, that carries the connotation of Jesus who said, "Anyone who has seen me has seen the Father." Jn 14:9.

Paul, in Galatians, counters this with the claim that the birth of God's own son among us, under the law, liberates us into filial relationship to God so that a new name is given to us by which we may address God, "Abba, Father." When we remember the importance that "naming," interpreting by titles, has always had in human experience and in human understanding, all these apparently disparate pieces about names and titles fit into the single mystery of the redemption. The message is that the event of Jesus in our world, our history, our midst, reinterprets everything and sheds new light on the meaning of our existence.

The Gospel reading is one more story about the radical nature of that reinterpretation and that new light. To grace the feast of Mary, Mother of God, we have the recital of the despised shepherds coming to the excluded couple to find the child cradled in a feeding trough. And this is interpreted as God with us, the Savior, the mothering of the divine into the world. Year after year, as we celebrate the event, we are tempted to confuse familiarity with understanding and acceptance. We have so ritualized the scene, that we have insulated ourselves against the shock, the scandal, the demand to look at the world upside-down and reinterpret everything in the light of this mothering of the divine in the world and this naming of the savior. Far from being welcomed into the existing order, Jesus is rejected by it, and therefore turns it upside down by fellowship with the oppressed and marginated. But we should stay here awhile, for it is here that it all comes together.

Feast of the Epiphany

READINGS: Is 60:1-6; Eph 3:2-3, 5-6; Mt 2:1-12.

Though darkness covers the earth, and dark night the nations, the Lord shall shine upon you and over you his glory shall appear. Is 60:2-3.

Those of us who read the newspapers regularly will find the description all too apt; there is a darkness over the earth in our days and it does seem that it is dark night for many nations in our times. Yet we celebrate the feast of Epiphany, of manifestation, of the showing forth of the glory of God. We separate the Nativity and the Epiphany feasts in our liturgical calendars; not only do we declare our faith that in Jesus the saving grace of God has entered the world, but we proclaim that it will be manifest to the nations, evident in the affairs of the world in all their complexity and intractable oppressiveness.

It is often tempting to look at the long stretch of history that separates our times from the life of Jesus, and wonder what difference it has made and what difference it can ever make in the large events of the world. Yet the wonderful showing forth of the glory of the Lord of which the Isaian passage speaks was, after all, in the literal sense just one such historical event for Israel, coming back from exile and beginning national life anew. In the passage from Ephesians we hear of the secret of Christ as one which draws us, the gentiles with our worldly affairs, into the mystery of the sacred history of Israel. In the secret of Christ, nothing remains profane; nothing is outside God's power and the manifestation of God's glory in justice and reconciliation and new hope among peoples and races and classes.

Of the many ways in which we might picture and consider the mystery of Epiphany, God's glory shining forth in the world, the Gospel reading presents us with the journey and visit and gifts of the Magi. We are so used to this that we forget to be surprised. After all, astrologers are not in good repute among Christians. Yet what better way is there to represent the task of reading the signs of the times, than by the star-gazers who follow their inspiration and vision until they truly find Christ, acknowledging his rule of peace by their gold, his mystery by their frankincense, and his tragic role in our troubled history by their myrrh. Their presence in the Gospels is a little like that of Melchisedech in the story of Abraham; they come mysteriously with wisdom and gifts, to seek one greater than themselves, and they disappear again without a trace. But they are symbols of hope, representing the unexpectedness, the gratuitous character, the wonder of God's glory breaking through the darkness of the nations. They come from afar, from nations outside the covenant of Israel. They are unexpected, expressing the yearning of all peopels for a better world, a better life, community with one another, and communion with God.

The Baptism of the Lord

READINGS: Is 42:1-4, 6-7; Acts 10:34-38; Mk 1:7-11.

He will make justice shine on every race, never faltering, never breaking down, he will plant justice on earth.   Is 42:3-4.

The passage that we read today from Isaiah's first "servant song," promises one sent from God who will put things right in our world, one who will be compassionate, full of the divine spirit, making justice shine among the nations, working powerfully but subtly to rescue the oppressed. Peter's sermon, which we read in the passage from Acts, assures us that it is Jesus who comes to us with this Spirit and power, that Jesus is the compassionate one whose healing and redeeming work continues in the world. To this Peter adds that no one is excluded, for God has no favorites.

None of this should surprise or puzzle us, but what ought to give us pause for thought and question is Mark's blunt, brief statement about the baptism of Jesus by John in the Jordan. If the iconography of it were not so familiar, we would be wondering what it could possibly mean that Jesus should be baptised in John's baptism of repentance. The New Testament has a far more inclusive and allusive sense of the significance of baptism than the one which we have today. It is not only a redemption from sin. For them the action was quite literally total immersion. To be immersed by John in the Jordan evoked many memories, not least of them the entry into the Promised Land through the river Jordan, with all that it meant of assuming the vocation of the chosen people. That Jesus chose to be so baptised certainly implies continuity with the calling of Israel to be God's witness people—the assuming of the legacy. But Mark makes sure that we realize that it means more than that when he tells us that in Jesus the vocation is fulfilled. The Spirit of God descends upon him and he is acknowledged as the beloved Son, the chosen of God. In him God's call to Israel is taken up anew, so that the task of witness and covenant fidelity may be brought to fulfillment.

The link and the symbolism go further than this. Elsewhere we learn that Jesus referred to his coming death as a baptism with which he was to be baptized (Lk 12:50). From the beginning, Christian baptism was seen as immersion in death with him, to rise to a new life of reconciliation, justice and peace. In today's reading, John the Baptist proclaims that this Jesus who is baptized into the destiny and inheritance of Israel will, in turn, baptize others in the Holy Spirit. There is both continuity and urgency in the proclamation, both assurance and exigence, because all that is said about Jesus carries implications for Christians. If Jesus is to make justice shine on every race, it will be through his embodiment in his followers in all generations. We also enter into the vocation which Jesus accepts in his baptism by John, and which the Spirit seals with power—the power of far-reaching renewal.

Ash Wednesday

READINGS: Joel 2:12-18; 2 Cor 5:20–6:2; Mt 6:1-6, 16-18.

Turn back to the Lord your God, for he is gracious and compassionate.   Joel 2:13.

For generations, I suppose, Catholics such as I have shaken their heads and chuckled over the vagaries of a Church that in its ritual marks the foreheads of the congregation very conspicuously with ashes, and then proceeds without apparent embarrassment to proclaim a gospel passage that warns against people who let the world know that they are embarked upon the works of repentance. No matter—it appears from today's three readings that the paradox is insoluble.

All three readings are concerned with the time-honored enumeration of three main aspects of repentance: prayer, fasting and alms deeds. Joel is certainly more compatible with the Ash Wednesday distribution of ashes, because of his insistence that it is the people as a whole, the whole people acting together, who must turn to God. His chances of getting a favorable response were good because he spoke at a time of panic when a fearful plague of locusts was advancing through the land, leaving behind a scene of utter devastation—a scene such as has occurred in Ethiopia and parts of the Sudan in our times. At such a time it is both critically important and exceptionally easy for the whole community to respond together, to turn to God, to renounce self-interest, and to help others. Joel expresses his conviction that when they do they will discover that God is not only gracious but compassionate in the deepest sense of the word; God is involved in the situation with them, and if they repent then God also will repent of the affliction he has allowed them to suffer.

Paul, in the passage from 2 Corinthians, reminds us that Christ is the vivid realization and fulfillment of that divine compassion taken to its ultimate possibilities, and that in him the day of deliverance has come; the reconciliation has begun in a way in which all can share. It is our opportunity of being made one with the goodness of God, as Paul puts it. It is not too late or too early. It is not hopeless; a real conversion of human life to its divine purpose is possible. But this message is not only for Paul's age, but for our age and every age. Even the complexity of the arms race and of worldwide economic problems is not beyond divine redemption.

In spite of the point made by Joel about the importance of the community's joint response of repentance in the proclamation of a public fast throughout the land, the gospel reading warns against the danger that piety, penance and good works can so easily become play-acting. The reality of conversion goes on rather secretly in the sight of God. The authentic attitude of prayer, genuine renunciation of self-interest and true concern for others are not publicly evident but are manifest eventually in the outcomes. Perhaps that is not only a warning but an encouragement. After all, most of us wonder sometimes whether our personal piety really changes anything, whether the renunciations of individual people are of any use to starving millions and oppressed populations, and whether donations of money, time and effort will really bring any measure of peace to a troubled world. The message of the gospel reading seems to be that we do not have to worry about that. God sees and grants the outcome, but we are called to repent and be reconciled to God's ways.

First Sunday of Lent

READINGS: Gen 9:8-15; I Pet 3:18-22; Mk 1:12-15.

Christ also died for our sins once and for all. He, the just, suffered for the unjust, to bring us to God.   I Pet 3:18

We Christians do not pay as much attention to the covenant of Noah, the covenant of the rainbow, as we might. But it is a good Lenten symbol. As renewal of the blessing and covenant of creation, it involves the whole human community. The covenant of Noah demands a moral life, respecting the sovereignty of God, the rights of others, and the natural order of creation. On the other hand it promises that when people live morally there is a harmony in creation, and that the waters of chaos will not submerge the earth again. The covenant of the rainbow is a beginning, involving all of us.

I Peter makes a swift transition when it compares the flood in Noah's time with baptism. But that is because the early community understood that when we are baptized as Christians we are baptized into the death of Christ, emerging from the water into his risen life. Christ died once for all. In that death the waters of chaos did their very worst and when they receded there was, in the Resurrection of Christ, a new beginning which could never be undone. Nothing could ever reverse what had happened. That is why the New Testament writers and the Church Fathers saw Noah's ark emerging from the flood as an important prototype of salvation. In this reading we are recalled to the new covenant to which we as followers of Jesus are party. We have become heirs of a blessing we have not earned, members of a new creation we have not deserved.

The gospel reading from Mark presents an account of this blessing in stark simplicity. Jesus, coming newly from the desert where the voice of John has been forever silenced, utters a declaration, a promise and a call. The declaration is that the time is now—that time that everyone has learned to expect—a time of fulfillment, of vindication, of power. The promise is that God's own rule in human society is at hand. It is in some ways the same promise as that of the covenant of the rainbow; God is faithful, God guarantees that creation can work in harmony by the Creator's laws. Yet it is also, in another sense, a new promise; Jesus in his person is the reason that God's rule is at hand in a way it never was before.

But there is also a call. As in the covenant of the rainbow, there is an exigence. There is a response called forth from the freedom of human creatures, to participate in the harmony of creation and in the renewed harmony of redemption. Jesus asks for two attitudes. He asks for repentance—for a turning around, a willingness to begin again, a willingness to change one's mind and perceptions and behavior. He also asks for faith in the Good News. He asks that we do him the courtesy of believing that it is true, that it is possible, that it can happen. In other words, he asks us to remember the covenant.

Second Sunday of Lent

READINGS: Gen 22:1-2, 9-13, 15-18; Rom 8:31-34; Mk 9:2-10.

A cloud appeared, casting its shadow over them, and out of the cloud came a voice: 'This is my Son, my Beloved, listen to him.' Mk 9:7.

The juxtaposition of readings this week makes the extraordinary, indeed the extravagant, claim that it is not we who are called upon in the tragedies of a sinful history to sacrifice what we hold most dear, but it is God who makes that sacrifice. It is God who feels all the anguish of the world with those who suffer. It is God who is most intimately involved.

Jews have had frequent occasion to reflect upon the meaning of the Genesis story to which they commonly refer as the "binding of Isaac." It carries all the pathos of tragedy brought on by fidelity to God's covenant and command. It provided a paradigm for the Holocaust suffered under the Nazi regime: by raising them according to the Covenant and the Law, faithful Jews had bound their children, and indeed the whole next generation, and placed them bound on the persecutor's pyre. And that paradigm extends to every persecution of those faithful to the tradition. But the impact of the paradigm is hopeful also, because it carries the promise the God will not be outdone in generosity.

Out of the experience of persecutions and suffering grew the traditional Jewish commentary on this passage, which maintained that God already knew the fidelity of Abraham but gave him the opportunity of actually expressing the generosity and goodness that was potential in him. In this way he would become more like God, because we are all created for just that, to be the image and likeness of God. In the last analysis it is God who is totally good and totally generous. For Abraham to sacrifice Isaac was to surrender the grounds for all his hope, all his future into God's hands. There is a suggestion here that that is what God does in history. He delivers his hope, his plan, his historical future into the freedom of human persons. His trust rivals his generosity in dealing with the human race.

Paul, in the passage from Romans, cannot but think of that, allude to that, when he reflects on the death of Jesus, and extols the generosity of God who does not withhold what is most dear to him—Jesus who is uniquely his Son. Paul sees this as the ultimate pledge which shows that God will withhold nothing from us which he has to give—the fullest reconciliation and the most enduring love. Abraham was saved at the last minute from the consequences of his sacrifice, but God gave Jesus up to a sacrificial death that he might be our champion, our ambassador. There could be no greater gift, no greater compassion, no greater sharing of our troubled history.

The Gospel scene of the transfiguration completes the representation of the exchange and of the parallel. The transfiguration offers a pictorial expression of the crossing over of Jesus, in the perception of his followers, from being simply a man among them who was good and gifted and prophetic, to being a mystery of divine presence and power in their midst. Some would put it that it expresses the transition from the Jesus of history to the Christ of faith. Mark places this scene six days after the conversation in which Peter confesses Jesus as the Christ, and Jesus enjoins them to silence and begins to prepare his followers for his own Passion and Death, and for their calling to follow him by radical renunciation. That placement suggests the purpose of the scene that is presented for our contemplation and reflection.

There is, of course, much in this text that suggests the moment of a great revelation. Jesus and three intimate disciples climb up a high mountain to be alone, just as Moses did, and just as Elijah did. He is transformed before them by an unearthly brilliance. These circumstances suggest a vision of great significance. Jesus is in conversation with Moses, representing the whole Law on which Israel's traditions and way of life rest, and with Elijah, representing all prophecy, all hope and most particularly that ultimate hope of messianic salvation, for Elijah is to prepare the way for Messiah in the popular expectation. We latter day disciples of Jesus can look back on this scene and realize that the whole life and being and impact of Jesus do indeed place him in dialogue with the traditions and authorities of Israel that came before him. His meaning and role are defined with reference to them. Lest we should miss the point, however, when Luke tells the same story more elaborately (Lk 9:28-36), he specifies what the conversation with Moses and Elijah was: Jesus was discussing with them his Death, the destiny he was to fulfill in Jerusalem.

There is something profoundly moving in this, because Jesus must indeed have come to the decision to set his face towards Jerusalem and the confrontation and death that surely awaited him there, in dialogue with the heritage of the Law and the Prophets that shaped his thinking and expectations as a Jew. There is also something profoundly moving about Peter's response. Which of us, after all, would not gladly seize a peak experience of consolation and remain there? The scene suggests the feast of tabernacles, the memory of the desert "honeymoon" of Israel, in which (or so it seemed to later generations) the people had been on terms of easy familiarity with God who dwelt, so to speak, in tents with them.

The high point in this story, however, is the cloud which casts its shadow and sends forth a voice. God had led Israel through the desert in a pillar of cloud by day, and the image of the cloud remained a symbol of the presence of God among the people. The voice that comes out of the cloud, focuses clearly and sharply in the person of Jesus what Jewish tradition has said was the real meaning of the story of the binding of Isaac: it is God who sacrifices what is dear to him; if people are asked for great renunciations it is only that their potential to become like God in goodness and generosity might actually be realized. Even the formula, "my only Son, my Beloved" echoes the story of Abraham and Isaac exactly, and indeed early Church tradition seized upon the parallel of Isaac, the son of the promises, the only, the beloved, with Jesus.

But if we are to take these three readings in their juxtaposition in total seriousness, we cannot fail to realize that Jesus himself accepted the Jewish interpretation of the story in great breadth. It is God who suffers in every victim because each is infinitely precious, infinitely loved. Jesus expresses this in his saying that what is done to the least important of human persons is done to him, the dearly loved of the Father. God has surrendered into our hands, into our decision-making power, his dearly beloved about whom he cares passionately—the starving Ethiopians, the illegal immigrants, the refugees of the world, the unemployed and marginated of our own socity, the war-weary peoples of Central America, the crushed black communities of South Africa. God assures us in the story of the binding of Isaac that he does not desire human sacrifice, but there is always the danger that we might sacrifice people to other gods.

Third Sunday of Lent

READINGS: Ex 20:1-17; I Cor 1:22-25; Jn 2:13-25.

He knew men so well, all of them, that he needed no evidence from others about a man, for he himself could tell what was in a man.   Jn 2:25.

Granted that the translator of this text should have used "people" and "person" instead of "men" and "man," this sentence is an extraordinary way of summing up the day's readings. Confronted by this sentence alone, one might well wonder whether it is more a consolation or a threat to be in touch with someone who has that kind of insight into one's innermost depth. Further reflection on the three readings may shed some light on this.

The scene about the trade and traffic of merchandise in the Temple, like almost everything in Johns' Gospel, is full of allusions and double meaning. Nowadays we tend to miss that because of a common preoccupation with the question whether Jesus was violent in chasing out the money changers and live-stock merchants, and whether by his actions he sanctioned violence among his followers in our own generation when that violence is used in a good cause. The story as John tells it seems not to be concerned with that question at all. If indeed it represents one particular incident in the ministry of Jesus, rather than a dramatic presentaion of the effect which faith in Jesus had on his followers' evaluation of Temple worship and the observance of the ritual code, then that incident is nevertheless concerned with the messianic claim and not with the question of violence. What is described in the turning over of the tables is a typical prophetic act, and the whip that John mentions was probably the customary means of driving the animals out. It need not even have been used to strike them; cracking the whip would have sufficed.

What is much more pertinent is the fact that Jesus was not the first to be concerned about trade in the Temple. Jeremiah, Zechariah and Malachi had all spoken about it prophetically with more than a hint that in the messianic time, the time of fulfillment of all the promises, the Temple would be cleansed of all these activities that were not worthy of it as the house of God. As John describes the actions of Jesus, there is certainly the suggestion of the fulfillment of messianic prophecy. Moreover, there is a suggestion that Jesus was attacking not only abuses against the Law, but the existing interpretation of the Law which put such emphasis on the ritual observances. The money changers were there because of a strict interpretation that the animals for sacrifices could not be bought with Roman coin. The animals were there because animal sacrifice had been given such a central role that such live-stock trading in the sacred precincts did not appear incongruous. The words of Jesus seem to imply that such concerns have little to do with the real purpose of the Temple as the place of more solemn encounter with God. Indeed, John links the action of Jesus with a quotation from Psalm 69, which not only anticipates persecution for the one who does such signs, but also states that sincere prayer of praise and thanksgiving is more pleasing to God than animal sacrifice. Jesus recalls the terms of the Covenant which God made with the people at Sinai. That is to say, he points to the real heart of the matter. This may be why the liturgy gives us the proclamation of the Ten Commandments as the first reading, in preparation for the message of Jesus in the cleansing of the Temple.

Because the claims made by implication in the incident are so extensive and so radical, it is reasonable enough that the "Jews" should challenge his authority for making them. Of course, John uses the term "Jews" in two different ways—sometimes for the people as a whole, but sometimes for that religious leadership which rejected Jesus. If we are honest with the content of the term, we ought probably to think in this case of "the religious leaders," "the clergy," "the Congregation for the Doctrine of the Faith," as the contemporary equivalents. That seems to indicate the nature of the confrontation between the prophetic figure of Jesus and the established order. The guardians of that order want a sign commensurate with the claims. Of course, the Temple itself was supposed to have been a sign—a sign of God's dwelling in the midst of the people. The followers of Jesus see him in the light of an analogy with the Temple—the new place of intimate encounter with God—and the sign that is beyond all signs is the ultimate triumph and indestructibility of that new Temple, that new place of encounter with God.

There is an important reflection on this in the very short selection from I Corinthians. It is concerned with the problem of finding and reading the signs correctly. The devout (the Jews), he says, look for wonderworks that speak of the power and purpose of God. Outsiders (the Greeks) look for the inherent reasonableness or wisdom of any claim or proposal. Either path leads to truth for those who have not lost their capacity for wondering at those things that are really wonderful, or for those who become wise in the manner of the wisdom of God. What is so difficult to recognize is that the self-gift of Jesus crucified is the real wisdom and the real power to redeem the world. The Gospel selection ends with the observation that there were many people who were impressed by the signs that Jesus performed, but that Jesus was aware that they had not really understood their meaning.

This reading seems to leave us with the sobering question of what difference faith in Jesus has really made in our relationship with God. Has it really brought us closer to the heart of the matter, or has it just substituted one set of ritual obligations for another? Have we really accepted the terms of the Covenant or are we forever trying to "tame" the exigence of the living God by trapping it in a dead code of ritual obervances? Or, to put it in another way, do we recognize the trading and trafficking which does not belong in the Temple because it is the house of God, the house of prayer?

Fourth Sunday of Lent (Laetare)

READINGS: 2 Chr 36:14-17, 19-23; Eph 2:4-10; Jn 3:14-21.

For it is by his grace you are saved, through trusting him; it is not your own doing. It is God's gift, not a reward for work done. There is nothing for anyone to boast of.   Eph 2:8-9.

As we celebrate the Fourth Sunday of Lent we are supposed to rejoice over it. The rejoicing does not seem to come quite as spontaneously nowadays as it used to when Lent was, for the most part, far more rigorously observed. Yet, according to these readings, it ought to come more spontaneously than ever, because redemption is pure, an undeserved gift. The story in 2 Chronicles is a kind of miniature of the story of salvation. Things go from bad to worse: the people as a whole and the leaders who ought to know better are unfaithful and immoral; God sends prophets to warn them and the prophets are ignored and ill-treated; and at last the cumulative effect of their wickedness caves in upon the people and their leaders in unspeakable sufferings and total disaster. Then, as though out of nowhere, but really out of the ever-loving and unquenchable compassion of God, arises a savior figure. The circumstances are the most unlikely, the rescue the most complete.

The letter to the Ephesian wants to make quite sure we realize the implications of this message of salvation: we do not earn salvation; it is given to us, and indeed is far beyond anything we could possibly merit or deserve. God, who is overflowing love and bountiful mercy, rescues us from the cumulative consequences of evil human deeds throughout history, out of sheer benevolence. And it is this munificence and magnanimity which liberate us to do the good deeds for which we are created and recreated in Christ.

This is a message most apt for our times. As we look at the world situation, the economy, the arms race, world hunger, many endless small wars, many cruel and unjust regimes, it is really easier to see the first half of the story in Chronicles being acted out—things get worse and worse, leaders prove untrustworthy, prophets are despised, disasters follow upon one another with alarming frequency. It is truly a matter of faith to see and to acknowledge that the grace of God in Jesus Christ has practically and effectively set us free to do good deeds of justice and reconciliation and compassion. There are really two quite different ways of assessing current affairs and situations: there is a perspective which claims to be that of common sense, but is actually that of timidity and lack of faith, seeing no possibility of the radically new, the unexpected, the creative; and there is a perspective which is often condemned as unrealistic because it does not accept the limitations of the present situation as the last word to be said, but rather speaks prophetically of what might be in a world of converted hearts.

The Gospel reading also speaks of the undeserved love of God, intervening quite concretely in history through the gift of Jesus to the world. There is a curious poignancy in the comparison of the crucified Jesus with the brazen serpent lifted up by Moses. Cyrus, king of the Persians, was certainly an unlikely savior for God's people. But nothing could be more unlikely or more startling in its symbolism than the brazen serpent, held up as a symbol of salvation for those who were stricken by the plague of serpent bites. Yet it serves aptly to prefigure the astonishing paradox of the unjustly, senselessly crucified, lifted up as a sign of hope and salvation to all who are caught up in the injustices, brutalities and perversions of human history. We can never afford to forget that the Cross, before it is the sign of salvation, is a forceful symbol of suffering, rejection, and final frustration. But the Gospel seems to hint at another allusion to the unlikely with the statement that God loved the world so much that He gave his only Son. The story of Abraham's readiness to sacrifice Isaac interprets the death of Jesus as God's extravagant and unlikely gift for our reconciliation.

Again, the message is of the gratuity of the rescue that is offered in the midst of our so horribly distorted human history. The house of the Lord is to be rebuilt—not only the Temple of stones, but the household of the faithful and the community of all God's people. What is offered is salvation, not condemnation. Yet a judgement inevitably takes place. The test, John's Gospel maintains, is that very gift of salvation, for it brings a new light into the world and people judge themselves according to whether they respond by living in that light or withdrawing into the shadows and denying the light. But to live in the light is to rejoice because salvation is ours by gift and we are liberated to do the works of the light.

Fifth Sunday of Lent

READINGS: Jer 31:31-34; Heb 5:7-9; Jn 12:20-33.

Son though he was, he learned obedience in the school of suffering, and, once perfected, became the source of eternal life for all who obey him. Heb 5:8-9.

It comes as something of a shock to hear about Jesus that he "learned obedience" by what he suffered. Accustomed to thinking of Jesus as sinless and indeed divine, we are not inclined to imagine him puzzling, struggling or experimenting in order to come to the right decision, the right attitude, the right course of action. But perhaps our discomfort with these verses is increased by an oddly narrow idea of obedience. From the time that Israel promised "to do and to obey" at Sinai, there was in the Hebrew heritage the sense that beyond the doing or literal execution of commandments, lay a further exigence of obeying. Jesus appealed to this distinction when he spoke of the letter and the spirit of the law. Obedience involves reading between the lines of the commandments, trying to discern the will of God in changing circumstances and unforeseen situations, tuning one's sensitivity and perceptions and judgments to the divine will and the divine self-revelation.

These verses from the letter to the Hebrews place Jesus at the heart of the human situation, at the very center of the task of human freedom, wrestling humanly with failure and rejection, with suffering and powerlessness, and finding the focus which can draw everyone back into a restoration of creation to its purpose and its meaning. That is why these verses really are a commentary both upon the Gospel selection and upon the excerpt from Jeremiah. We are introduced to a new covenant which is not like any code formulated into conditions and terms of contract, but rather like a deep personal bond of empathy and loyalty, of affection and mutual understanding. It is a covenant of intimacy such as we could only have by sharing it with Jesus Christ.

Prepared by those passages, we are in a better position to consider the meaning of today's Gospel reading. In the verse just before this reading, the pharisaic leaders have lamented that all the world seemed to be following Jesus. We now have that confirmed by the arrival of Greeks who are anxious to see Jesus personally. But this approach of the Gentiles seems to be a sign for Jesus that the time of the consummation, of the great confrontation, has come. As John the Evangelist sees it retrospectively, from his single death Jesus expects a great burgeoning forth of new life. His death is to be the fulfillment of his mission, testimony to the Father and his own glorifying.

Yet even John, whose Gospel is so full of solemn speeches and theological explanations that are clear only because they are made in retrospect, gives us a passage similar to the Gethsemani story. Even John tells of inner turmoil, of anguish and anxiety, and of the response of divine consolation and confirmation of the determination to which Jesus has come. In fact, it is in this human choice of Jesus that John sees the judgement by which the power of evil is broken, and by which the ravaged and scattered human race is to be drawn together again. It is by being "raised up" in crucifixion, as John indicates, that Jesus is to have a magnetic attraction for his fellow human beings.

We are asked to enter into a deep mystery here, and as is the case with mysteries, it is offered to us in a paradox. The one crucified is accursed, isolated from human society, a sign of terror and of warning. But it is in seeing into the abyss of that terror and isolation that Jesus arrives at the very heart of the human tragedy as the self-utterance of the divine compassion. It is in this self-commitment of Jesus that we are given to know and to experience that God does not stand over against sinful creatures in condemnation but takes their side, standing with them in vindication. If we could but take this seriously, it would turn our whole perception of the world and human history upside-down. If we could but accept the salvation that is offered to us on these terms, it would change in radical ways our attitudes to the unsuccessful, the powerless, the shiftless, the poor, the enemy, the condemned.

But we look at the message of this Gospel passage and the invitation to the following of Jesus which it contains, we see the implication of death and self-surrender, and we find ourselves with that vertiginous feeling that the leap is too great and the risk too terrible. From year to year we have a tendency to conclude that we must, after all, be reasonable; wisdom is in moderation; Christian faith and practice cannot be so extreme but must accommodate the capacities of ordinary people. But from year to year the Lenten liturgy brings back these readings an meditations to disturb our established compromises.

Passion Sunday

READINGS: Procession of Palms: Mk 11:1-10 (or Jn 12:12-16).
Eucharist: Is. 50:4-7; Phil 2:6-11; Mk 14:1-15:47
(or 15:1-39).

Bearing the human likeness, revealed in human shape, he humbled himself, and in obedience accepted even death—death on a cross.   Phil 2:7-8.

Contemplating the execution of Jesus is not something that most of us do spontaneously. That may be in part because our earlier training too often focused attention exclusively on the intensity of the various kinds of physical pain that Jesus endured in the course of a protracted torture death. It may also be in part because the passion of Jesus has too often been presented in terms of expiation—an enormity of suffering weighed out and measured to be commensurate with the enormity of the world's sin, expressing an image of God not seen in the parables and prayers of Jesus.

Yet there seems to be a deeper reason for a spontaneous repugnance in confrontation with the Passion and Death of Jesus. It speaks of dimensions of the human situation which are terrifying. It expresses paroxysms of hatred and fear all too well known in the contemporary world and it demonstrates with unmistakable clarity the selflessness that is needed to counter such hatred and fear. Beyond all this, the story of the Passion shows us that God is in a certain sense powerless; God does not intervene to cancel the consequences of destructive deeds or to substitute for human freedom. Redemptive grace is the empowerment of human freedom and human action.

It is, perhaps, for these reasons that the liturgy insists on our contemplation of the Passion of Jesus by placing the Eucharist at the center of our worship, by making the Cross the central icon in both graphic and verbal symbolism, and by shaping the liturgical year as well as the liturgical week around the Paschal Mystery. And to make the matter more secure, the readings are so arranged that even those of us who take part in the Eucharist only on Sundays, cannot simply pass from the "Palm Sunday" scene of the entry into Jerusalem to the Easter Sunday Resurrection appearances. We are deluged with readings on the Sunday of the Passion, and all these readings pass before the mind's eye scenes that interpret the meaning of the death of Jesus.

The entry into Jerusalem sets the stage. Jesus is welcomed in acclamations fitting a conquering hero. He responds in symbolic action bespeaking non-violence and unpretentious service. The liturgy moves us from this to the Isaian passage. We hear of a calling to teach and console and discern the voice of God—a calling accepted with unshakable resolution in the face of persecution and contempt. The third of the "suffering servant songs," is invoked to explain what Jesus is doing. Paul in the letter to the Philippians quotes an ancient Christian hymn to say this even more explicitly. Unlike the first Adam, created in the divine image and "snatching equality with God," Jesus restores the truth of the relationship, accepting the limitations of the human, accepting death, even the appalling death on the cross.

When we return to the Gospel, the scenes continue to flash by, each super-imposed on the last, giving depth of meaning to the whole. There is the plot that miscarried, threaded through the whole recital: he must be gotten out of the way, but not killed on the festival day which would give him too much exposure to the impressionable crowds. In the event, he dies during the festival gathering and in the course of history it is the Cross that becomes the rallying point. Then there is the anointing at Bethany. Anointing makes the Messiah in the root meaning of the term, and the anonymous woman who does it certainly recognizes in Jesus a person of special significance before God and among the people. But the response of Jesus reinterprets the action: it is for his burial, for his death as the rejected one. Similarly at the Last Supper, the farewell meal, within the accustomed ritual actions the meaning is refocused: the host becomes the hospitality, the homilist becomes the homily.

Next, the scenes that pass before us are concerned with three trials. Gethsemani is the trial before God and conscience, the trial of purpose and discernment, a trial not only of Jesus but also of his disciples. Jesus saw what must be done; the disciples fled. The second trial before the High Priest and Council is presented by Mark as a kind of parody, for they were only able to condemn Jesus on his own voluntary testimony in the end. At the third trial, before Pilate, according to Mark Jesus is condemned by his own voluntary silence. It is not accidental that the Holy Week liturgy through the centuries echoed with the refrain, *quia ipse voluit,* because these three scenes leave us with the impression that it is Jesus who is in charge and that it is the world that is on trial before the clarity of his vision, his purpose and his practical commitment to see the matter through.

After this we are prepared for the irony of the mocking scene and for the curious impression of the crucifixion as enthronement and the death scene as one of holding court. Here again it seems that the crude brutality of the execution is reinterpreted for us: Jesus is enthroned and vindicated for ever, but the evangelist summons the enemies of Jesus to the scene to be judged by their stance in relation to the crucified, as the temple veil is torn in two, one era ending and a new one dawning with the centurion's testimony and the great Sabbath rest.

Easter Sunday

READINGS: Acts 10:34, 37-43; Col 3:1-4 (or I Cor 5:6-8); Jn 20:1-9 (or Mk 16:8).

God raised him to life on the third day, and allowed him to appear, not to the whole people, but to witnesses whom God had chosen in advance—to us who ate and drank with him after he rose from the dead.   Acts 10:40-41.

Even those who were the first witnesses did not manage too well to explain in words what that event was that so completely changed their lives and their perceptions. We, who in Eucharist and community also eat and drink with the risen Christ, and who are also chosen in advance as witnesses, are hard-pressed to give an account of the hope that is in us and of the founding experience on which that hope rests.

Those who are fortunate enought to be present at the Easter Vigil need little added commentary. The stories of creation and liberation, hope and peoplehood and covenant, speak powerfully with their symbolism, and it would be difficult to say more without dulling their impact. The rituals of the kindling of new fire, the lighting of a multitude of little candles, the coming up out of water and the wearing of new and radiant garments, the haunting melody to the *Exsultet,* the midnight timing of the celebration, are all in themselves so eloquent that added words of explanation tend only to restrict the range of meaning which the symbols have in themselves.

The Sunday morning worshippers, however, who have not been party to the celebration of memories and hopes, and to the explosion of light and song during the night, are somewhat cheated of the full experience of the great feast of the year—the feast that gives meaning to everything else in Christian life and worship. For them it is necessary, after all, to put something into words, to draw out the message of the Scripture texts and to situate ourselves and our times within that great mystery which is Easter.

There is a certain austerity in the way Peter's speech before Gentiles (as told in Acts 10) expresses the great news of salvation; Jesus came in the power of God's holy Spirit, bearing healing and reconciliation, offering peace; the world did its worst to him in a criminal execution; but Spirit and truth prevailed. God raised him to the life on the third day; witnesses have seen him; he is become the pledge for all peoples that God's saving act prevails over death. Jesus, in his death and in his life of the third day, is become the judge and the criterion by which all of us may understand where we really stand before God. To believe in him is to know forgiveness of all sin, error and stupidity, and to become a living witness of reconciliation and peace in public and private life.

The selections from Colossians and I Corinthians emphasize in two distinct ways that we have not understood the message of the Resurrection of Jesus if we do not in fact witness that we are living the life of the third day with him. Jesus has broken through into that other day, that other age, not alone but as the first of many people linked by the closest ties. We are driven to ask what is this life of the third day, for the New Testament emphasizes not the utter discontinuity of Jesus' risen life from our own experience, but precisely the continuity and familiarity. From the readings chosen for the Mass of the Day, it appears that the life of sin and alienation is overcome by the crucified and risen Jesus, but also by those baptized into his death and living the new life in and with him. The life that we have now is that of the new age, the third phase, beyond fear and recriminations, beyond defensiveness and compromises with evil, beyond the old feuds and factions and divisions. It is the life of reconciliaton and restoration of all things that is offered to us now.

Because the implications of this are so great and far-reaching in all our relationships with one another, in the large issues of social justice and peace as well as in our more intimate encounters, there is always the temptation to reduce the message of Easter to something less than it really is. That is perhaps why the two Gospel passages offered to us today focus so sharply on the empty tomb. Our own century has seen much argument about the meaning of the empty tomb stories, centering for the most part on the question whether the emptiness is to be understood in a physical sense. But this discussion may be a distraction from a far more significant question: whether we ourselves are content to linger at the entrance of the tomb and seek no further, or whether having gone in we are prepared to believe what we see; whether having believed we respond with awe and not a little anxiety and go away and tell no one, or whether we realize and proclaim that the tomb is empty because Jesus is among the living, and because a whole new age has begun for this confused and troubled world.

It seems sometimes that we would prefer to have Jesus safely and decently buried in antiquity and in our Churches. To have the risen Christ abroad in the world, turning up in unexpected places and situations, appearing to the witnesses that God has chosen beforehand, exploding our prudently limited ideas of the practicable as we eat and drink with him in Eucharist after his rising from the dead—all this is really very disturbing in its own way, very challenging, very disconcerting. But the way into the tomb, like the way into the Garden of primal innocence, is blocked by an angel who warns us not to try to go back. He is risen as he said.

Second Sunday of Easter

READINGS: Acts 4:32-35; I Jn 5:1-6; Jn 20:19-31.

The whole body of believers was united in heart and soul. Not a man of them claimed any of his possessions as his own, but everything was held in common, while the apostles bore witness with great power to the resurrection of the Lord Jesus.   Acts 4:32-33.

Luke's account of the early community of followers of Jesus may be rather idealistic, but it does express clearly and in very practical terms the outcome of true resurrection faith. Such faith means that one has found one's true hope, joy and security in the saving power of divine love, and therefore no longer needs to cling to wealth, power or status. There is a spontaneity of fellowship expressed in detachment and sharing. People are provided for according to their needs and not according to any scale of deserts. It sounds like communism, and it is such, though not with the capital "C" suggesting that such generous sharing must needs be grounded in atheism.

Perhaps the other readings, both from John, help to explain the phenomenon here described by Luke. In the passage from the first letter, John insists that faith in Jesus as Christ, the Savior, the Son of God, is a totally transforming experience, because it means a love of God which includes all God's family. To love God is to respond to the will of God and that is to care for other people without exception. John connects this with victory over the "world," that is over structures and values of society pitted against God. Jesus is totally victor over the world and those who live by faith in him are privileged to share his victory. It is a victory that restores the God-given order of things in which peace and fellowship and goodwill are seen to be far more precious than wealth and status and power.

John finds testimony to the reality of that witness in "the Spirit, the water and the blood," a symbolism that is very strange to our modern ears, though evidently of great significance to him. The Gospel of John also mentions water and blood in the same breath, as it were, in Jn 19:30-34, with reference to the death of Jesus, who breathed forth his spirit, and from whose pierced side flowed water and blood. But it may be that the reference is rather to the proclamation of Jesus as Son of God at the baptism in the Jordan in water, the testimony of his death in blood, and the power of his resurrection in the gift of the Spirit. And it may also be that when these lines were written at the end of the first century, they already suggested to the members of the Christian community the testimony of their own experiences of transformation in baptism, Eucharist and the prophetic power of the spirit among them. Certainly their own changed lives were the foundation for that witness with great power that went out from the community to those about them.

The passage from the Gospel speaks of the origin of that power in terms of peace, joy and reconciliation conferred on the disciples and entrusted to them by the risen Jesus. We are told that the disciples were gathered behind locked doors on the first day after the great sabbath—that is, the first day on which the persecutors of Jesus could have continued their pursuit and arrested some of his followers. Who these disciples were is not specified. They seemed to be more than the Twelve, and according to Acts 1:14 they seem to have included women as well as men. To this group Jesus appeared suddenly with the familiar greeting, Shalom, bringing them peace in reality, and evoking great joy. Jesus, who at the beginning of John's Gospel was introduced as the one who would baptize in the Holy Spirit, now fulfills that promise. More than that, he who was identified at the beginning of the Gospel as the Word by which God first created, now breathes the new life of the Spirit into his disciples, making them a new creation.

The passage is dense with symbolism and allusion of a kind our present-day minds are not used to catching. But perhaps the most interesting and puzzling aspect of that first encounter with the risen Jesus is the mandate that John sees in it. The gift of the Spirit means a task of reconciliation, of forgiveness, laid on the gathering of the followers of Jesus. The Spirit, or life, he passes on to them is his life, and the task with all its responsibilities, is his own task of universal reconciliaton by offering the redeeming love of God. John has written in many places that to meet that redeeming love in the person of Jesus, is to stand judged according to whether one accepts it in faith or rejects it in scorn or disbelief. The task of palpably presenting that redeeming love which confronts people with God's judgment, is now the challenge of the community of the followers of Jesus.

Lest we should think of all this as interesting past history to be admired from afar, John's Gospel quickly adds another story—that of Thomas. Most of us have no doubt about it that it would have been so much better and easier to have known Jesus in the flesh, to have been present to see and hear and touch, to have empirical proof. Thomas is there to represent us, availing himself of such proof, only to learn that what he has attained is less valuable than the faith of those who have not seen Jesus in the flesh. The Gospel of John culminates with a new beatitude: blessed are they who have not seen and have believed. And it is perhaps in that statement that the text from Acts becomes clearer: the Resurrecton becomes a tangible fact in a very different way from that which we should expect. Not by direct empirical verification but by the radical transformation of the community into a fellowship of justice, truth, compassion, reconciliation and sharing of all things, is the presence and power of the risen Jesus known.

Third Sunday of Easter

READINGS: Acts 3:13-15, 17-19; I Jn 2:1-5; Lk 24:35-48.

Then he opened their minds to understand the scriptures.   Lk 24:35.

All three of the readings chosen for today are concerned with the revelatory impact of the Resurrection of Jesus, in the light of which we are enabled to reinterpret the whole human situation as though understanding the scriptures for the first time. And the burden of this oft-repeated message is the revelation which we thought was too good to be true.

Peter's comment on the cure of the cripple in the Temple is rather straight forward: the fidelity of God overcomes the infidelity of human society; the God whom Abraham, Isaac and Jacob trusted has fulfilled his promises. God sent his servant, Jesus, to bring life. The people rejected him in favor of a murderer, of one whose mission it was to bring death. But even so God raised Jesus from death and he continues to bring life, though his witnesses, challenging ignorance and confusion in the face of persecution.

The excerpt from I John gives a rather similar message of the indefatigable fidelity of God. We who are reborn in the life of the Risen Christ, should not sin, but to the extent that we do we have one to plead our cause, for Jesus himself is the remedy for sin, and we know it when in our obedience to the commands of Jesus, divine love comes to a certain perfection among us. This may seem at first to be a strange saying, but in the sequence of these Easter readings it gains a degree of luminosity.

The Gospel reading places us in the series of apparitions of Jesus in which he clarifies for his disciples the meaning of all that has happened, in preparation for the commission he is to give them for an apostolate to the whole world. The apparition of which we hear in this passage is linked with the Emmaus story by the exchange of testimonies between the travellers and the community of Jerusalem. In both stories the emphasis is on the authentic continuity between the Jesus of history and the Christ of faith. The Jesus of history is not irrevocably lost but transformed and vindicated; what has happened is not the denial but the confirmation of the scriptures, not the failure but the fulfillment of the promises of redemption.

The earliest disciples evidently had a great deal of trouble accepting this interpretation of what they themselves had seen and lived through. They were not easily persuaded of the continuity and of the truth of the Resurrection as something more than hallucination or wishful thinking. If we today do not have similar difficulties that may be because both the Death and the Resurrection of Jesus remain so peripheral to our lives and our sense of meaning and purpose for our lives. The difficulty for us is rather that of grasping that everything in history really depends on whether there is truly such a continuity between the Jesus of history and the Christ of faith, in other words whether the covenant fidelity of God triumphs over human infidelity in the Resurrection of Jesus of Nazareth.

Perhaps it is an inadequate sense of sin that makes all three readings for this Sunday appear a little remote. The true tragedy of sin is not that a vengeful God arbitrarily exacts suffering by way of compensation. The true tragedy of sin is that it is so fertile, so prolific of its own progeny. Sin is, so to speak, its own punishment. Once the disorientation from God has begun, the focus of creaturely existence becomes more and more distorted and obscure; fear, violence and confusion spread, and there appears to be no way back. Moreover, the true tragedy of sin is that in our human situation of interdependent freedoms unfolding in relationships with others in society, the distortions and disorientation of sin spread like yeast, like bacteria through the whole mass of human relationships, and there appears to be no escape.

It is surely in this context that we can indeed recognize Jesus as the remedy for sin, the one to plead our cause, because in him there is a way back, there is a way to stop the spreading contagion and escape the disaster. When Peter spoke with such conviction it was because he and those around him had already experienced in their own community and in their impact on outsiders, that Jesus had indeed turned the tide of history. When John wrote that Jesus was the remedy not only for the sins of individuals within the community but for the sins of the whole world, it was because he and his community had already experienced the reversal of the terrible powers of sin and the coming to perfection of the love of God in the human community. And the Lucan story which is so concerned with the reality of the Resurrection as the fulfillment of all prophecy and the realization of hope, is followed by the declaration that because of this the forgiveness of sin may be proclaimed far and wide to the nations.

The challenge to us today is just as real, because among the intrinsic punishments of sin is cynicism—the obstinate conviction that there is no way out, that war and greed and far-flung injustices and oppressions are inevitable, even that the world is necessarily caught in a rising spiral of violence that must end in total destruction. But if we believe in the Resurrection, we know that Jesus is the remedy for sin because he has reversed the tide of history.

Fourth Sunday of Easter

READINGS: Acts 4:8-12; I Jn 3:1-2; Jn 10:11-18.

I am the good shepherd; I know my sheep and my sheep know me . . . and I lay down my life for the sheep . . . I am laying it down of my own free will. I have the right to lay it down, and the right to receive it back again; this charge I have received from my Father.   Jn 10:14-15, 18.

All three readings for the day are concerned with naming, appropriating, interpreting, the events of the death and Resurrection of Jesus. Peter and John, arrested, imprisoned and brought to trial before the Jewish rulers for causing disorderly assemblies in the Temple, are interested in just one thing: explaining to all who will listen the radical difference in human life and prospects that has been brought about by Jesus through his death and resurrection, making him the one true channel of salvation. The reading from John's first letter assures the followers of Jesus that this has already made a difference to us, Jesus has established a filial relationship with the transcendent God, which we cannot fully appreciate now but which is to unfold into unmistakable clarity and transformation. The transforming power is the love of God expressed in Jesus, which we shall come to understand more fully when we have become like God as God is expressed in Jesus. And we glimpse this deeper understanding when we have begun to see him as he is—creative and redemptive love.

These two readings give us a story of courage and reconciliation, and a message of consolation. The third reading gives us an image, a symbol, which embraces and interprets both. The image of the shepherd has a long history in Israel. God has been imagined as the shepherd of Israel (Ps 23, Ps. 80), Israel's best loved king came to the throne from a youth spent as a shepherd. Ezekiel 34 laments the treachery of the hired shepherds who are the leaders of Israel, and promises that God in person will shepherd the flock. Jesus was fond of the image of the shepherd and used it for God in one of his striking parables about forgiveness (Lk 15). The image of the shepherd seems to be used because the shepherd leads the flock into safe pathways, to places of nourishment, protecting it against attack, providing the focus that unites the flock and gives it a sense of direction and purpose. But beyond all this, the shepherd is a symbol of compassion in the root sense of that word, for the shepherd fulfills all those tasks by entering into the life and experience of the flock, sharing its risks and hardships, becoming responsible for its fate.

According to the reading from John's Gospel, it is because of that attitude in Jesus which is represented by the role of the shepherd, that Jesus willingly goes into death. His death concludes his entry into the whole experience of those for whom he accepts responsibility—his entry into the risks and hardships of their lives. It is because he carries his concern to its logical conclusion that we are able to recognize him as the true shepherd, the one promised, the one who really makes the difference. John's Gospel contrasts this with false shepherds, motivated by self-interest, who lead the flock to destruction. During the lifetime of Jesus there were, of course, many of these, and several times after the death of Jesus there were those who led Israel into uprisings that were catastrophic in their outcome for the oppressed. But we would miss the point of the day's readings if we were to refer them only to past history. Jesus remains forever the image of the true shepherd, and any leadership that contradicts his guarantees some kind of destruction just as catastrophic as the fall of Jerusalem and the destruction of the Temple.

What is so important for us to try to discern is what this means in our own lives—the imagery and interpretation of the laying down of the life of Jesus and his receiving of it again at the hands of the Father. In the readings from Acts, Peter uses the complementary image of the rejected stone which has become the keystone, to warn us how radically our thinking about human affairs must change if it is to be in line with God's creative and redemptive intent so that we may be co-builders with God. It is by the name conferred on Jesus, the crucified, the risen, the savior, that the wonderful works of God among us are realized. Just as the image of the shepherd bears allusion to God, so does the invocation of "the name," for "the name" is one of the circumlocutions used for God in Jewish tradition. But Jesus, in his life, Death, Resurrection and impact on his followers, gives body to this ethereal circumlocution for the divine. "The Name" comes to be a naming of shepherd, rock, healer, friend and companion, self-sacrificing life-giver, and compassionate.

Reflection on these names suggests what John might mean by writing that we shall understand what it means to be children of God, when we come to be like God as revealed in Jesus, because we see him as he is.

Fifth Sunday of Easter

READINGS: Acts 9:26-31; I Jn 3:18-24; Jn 15:1-8.

If you abide in me and my words abide in you, you shall ask what you will and it shall be done unto you. Herein is my Father glorified, that you bear much fruit; so shall you be my disciples.   Jn 15:7-8.

The Paschal Mystery is, of course, not only to be admired from afar, but to be lived and be allowed to penetrate all aspects of our human existence. The readings for this Sunday are intent upon this realization. They offer us a story, an exhortation, and a parable with strong and allusive imagery. The story is that of Saul's acceptance into the community of the followers of Jesus and into their apostolate soon after his conversion. It seems that although they themselves had undergone conversion to and in the Risen Christ, the Christians of Jerusalem were still skeptical about the power of the Paschal Mystery to transform the vision and goals of a persecutor such as Paul. There is something strangely moving and immediately relevant to our times in this reluctance of theirs. We ourselves do not readily believe that the world can really be transformed in the mystery of the risen Christ—at least in its more intractable elements, such as the great ideological oppositions of our own times, or the economic and political structures of power.

There is another aspect of interest in this short story about Saul. The story illustrates the way the challenge of the gospel of Jesus Christ works. The presecutor is won over to faith, but inevitably becomes in turn the persecuted, because the conversion questions the entrenched positions and beliefs of others—convictions by which people define themselves and in which they rest their security. To be converted to Christ, to live in Christ, necessarily means to share this experience of reversals in some measure. For most of us this does not involve the dramatic aspects of actual persecution, but there is a movement of conversion in which the judgmental become the judged, the contemptuous become the despised, the exclusive become the excluded, and so forth.

This, however, is not the heart of the matter, it is a consequence of conversion. The reading from I John, like so many Johannine texts, insists upon the heart of the matter; love is not expressed in words but in action; to believe in Jesus is to love one another, and it is love which fulfills all the commandments. God is not waiting to judge and condemn but rather to convert to the truth, and the truth is to be found in Jesus and in the authentic charity that has been made possible by him and in him.

The parable of the vine and the branches speaks directly to this point; so much becomes possible in the risen Christ, which we on our own are not capable of achieving. One cannot really appreciate the imagery of the vine and the branches without realizing the role that the vine and the vineyard have played in the history of Israel and in the expression of its vocation of peoplehood in harmony with God. The image of the vine speaks of an intimate communion of life, of fruitfulness, and of responsiveness to the one who plants and tends. Yet the allusions to vine and vineyard in psalms and prophecies are ambivalent; they speak of divine longing and outpouring and of human failure and unresponsiveness. They tell of divine persistence and undaunted fidelity in the face of constant rejection. Jesus himself presented the theme in a new light (Lk 20) when he told of the vineyard and the unfaithful tenants who appropriated the fruit and killed the messengers and the owner's son.

In light of these other references, the claim of Jesus that he is the true vine comes into sharper focus. It is a claim to be a new beginning, a new foundation for peoplehood, a whole new communion of life. It is a claim to open hitherto undreamed-of possibilities. It is a challenge and an invitation into the new life of the Paschal Mystery.

Sixth Sunday of Easter

READINGS: Acts 10:25-26, 34-35, 44-48; I Jn 4:7-10; Jn 15:9-17.

There is no greater love than this, that a man should lay down his life for his friends ... This is my commandment to you: love one another. Jn 15:13,17.

By this time most of us have laid aside the festive mood of Easter and lost ourselves once more in the dust-drab tasks of making a living and simply surviving in a complex and competitive world. But the liturgy insists on our returning into the presence of the risen Christ until the full forty days have run their course. More than that, the readings bring us back not only to the resurrection but to the issue of the death, reminding us that the issue is love. Lest we think of the Easter spirit as a momentary luxury, or as an event that remains forever outside of ourselves and in some measure alien, all three of the readings make it clear that the earthly glory of the risen Christ is our empowerment to overcome all obstacles by divine love, so that life can never be quite the same for any of us.

Because of the distance in time and culture, we do not easily realize the magnitude of the obstacles that were overcome in Peter's baptizing of the family of the centurion, Cornelius. But we must believe that they were at least as great as the barriers erected by racism in our own society, and anyone who has tried to break them down knows how intransigent these latter are. We must know too, how difficult it is to accept literally in our own times Peter's discovery that "God has no favorites." Our historically cultivated national sense of "manifest destiny" seems so indisputably to establish our special merit and exclusive divine election over and against the peoples of the Communist and Third World countries. Among ourselves it seems that economic and professional success most surely signal moral and spiritual worth that sets us far apart from the faceless and unsuccessful—the welfare families, the unemployed, the homeless, the "skid row" people, those in the lengthening bread lines, those targeted by the Campaign for Human Development. But the revelation to Peter is as fresh and pertinent today as it was then: God has no favorites. The barriers are of our own sinful making. God hears the cry of the poor, the oppressed, and the excluded.

However, the message that reaches us on this Sunday is not one of condemnation but of hope. For John assures us that all the talk about transforming love is not simply a command to us to change, but a gift of empowerment; the love of which we speak is that by which God first loved us into new possibilities and new creativity. If there is talk of laying down one's life, or one's prejudices, or one's special claims to wealth, status or power over others, it is in the context of the death and resurrection of Jesus who has brought about a whole new creation with new possibilities. John's point is that there is really a whole new beginning. What was not possible before in human ralations and human community has now been begun by Christ.

John's language is so poetic and lofty, that is is all too easy to miss the compelling practical quality of his teaching. He presents the message of Jesus as startlingly simple but all the more exigent for that simplicity. Radical transformation of all human activities is possible because love is from God.

Ascension Thursday

READINGS: Acts 1:1-11; Eph 1:17-23; Mk 16:15-20.

So after talking with them the Lord Jesus was taken up into heaven, and he took his seat at the right hand of God; but they went out to make their proclamation everywhere, and the Lord worked with them and confirmed their words by the miracles that followed.   Mk 16:19-20.

There is much pathos and longing in the story of the ascension which these readings give us twice. The story contains on the one hand the theme of the exaltation of Jesus to the right hand of the Father, as we have preserved it in the creeds—the theme of the vindication of Jesus and of all he stood for and all he taught. But the story contains, on the other hand, the sending of the followers of Jesus to continue his mission, to be his presence in the world. That is why there is a gentle irony in the question raised by the assembled disciples in Acts 1. Is this the time at which Jesus will establish his Kingdom, restore sovereignty to Israel? It seems that they who are sent have by no means grasped even now what is the nature of Christ's kingdom and what is the nature of the hope that is offered to them.

The Ascension story really raises all the important questions about the nature of that hope not only for the disciples of those first years, but for all of us even in our own times. The Ascension means that there is no magic answer to the troubles of the world—no answer that can bypass or dispense with true conversion and transformation of our human society with all its distorted values and inauthentic relationships. The Ascension challenges us to realize that the grace of God does not work above or alongside of our own freedom but within it, and to know that what is accomplished within the human freedom of Jesus cannot substitute for our own conversion but must yet come to include it.

Even the apparently simple imagery of the Ascension story is important. Jesus has gathered his disciples about him one last time, giving final instructions and encouragement. Then he was "lifted up" and enveloped in a cloud. It is an image that recalls the presence of God with Israel in the form of a cloud. It also recalls the passing of

Elijah (who was expected to return at the end-time) in a fiery chariot. And the two white-clad figures are like those at the tomb, exhorting the disciples not to look here into the past, but out to the community and the future, knowing what is the hope in which they live and reach out to others.

Seventh Sunday of Easter

READINGS: Acts 1:15-17, 20-26; I Jn 4:11-16; Jn 17:11-19.

Though God has never been seen by any man, God himself dwells in us if we love one another; his love is brought to perfection within us. I Jn 4:12.

We are already in the novena of prayer that leads to the promised bestowal of the Spirit. But we are reminded that the Spirit that is to come upon us in power and newness is after all the Spirit of Jesus. We are called to witness to his resurrecton by the newness of our lives. There is the passive witness—our own experience of a break-through, a new beginning, undreamed of possibilities. And there is the active witness—the giving of the good news to others. It is a matter of making the presence of the living God visible in the world, so to speak.

The story from the Acts of the Apostles, in which Mathias is elected to take the place of Judas, is concerned with this task of being a witness to the resurrection of Jesus. But the community is looking for more than faith and good will and membership of the congregation of believers. The community at the time of Luke's writing is already concerned with something that is important for us also—the historicity of the events of the life and death of Jesus. It is necessary to complete the number of the principal witnesses upon whose testimony the whole tradition must rest. There is a sense in which we all share their task, but there is also a sense in which they stand forever apart, because they must assure us that the good news is rooted not only in fond hopes but also in a solid historical past. The symbolic number "twelve," corresponding to the tribes of Israel, speaks of the completeness of the founding testimony. The failed vocation of Judas leaves a gap that must be filled, but ultimatly it is God who chooses whom to send.

John's letter refers to the task of witness as we all share it. Much of the Johannine literature seems preoccupied with the realization that we do not see God face to face, but that we can see God in the faces of other people and that we can make God visible to others in our own faces. The passage read today echoes the conversation of Jesus with Philip in the Last Supper discourse (Jn 14:7-11). The only way in which Jesus can show his disciples the face of the Father is by the image that reflects it in his own face, and this we are all called to do in some measure for one another. But John's letter does not leave the matter there; it becomes quite specific. Making God visible for one another is realized by love for others, indeed by mutual love within the community of the witnesses, because it is this which expresses the Spirit which is received from Jesus, and it is this love also which constitutes the authentic confession of Jesus as the Son of God.

The Gospel reading completes these reflections by drawing together the feasts of Easter, Ascension and Pentecost. It speaks of the spiritual legacy of Jesus to his followers. He leaves them the gifts of divine protection, unity, joy and consecration by the truth. In his mortal life, his presence was the power that kept them loyal to God and protected them from "the evil one." In parting, he assures them that he will not leave them unprovided. He wants them to know that the divine presence will not leave them, so that their joy may know full measure even while they struggle in a world full of bitterness and persecutions. They are to know the consolation and strength of the divine protection when they experience the ability to become one among themselves in profound harmony, even as Jesus and the Father are one. It is the miracle that is recalled again and again in the Acts of the Apostles, and described so wistfully in the letters of Paul and John.

But the legacy of Jesus to his followers also includes a "consecration by the truth." We may well ask what that may mean. Jesus offers himself and his own dedication in death as the model that explains the meaning. Consecration by (or in) the truth has reference to the word of God which is truth and to the mission to proclaim it with one's life and, if opportune, with one's death. In our own times, such consecration in or by the truth of God's word seems to carry far-reaching consequences for social justice and peace, for policies of community sharing and caring, for structures of compassion and reconstruction. It is a calling that presupposes protection from destructive spirits of all sorts, along with a gift of unity and profound joy. In describing this legacy, Jesus seems to sum up what it means to become witness to his Resurrection.

Pentecost

READINGS: Acts 2:1-11; I Cor 12:3-7, 12-13; Jn 20:19-23.

In each of us the Spirit is manifested in one particular way for some useful purpose . . . For indeed we were all brought into one body by baptism, in the one Spirit, whether we are Jews or Greeks, whether slaves or free men, and that one Holy Spirit was poured out for all of us to drink. 1 Cor 12:7, 13.

In some of the traditional Catholic communities of Europe, it was the custom to write out on white slips of paper at Pentecost the gifts and fruits of the Spirit as listed in the catechism (and garnered from the New Testament letters of Paul). They were turned upside down in two baskets, and in families, classrooms and sometimes churches, each person present would draw one slip from the gifts and one from the fruits. It might have been seen as a mysterious way of finding out with which charisms each was endowed by the Holy Spirit, or that one was supposed to pray for those particular endowments. But perhaps the truly useful purpose it served was to make the community reflect at least once a year on what should be the characteristics manifest in a Spirit-filled gathering of believers.

Today's readings seem to warn against the tendency to think and act as though the movements of the Spirit could be institutionally controlled—the tendency to suppose that the initiative is ours rather than God's. The passages from the Acts of the Apostles and from John's Gospel seem to tell the same story in different ways, but both emphasize that the initiative is divine and that it comes to us from the crucified and now risen Jesus. The story in Acts is richly allusive. The Spirit's coming is placed within the festival of the Sinai covenant which was celebrated fifty days after Passover. As on Sinai, the place shakes under the participants' feet as in a great storm, and the presence of God is made known under the form of fire. As on Sinai, a new people is formed, the people of God, made up of the reluctant and the fearful, wonderfully transformed in great power. Here in the upper room, as there on the mountain, what is brought forth is a witness people to tell to the whole world the wonderful works of God.

However, the scene in Acts not only parallels that earlier gathering of God's people; it also offers a contrast to the still earlier story of the scattering of God's people at the tower of Babel. In that sad tale, the people built and climbed in order to usurp God's place; they captured the control tower, so to speak, or so they thought. And everything fell apart. No longer could they understand one another's utterances. At the disciples' Pentecost it is a humbled remnant that climbs to the upper room to beg that the divine Spirit may descend to direct human affairs once more. And the people converge, each understanding the message in a familiar tongue.

When John tells the story, it is simpler. The risen Jesus comes in person, assuring his disciples that he is indeed the crucified, and breathing his own spirit, which is the Holy Spirit, into them, offering them the gifts of peace and joy and the power fo reconciling others. The scene carries the suggestion of the new creation. In the first creation, God breathes the divine breath (spirit) into the human person who thereby becomes a living being. In a history of sin and the disastrous consequences of sin, the breath of God blows again and again for freedom—in the drying up of the great flood, in the escape from Egypt, in the vocation of the prophets, in Mary's conception of Jesus. And now Jesus, who has given human shape to the divine breath, breathes it forth into his followers, transforming them with new life, recreating them in his own image and likeness. The face of the earth is, in a true sense, renewed. But we need to be told, to be reminded, because this does not happen all at once. It did not happen long ago without our participation, nor by sheer evolution without any struggle.

As so often happens, Paul makes it specific and explicit and practical. There is need for some criteria as to who speaks in the Spirit. The criteria are offered us by the person of Jesus, rooted in history, made present in the community. The gifts of the Spirit to the members of the community are for the building up of the whole body, for its unity in complementarity. They are not privileges for the benefit of the recipient, giving some more dignity and more rights than others; they are for the common good. Our task is to discern the gifts of the Spirit in all their variety, wherever they are bestowed, and to thank God and accept these gifts. It is not ours to assign the gifts of the Spirit, to ration them out, or to set limitations concerning those to whom they may be given. That task is divine. We have our individual vocations and they unfold for us in the talents for ministry which we discover. It is in our plurality, our variety, that we become one body in Christ. To deny the talents of any is to diminish the body of Christ, the presence and ministry of Christ in the world ready for redemption.

Paul gives us the most concrete indication of what it is to be reborn in the Spirit when he insists the barriers between Jews and Greeks, between slaves and free men, and all prejudicial and oppressive distinctions cease for those who truly live in the Spirit. For it is the same Spirit that has been poured out for all of us to drink.

Trinity Sunday

READINGS: Deut 4:32-34, 39-40; Rom 8:14-17; Mt 28:16-20.

For all who are moved by the Spirit of God are the children of God. The Spirit you have received is not a spirit of slavery leading you back into a life of fear, but a Spirit that makes us children, enabling us to cry, 'Abba! Father!' Rom 8:14-15.

The mystery of the Triune God makes a difficult topic for meditation or preaching. There is a danger of theological abstraction that offers no edification for Christian life. There is a danger of claiming considerably too much for human knowledge of the transcendent God. The one sure way to avoid such dangers is that which both liturgy and Scripture follow. We come to celebrate the mystery of the Triune God as the culmination of the Church's year of grace-filled memories. We have recalled the ancient mercies and centuries' long fidelity of Israel's one, almighty creator God, and that God's promises of salvation from a tangled history of sin. We have retraced the disciples' steps in discovering the mystery of God-with-us in the person of Jesus seen in the radiance of the Risen Christ. We have learned to recognize the Spirit of God dimly in the great prophets and distinctly in Jesus, and have joined the earliest disciples in being overwhelmed by the gift of the Spirit to us, experiencing the immanence of the divine as an unfailing presence in our midst. And it is at this point in the liturgical cycle of the year that we pause to consider what it means to say all this of God.

It begins really with that sense of wonder, gratitude and recollection which is evoked by the first reading. The passage from Deuteronomy 4 invites *anamnesis,* grateful recall of the mysteries of power that have touched us in our own lives and in that earlier history that shaped the possibilities of our lives. We are prompted to remember not only the history of Israel, which goes into the shaping of the Christian sense of God, but all our history from Jesus to the present. Moreover, we are challenged not to forget the natural phenomena about us and the history which we call secular. We are called to open our eyes, to appreciate the works of God's power, wisdom and affection, and to tread reverently in creation and history, gaining confidence from learning what manner of God it is that we worship.

The excerpt from Romans 8 gives Paul's sense of what it means to do this as a follower of Jesus. It is in intimacy with Jesus, in close identification with his life, his attitudes and actions, his Death and Resurrection, that we are able to know God as intimate, as Father. And it is that sense of familiar intimacy that lifts believers beyond the experiences of fear and of oppressive alien commandments. It lifts them into the spontaneity and creativity that is testimony of the divine Spirit become internal to human freedom, liberating human freedom to be truly such, not self-destroying, self-defeating. A new freedom, spontaneity, integrity is the sign and seal of the divine Spirit. A new image of God emerges in this experience. A new way of knowing and encountering God gives confirmation and solidity to the old way of knowing by looking outwards to creation and history.

The Gospel reading links the two ways of knowing and encountering God together. It is the gift of Jesus, God-with-us, that bestows the Spirit. But the testimony of Jesus in history and community remains—another way to know God by seeing the human face of God this one time in unambiguous clarity, such that it might be reflected many times, in many human faces. In the human face of the risen Christ, the first disciples recognized the call to worship and acknowledged promptly that all authority was vested in that human face of God. But the matter could not rest there. They could not give a notional assent to such an experience, such a realization, and remain themselves unchanged by it. Nor could they accept this gift for themselves without feeling the call to share it far and wide with the visionary hope of creating a wholly renewed world of justice, community, peace and undiscriminating compassion.

To know God in these three different ways is to know also that God does not deceive in the divine self-manifestation, that the divine being of God is in truth as it is revealed. And so Christians speak with reverence of the Triune God, unwilling and unable to translate the paradox into the canons of human reasoning, but unwilling and unable to relinquish the living truth of experience that assures us that all these ways of knowing God lead to the heart of the mystery. In Scripture and in liturgy, the Christian tradition enshrines this conviction in narrative forms that make no attempt to reconcile by systematic formulation. In Christian life, the community expresses its experience and its convictions not only in devotional practices such as the sign of the cross and the doxologies, but in a missionary thrust to go out and invite others into the fellowship of Father, Son and Spirit, and in the confidence that sees no aspect of life as profane and no dimension of human experience as obscuring the self-communication of God.

The Triune God is the ever-present, magnificently powerful, affectionately intimate and irresistably reconciling God.

Solemnity of Corpus Christi

READINGS: Ex 24:3-8; Heb 9:11-15; Mk 14:12-16, 22-26.

This is my blood, the blood of the covenant, shed for many.   Mk 14:24.

The symbolism of blood in the Hebrew Scriptures, with its references to sacrifice and covenant, is not only strange but also repugnant to our contemporary consciousness. Yet we cannot understand what the New Testament is saying about the death of Jesus, and about our link with that death in the Eucharist, without considering the ancient symbolism of blood.

The reading from Exodus presents that symbolism starkly. The people have been summoned to the solemnizing of the covenant with God. The "words" and the "laws," that is to say the Ten Commandments and the ritual code, have been formally proclaimed, and the people have accepted them: "We will do all that the Lord has told us." It has all been officially recorded in writing, and the time has come for the sacrificial ceremony that completes the covenant. An altar is set up at the foot of the mountain and animals are slaughtered as offerings to be consumed. The blood is drained from them, and divided into two. Half is poured over the altar that represents God. The covenant terms are read again in God's name and are accepted again by voice vote of the people, and when that is done the remainder of the blood is poured or sprinkled over the people. Moses declares solemnly that this is the blood of the covenant which the Lord has made with the people according to the terms that were proclaimed, that is according to "this book."

The ninth chapter of the Letter to the Hebrews refers to this covenant and its ordinances, especially its ritual observances. Recalling particularly the sanctuary and the high priesthood with the annual offering of blood in the inner sanctuary, the text offers an analogy that interprets the meaning of the death of Jesus. And this is the passage that is selected for today's liturgy. Jesus is depicted as entering once for all into the true inner sanctuary of God's presence, joining the human and the divine in his own sacrificial blood, thereby dedicating the new people. It is all couched in a language and an imagery that looks back to the ritual tradition familiar in Israel. It demands that we try to imagine and understand the analogy so that we may consider what it may mean in terms of our own experience. Meanwhile, the author of Hebrews has already broadened his cultural context by mixing another metaphor into the discourse— that of a dying testator leaving a "last will and testament" which is set in motion by the death itself.

Mark's Gospel gives us a terse description of the farewell supper. The conflict has come to a head; all that is wanting is the convenient moment for the betrayal that will take Jesus to his death. Passover arrangements are made secretly and swiftly, and Jesus gathers his disciples for a last supper that is built around the covenant theme. The traditional blessings of the unleavened bread of Passover and of the last of the four ritual cups of wine, recall the ancient covenant of God's people but are also invested with the entirely new significance of a covenant about to be completed in a new outpouring of blood. It is in one sense always the same covenant renewed and expanded to include more people, though in another sense it is a new covenant. It is new because it has come to the heart of the matter, and old because the matter in hand is still the reconciliation of the human community to its God by a promise and commitment of peoplehood.

Thus this strange theme of blood of the covenant turns out to be another expression for the more familiar Pauline theme of I Corinthians, the theme of the body of Christ which is made present in Eucharist, incorporating the worshippers into the Death and Resurrection with all their implications for human life and human community. The theme of the sacrificial covenant blood, like the theme of the body of Christ in the Eucharist, turns out to be practical because it is concerned with reconciliation. Like the Sinai covenant, the new covenant in the blood of Jesus envisages communion with God only on terms of peoplehood, on terms of non-exclusive communion with fellow human beings. That is precisely what is spelled out in the terms of covenant which Moses read out so painstakingly to the people to make sure they understood the terms within the peoplehood of Israel. That is also what is spelled out explicitly in many passages of the New Testament—in the Last Supper discourse in John's Gospel, the First Letter to the Corinthians, the Letter of James, and so forth.

We cannot afford to read the terse recital of Mark without taking into account what it means when Jesus calls his own blood shed in death the blood of the covenant. We cannot celebrate the feast of the body of Christ without trying to understand what our Eucharistic incorporation in the risen Christ means in terms of a community that knows no prejudicial divisions, no boundaries that could exclude the poor, the needy, the distant or the disreputable from fellowship and practical help under the terms of covenant in the blood of Jesus. To celebrate Eucharist is to renew and deepen our participation in the terms of the new covenant. It is a pledge and a source of stength to fulfill the pledge. It is a far-reaching pledge whose implications pervade all the relationships and structures of human society. It is a pledge made in the blood of Jesus which is the blood of the everlasting covenant.

Second Sunday of the Year

READINGS: I Sam 3:3-10, 19; I Cor 6:13-15, 17-20; Jn 1:35-42.

When he turned and saw them following him, he asked, 'What are you looking for?' They said, 'Rabbi' (which means a teacher,) 'where are you staying?' 'Come and see,' he replied. So they went and saw where he was staying, and spent the rest of the day with him. It was then about four in the afternoon.   Jn 1:38-39.

We have three stories today about discipleship and about the intimacy of the bond that is implied in it. It is unfortunate for Catholics that we have so long thought of "discipleship" as a Protestant word. It is a good word, for it has to do with listening and learning, with acquaintance and apprenticeship, and therefore with following or patterning oneself after a master with whom one is on intimate terms. All three readings are concerned with these components of discipleship, and hold up models for us to consider and imitate.

We glimpse both Samuel and the first disciples of Jesus at the moment of their first calling, and both stories are told in allusive language full of meanings. In both cases these are people already in God's service, Samuel in the Temple, and the three young men as followers of John the Baptist. But what we are told in the stories is that there comes a point in their lives when they begin to "hear" the divine call at a deeper level, in a more personal and intimate way. Samuel's name means "God has heard," given him because of his miraculous conception by a barren woman, and now the story revolves around what Samuel hears. In the simplicity of a child he is totally present, intent, ready to respond to the call.

The story of the first followers of Jesus, though just as short, holds more for our reflection. John the Baptist points to Jesus and two of John's followers immediately walk after Jesus. But perhaps we are to understand that they did not really know what they were getting into, for Jesus asks, "What are you looking for?" Of course, that is a very practical, ordinary kind of question, but John's Gospel seldom records such a detail without intending that we look for a further meaning in it. In any case, it is a very good question for us to ask ourselves: what is it we desire and seek in following Jesus? They declare themselves disciples, apprentices, when they address him as "Rabbi," but it is the question that follows which has such depth. One can of course read it with a number of quite different inflections of voice. It could be casually practical, and so could his answer. But there can be much more to it than that. It could be a polite way of fishing for an invitation, but it could also be more personal than that.

When I read this question in its context, it seems to me to hold worlds of meaning, for I hear in it a great depth of longing—a longing to be close to him, to be allowed to stay there all day, the "rest of the day" as the text puts it, for it is already four in the afternoon. They have been on the spiritual quest for some time, and in that sense it is late in their day, and they want most urgently to be with the Servant of God, the deliverer, "the Lamb" whom they have been expecting. It is a moment of suspense. They are so close, yet the initiative must come from him to call them. It is a scene to dwell upon for it describes such a typical moment in the life of any follower of Jesus.

What the outcome of that evening in their lives was we can guess from the precipitation with which Andrew fetched his brother, Simon, and was able to persuade him. Simon's call is interesting because his name, "he who hears," son of John, "God's gift," is enhanced with the additional appellation, "the Rock." Naming was always important in the Hebrew Scriptures, and seems to have marked great turning points, as in the renaming of Abram who became Abraham and of Sarai who became Sara, as also of Jacob, who wrestled with God and became Israel, "he who prevails with God." The names of Simon Peter certainly conjure up a symbolism rich for reflection on discipleship.

The theme of intimacy in discipleship which is at play in both these texts seems to occur again in the reading from I Corinthians. One might at first read this as a Pauline rejection of a natural law morality that is based on the physiological functions of bodily organs! For Paul certainly maintains that Christian behavior is not to be determined in this way. But his point lies beyond this, stressing intimacy of union with Christ as the criterion for a Christian life. His analogy of physical sexual union—a favorite symbolism of the Hebrew Scriptures in relation to Israel's closeness to God—suggests the intense degree of spiritual intimacy which Paul sees as the condition of Christian discipleship. Today's three readings leave us pondering the implications of this for our own lives.

Third Sunday of the Year

READINGS: Jon 3:1-5, 10; I Cor 7:29-31; Mk 1:14-20.

Buyers must not count on keeping what they buy, nor those who use the world's wealth on using it to the full. For the whole frame of this world is passing away. I Cor 7:30-31.

Most of us can sympathize readily with the prophet Jonah. Admonishing other people is a thankless task, and being made to look foolish in the process adds insult to injury. However, the focus of today's first reading is not on Jonah himself and his exasperating experiences. The focus is on the message: the call to repentance is urgent and holds not only the threat of disaster but also the promise of radical transformation for the better. Oddly enough, in our generation people seem more inclined to listen to prophets of terror and doom than to promises of genuine, far-reaching change for the better in the affairs of the world.

The point of the whole story of Jonah, and of the Baptist's preaching and of that of Jesus himself and that of Paul, is that our future is not in the power of blind fate but in the hands of a passionately concerned and involved God. We are not helpless on the threshold of inevitable tragedy—not even in our times when the spiralling nuclear arms race siphons the resources of the world from the hungry and homeless and otherwise needy, drawing the gifts of creation into a vortex of ever-increasing fear and distrust. Even in our times we are at the great crisis, the point of decision and commitment, faced with all the promise and the exigence of the Reign of God in creation and history. It can all be so wonderful—a story of happy endings—but it can only be so on the creator's own terms.

Paul's rather puzzling and paradoxical advice to the Corinthians seems to caution us on the need for a certain degree of detachment, a willingness to change and to have things changed in quite radical ways. It warns us not to be too dependent upon the possessions and positions and relationships that we enjoy in the present order of society, because that order is exactly what must and will pass away to make room for the very different order of God's own rule in human affairs. Paul's paradoxes rest on his own conviction that the present order of things cannot be taken as the will of God, but must be seen as an order produced by rebellion against God—an order that has brought us to the crisis on such harsh terms.

The earliest followers of Jesus were apparently precisely those who grasped this truth unhesitatingly in their pagan enivironment. In our own society where the term "Christian" is far too widely applied, we seem to have more difficulty in taking Paul's paradoxes seriously. Because we think of ourselves as a Christian people, it is all too easy to suppose that in our case power, privilege and possessions are the rewards of virtue and the sign of God's favor. That, no doubt, is why the liturgy brings us face to face with Paul's admonition. It conjures up that rallying cry of recent Popes: if you want peace, do justice. It also suggests the current preoccupation of the U.S. Bishops: do not take the economic and defense systems and their structures for granted as a necessary given, but find out what they do to people at home and abroad. The good news is that the present order both must and can pass away to yield to God's own rule in the world and among its peoples—a rule of justice and peace for all.

The Gospel gives us Mark's version of the same story that we saw through John's eyes last Sunday—the circumstances of the call of the first followers of Jesus. Mark links it with the arrest of John the Baptizer, who had preached repentance and expectation of one who was yet to come. As Jesus picks up his mission in succession to John, his message is not only a call to repent, but a call to repent and believe the good news that the time is now, the reign of God at hand. In our own rather cynical age scholars have raised the question whether Jesus was simply mistaken, deluded, in his optimistic proclamation, because no great and radical change seems to have occurred then or since. But the words of Jesus are a prophetic utterance not a prediction. His message and proclamation are addressed to human freedom. He invites and does not compel or manipulate. In every age and every situation, that call is as fresh and pertinent and immediate as it was when Jesus set out to call the first disciples in Galilee. The invitation is still held out to us to repent and believe the good news that it can really all be very different, because the time has come, and the reign of God is at hand.

Fourth Sunday of the Year

READINGS: Deut 18:15-20; I Cor 7:32-35; Mk 1:21-28.

His teaching made a deep impression on them, Because unlike the scribes, he taught them with authority.   Mk 1:22.

The authority of Jesus is a favorite topic of Mark's Gospel, but on first sight the claim here made is a strange one. In one sense, after all, the scribes had as much authority (or as many authorities) as a Ph.D. dissertation, because they delighted in quoting many sources to substantiate any position they took. Evidently the tradition of the early Christian community was concerned with authority in another sense, perhaps at first the sense of a rabbi's claim to give a binding interpretation of the laws of the covenant, but by the time of Mark's gospel a sense that went further than that. Mark implies a special divine authorization or mandate—the empowerment of a prophet, indeed of *the* prophet, the messianic or saving power. That is why the liturgy can link this gospel reading with the passage from Deuteronomy; the notion of authority given by divine mandate implies not only the right to teach but the efficacy of the teaching

However, it would be a mistake to think of this in purely juridical terms or in any way that bypasses human freedom and ordinary human experience. If we read the story quite simply and without being too subtle, it evokes analogies from our own experience. It suggests the difference between hearing someone dispense book learning and hearing someone speak from experience. Most of us have had experiences of sudden breakthrough when something we had been taught and which did not hold much practical, personal meaning for us, came vividly to life when presented by someone with evident personal experiential grasp of it. The Deuteronomy passage seems to make this link; the people have expressed their fear of direct encounter with God, wanting to delegate Moses to "meet with God" and mediate the covenant to them. Moses is the great mystic, the prophet who speaks from his personal experience of intimacy with God and of receiving divine revelation. There is the problem whether there will be a successor to Moses who can continue and fulfill this task, and the successor is promised.

The early followers of Jesus understood that this successor was, in truth, Jesus, who fulfilled and completed the prophetic role because his teaching was effective in reaching hearts and turning them to God. Indeed, the early followers marveled that even "unclean spirits" responded to the commands of Jesus. He accomplished what was thought to be the impossible. Today we are not generally concerned about "evil spirits" because we tend to think we can find a scientific explanation for everything and a "technique" for dealing with everything. But we have to admit that in one respect we are still very much like those Israelites in the story about Moses and the promised successor. We are still exceedingly shy of personal encounter with the transcendent God. It is worth some reflection to consider what our faith in God and our relation to God might be like without the concrete historical event of Jesus of Nazareth. We have someone who speaks with authority, a self-validating claim to truth and power, in the matter of human destiny and ultimate reality. The sheer encounter with the transcendent God is terrifying in its silent and formless simplicity, and we are constantly in need of mediation to guard against illusion, and also to make the encounter with God bearable.

The rather strangely matched passage from I Corinthians seems to exemplify this kind of mediation, grounding its trustworthiness in the relationship to Jesus Christ. The passage must be understood in its context within the whole letter. Asked whether Christians should renounce marriage or its physical consummation, Paul defends the goodness of marriage *and* the special gift of those whose calling is to remain unmarried. Asked more particularly about celibacy (and perhaps whether some celibates in Corinth ought to abandon their celibacy and marry), he answers that celibacy is good particularly because of the freedom for total dedication to the "things of the Lord." This week's reading, taken out of context, might give the impression that marriage is deprecated. In context this is not so. However, what is perhaps most interesting is that the whole passage is prefaced by a concern of Paul to distinguish between those judgments that come "from the Lord" and are binding, and those others which are his own opinion and are not binding. Paul seems to be concerned here with different kinds and degrees of authority, and he also evidently thinks of Jesus Christ as the one whose teaching makes a deep impression because, unlike those who are learned from human sources, he teaches with messianic authority, which is the power of the Holy Spirit—power to touch and transform everything in creation.

Fifth Sunday of the Year

READINGS: Job 7:1-4, 6-7; I Cor 9:16-19, 22-23; Mk 1:29-39.

After sunset they brought him all who were ill or possessed by devils; and the whole town was there, gathered at the door. He healed many who suffered from various diseases, and drove out many devils.   Mk 1:32-34.

Today's reading from the Gospel of Mark seems to spell out God's redemptive answer to the human situation. Perhaps that is why the first reading, taken from the book of Job is so dreadfully gloomy. Job is a kind of extended parable of the human situation: the existence and condition of any human person in the world is very fragile—more fragile than most of us in privileged positions in a rich society are willing to admit. When misfortune strikes, it is seldom possible to explain why—why it should have happened to this good person and not to some evidently guilty party. Morover, when suffering invades one's life from many directions, it is easy enough to become very depressed and to question the meaning of life in tones of despair.

What seems to be important about this reading as selected for today, is that it stops there. It does not quickly skip forward to Job's vindication by God, the end of his sufferings and his reinstatement as a powerful and respected patriarch. This reading simply states the human situation from its gloomiest angle in powerful poetry. And there are so many people in the world who must recognize their own situation described in it—the starving of Ethiopia and other regions, the bitterly oppressed under harsh dictatorships and in places of constant warfare, political prisoners, the wretchedly and permanently poor even in our own country, so many of the elderly among us, all who are abandoned to their suffering without compassion or relief.

It is surely in this context of the human situation in a world shaped by a long history of sin, that Paul expresses the inner compulsion to preach the Good News. He cannot help himself; the exigence of preaching the gospel simply overwhelms him, and the preaching of the gospel becomes its own reward. But the major interest of today's readings seems to me to lie in the Gospel selection. Though its implications are universal, it is a colorful and quite specific human interest story. On this same day he had taught in the local synagogue. It was not unusual for a visitor to town to be invited to read and comment upon the Scriptures, but he had left them all astonished not only by the immediacy of his teaching but also by the power he exercised over an "unclean spirit." Then he had gone to the house of Simon and Andrew. That was not unusual either—he may have been staying with them or it may have been the Sabbath visit for a little conviviality. Finding Simon's mother-in-law in the grip of one of the many dreaded, undiagnosed and often fatal fevers, he raised her to her feet and she recovered. It is the first miracle of healing reported by Mark.

The news evidently spread rapidly but the people could not invade his privacy until after sunset because it was the Sabbath. Only when Sabbath officially ended at sunset could they legitimately carry sick persons to that place. But now Jesus is squarely confronted with the challenge of untold human misery, and the question is: how will he, how can he, respond to it all? He does what he can that evening, healing many, but early in the morning he slips away quietly to a solitary spot to pray. It is not long, however, before Simon finds him and insists that there are many more people in distress and all are waiting for him. If we were not so used to the passage, we might be surprised at what happens next. At first it looks as though there were no connection between the foregoing sentences and what follows. They tell him everyone in town is looking for him to continue the ministry of healing he has begun the evening before, and he answers that they had better set out for the other towns to proclaim his message, because that is what he is really supposed to be doing.

Reflection on this extraordinary sequence of events suggests in the first place that the miracles of healing were not random acts of mercy but were supposed to carry a message—the message that suffering is not intended by God, and indeed that God's intention is that suffering be ended. There were, as the Gospel makes abundantly clear, vast numbers of suffering people seeking help and one person could not respond to them all. In that situation after praying in solitude, Jesus feels a great urgency to proclaim his message of God's redemptive love, and continues from village to village and town to town. The question this prompts is, of course, how this was going to solve the problem. The answer of the Gospel taken as a whole, and the answer of the Christian community that sprang up after his Death and Resurrection, is that the preaching and actions and life and Death of Jesus were like seeds cast wherever he went, to sprout into communities of disciples who would do as he did—who would live by compassion, who would respond in practical (and perhaps very ordinary) works of redemptive healing and rescue. The telling of Mark's story would have missed its point if we did not realize that it is a message addressed directly to us, concerning the will of God to end suffering and concerning our calling to do the work of Christ by implementing this.

Sixth Sunday of the Year

READINGS: Lev 13:1-2, 44-46; I Cor 10:30–11:1; Mk 1:40-45.

Jesus stretched out his hand, touched him, and said, 'Indeed I will; be clean again.'   Mk 1:41.

The fate of a leper is a sad one in any society. Those of us who have met lepers in the Third World countries, outcast and begging, have known what it is to recoil involuntarily with a nameless dread that reaches far beyond the danger of catching the disease. In Israel at the time of Jesus there was more involved; leprosy, and various contagious skin conditions which were not distinguished from leprosy, evoked a kind of moral condemnation from many people— analogous in some degree to the response our society gives to AIDS. Linguistically, leprosy was linked to plague sent as punishment by God. The passage from Leviticus read today contains an admission of helplessness in the face of leprosy. Because curing leprosy was proverbially as difficult as raising the dead, the Law emphasized the protection of the community from contagion, at the price of isolating and abandoning the leper. In a society with rigorous laws of ritual purity, the leper embodied all that was unclean—a living representation of contagion, corruption and sin.

In the light of this heritage the cure of the leper by Jesus carries more meaning than we in our times would at first suppose. When Jesus touches the leper he does the unthinkable and involves himself in ritual impurity as well as the risk of contagion and the overcoming of a certain revulsion. But when Jesus heals by his touch he challenges the division between the ritually pure and the impure as well as accomplishing that which was thought to be as difficult as raising the dead. The form of this healing and the words that go with it are those of an exorcism. In Mark's account it results in a joyful explosion of missionary zeal and proclamation of the good news on the part of the former leper.

This story had surely been told in many ways and in many contexts before Mark seized upon it to incorporate it in this early part of his Gospel, but when Mark tells it it suggests comparison with baptism in no uncertain terms. In baptism, the believers have been touched by Christ, cleansed of sin, released from any distinction between the holy and the unholy or the ritually acceptable and the ritually impure. All distinctions like this are supposed to have fallen away. In Christ there is no question of condoning categories of excluded, disgraced people in order to preserve the community at their expense. In Christ there are no categories of people beyond the protection of the law, beyond the reach of grace, or beyond the power of healing and forgiveness. In Christ no one is abandoned.

In this context, the reading from I Corinthians acquires new depth and content; it is true that Jesus has broken down the barriers between the ritually clean and the ritually impure, but his concern is not with food but with people. It is true that technically for Christians there is no impure and ritually forbidden food, and that therefore in principle anything edible may be eaten. Yet the real issue is whether it drives a dividing wedge between people. To scandalize others needlessly is to introduce new divisions. The christian way is to respect the needs and even the scruples of others in the endeavor to build true community among human persons. It is this, Paul maintains, that marks the true follower of Christ. In itself indifference to matters of ritual purity is not what is redemptive of the human situation.

As Mark retells the story of the healing of the leper, Jesus tells the latter to follow the Mosaic law in obtaining the proper certificate of cure, but not to spread the story about that it was Jesus who cured him. The leper, however, told the good news of his cure far and wide. That may be Mark's understanding, because the Gospel of Mark constantly treats the messianic identity of Jesus as a secret not to be revealed until the end—a secret made manifest by the unfolding of the life of Jesus and the impact of his deeds on those about him. Perhaps this holds some important analogies for the community of the baptized. When we know that Jesus is indeed that promised savior of the world because of his gift to us, it is not appropriate to pass on a hearsay message. It is appropriate to pass on the living experience of transformation, so that the truth may unfold through life and action and through the impact that the touch of Christ has in the world. The Gospel suggests that when true testimony of that sort is given, people flock to Jesus from all sides without further bidding.

One cannot but pursue this one step further to ask what such testimony might look like in our world today. Certainly to proclaim the good news of salvation by doing as Jesus does in this particular gospel scene, must be a matter of breaking down divisions which seem inevitable to us today. It must be a matter of caring for, touching, people who seem beyond redemption today, rather than excluding them in order to protect the rest of society. Certainly it must be a matter of confronting in faith the problems that seem as difficult as raising the dead. One wonders whether it might be pertinent to question whether widespread and bitter poverty is really the unavoidable product of any economy we can devise. Would Jesus respond with passionate anger over the plight of the destitute in our world of plenty as he did over the plight of the lepers? Would he refuse to accept the outlawing of peoples and countries from consideration of life and livelihood once they have been defined as Communist? What would he say about death-row where we isolate those for whom we cherish no hope, abandoning them out of fear, for the protection of society? How would he look at situations in which a differential value is placed on human lives according to which race, or economic class or nation is involved?

An interesting detail about this Gospel reading, pointed out by some exegetes, is that there is more emotion expressed in this story than anywhere else in the four Gospels. It is expressed in the kneeling and pleading of the leper, and it is echoed in the passion with which

Jesus responds. It seems to express the desperation of someone who has been totally abandoned by his society and who does not count or matter to the society any more. It also seems to express the passionate and compassionate judgment of God in vindication of such persons. The liturgy makes us wonder just where we stand in this.

Seventh Sunday of the Year

READINGS: Is 43:18-19, 21-22, 24-25; 2 Cor 1:18-22; Mk 2:1-12.

He is the Yes pronounced upon God's promises, every one of them. That is why, when we give glory to God, it is through Christ Jesus that we say, "Amen."   2 Cor 1:2.

The readings for this Sunday are all concerned with the over-whelming goodness and compassion of God and with our unceasing reluctance to believe in that goodness. There is a certain impatience in the first reading. It is taken from the Second Isaiah collection which seems to have been an attempt to rouse new hope in the Hebrews in Babylon towards the end of their sixth century exile. The author wants these dispirited people to stop brooding over the past and to trust that God is indeed coming to the rescue. They should be attentive to the signs and prepared for God's coming, but a certain lethargy has set in; so that they neither observe the traditional requirements of Hebrew life and worship, nor look with confidence to the future. Yet God will rescue them because it is the nature of God to be compassionate and to care.

The passage from Paul's letter to the Corinthians seems to echo something of this, when he roundly maintains that God's Yes is unambiguous and does not vacillate as human responses do between Yes and No. But Paul also wants his readers and listeners to understand that Jesus is the Yes of God to the redemption and reconciliation of the world, and that God has sealed us and given us the Spirit of Jesus that we might be steadfast and unambiguous also. Such fidelity is essential to the restoration of all things in Christ, and Christians therefore need to give evidence of this fidelity and loyalty to one another. Paul seems a little concerned that his own change of plans in his travels might be take for vacillation, and makes an occasion of it to write about the fidelity of Christ.

The story in today's Gospel reading is also about the consistency of God's Yes in the redemption and about the difficulty some of the contemporaries of Jesus had in taking that quite seriously. They found difficulty in believing that God's forgiveness of sin could be dispensed in the unpretentious, human way in which Jesus acted. But the story is rather obscure to us today until we realize that the contemporaries of Jesus understood that there was a close connection between sin and illness. There seems to have been some speculation about whose sin and what sin was being punished. This must have added a further burden of anxiety and depression to the suffering involved in illness and disability. The assurance of forgiveness may have been the most consoling word that the paralyzed man could have heard. The answer that Jesus gave to those who took scandal at it seems to imply that for Jesus both physical healing and forgiveness were integral to the redemption and reconciliation that was his mission. He is consistent in expressing in his person God's Yes.

Eighth Sunday of the Year

READINGS: Hos 2:16-17, 21-22; 2 Cor 3:1-6; Mk 2:18-22.

No one puts new wine into old wineskins; if he does, the wine will burst the skins, and then wine and skins are both lost. Fresh skins for new wine!   Mk 2:22.

The readings for this Sunday are full of proclamations of new beginnings. Hosea's prophecy in its entirety is about this, and today's selection catches the gist of it. God's command to Hosea was that he should reflect the divine love and compassion by taking a wanton woman to wife and begetting children of her. Those children were to be named "loveless" and "not my people," to mirror the condition of Israel at the prophet's time, but the children were to be reared lovingly nevertheless until they would finally belie their names. It was a strange parable in action, but it does seem to tell the story not only of Israel of old but of the Church in all the ages, with its constant need of conversion and renewal.

The excerpt from 2 Corinthians seems to insist that such a fresh beginning has already been made in Christ. Unworthy as Paul himself might be, he has been sent to dispense the new covenant with God made through Christ and maintained in the Spirit. In that new covenant there can be no question of personal qualification or merit because it is God's goodness that transforms the old situation into a radically new one. The community itself is the letter of credentials. The intentions and actions of God are written in that community.

The Gospel reading gives us once again a passage from the early teachings of Jesus as recalled in the Gospel according to Mark. The passage is familiar and both sections of it are about newness. According to this story some observers were judging the followers and movement and teaching of Jesus by measuring them up against the old. John's disciples as well as the Pharisees were observing a fast that was not strictly required by the Law, and people evidently expected that Jesus would require his disciples to keep this fast also. In reply Jesus draws an interesting analogy: guests at a wedding were not required to observe even the obligatory fast; in fact they were admonished not to do so. The years of the public ministry are represented as being like a wedding feast, suspending ordinary time with a moment of refreshment and ecstasy. Indeed it is a moment of breakthrough to something radically new.

That leads to the second image that Jesus employs. It is useless to take new cloth to mend old garments; the old material of the garment cannot support the tension of the new. The new is lost and the old is not saved. Likewise pouring new wine into old wineskins is an exercise in folly; they are bound to burst, wasting both wine and skins. The imagery is powerful; redemption in Jesus Christ is not to be judged by whether it fits the old categories, because it is radically new. In particular, it is not to be judged in terms of customary ritual observances, because it utterly transcends these in the simplicity of the reconciliation which Jesus offers.

Ninth Sunday of the Year

READINGS: Deut 5:12-15; 2 Cor 4:6-11; Mk 2:23–3:6.

The Sabbath was made for the sake of man and not man for the Sabbath.   Mk 2:27.

All religious life seems to be marked by a certain tension between the human need for ritual to express faith and build a total vision of faith on the one hand, and the even greater need to put reality above ritual on the other. The preaching of Jesus, perhaps in part because of the particular excesses of his own society, leaned very heavily towards a de-emphasizing of ritual observances and a focus on the ordinary, immediate needs and sufferings of ordinary people.

The commandment of keeping the seventh day holy, as it is given in Deuteronomy, expresses a careful balance in this respect. The free people of Israel are to observe the Sabbath rest scrupulously in acknowledgement of God who set them free from slavery and foreign domination so that they might exercise such rights. But they are also to remember what God has done for them by sharing the day of rest fully with those who now are slaves or aliens. The gift of God becomes the obligation to pass on blessings to others. There is a simplicity in this outlook that counterbalances any tendency that there might have been to observe the Sabbath simply as a ritual obligation.

The text from 2 Corinthians does not address this theme directly, yet it has a certain relevance. Paul writes of the light that has shone in Jesus and which must shine through the community of his followers. That light of revelation by which the glory or radiance of God reaches the world is made present by the whole life of the Christian community. It does not matter what their circumstances are, nor even whether they are dying or living, as long as they do everything in the spirit and image of Christ who is the restored human image of the transcendent God. That thought is very much in line with the theme of the simplicity of Jesus in his direct concern with human needs.

The Gospel reading gives us two stories which become the basis for the teaching of Jesus. In the first of these, Jesus and his disciples were walking through a field of grain on the Sabbath. Existing law and custom did not forbid them to do that, nor would it forbid them to pluck a few ears to eat if they were hungry on a weekday. Whether such satisfaction of hunger on the Sabbath constituted forbidden work was a very fine point indeed. It suggested a great eagerness in fault-finding for its own sake. Jesus offers a precedent with which no one would dare to find fault, but also gives the reason for his position: ritual obligations do not exist for their own sake, nor by inner necessity, but rather as a help in the human relationship with God and with other human persons.

The second story, matched a number of times in the Gospels, concerns an act of healing done on the Sabbath. Again, Jesus shows that he knows and respects the Law of Moses, but wants that Law to serve its true purpose—the saving and guarding of a truly human life. This text even says of those who were trying to trap him that he looked around at them with anger and sorrow over their obstinate stupidity. The question and the problem is by no means confined to their times but is very much alive in our own. There is a human inclination to opt for what seems safest. The explicit nature of ritual commands makes it easier to know that one has fulfilled them than is the case with positive commandments like love of neighbor. The call of Jesus is to move away from the safe and be creatively daring in appropriating the gift of redemption.

Tenth Sunday of the Year

READINGS: Gen 3:9–15; 2 Cor 4:13–5:1; Mk 3:20–35.

How can Satan drive out Satan? . . . if Satan is in rebellion against himself, he is divided and cannot stand; and that is the end of him.   Mk 3:23, 26.

The shadowy figure of Satan lurks throughout the Scriptures but seldom becomes clearly defined except in extra-biblical legend. The Genesis passage about the ultimate source of human temptation is really very unsatisfactory, because it does not resolve the question but files it away. Oblique reference is made to the story of a prior, spiritual creation, and to angelic spirits who under a leader, Satan, rebelled and refused to serve God. This seems to be a reference to the apparently super-human power of temptation and sin. For the Hebrew people who passed on the stories of Genesis, as for us now, there is a sense that sin and sinfulness are prevasive forces that are greater than any one person, but seem rather to be over-arching, super-human forces of distortion.

The Genesis 3 account wrestles with the awareness that we all have of being only partially responsible for destructive attitudes and actions in our lives. Our values and expectations are shaped before we make any free decisions of our own, and they are shaped by the patterns which our society (the companionship that God has given) offers us. Yet society could often say that the problems and distortions of value which are rampant seem to be beyond everyone's control, and seem to come from forces that are in some sense above the society also. The passage from 2 Corinthians, though not chosen as a comment on this, offers a reassuring complementarity. Redemption has its own solidarity and interconnections. There is reason to believe and to speak out in confidence, because all things are being reordered in Christ. The grace of Christ is also a power that transcends the possibilities of individuals and of societies—a power to reconcile and heal.

What the Gospel reading seems to say is that people are very slow to believe in the power of such reconciling and healing grace. Their experience leads them to distrust the promise of redemption at any level, and indeed to suppose that radical and ecstatic conversions must be the manifestation of another kind of diabolic activity. When the mission of Jesus arouses such enthusiastic response from the crowds that Jesus and his disciples scarcely have time to eat, the response of those who knew him was that he must have gone mad to attract so much attention. The response of the devout and learned was that this must be a manifestation of Satanic power. There is something pathetically human in not wanting to acknowledge anything that goes against the security of our accustomed assumptions—anything that undermines our competence by raising new hopes and possibilities. In moments of critical decisions many of us tend to opt for maintaining our privileged and established positions in the existing order, rather than welcoming new hopes for the society as a whole and for the underprivileged within it.

The response of Jesus is very simple: Satan driving out Satan does not make sense. Healing, reconciliation and hope as a way of inflicting further damage is an absurdity. There is a sin against the Spirit that destroys everything, even the possibility of forgiveness and conversion. As it is presented here, that sin against the Spirit is a cynicism that devotes all its strength to resisting and ridiculing revelation and grace for the sake of holding on to an uneasy compromise with a hostile world. The sin against the Spirit seems to be an unwillingness to risk transformations of grace, but for those who are open to grace even the exclusivity of family relations breaks down to embrace the whole family of God.

Eleventh Sunday of the Year

READINGS: Ezek 17:22-24; 2 Cor 5:6-10; Mk 4:26-34.

The Kingdom of God is like this. A man scatters seed on the land; he goes to bed at night and gets up in the morning, and the seed sprouts and grows— how, he does not know.   Mk 4:26-27.

It is most opportune that these texts appear together just on this Sunday, as we return to ordinary time in the liturgical cycle. All three of them offer hope for the "time between." All three of them encourage Christians to learn to see familiar realities by the light of faith, discerning God's power and providence at work in them. Moreover, all three readings are concerned with waiting, but with the right kind of waiting.

The passage from Ezekiel makes a picturesque blend of the familiar with the unexpected wonderful works of God. The ordinary ecology of the forest with which we are all familiar is, of course, that tall, proud trees dominating the vegetation drop acorns or chestnuts or cones that fall helplessly to the ground, but which sprout and spring up in their turn and eventually assert themselves and displace the old tree. That is a miracle of nature, but one which we take for granted. Ezekiel pictures a special divine intervention, preempting the expected order of things, with the imagery of plucking and planting. The Lord will pluck a shoot from the tip of the tall cedar and will plant it and tend it on the heights of Israel until it becomes a mighty tree, fruitful and shady, sheltering all manner of birds.

It would be difficult for Christians, especially in this season with the Paschal celebrations scarcely behind us, to contemplate this imagery without thinking of Jesus, plucked as it were from among his people and tradition, plucked from the land of the living, and planted so to speak on the heights of human history and experience to take root and become a fruitful and sheltering presence for all the peoples of the earth.

The parable of Ezekiel turns up again as a parable of Jesus in a slightly different setting. The context of forestry has given way to a context of ordinary farming, and the focus is on the extraordinary character of the ordinary and expected. The smallest and most insignificant seed grows to be the large shrub sheltering the birds of the air. But for us the mention of seed is bound to trigger other memories. Seed can grow to bear fruit or can waste in inhospitable soil. Unless the seed falls into the ground and dies, it remains barren as isolated grain. Moreover, the growing of the grain is utterly mysterious, for the farmer sows, tills the ground, anticipates the rainy season, but it is nevertheless God who causes the seed to sprout and grow and bear fruit for the harvest.

We can think of all this, of course, in terms of Jesus moralizing and preaching from an exalted and detached position, but it would be quite false. It is Jesus, above all, who sows and must trust the Father to bring about germination, growth and fruit—to bring it about after the death of Jesus. It is Jesus who is personally like a very small and insignificant seed cast into the ground to die, only later to become the great tree. Likewise, it is Jesus who sows his own words that seem in history like a ploughing under of scarcely noticeable mustard seeds. It is he who must trust that the Father really makes great things grow from such modest beginnings. It is he who must first really see the Kingdom of God coming in such small events swept under in the tide of histroy, in order to give faith and courage to others to enable them to see it also.

Paul, writing again to the Corinthians, is also concerned with the vision that is shaped by faith. He is concerned with the kind of detachment from personal questions of life or death, waiting or realization, hope or present experience, which makes the circumstances of life transparent to the powerful working of God among us. He also is concerned with the truth that, although we may sow, it is God who gives growth and increase; it is not for us to decide the times which the Father has determined, though we may indeed attempt to discern them. A vision shaped by faith sees everywhere the signs that God's purpose is being accomplished.

There are different kinds of patience, and different kinds of waiting. There is a certain lethargic impassivity that lets things go by because there is no hope and no commitment, and therefore there is no readiness for effort and self-sacrifice. That obviously is not the kind of patient waiting of which Paul writes. Neither is it the attitude suggested by Ezekiel's parable or by the parables of Jesus. The point of the three readings, about the analogy from forestry and the analogies from farming and the reflections on the uncertainties and obscurities of living in the "time between," is a different kind of patient waiting. It is a kind of patient waiting characterized by prayerful discernment of God's work in nature and history. It is marked by an attitude both of gratitude and of collaboration, and therefore it is a matter of doing the human tasks, knowing that what seems so insignificant as to be hardly worth doing, is like the mustard seed of the parable, growing to a harvest proportioned not to the human effort but to the divine intent.

The Kingdom of God is like this.

Twelfth Sunday of the Year

READINGS: Job 38:1, 8-11; 2 Cor 5:14-17; Mk 4:35-41.

When anyone is united to Christ, there is a new world; the old order has gone, and a new order has already begun.   2 Cor 5:17.

At a time of year when thoughts are turned to summer vacation, and a longing for seashore and lakeside, fishing and swimming, takes over, readings about the majestic and dangerous power of the water are very apt. Summer is always a good time to contemplate nature and to find God in the wonders of creation. For us city dwellers, who tend to see the world as largely man-made, summer vacation is often a time to rediscover the world as gift and wonder. It is a time to recover our sense of gratitude and our trust in the underlying goodness of the world as it comes from the creating God. It is a time also to realize anew that in the last analysis, control of the world is not in our hands but in the power of the creator.

Such a journey of recovery is that long meditation in the book of Job of which this Sunday's excerpt forms a part. One great marvel of nature after another is brought forward for consideration, suggesting how small we are in the order of creation, yet how blessed—how insignificant, yet how lovingly and lavishly provided with comfort and beauty and mystery. But the image of the ocean with all its power is particularly appropriate. We see the ocean poured into its proper place, balanced within its proper boundaries, so that the swaying tides and heaving waves know where to stop, and obey their maker. It is a magnificent symbol of divine rule in the world.

No doubt it is because this image of divine power is so striking that the passage was chosen to set off the gospel story of Jesus in a boat caught in a sudden dangerous storm on the Sea of Galilee. The story must have been a great favorite in the early Church, because it is told in almost exactly the same way by three of the four evangelists. It is rich in symbolism and levels of meaning. There is, for instance, the total trust that Jesus has in the creating presence of the heavenly Father who has set the bounds—a trust that enables him to sleep peacefully in a very threatening situation. There is also the fear of the disciples—a fear that most of us could readily match in our own lives—that even the presence of Jesus with them cannot save them from disaster. The image is powerful because a storm at sea and a threatened boat are so obviously symbolic of a host of threatening "stormy" situations, both outer and inner, which people experience as likely to "capsize the boat."

However, the story makes its most important statement when Jesus wakes and calms the raging waters, leaving the awestruck companions wondering who this is, for to quell wind and sea is divine. In the terrible persecutions which the early Christians faced, they must often have comforted themselves with the recital of this incident of the boat in the storm. But it is no less appropriate for us as for them to remember it when the waters of chaos seem poised to overwhelm the world again, whether through nuclear war, or famine, or sheer corruption of societal structures. The story of the boat in the storm has a meaning that is larger than some single incident in the travels and preaching of Jesus; it is, in brief, the story of his whole life and redemptive mission that he trusted the divine power quietly even when caught in a raging storm of cruelty, injustices, and oppression, and that he arose on the third day from the sleep of death, giving the divine command that calms the storm.

For us, as for the disciples of Jesus, and for the Psalmist long ago, there are many times when it seems as though God is sleeping and must be aroused. Indeed the passion and death of Jesus must have looked like that, and so must the times of bitter persecution. The Psalmist says bluntly to God, "Wake up, why are you sleeping? Attend to your business and rescue us!" The disciples in the boat echo that cry, and suggest to us how fitting it is to express the terror and abandonment that we feel in times of crisis. They suggest we should "wake" God and "wake" Jesus with realization that we are in crisis, and that though the crisis may be of our making, its resolution is a matter for the divine power.

Curiously, the passage from Corinthians (not particularly chosen as a match, but because we are moving systematically through the letter) reads like a concluding admonition on the same theme. Paul, as always, wants to preach only Christ and him crucified, as remaking the whole meaning and direction of human history. He begs us to realize that with the death of Christ and our incorporation into it, a new creation has in truth already begun, so that we can live and behave accordingly. Just as it is necesary to realize that God remains in control in the first creation, that God holds all creatures no matter how powerful within the guidance of divine providence, so Christians must know that Jesus has risen from the sleep of death to calm the waters of chaos, and that we have a new creation. We have no reason to regard nuclear war and armaments build-up as inevitable, or the vast oppressions and injustices of the world as inconquerable, for a new order has already begun.

Thirteenth Sunday of the Year

READINGS: Wis 1:13-15; 2:23-24; 2 Cor 8:7, 9, 13-15; Mk 5:21-43.

God did not make death, and takes no pleasure in the destruction of any living thing; he created all things that they might have being. The creative forces of the world make for life; there is no deadly poison in them. Death is not king of earth, for justice is immortal.   Wis 1:13-14.

In these days of nuclear strategy and nuclear fear it is quite tempting to think more seriously of the reign of death and terror in the world than of the reign of God mediated by the reign of Christ, the prince of peace. Lest we should pass too lightly over the gospel passage about the raising of the daughter of Jairus, the liturgy juxtaposes that text with a little known excerpt from the book of Wisdom. It is characteristic of God to give life, to sustain life and to desire not death but the fullness of life. What is crushing and deadly is not from God but from human corruption. It is out of our own recurrent human pettiness that we tend to see God as wielding vengeance and dealing out death as just retribution for insubordination. But it is not so, and the liturgy offers a swift transition to the story of Jesus as life-giver in the face of certain death.

The story of the young girl who is recalled from the dead and the interpolated story of the woman cured of chronic bleeding are packed with allusions. The language of curing and saving seems intended to refer not only to physical healing but to spiritual saving and immortality. Jesus restores life, but he has to summon forth a deepening faith in the woman and in the parents of the girl, so that they may be open to receiving the gift of restored life. That is a powerful message for our times. God, acting through the Spirit of the Risen Christ, offers restored life to the human community, but there is great need of deepening faith to receive the gift of that restored life. This is most certainly true of the nuclear crisis, the permanent condition of cold war, the huge number of famine deaths, and other catastrophes.

It seems at first that there is little link between this theme of the life-giving God, and Paul's plea for generous sharing with the needy of another land whom his hearers have not met. But there is an immediate connection which we do not easily see because of the abbreviation of the Wisdom passage. Taken at full length without the omitted verses in the middle, that text connects absence of faith in the life-giving and saving God, with desperate grabbing for pleasure, pomp and profit, to the exclusion and oppression of the poor and powerless and to the outright persecution of the prophet who speaks for the poor. It is because they have no faith in God and no hope of immortality, that people come to be cruel and uncaring in their selfishness.

Paul appeals to the generosity of Christ as the ground for the generosity he expects of Christians. Paul reassures his hearers that they are not being called to impoverish themselves to the point of hardship to rescue others from hardship. The goal, he writes, is equality. We could do worse than reflect on what that would really mean in today's world, and to ask ourselves how effective in our lives our faith in immortality is.

It is true that the connection between sharing of goods and entrance into the reign of God must have been more readily evident to the first Christians than to us. They, after all, were a small and persecuted community who expected the great breakthrough any day, at any hour. Yet even in a long and complex history, that connection between genuine human community and the reign of God is the foundation for the deep conviction that death is not king.

Fourteenth Sunday of the Year

READINGS: Ezek 2:2-5; 2 Cor 12:7-10; Mk 6:1-6.

I am well content, for Christ's sake, with weakness, contempt, persecution, hardship and frustration; for when I am weak, then I am strong.   2 Cor 12:10.

Even if we did not have the word of Ezekiel and of the other great prophets of Israel, and even if we did not have the words and life-story of Jesus himself, the fate of prophets of all kinds would be all too clear. Our national newpapers re-echo with the fate of "whistle-blowers"; we learn what happened to trade union leaders in Poland; we see ridicule and hostility poured out on those who return from Central America to speak the truth that has been shown to them. The reading from Ezekiel is eminently practical, for it points to an inevitable dynamic set in motion, and counsels perseverance. To challenge what is amiss in any place or time or society is to become a threat that is resisted, rejected, and if possible, eliminated. But the very reaction that is provoked shows that the message is understood and cannot be silenced, and therefore the suffering of the prophet is justified because in the long run it is fruitful.

Paul knows that. Hence his curious boast of finding pride and joy in his very weakness and humiliation, and hence his odd confidence that the grace of God is more effective when exercised through human inadequacy. This paradox of divine power, which he takes from the example of Jesus himself, is such a challenge to assimilate into one's own perspective on life, that it is tempting to let the reading slide by and focus quickly on another point. One might, for instance, move promptly to the gospel reading. But here we are trapped, for the passage assures us that not even Jesus could escape the frustration and defeat of the prophet.

Coming immediately after the raising of the daughter of Jairus in Mark's account, this passage is particularly poignant and particularly interesting. The wisdom and the healing power of Jesus are devalued because of his familiarity and their lack of faith. He is too ordinary and too close to them to be believed. If someone should come from a distance, shrouded in mystery and accompanied by pomp and ceremony, wondrous works and wise words might be acceptable. From one so ordinary, so simple and unpretentious, and above all so familiar, they are not acceptable. It seems that the folk of Nazareth are all too typical of human behavior. We demand that God's word and deed should come to us through our kind of power and not through God's kind of power. And so we resist and persecute the prophets of our own time, and it becomes true again that the power of God's grace is manifested in human weakness and defeat.

However, the desire for a great, dramatic divine intervention is also perhaps a desire to remain personally uninvolved. It seems to be a desire for a redemption that makes no demands because it remains quite external and alien to us. That may be why we also are reluctant to accept prophetic voices in our midst. And that may be why the Gospel reading for the day confronts us with the challenge to recognize the prophet's call in our own immediate social context.

Fifteenth Sunday of the Year

READINGS: Amos 7:12-15; Eph 1:3-14 (or 3-10); Mk 6:7-13.

He has made known to us his hidden purpose . . . to be put into effect when the time was ripe: namely, that the universe, all in heaven and on earth, might be brought into a unity in Christ.   Eph 1:9-10.

The theme that binds the day's readings together is that of vocation—the exigent character of God's calling, the unpredictable and unlikely selection God makes of divine emissaries, and the conditions for authentic witnessing to God's word. However, the most substantive reading in these selections is that from the letter to the Ephesians, and its main theme is something else. It is concerned with the whole divine plan of redemption, seen as a great reconciliation bringing disparate and warring elements into the harmony intended by God.

In this reading from Ephesians we are drawn into a hymn of praise, which might be described as a hymn of all creation, and more accurately as a hymn of redeemed creation. It seems to be a recital of blessings linking creation and redemption in the remembrance of the joys God has offered. Like the Passover hymn, *dayenu,* ("it would have been enough"), this hymn recalls a whole series of wonderful events in our history as a people: a calling to live in the manifest love of God; association with Jesus through which our possibilities are transformed; redemption by the death of Jesus; the sharing of God's wisdom by which we can know and appreciate God's plan of redemption; the call of Israel; and the call of the Gentiles.

If this enumeration of blessings seems to us rather odd and based upon an obscure kind of logical sequence, that is of course in part because of the great cultural and experiential gap between the setting of this early Christian community and our own. However, it may also be in part due to our general failure to appreciate the gifts of our own history, even in realms we regard as profane. What this hymn really invites us to do is to reflect how it would have been, or might have been, had each event not happened. It invites us to imagine ourselves living in an unredeemed world, allowed to fall apart from the effects of sin, and then to realize by contrast that in face of all the tragedies and horrors of our own contemporary world, the redemption is at work by the hidden purpose of God, revealed to us so that we might become cooperating partners in that work of redemption.

It is in this context that we might look back over the vocation theme that runs through the readings, and realize in a new way why God's choices are so oddly unpredictable, why the call is so exigent, and why the conditions favoring authentic apostolate may well include simplicity and paucity of resources. Amos must have seemed an unlikely choice as a divine messenger—the more so when it became clear that he did not even belong to a band of "professional" prophets such as existed in his time. Amos claims to be a plain-speaking simple small-scale farmer or farm worker. His words must have been very uncongenial to the arch-priest of the royal shrine of Bethel, and indeed to the king himself. But Amos is a sturdy prophet because he has nothing at stake for himself in the corrupt regime.

The mission on which Jesus sends the twelve echoes this sense of the necessary detachment and freedom of those sent to proclaim God's judgment. Mark gives a stark account of the conditions of their missionary expedition: they might take the clothes and sandals they wore and a staff, but neither money nor provisions. They were to live in expectation of, and dependence upon the hospitality of those they would visit. Their message was repentance and their work healing and reconciliation. In this they would be advance heralds of God's hidden purpose.

Sixteenth Sunday of the Year

READINGS: Jer 23:1-6; Eph 2:13-18; Mk 6:30-34.

Now in union with Christ Jesus you who once were far off have been brought near through the shedding of Christ's blood. For he himself is our peace.   Eph 2:13-14.

Unfortunately, the image of sheep without a shepherd is so remote from our everyday experience that it does not suggest the powerful analogy which it must have implied for the first generations of Christians, and before that for Jeremiah's audience. Jeremiah's allusion to shepherds may sound to us like a reference to strictly religious leaders, but was in fact a reference to the kings, the rulers of Israel. What Jeremiah wrote then, is just as true today: the poor and powerless of the world are scattered as refugees, taken captive and oppressed, subjected to drought and famine and inflation, all because of the failure of rulers and governments to fulfill the trust that is vested to them. This much is as true today as it was in Jeremiah's time.

Jeremiah directs our attention to a promised futures. He envisages a ruler, a descendant of David, who will gather the dispersed and terrified people, who will care for them, maintaining justice and peace. The symbolic name of this ruler is to be: The Lord is our righteousness. In the light of that text, and others like it (such as Ezek. 34), there is great depth of meaning in the apparently casual remark of the evangelist, Mark, that Jesus had compassion for the crowds that clung to him in times when he needed some solitude and quiet, because Jesus saw that they were like sheep without a shepherd. It implies the vocation to gather and guide, to show the way and offer a sense of purpose and a reason for hope. It implies a calling to reshape human society by an entirely new principle. Negatively, it also implies a judgment about the collaborators with the Romans, who maintained their own privilege by helping to subject and oppress their people.

This Gospel text is one of the rare passages that gives us a more intimate glimpse into the life-style of Jesus during his public ministry. Even though he had sent his close disciples out in pairs to extend his ministry and presence, we are told that he was constantly mobbed by people. We also learn that he was keenly aware of the need for rest and quiet for himself and his disciples, and that it was not easy decision on his part that led him to welcome the crowds who outwitted him and came around the lake to find him. The saying about sheep without a shepherd suggests that Jesus saw the plight of these people as desperate indeed.

Although the reading from Ephesians is in a sequence of its own, and not chosen to match the other readings, it is curiously apt because it also is concerned with Christ as creating a new order in the world, reconciling, restoring, bringing hope. It is easy for us to pass over these passages with little attention, because they speak of reconciling Jews and Gentiles. But if we take that as an example of the healing effect of Christ in human society, it becomes far more pertinent. The thrust of this passage has to do with the forming of a new humanity of cooperation and peace, eliminating rivalries, feuds, hatred, prejudice. Christ is a new order of things. Christ is our peace. If this is not happening, so today's scripture readings suggest, we have not yet really understood the meaning of Christ in the world.

Seventeenth Sunday of the Year

READINGS: 2 Kgs 4:42-44; Eph 4:1-6; Jn 6:1-15.

They will eat and there will be some left over.   2 Kgs 4:43.

We are used to relating the miracle of the loaves and fishes directly to the Eucharist, and to think of the Eucharist in so "churchy" a fashion, that there is real danger of missing the basic practical meaning when this Sunday's Scripture texts are read. The readings from Kings and John's Gospel insist on the providence of God whereby there is enough for all if we share, and the reading from Ephesians recalls the restored unity that we have in Christ whereby our greatest concern must be for the common good and the common destiny.

The story of Elisha is one of a series in which Elisha mediates the power and will of God to provide far beyond the power and will of human persons to hope. In this particular story, Elisha is surrounded by about one hundred disciples at a time of famine. A follower has brought a gift of food from afar, intended for the personal consumption of the prophet. Elisha commands him to distribute it but the man demurs: if it is distributed no one will have enough and it will be wasted. The word of the Lord is that if it is shared, all will be satisfied and there will be some left over. And so it turns out.

The more familiar story of the multiplication of the loaves and fishes by Jesus is almost a replica of the Elisha story, but elaborated with further detail including the collection of the leftovers into twelve baskets, an overflowing fullness of divine bounty. It is clear that some of the elaboration in the story is deliberatley intended to point to the Eucharist. But this takes on new meaning if we look first at the obvious sense of the two stories: God's bounty to us is released by our sharing with one another, and in particular by our sharing in times of great need.

This is, of course, also the meaning of the Eucharist: to enter into the death and Resurrection of Jesus is to enter into a new human community. It is the community described in the text from Ephesians: one body living by one Spirit, in bonds of peace, in one hope and one calling. Eucharist is the anticipation of the restored, redeemed creation—a sharing of life and hope and all that sustains life, without exclusions because there is enough to share.

It seems to be a persistent temptation of religious people to focus on the extraordinary, to dwell on miracles in the distant past, and to see these as quite discontinuous with our ordinary lives. Yet the Scriptures are not intended to cater to curiosity or hold us spell-bound in amazement. They are intended to show us our own lives and relationships in a truer perspective and a clearer light. Again and again we are being shown in story and image that we are all guests of God's hospitality, invited to enjoy the gifts of creation together by sharing. As guests at one table we are called upon to notice one another's needs and respond to them. Even on a worldwide basis the believer knows that God's hospitality is not stinted, that there is enough to share.

Eighteenth Sunday of the Year

READINGS: Ex 16:2-4, 12-15; Eph 4:17, 20-24; Jn 6:24-35.

I am the bread of life. Whoever comes to me shall never be hungry, and whoever believes in me shall never be thirsty. Jn 6:35.

These readings continue the theme from the previous week, for the Gospel text gives a dialogue reflecting on the meaning and implicatons of the miracle of the loaves and fishes, and correcting some misinterpretations of the miracle of the manna and quail in the desert. In the Exodus story, God provides for the people when they trust in divine providence. When they are concerned first and foremost to obey the divine commands and do what is right, their communal and individual needs are met. In the dialogue taken from John's Gospel, Jesus points out that the crowd coming in search of him has inverted the order. They are concerned to care first for their material needs as though that were sufficient to give meaning and happiness to human life.

Perhaps the injunction to seek the unperishable food of eternal life, and the claim that Jesus is that bread of life, make most sense when we recall those other sayings of Jesus: his food is to do the will of the One who sent him; people do not live by bread alone but by every utterance that comes from God; to seek God's will and justice first is to find all other needs being met. These sayings suggest a clearer perspective on manna, miracle and Eucharist. They suggest a new way of thinking about "spiritual food," about grace, about the sharing of divine life. They suggest that for Jesus miracle and Eucharist are the call to deeper, fuller discipleship, not merely moments of passive receiving of benefits without further consequences. For Jesus the reception of divine nourishment is also the process of becoming, as it were, food for others, sustaining and nourishing the lives of others. Such is the meaning and power of God's wonderful deeds in our own lives. Such is the intent of Eucharist.

Perhaps this needs to be made more explicit. The whole mission of Jesus is to redirect human life and society towards God. This means a reordering of values and expectations, and it involves a rediscovery of the true foundation for security and the true source of sustenance. The long and rather complicated discussions in John 6 are all concerned to evoke an appreciation of this by allusions and figures of speech. Human yearning is not stilled by self-seeking or self-gratification, but by self-gift to God in trust and to other human beings in meeting their needs. To be nourished and sustained by Jesus means being empowered to live in this way.

Nineteenth Sunday of the Year

READINGS: I Kgs 19:4-8; Eph 4:30–5:2; Jn 6:41-51.

I am that living bread which has come down from heaven; if anyone eats this bread he shall live forever. Jn 6:51.

There are many kinds of hunger—the basic hunger for food and drink that offers physical sustenance, a hungering after fresh air and sunshine and pleasant surroundings, a hunger for friendship and recognition and personal dignity and freedom, a hunger for purpose in life and for hope in the future. Correspondingly, there are many kinds of nourishment, and many ways of being bread or sustenance for others.

In the story about Elijah, the angelic messenger offered a hearth-cake and water, but we are given to understand that the real hunger that Elijah felt was a hunger for hope and for a purpose in life. His situation is in many ways very like ours today, particularly like that of our young people. The juniper tree or broom bush under which Elijah sat is suggestive of the mushroom cloud of a nuclear explosion that haunts many people today with its threat to annihilate the future. The death-wish expressed by the prophet is no stranger in our midst. The food that is offered to Elijah, however, is full of implications beyond immediate physical nourishment; it recalls the manna in the desert and therefore is a reminder of the covenant fidelity of God in all time and all circumstances; it is a gentle act of hospitality and as such gives a taste of the goodness of God and the goodness of human existence as God's creation.

In the story, the hospitality is repeated, and Elijah draws strength from it—not only physical strength, but hope and courage to meet the future and to respond to his own calling. It suggests the kind of nourishment and encouragement that all of us can receive from repeated meditation on Scripture, from retreats and spiritual direction, and also from the liturgy, especially the Eucharist.

The excerpt from Ephesians is curiously appropriate in that it reminds us that sealed by the Spirit of God and empowered to live in and by the love of Christ, we ourselves are able to extend divine hospitality, offering both physical and other kinds of nourishmnent to sustain the life and hope of others and to be signs of the covenant fidelity of God. It is not difficult to see people and whole nations sitting under the shadow of despair in our times, waiting for death. And it is evident that the pledges of hope are in our hands to give. We can be bread of hope both to one another within the community of believers (especially in the local church), and also to the world at large where there is great need of hope.

The text from John's Gospel is, once again, a continuation of those significant sayings of Jesus in Chapter 6. They are difficult for

Christians of our times to understand because they are so allusive and use a symbolism not so familiar to us. But this is why the liturgy has carefully matched these excerpts with stories from the Hebrew Scriptures that shed light on the sayings of Jesus. Having reflected on the Elijah story we are invited to realize that we also are offered such heavenly remedies and sustenance.

The pledges of hope are in our hands because, as John reminds us, Jesus has become the true bread of life for us, heavenly bread of hope and immortality. Nourished by that bread in so many ways, we are called to become sustenance for others—to love in concrete and practical ways, as Christ loved.

Twentieth Sunday of the Year

READINGS: Prov 9:1-6; Eph 5:15-20; Jn 6:51-58.

You will live, you will grow in understanding.   Prov 9:6.

The passage from Proverbs seems to suggest that the invitation of wisdom to enter her house and partake of her banquet, is generally resisted, because people are loath to trust that the true wisdom, God's wisdom, is really life-giving, leading to a growth in understanding that gives more meaning and purpose to life. The invitation may sound more like a call to renunciation of all that is personally fulfilling.

The second reading dwells on a similar theme: it coaxes Christians to be critically alert concerning the various invitations to feasting that are heard in the world, discerning which lead to destruction and which to life. Indeed the text begs us all not to be caught up in the kind of feasting that is marked by drunkenness and dissipation, but to feast on the Holy Spirit, sharing joy and encouragement and gratitude with others in the name of Jesus. There are, of course, many different ways of self-destruction; and drunkenness and dissipation are representative. The endless quest for wealth beyond real need is certainly a contemporary form of dissipation, and so is the concern to impress others by style of living, dress, cars, and so forth.

John's Gospel assures us that Jesus himself encountered bitter resistance and hardness of heart in issuing his invitation to the heavenly banquet. He offers his life's blood and all that he is, to extend the divine hospitality to the world in his own person. And yet there is resistance., The news, like the invitation of wisdom in Proverbs, is too good to be true. It appears to demand too much risk in the acceptance. It calls for a turning, a somersault, a revolution in our thinking and our expectations. It calls for a frightening degree of trust, for the surrender implied in authentic discipleship. And for the greater part the crowds about Jesus, as John depicts them (and us), hesitate and back away. It is difficult to believe that in himself Jesus really gives bread for the life of the world. It is even more difficult to realize that by entering into his wisdom we are called upon not only to receive but in turn to dispense bread that others may live—bread that is in some sense ourselves, bread that nourishes the life and hope of the world.

There is a certain ambivalence in the response of Christians to the invitation of Jesus. On the one hand, while we think in ritual terms, we readily profess that Jesus nourishes those who believe in him both by word and by sacrament. But on the other hand, we are generally quite reluctant to link Eucharist with the death of Jesus in a practical way which would imply our own involvement in a death to many ways of self-assertion that we take for granted as part of life.

To believe that Jesus makes his very substance and being nourishment for others, and to receive that gift from him, is so fraught with consequences that we tend to prefer our own kind of wisdom which is generally more concerned with conquest than with sharing. But wisdom in the person of Jesus continues to hold out the invitation, offering food for the life of the world.

Twenty-first Sunday of the Year

READINGS: Josh 24:1-2, 15-18; Eph 5:21-32; Jn 6:60-69.

To whom whall we go? Your words are the words of eternal life. We have faith and we know that you are the Holy One of God.   Jn 6:68-69.

It seems to be such a general temptation in human life to float with the stream, to live from one day to the next, somehow never confronting really fundamental decisions, that we have even coined the slogan, "Not to decide is to decide." Something of the sort seems to be at stake in the covenant renewal story that is situated shortly before Joshua's death. It appears to Joshua that the generations of Israel born after the Sinai convenantal encounter, are drifting along without the benefit of a commitment that is fully their own. Joshua confronts them ruthlessly with the demand to choose who is their God, what is ultimate in their allegiance. Their response is obviously offered as a model to all of us, and perhaps as a warning to be prepared, because sooner or later we all do come to a point where the radical decision can no longer be evaded.

The Gospel story offers a parallel that is even closer to home. The claims and promises of Jesus arouse cynicism, ridicule, contempt, and the situation has come to the point at which the followers of Jesus must choose and must declare themselves. Either they are with him all the way, or they are against him. It is no longer the case that any who are not against him are with him, because now it is a moment of crisis, a time to choose and to stand by the choice. For Peter and his companions it is a moment that calls for covenant renewal.

Both stories are strong paradigms for situations that face us from time to time—in private decisions and relationships, and in larger issues of peace and justice, such as responses to illegal immigrants fleeing for their lives, participaton in the production and marketing of dangerous commodities, hiring and firing policies, investment, involvement in support of covert or overt wars, and so forth. All these are crisis moments at which a difficult and consequential choice must be made as to whether we stand with Jesus Christ or go our own way.

The reading from Ephesians suggests another paradigm—the covenant loyalty called for in a marriage, the total commitment it involves, the subordination of self-interest on the part of both parties. The mystery of two becoming so united in fidelity that they are as one, can refer, as the author of Ephesians suggests, both to Christ and the Church and to the marriage of individuals. The letter takes for granted elements of the social order of the time involving a subordination of women which is not accepted today, but this should not obscure the point of the passage. It is not about the proper hierarchy of authority in the family. It is about covenant fidelity and the subordination of self-interest which is implied for all concerned. There are times when we must choose and must stand by our commitment.

All three readings, then, in different contexts, remind us that we cannot drift through life taking choices, values, goals and relationships for granted. There are crisis points for which we must be prepared. There are moments of decision which set the direction of our lives and activities. If we do not recognize them as Christian vocational moments, we are likely to drift by choices inconsistent with our hope, just because others are moving in that direction. To be alive in Christ is to recognize the time to choose.

Twenty-second Sunday of the Year

READINGS: Deut 4:1-2, 6-8; Jas 1:17-18, 21-22, 27; Mk 7:1-8, 14-15, 21-23.

The kind of religion which is without stain or fault in the sight of God our Father is this: to go to the help of widows and orphans in their distress and to keep oneself untarnished by the world. Jas 1:27.

Israel was never allowed to forget that the election and the Sinai covenant was an inclusive way of life, not only a way of worship.

The Covenant structured society by principles of justice and peace that were to make Israel a witness people to all the nations, displaying the power and wisdom of God. Although the introductory admonition neither to add to nor to subtract from the laws of God, is a conventional form for such a proclamation as this, the juxtaposition of the text from Deuteronomy with that from Mark 7 is certainly intended as a commentary on the all too human habit of trivializing divine law by the way it is interpreted in human formulations.

This collection of sayings of Jesus deals with a theme that seems to have been very important to him—the contrast between ritual purity and true religious purity which is purity of heart. Ritual purity is constituted by observances which are, in the ultimate analysis, arbitrary. Though these observance may serve a useful purpose in maintaining the identity and coherence and focus of the People of God, they are not unconditionally binding. On the other hand, purity of heart and intention is concerned with the essence of the relationship with God and with fellow creatures. The Gospels insist on the distinction, not in order that we might condemn certain learned contemporaries of Jesus, but that we may be warned against such confusion of the two kinds of purity as is likely to arise in our own Christian experience. It is often tempting to be punctilious in the performing of ritual obligations while neglecting the weightier matters of divine law that have to do with justice and compassion, with peace and forgiveness, with responsibility and honesty. But it is necessary at all times to maintain a distinction between ritual observances that can always be omitted for a good reason, and the basic terms of human relationship to God and others, from which there can be no exemption even when they become very onerous or fraught with risk.

This passage from Mark lists a series of negative examples. The excerpt from James, however, is positive, direct and very practical. True religion is a simple matter of accepting the good news not only by listening to it but by acting upon it. There are plenty of ways of deceiving oneself over this, but one way is failproof—to come to the help of the poor and distressed, whoever these may be, and to resist assimilation into the values and power struggles of the world. Our faith is not a proposition calling for a notional assent but a way to live. And the message of this Sunday is that it is basically a very simple way to live. Nothing in these readings suggests that a Christian life should be easy, but there is much to suggest that a deep sense of reconciliation and harmony in one's own life is a spontaneous by-product of sincere, practical service to others in need. That is the meaning of the day's readings about an authentic way to live.

Twenty-third Sunday of the Year

READINGS: Is 35:4-7; Jas 2:1-5; Mk 7:31-37.

Be strong and fear not. See, your God comes with vengeance, with dread retribution he comes to save you. Then shall blind men's eyes be opened, and the ears of the deaf unstopped. Is 35:4-5.

When God comes to save, blind eyes are opened, the deaf hear, the lame leap, and the tongue-tied give forth loud proclamations of the good news that has overtaken them, so Isaiah expresses it. James puts it more bluntly, more inclusively: it is those who are poor in the eyes of the world whom God has chosen. It is the hallmark of God's saving intervention that it takes place among the unlikely, and that it looses bonds of suffering and frustration.

This understanding is, of course, deep in the traditions of Israel, for whom God is first and foremost the liberator of the Exodus event, who chose the suffering and oppressed slave tribes in Egypt as the people of divine election. God opens up new possibilities, heals what is broken, gives courage and vision where there is pervasive despair and deep darkness. God opens the ears of people long deaf to hope and prophecy, and gives a prophetic voice to those who have long been too discouraged to speak of divine promises or to proclaim redemption. God's saving actions mean release from suffering at many levels, from the most physical and immediate to the most sublime and ultimate.

The followers of Jesus, as well as his critics and the uncommitted bystanders, were keenly alert to the deeper levels of meaning in the opening of ears and unloosing of tongues. These were acts of promise, of proclamation. That is why Mark can state that their astonishment knew no bounds. Most of us, in any age, are not prepared for the wonderful works of God to touch us so closely, and for the redemption to unfold before our very eyes. In this case the onlookers responded with faith, for it was not only this particular deaf and dumb man who was released to hear and proclaim; the crowd around him has also heard and begun to proclaim.

The Church has retained accounts like this one, enshrining them in Bible and liturgy, because they speak of something that happens to us in greater or lesser measure as we enter into the mystery of Christ. Indeed, the baptismal liturgy makes it explicit: our ears are opened to hear and our tongues to speak. The letter of James adds an important reflection: we are rescued and chosen out of our need and not out of any excellence or achievement; therefore we have no right to despise anyone, but are called upon to respond to the poor and needy with the same grace that has been extended to us.

However, if strength and fearlessness are demanded, as the Isaian passage proclaims, this is not only so that we may do for others what has been done for us. The strength and fearlessness are needed in the first place even to hear with the ears that have been unstopped and to see with the eyes that have been opened. The self-revelation of God always comes as a challenge to the opaqueness of our world and the illusory security which it offers. The self-revelation of God in Jesus comes with a quietness and simplicity which challenges the noisy complexity and confusion in which we tend to hide. It involves risk in listening to what sems like silence. But that is how God enables the deaf to hear.

Twenty-fourth Sunday of the Year

READINGS: Is 50; 4-9; Jas 2:14-18; Mk 8:27-35.

Prove to me that this faith you speak of is real though not accompanied by deeds, and by my deeds I will prove to you my faith. Jas 2:18.

Clearly the good news to which God opens our ears does not come to us without making its own demands. In a sinful history and a world distorted by the consequences of destructive deeds, the glad news of a radical transformation comes also as a challenge to all that is not right in our lives and in our world. Every challenge carries some pain, and demands some renunciations.

The third servant song of the later Isaiah, which is read for this day, puts this in sharp relief. When the prophet's ear is opened, and he listens, and he speaks God's word with the eloquence bestowed upon him, he expects suffering and contempt. But he stands firm, knowing that ultimately the victory is God's, and that those who trust in God are vindicated. The opposition will wear out and disappear like a garment eaten by moths. It is God who is the self-same and endures forever. It is the covenant fidelity of God which never wears out.

The liturgy, of course, applies this song of redemptive suffering to Jesus. Mark's Gospel endorses that and carries it further. When Jesus is acknowledged as Messiah/Savior, he replies that his role involves provoking opposition, being rejected and put to death. Mark makes a point of it that he spoke so plainly, so bluntly, that Peter was shocked and tried to deny it, as we all tend to do. But Jesus had not finished his explanation. To follow him necessarily means, he insisted, to provoke opposition and risk loss, even the loss of life. Like Peter, we would all like to rewrite this passage. The age of martyrdom is over and the age of Christendom has come; we live in a Christian country and a Christian culture, so we like to think. But the liturgy brings us back from time to time to the blunt statements in Scripture to the effect that the struggle continues and that we are part of it. If our Christianity means nothing more than an endorsement of the *status quo* of a world full of unnecessary suffering and poverty and oppression, then we stand aligned rather with Peter's reluctance and self-deception than with the clear statement of Jesus. To live as a Christian is to be drawn into more and more clearly prophetic positions.

The passage from James offers its own perspective on the issue, by asking what faith can possibly mean if it does not issue in action. The type of action which speaks, according to James, is care for the needy, the underprivileged, the suffering. That kind of action is the proclamation of the good news of God's salvation. It involves willingness to sacrifice everything for the promises of God, as Abraham was willing to sacrifice Isaac. Such actions speak, and the message they convey is truly good news.

Twenty-fifth Sunday of the Year

READINGS: Wis 2:12, 17-20; Jas 3:16–4:3; Mk 9:30-37.

Justice is the harvest reaped by peacemakers from seeds sown in a spirit of peace. Jas 3:18.

One needs to listen to this saying of James carefully to catch its drift. We have become more accustomed in recent years to a slogan that sees matters the other way around: if you desire peace, do justice. James says that justice is the outcome of making peace. But the context in which the statement appears is a reflection on what it is that causes quarrels and murder: inordinate desires and unjust ambitions. Though the passage is not specifically chosen to match the other two readings, it suggests a curiously apt approach to the latter.

The Gospel reading presents a second prediction of the betrayal and death of Jesus, and again asserts that the prediction was incomprehensible to the disciples to whom it had been made in private. The next paragraph plays a favorite theme of the gospel, namely, that greatness is not in domination but in ministry to others, that is in servanthood. It seems that the two incidents are closely related: they could not understand his prediction of betrayal and death but they, meanwhile, were concerned about who should be reckoned the greatest among them. It is all too human. We want success, of course, but the problem lies in the ways in which we define success. For us, as for those first disciples, there is no doubt that Jesus is a challenge which again and again redefines our ideas of greatness and of success. His approach is that kind of peacemaking out of which justice can grow, and it comes at a high price.

The reading from Wisdom seems to have been chosen to underscore and also to explain this. From a worldly perspective people are always outraged at the "just" person whose life style, relationships and actions seem in themselves to carry a reproach to others. If such a person is right, then much in the structures and values of society which we take comfortably for granted, is sinful and ought to change. But we want to believe that we are surely the good people, the ones on God's side, and it must be those others, those outsiders, who are the sinners.

The passage from Wisdom suggests that this is a classic case; the person whose life is experienced as a challenge to the values the rest of us take for granted is bitterly persecuted. The Gospel applies it to Jesus, but we have seen it in our times in Gandhi and Martin Luther King and many others. In retrospect we see that their servanthood was true greatness, that their peacemaking brought justice, and that their way was true wisdom.

Twenty-sixth Sunday of the Year.

READINGS: Num 11:25-29; Jas 5:1-6; Mk 9:38-48.

He who is not against us in on our side. Mk 9:40.

It is true that Jesus, according to Mt 12:30 and Lk 11:23, also said the opposite; those who were not with him were against him. That suggests that we should interpret the saying with reference to its context. Surely we have all had the experience in personal relationships and social situations that those who did not acknowledge the problem *were* the problem, and that those who remained carefully neutral were in fact taking sides for the *status quo.* But here the situation is different: someone is acting redemptively though apparently without the proper credentials or mission.

The liturgy provides us with the Mosaic parallel by way of clarifying the significance of the story. In both cases the disciples are more concerned about procedure and ritual and credentials than about the substance of what is being accomplished. Moses, intimate with God, gives an answer that even suggests he may have been amused at this misplaced zeal. There is no reason for him to be jealous of his office and demand that the gifts of God's spirit be dispensed only through him. Rather, he rejoices over the lavish abandon with which God bestows such gifts. The Gospel shows Jesus endorsing this understanding that it is matter for thankfulness that the work of God is being done, and here moreover being done in Jesus' name, because it shows that although not officially designated, this exorcist also is aligned with Jesus. It is the substance that counts; people are to be rewarded for the good they do, no matter how insignificant, and punished for what is destructive, for that is the real evil to be feared.

This wise ecumenism is a rather important matter for our reflection because the issue is around us constantly. There is such temptation to judge by official credentials and ritual correctness, such a temptation to try to restrict the Holy Spirit within our own institutional expectations that we are in constant danger of denying the redemptive forces outside our own institutional preferences and preoccupations. A wise ecumenism looks to the substance of what is being done. It does not easily condemn people by attaching labels like Communist, atheist, infidel, heretic, and so forth. Rather, this ecumenical attitude looks to the substance of what others do or propose to do, and judges whether the action is helpful.

Meanwhile the passage from James seems to warn against a

foolish, false ecumenism, one that accepts the standards of the world and assumes that the human order of things is good enough, needing no counter-cultural adjustments. Again, the temptation is pervasive to live hoarding riches and making sharp bargains at the expense of the powerless, because these things are generally done and look respectable enough. James points ruthlessly to the substance of what is being done and to God's judgment on these attitudes and actions of amassing wealth and comfort at the expense of others. True wisdom sees our social and ecomonic relationships as they appear before God. And this may lead away from alliances we have taken for granted and into a new but better range of ecumenism.

Twenty-seventh Sunday of the Year

READINGS: Gen 2:18-24; Heb 2:9-11; Mk 10:2-16.

In the beginning, at the creation, God made them male and female. Mk 10:6.

Challenged with a question about the legitimacy of divorce in the Mosaic law, Jesus admits without hesitation that Deuteronomy 24 assumes the legitimacy of divorce under certain conditions (though the exact conditions were apparently under dispute at the time of Jesus). However, Jesus does not leave the question within the legal framework in which it was proposed, but proceeds to give some radical reflections on the relationships of men and women. Referring the matter to the context of the divine purpose in creation, he claims that unconditional, lifelong fidelity is what God really intends in marriage, although the Mosaic exemption may be necessary in the historical conditions of a sinful world.

So that we might more easily grasp the sense of this gospel passage and its application to our own times, the liturgy juxtaposes it with the text that Jesus quotes, from Genesis 2. This reading seems to be a reflection on the experience of sexual differentiation among human persons and the attraction of complementarity that overcomes the division of the sexes. Some medieval Jewish comentators, notably

Rashi and Ezra, translate "side" instead of "rib", because they conjecture that the story means to imply that originally the human person was androgynous and that God found it good to separate the two sides, dividing the woman from the man and creating interdependence of human persons. The reason for it is that it is not good for the human person to be alone as though self-sufficient like God. The two separated sides are akin, equal but complementary, and intended to come voluntarily into fullest communion as a basic cell of a wider community. Ideally, the commitment involved is total and the fidelity unbreakable.

There seem to be some important elements in the way Jesus cites this passage which might elude us until we learn something of the law and practice of the time. The question put to him was whether it was lawful for a man to divorce his partner because, except in the most extraordinary circumstances and through the intervention of a court, it was not possible for the woman to do so. The answer Jesus gives seems, in the first place, intended to put the woman on a par with the man, as the intended partner of creation. When the disciples pursue the matter with him privately, he says something that seems obvious to us but may have seemed radical to his listeners. Adultery was seen as a sin of injustice against the husband of a married woman, committed by another man who had intercourse with her. Jesus says that what is wrong when a man divorces and marries again is that it is an injustice against the wife he has dismissed, with or without the legally required note of dismissal. It was apparently only for Gentile readers of the Gospel of Mark that the parallel of the wife divorcing her husband was added.

It is clear from the various encounters of Jesus with women, as recorded in the Gospels, and from the role that women disciples played in the ministry of Jesus and the very early church, that Jesus himself saw the complementarity and equality as extending into society more generally, and not only in marriage. The intent of the Genesis passage is certainly to suggest that the complementarity of the sexes is God's way of creating community, not division and isolation. In that context one might be forgiven for wondering what Jesus in person would reply to the question, "Is it lawful to exclude women from ordained ministry and decision-making in your Church?" Might he, for instance, respond, "Canon Law has done this because of the hardness of your hearts, but in the beginning, when I gathered my disciples, it was not so, because God has made them male and female"?

Whatever the answer to that question, the passages having to do with marital fidelity in the New Testament are all ultimately set against the background of the fidelity of God to the human community as expressed most concretely and particularly in the total self-gift and fidelity of Jesus to the Church. The self-gift and fidelity of Christians to each other in a marriage is intended to be a sacramental expression of that more comprehensive fidelity, and it is in that context that Christians are encouraged to be faithful even in tragic situations.

It is rather appropriate, therefore that the brief reading from Hebrews should be concerned with the irrevocable commitment by which Jesus becomes one with the whole sinful human race, and remains loyal to the bond in the face of extreme suffering and of death. Although the theme of Hebrews is the priestly mediation of Jesus through his obedience and death, the notion of covenant and of covenant loyalty is pervasive here as everywhere in Scripture. But the most common and fundamental covenant in human experience is the marriage bond. It is through marriage that people most commonly experience the reconciliation of opposites in complementarity, the solidarity of human community overcoming self-centeredness and isolation, the experience of another as promise rather than threat, as companion rather than rival. And that is all in the plan of the creator which makes us not androgynous but essentially interdependent, so that what God has joined ought not humanly to be pulled apart and broken.

Twenty-eighth Sunday of the Year

READINGS: Wis 7:7-11; Heb 4:12-13; Mk 10:17-30 (or 17-27).

Jesus looked around at his disciples and said to them, 'How hard it will be for the wealthy to enter the kingdom of God!' Mk 10:23.

There is no doubt about it: from the beginning of Christianity there has been a certain bias against the rich and a preferential option for the poor. It makes for a very definite clash of values in a wealthy capitalist country where the work ethic is in the air we breathe, and financial success seems to be the just reward of highly valued virtues such as diligence, prudence, ambition and tolerance of delayed satisfaction. The Gospel suggestion, that in the eyes of God being rich is likely to be quite a disadvantage, almost sounds as though the remark came from the wrong side of the Iron Curtain.

The word of God, according to the short reading from Hebrews, is dangerous to one's complacency, piercing to the hidden center of things, and sifting purposes and thoughts of the heart. That seems to be particularly so in the matter of riches and one's attitude and relation to them. The wisdom of Solomon is proverbial, and it is invoked as commentary and background to the Gospel text in an interesting way. The Wisdom passage is put in the mouth of Solomon, recalling that other account in I Kings 3. Solomon, we learn, put aside desire for riches, long life and conquests, in order to beg God for wisdom—not some abstract, ethereal kind of wisdom, but a listening heart that he might govern his people justly, discerning good and evil and realizing that to be vice-regent for God he was to be totally dependent on God. Solomon is exemplary because he reckoned riches as nothing beside the gift of God that enabled him to respond to the call of God.

This is such an interesting background to the Gospel story. The stranger who ran up and knelt before Jesus was certainly in quest of wisdom—of that special wisdom that he was convinced Jesus could dispense. Jesus suggests that the questioner is already in possession of the key to answering his own question, for God has shared the divine wisdom in giving the commandments which are the guide to a good life. The stanger's answer is the answer of the devout, the professionally religious, the Sunday church-goers; he could truthfully say he had been plodding along all his life, keeping the commandments. But he knew that that was not the answer to his question or his quest.

Perhaps of all the Sunday Gospel readings to reach the ears of the devout, this is one in which the two edged sword of the word of God most surely reveals the purposes and thoughts of the heart. No one who meditates the Scriptures and sets out day after day to live by them can long remain unaware that there is a vast chasm between the faithful performance of moral and religious duties as commanded, and the real surrender that places trust in God alone. The test of that surrender in this story is the willingness to abandon great wealth and all the privileges and inflated importance afforded by such wealth, and to share with the needy without reserve. In every age there have been saints and radicals who responded to this saying in a shockingly literal way. The rest of us found that it worried us that Jesus said this and that we hoped he did not really mean it. Even at the end of the second century, Clement of Alexandria was already busy trying to make the saying sound more reasonable to his fellow citizens. But, to tell the truth, Clement's reassurance about the rich man who *can* be saved, makes so many demands on that rich man's purse that it does not seem that he would long be rich while fulfilling the conditions proposed.

In a world full of poverty, hunger and oppression, perhaps the test is always whether we will abandon wealth, with the privileges and status that goes with it, in order to share with the needy. To have exceptional wealth, power, privilege or status always carries the temptation to define oneself by these things, to fashion a self-image out of them. In proportion as one is poor, powerless, unprivileged and constantly dependent on others, there is less possibility of this and therefore less danger and therefore also less of an obstacle to a message of dependence on God and community with others simply because they also are human, children of God, called to be the people of God. In a world such as we know, the wealth and privileges and power we hold are not irrelevant to our relationship with God and other people. That is so whether we are thinking of individuals or of whole social classes and nations. The wealthy are not simply so by chance or predetermination; they remain wealthy in the face of others' need only by their own choice. For Christians that raises the question, why? When the message is total trust in God and not in one's own resources, and total identification with others in their human dignity and destiny and need, why would Christians withhold their wealth from others in desperate need?

In the Gospel reading, Jesus looks around, not at outsiders but at his own disciples, and remarks how difficult it is for a rich person to enter into that transforming reign of God in which all things are revalued—in which community rather than individual advantage is the foundation of security, in which trust in God's creating and redeeming goodness makes anxious getting and hoarding unnecessary, in which divine wisdom is preferred to all manner of riches.

Twenty-ninth Sunday of the Year

READINGS: Is 53:10-11; Heb 4:14-16; Mk 10:35-45 (or 42-45).

For ours is not a high priest unable to sympathize with our weakness, but one who, because of his likeness to us, has been tested in every way, only without sin. Heb 4:15.

All three readings for this Sunday are concerned with the price to be paid in liberating people from the effects of sin in all their tragic complexity. Although the liturgy applies the Isaian text from the fourth "suffering servant son" to Jesus in his Death and Resurrection, that text seems originally to have referred to the vocation of Israel as God's chosen people. Even today it is not inappropriate for Christians to read this text and to think of the sufferings of the Jews throughout the ages, and most recently in the Holocaust, remembering that it was in large measure vicarious suffering in which the prejudices, fears and hatreds of the world were exposed and therefore challenged. The suffering servant songs tell of something that is a classic situation in human history: the price of liberation for the people is the blood of prophets, or soldiers or other martyrs for the cause.

The short text from Hebrews points out that Jesus himself did not have a privileged way of redeeming from the tragedies that sin has caused in human history, that he did not have a way of by-passing the price to be paid, that he confronted the horror of the evil in the world on genuinely human terms of weakness. The writer of this text seems to have been concerned to encourage the readers or listeners, and to warn them against the temptation to settle for something less than total personal consecration and commitment. Followers and imitators of Jesus are being reminded that Jesus himself faced no less to liberate people from evil. He did not escape the classic trial, the price to be paid.

There is a certain pathos in the text, because we all tend to have that surreptitious sense now that the Church is established, now that Jesus has long ago died for us, now that we have the structures of the Church and the sacramental life—that now the Christian life should not make any unusual demands, that there should no longer be a high price to pay in the process of redemption, in the liberation from sin and its tangled consequences in the world.

It is perhaps this sense that Christian life should now be more routine and less conflictual or difficult, which prompts protests when Pope or Bishops or priests in Sunday sermons address the large social issues in which the consequences of sin so powerfully express themselves in our times—issues of race, of peace, of social justice, of world hunger or local poverty, of developments in the national or international economy, and so forth. Most of us have the spontaneous reaction that our faith is supposed to provide us with consolation, serenity, inspiration, that it is not supposed to get us entangled in matters that are so complex, so conflictual, so worldly. Oddly enough, though Lutherans have better reasons for it in their theology, we Catholics often practice our sacramental spirituality in such a way that we implicitly claim that the death of Jesus was "substitutionary". It is as though significant involvement in the redemption of the world were all in the past and we were called only to receive and enjoy the fruits of it. Yet our world is not like that. It is still a world in which the freeing of people from suffering, caused by sin through the centuries, calls for total commitment, for the dedication of one's life and resources, in some countries and circumstances even to the point of a violent death.

Mark's Gospel account of the circumstances of the third prediction of the passion by Jesus, assures us that it was so from the beginning. Some of those whom we revere as founders of the first churches were quarreling over the privilege of a status close to Jesus with no realization at all of the cost of what Jesus was doing. They spoke as though they could claim the glory of the victory without participating in the blood and tears of the struggle. Then, as now, the word of Jesus to his followers is that we must think quite differently about authority, status and importance. The authentic redemptive transformation does not come about by a process of bullying other people, making them "feel the weight of authority", commanding them and expecting subservience. The transformation comes about through sacrifcing oneself for others, being dedicated as totally as a slave, giving one's life as a ransom. It is, of course, a truth that every revolutionary, whether violent or peaceful, realizes sooner or later. The liberation of the human race from sin and all its expressions in the values, relationships and structures of our society, is a very fundamental kind of revolution.

There is an inescapably quality in the readings for this Sunday. They question our understanding of the very essence of being Christian, of our own role in the mystery of redemption, of the nature of ministry, and of the content and quality of our hope. They speak to us of true liberation.

Thirtieth Sunday of the Year

READINGS: Jer: 31:7-9; Heb 5:1-6; Mk 10:46-52.

Jesus said to him, 'Go; your faith has cured you'. And at once he recovered his sight and followed him on the road. Mk 10:52.

The day's eucharistic liturgy presents us with three texts very loosely connected to one another. From Jeremiah we have a poem of consolation (one of a series) that promises the end of 100 years of bitter oppression and exile. It promises a moment of salvation, a day of deliverance. Among the suffering who will be gathered from the ends of the earth for the great return, the poem mentions the blind, who will be led gently over a smooth path so that they shall not stumble. From Hebrews we have some reflections on the character of the mediating (or priestly) role which Jesus plays, and particularly on the intimacy of his sharing of human suffering and alienation. In some rather tenuous sense, the Gospel reading picks up both those themes, that of the blind being led to the great return of the moment of salvation, and that of the intimacy with which Jesus shares the suffering that is involved.

The focus of the day's readings is in the story from Mark which seems at first sight so simple that there is little to be said about it by way of commentary or mediation. Actually, the story seems to address Christian believers on many levels of understanding. At the simplest level of the story, a suffering, deprived, neglected person who is not only blind but a beggar, thrust out of the way by the people around who tell him to be quiet when he pleads for help, calls to Jesus for help and is heard and helped and vindicated. This would be enough to make it worth meditating upon; it shows Jesus as helper, healer, friend of the poor and suffering and oppressed, champion of the people who "don't count" according to worldly evaluations.

But the story also invites symbolic interpretaion, for there have been other blind persons healed in this Gospel, and in Scriptures as in everyday language, blindness is a ready metaphor for failure to recognize and understand in the spiritual realm. Since early Christian times the baptismal liturgy has used the symbolism of opening the eyes of one who has been blind, of shining a light into darkness so that people truly see reality for the first time, to represent the change that happens when people begin to see themselves, their world and God as revealed by Jesus Christ. Seen in this light, the story is about ourselves, the readers and listeners, who come in our poverty, asking to see, asking for life to make sense, to offer meaning and purpose. In the story Jesus says to us that it is faith that cures or saves us, and he invites us to follow him on the road.

Even without much searching into the structure of Mark's Gospel or the allusions contained in the passsage, Christian believers can hear themselves being addressed in this passage in this way. However, further reflection and study brings this particular blind beggar to life in startling ways. Whether any special allusions are intended or not, the placing of the incident in Jericho is very suggestive. This oasis in the desert near the Dead Sea has a very ancient history; the story of Joshua's victory by a liturgical procession of trumpets and earthen jars is told about Jericho. The city resonates with the memory of Elijah, for its excellent fresh water spring is named after the prophet. Simon Maccabaeus was killed there by treachery. In the New Testament the story of the Good Samaritan is placed on the road to Jericho, and the story of Zacchaeus is located in the town itself. Zacchaeus also could not see—in his case a matter of lack of stature—and, for his great desire to see Jesus, was affectionately welcomed by him.

The name of the blind beggar may be fortuitous but is similarly suggestive; he is identified only as "son of the honored one" while evidently living in deprivation and despised. His addressing Jesus as "son of David" is certainly not fortuitous but clearly intended to convey expectation of salvation, recognition that Jesus is the expected one through whom deliverance is to come to the people, initiating the end of a time of misery. The earliest Christians called themselves, among other designations, the followers of the way, so that the unobtrusive last sentence is pregnant with meaning. That he recovered his sight and followed Jesus on the road, or on the way, strongly suggests that he followed as disciple. This is even clearer from the fact that this story follows directly upon that of James and John seeking a favor from Jesus. In both cases Jesus turns to the petitioners and asks what it is they want him to do. The sons of Zebedee, represented in the Gospel as belonging to the inner circle, have understood so little that they ask for special status. The blind outsider only asks to be allowed to see and, being granted this, follows in discipleship.

The placing of the passage in the structure of Mark's Gospel makes this particularly vivid and stark, for the story of Bartimaeus makes the transition from the peripatetic preaching to the entry into Jerusalem for the final conflict. It is a moment of clear declaration in the pattern of the Gospel; Jesus does not rebuke or discourage the blind man from giving him the title, Son of David: the cure and the commitment to discipleship are instantaneous, and the drama of Jesus' own vocation moves swiftly to its end. We who meditate on the text are left with a riddle, for we are made party to the vision of the blind man.

Thirty-first Sunday of the Year.

READINGS: Deut 6:2-6; Heb 7:23-28; Mk 12:28-34.

Love the Lord your God with all your heart, with all your soul, with all your mind and with all your strength . . . Love your neighbor as yourself. Mk 12:29-31.

The liturgy has skipped about two chapters of Mark's Gospel which are more suited to Lent and Passiontide, and that is why we find ourselves quite suddenly in the story of the lawyer and his question—reminiscent, though not exactly identical with the young man who wanted to know what to do to be saved. The readings speak of two tensions or polarities in Christian life. Deuteronomy and Mark's Gospel point to the paradox that on the one hand to realize the divine purpose of our existence is ineffably simple but that on the other hand we really do need to determine the specific ways of realizing that purpose. The text from Hebrews which has been insisting week after week, Sunday after Sunday, that Jesus our High Priest is just like us, now suddenly tells us how uniquely different he is, and that our salvation depends upon this. The two paradoxes have a certain bearing upon each other; Jesus exemplies the utter simplicity of what is actually involved in salvation and reconciliation, but he effects that reconciliation and salvation because he shared the complex tragedy of our human history in which the sublimely simple becomes so complex that it must be spelled out in specific commandments.

The passage from Deuteronomy to which Jesus referred is set between a brief form of the commandments of the Law and a summary of the promises and the ways the promises are to be passed on through the generations. The linking passage presents the covenant relationship between God and Israel in its utter simplicity and its total exigence. It became, of course, not only the introduction to private prayer and public worship, but also such a rallying cry of Jewish vocation and identity that it was often the last utterance of the death-camp victims of the Holocaust in our own times. Because we have only one reading from the Hebrew Scriptures at our Sunday Eucharist, we do not hear the context from which Jesus quoted the other half of his answer. In Leviticus 19, after three separate lists of the duties that all have towards their neighbors, many of them dealing with justice to the poor, fair payment of laborers, respect for the handicapped, decent behavior towards aliens, and the correction of corruption and prejudice, the matter is summed up very simply as a matter of caring for the neighbor as a person just like oneself.

Of course, what Jesus said was obvious—after he said it. He simply referred to the first text that a Jewish child would have learned to pray and meditate upon and treasure from the age of seven. It was taught first because it was basic, and because one could turn back to it any time in life in order to find the center and to renew one's perspective. But Jesus matches with this text the necessary complement that makes it practical for everyday living. We cannot be sure that this was entirely original to Jesus. Mark's Gospel seems to use the incident to show that Jesus was quite orthodox and faithful to the best Hebrew tradition. Certainly, the scribe, described as a lawyer because he is learned in the Law of Moses and its interpretations, is very satisfied with the answer.

The observances of the Mosaic Covenant were and are complex and elaborate, much more so than Catholic observances have ever been. It is not to be wondered at that the question the scribe asked represented a persistent scribal concern: was there a way to reduce the complexity of the commandments to a central guiding principle from which the whole of the Law could be derived or elaborated. All of us feel that tension sometimes between the complexity and multiplicity of the demands made on us and the need for a single guiding principle to cope with it all. It seems that in religious traditions there is always a temptation to simplify too far, reducing all either to a facile command to love and serve God (with not much content in it) or to be a good moral person (with no relationship to God in it). History and contemporary society are replete with examples of both a reduction to mere religiosity and a reduction to secularity, both in the Jewish and in the Christian community.

It is certainly not by accident that the focus of Jesus on the centrality and inseparability of the two great commandments of love is mentioned several times in different contexts in the Gospels and becomes a kind of refrain of the New Testament Letters of John. We seem very often to be in the position of the scribe of this story. We are in danger of missing the wood for the trees, and when we see our way of life reduced to basic principles we want an assurance that we have not lost the essentials. Those of us who are theologically sophisticated seem to be the most at risk of making the matter unnecessarily complicated or unnecessarily uncertain, because we are so far away from what we learned when we were seven and have constructed so much complexity over it since. There is something delightfully refreshing in the relief of the scribe when he recognizes the obvious rightness of the answer that Jesus gives—rightness both in terms of fidelity to the traditions of the past and in terms of adequacy to the challenge and possibilities of the future. There is something relaxing and cheerful about it.

Thirty-second Sunday of the Year

READINGS: I Kgs 17:10-16; Heb 9:24-28; Mk 12:38-44 (or 41-44).

Those others who have given had more than enough, but she, with less than enough, has given all that she had to live on. Mk 12:44.

The liturgy draws our attention to the second half of the Gospel reading by setting it alongside of the story of the widow of Zarephath in I Kings. In that story God directs Elijah to seek food during the famine not from some wealthy family that might well have stores put away, but from the proverbially poor, the widow with a single young child. According to this text, God, the provider of all good things, expects a generous response and willingness to share not from those who are amply endowed but from those who have less. In the story, the prophet is not turned away, just as in the Gospel the widow does not refuse God hospitality but contributes out of her desperately needy situation to the furnishing of an earthly dwelling for God's glory among the people.

All who have lived and worked among the poor have at some time come to wonder at the generosity and sharing of those who have least. It may well be that such people cannot trust in their possessions or in the power or status that possessions can command, and that therefore they know their own dependence and are ready to place their trust in people, in sharing, in community, in divine providence. In any case, it is clear that Jesus, as he stands opposite the temple treasury chest with his disciples, watching people file past to make their contributions, wants to challenge all his followers as to how they value those contributions. It is not the money value of the gifts that makes the true splendor of the divine dwelling among the people, but the self-dedication that is expressed in those gifts.

It is so easy for us to assent to that evaluation in principle, yet it slips away from us so quickly in practice. We all tend to value the contributions people make to the parish, the country, the family, or to any other enterprise by their material content, their market value, their cash equivalent, even while we know how arbitrary that equation is. The remark that Jesus makes in this passage seems so casual, so unpremeditated, that it might well slip by without our realizing that he is asking us to turn our whole sense of values and of social order upside-down. It is an appeal to our imagination to construct the meaning of society and social relations in a whole new way.

There is an unexpected consonance of this with the passage from Hebrews. The author of that document seems to intend the passage we read today as a quick summary of what has gone before, but in the liturgical context in which we read it, Jesus himself comes to look very much like the poor widows of I Kings and Mark 12, contributing the last things they have. What Jesus has offered effects reconciliation once and for all, because it is neither symbol nor title but the whole reality of himself. It is the gift of the poor because he did not die as the victorious warrior in a great battle of national liberation, nor did he negotiate from a position of wealth, power or prestige. The life that he surrendered when he died was stripped down to the simply human. The unimportance of Jesus by any ordinary human standard is a scandal that we have forgotten, and that forgetting may tend to obscure our christian evaluation of other people.

Although these readings really carry a far-reaching challenge to rethink our hierarchy of values, they might leave a bland and sentimental admiration for heroic generosity on the part of needy people, if the shorter version of the Gospel selection is read. The additional verses in the longer version are anything but bland. The novels of Dickens, the early drawings of Van Gogh, and the diatribes of Marx are mild in their social criticism beside the comments of Jesus about those who take advantage of the poor and oppressed in the name of religion. Evidently, for Jesus, it is one thing to admire the generosity of the poor, their willing hospitality, their eagerness to sacrifice their own resources to contribute to beautiful liturgies and magnificent places of worship, but it is quite another thing to accept the reverence and the sacrifices of the poor to build up one's social standing and privilege.

Actually, Jesus seems to issue two warnings in the first half of the longer Gospel selection. The first warning is to the crowds of ordinary people who are listening to him, that they should beware of people who claim special respect because of their religious functions or observances. We are not told here why we should beware of them, though the context in Chapter 12 seems to suggest a danger of being led astray. The second warning goes directly to those who oppress the poor in the name of religion. It is a warning that they should expect a terrible judgment.

These Scripture passages, taken together, seem to confront us with some incisive questions: "Where do you stand? In what or whom do you place your trust? How do you respond to those in need?"

Thirty-third Sunday of the Year

READINGS: Dan 12:1-3; Heb 10:11-14, 18; Mk 13:24-32.

The present generation will live to see it all. Heaven and earth will pass away; my words will never pass away. But about that day or that hour no one knows, not even the angels in heaven, not even the Son; only the Father Mk 13:30-32.

In our nuclear age there has been renewed interest in the apocalyptic passages of the scriptures, and often enough that interest has assumed a fundamentalist interpretation of those passages. Curiosity about the future and speculation about the chronological beginning and end of the human species is not surprising at any time and certainly inevitable in our time of extended technical capacity both to create and to destroy. However, a fundamentalist reading of biblical apocalyptic is to be avoided on two counts. In the first place, it destroys the meaning of the scriptures—the meaning of the original composers, the meaning of the Church that included the texts in the canon of scripture, and the meaning that the liturgy presents by the way the texts are selected and juxtaposed. Secondly, a fundamentalist reading is to be avoided because it tends to bypass or deny human responsibility for the course of human history, for instance for the outcome of the nuclear armaments race.

Yet these passages clearly have a meaning that is important for Christian life; otherwise they would not be in the canon and in the liturgy. The reading from Daniel is a poetic ending to a prophetic utterance that tells of wars and very great sufferings. Yet these concluding verses frame all the suffering and fear within a hope and a promise that surpass everything. Michael, leader of the heavenly host will come to the defense of the people, the dead will rise, and wise, just leaders will be forever recognized as such and honored. If we ask ourselves what this message and promise might mean to us now, thousands of years later, it does seem that they speak of a divine providence that has not abandoned human history, a God who has not lost control. These verses hold out great promise of ultimate vindication of those whose "names are written in the book", supposedly the just who place their trust in God as Redeemer, no matter what the events and circumstances of history.

The passage from Hebrews, though not directly related, makes a similar point. We are not caught in an endless cycle of repetitions of the same tragedies and disasters, the same sins and reconciliations. Christ has changed the possibilities of the human future once and for all. Quoting the vivid imagery of Psalm 110, this reading depicts Jesus as enthroned at the right hand of the Father, waiting calmly for all the enemies to be subdued, to be "made his footstool." Again, when we ask what this really means for us in practical terms, we cannot escape the realization that it is offered as a guarantee, a promise of ultimate victory, ultimate fulfillment.

All this is strengthened by the Gospel reading. Mark offers the same recognition of disasters, terrible sufferings, historical tragedies, and the same reassurance that precisely in the midst of all that agony, the Son of Man will come in power and glory, initiating a final judgment and resolution. Indeed, Mark goes so far as to say that in great conflicts and disasters we should see signs of the coming end.

The cosmic imagery that is used is a kind of mosaic of references to the language of expectation in the Hebrew Scriptures, and the point that is being made has to do with the urgency, the immediacy of the end-time and the resolution. But it seems to be a promise, not a threat. Christians of the late first century would probably have read this passage in the light of the destruction of Jerusalem in the year seventy. Yet the emphasis on the present generation as witnesses and participants is as relevant now as then, for none of us is so placed in history as to escape the ultimacy of the exigence or the finality of the promise. Every present generation will live to see it—will live to see the transcience of everything except the divine fidelity, the divine word.

The temptation to treat such texts as mysterious predictions, soothsayings, must have been strong from the beginning, because Mark assures us that Jesus himself insisted that it was quite useless to speculate about when things would happen or how the end would come—to try to calculate this from prophecies or decipher it by breaking some esoteric code. The point rather, is that we are to be alert at all times, living in the awareness of the coming judgment and salvation. The texts are meant to tell us that the end is always imminent. One could, of course, respond to this in two quite different ways. On the one hand, one could assume that human history has been taken out of our hands and we are left with neither freedom nor responsibility in the public sphere, for the destiny of the world is predetermined. But this is certainly not what is intended. One can, on the contrary, see in these texts that kind of divine assurance which validates all action for peace and social justice and betterment, simply by giving the assurance that it is not in vain because the divine power works within our freedom towards the coming end.

The Last Sunday of the Year: The Feast of Christ the King

READINGS: Dan 7:13-14; Rev 1:5-8; Jn 18:33-37.

My kingdom does not belong to this world. If it did , my followers would be fighting to save me from arrest by the Jews. My authority comes from elsewhere. Jn 18:36.

The conversation of Jesus with Pilate in John's Gospel is perhaps the most important conversation ever captured in literature. It allows much scope to imaginative interpretation. Christian fantasy has run riot through the ages filling in the character and motivation of Pilate. Less obviously, Christians have used their imagination to supply the meaning of Jesus' qualified disclaimer, and unwittingly they have projected back into the scriptures notions of the kingdom of heaven drawn from later experience. None of us can avoid this kind of projection of meaning into the text, so it may seem that the best recourse is scholarly analysis. However, a survey of standard commentaries on this text leaves the reader very disappointed. In fact, the text can only be read in the context of living faith, that is to say in the context of our own experience as we live, or try to live, the implications of our faith in Jesus as Christ.

As always, the liturgy gives some direction to our interpretation by the juxtaposition of the texts for the day's Eucharist. Daniel's vision is placed within the context of a heavenly court sitting in judgment and apparently surveying in an apocalyptic sequence the drama of human history in which great oppressive powers (conquering kingdoms) are finally totally destroyed. At last there appears the figure of a man, mysterious, coming in the clouds of heaven (unlike the monstrous beasts who are destroyed in this vision, and who came from below). Presented before God, the Ancient of Days, this mysterious one has ultimate kingly authority vested in him over all peoples, for all time, in full measure. The imagery is one of power and splendor and peace—divine vindication of God's people and the resolution of conflict. It is a vision offered as consolation to those suffering persecution. The particular Gospel text of John does not seem to intend direct reference to that vision of Daniel, but the Church's juxtaposition of the two texts in the liturgy gives a new aspect to the conversation.

The passage from Revelation does intend to refer to Daniel's vision, and intends to interpret it with reference to Jesus, crucified and risen as the firstborn of the dead, to assume the rule over all the kingdoms. Thus, this text sees the powers of evil and destruction as already conquered. It is not any of the great emperors, not Caesar, who rules, but God who rules through the person of Jesus who has come and who is yet to come in full realization of Daniel's vision— Jesus who is yet coming with the clouds, drawing together the beginning and the end. Like Daniel's vision, this text is a message of consolation to the faithful who suffer persecution, and who cannot see much practical change in the world as the outcome of divine redemption.

Reading the gospel text in the light of the other two selections, we are still confronted with the question about the disclaimer that Jesus makes, saying that his kingdom is not of this world. Does it mean that we should not expect redemption to happen within history, in the affairs of the world of our experience in the way power is wielded over peoples and nations, in access to the resources of creation? In Daniel's vision the distinction is not between a world of historical human experience and another realm that is outside history and inaccessible to experience. The contrast is between the oppression of the present and the vindication or liberation that is to come in the future. In the passage from Revelation there is a similar contrast. But both these texts speak of a power above the powers of kings, not of one kingly power among others.

Pilate's question is a political one—whether Jesus is a claimant to the throne of Israel, and therefore is likely to organize an insurrection against Rome. Some translators have noted that there seems to be emphasis on "you" in Pilate's question, "Are *you* the king of the Jews?", suggesting that Jesus is a very unlikely candidate. Jesus asks what Pilate really understands by the question, and explains that the term kingdom (introduced, as the narrative implies, by his enemies) has to be understood rather differently from the way Pilate assumes. Indeed a little later in the account, Jesus points out that it is not he who introduced the word "king" into the conversation, and that he is aware that it can easily be misunderstood. In that context, "not of the world" bears reference to the meaning and implications which the words "king" and "kingdom" would ordinarily have for a Gentile of the ancient world. What it is that is set in contrast to this Gentile understanding, could only be understood in the light of that long Hebrew tradition that speaks of the Kingship of God and of how that divine rule is quite different in its way of working and in its effects, from the sort of government we have come to expect from our fellow human beings.

John's Gospel seems, however, to suggest that a shortcut to understanding what it means is to be found in the person of Jesus himself as witness to the truth of our existence, to the fidelity of God, to the divine order of creation and grace, to the demands of the love of God and the love of every other human being in practically effective ways. If we are tempted, then, to suppose that "not of this world" means that change is not be be expected in the public affairs of the world as we know it, we should perhaps ask ourselves whether that interpretation could be influenced by self-interest—by fear of what advantages and privileges we might lose in the context of a different kind of kingship.

Year C

First Sunday of Advent

READINGS: Jer 33:14-16; I Thess 3:12-4:2; Lk 21:25-28, 34-36.

When all this begins to happen, stand upright and hold your heads high, because your liberation is near. . . . *Be on the alert, praying at all times for strength to pass safely through all these imminent troubles and to stand in the presence of the Son of Man.* Lk 21:28, 36.

At this time of year, the crops have been harvested and stowed and shipped; the leaves have been raked; most of us have resigned ourselves to rain or snow and winter storms; and we have, so to speak, battened down the hatches and withdrawn into the relative privacy of winter. But it is precisely at this time that the Church's year begins with enthusiasm and great momentum, warning against any sense that things are over, that we can relax and let the world go its own way out in the storm.

Year after year, commercial advertising flavors this season with a wistful backward glance—a nostalgia for childhood, for times of simpler living and closer families, for wonderful folk festivals and celebrations, indeed for times that never actually were. And year after year, the liturgy calls us to look forward, placing those wonderful times where they really belong—in the days that are coming, the days of the Lord, the days of salvation. The Church's Advent season is an invitation to hope, and that is always an invitation both to trust and to action. It is an invitation that summons jaded and shrunken desires to new vigor and boldness.

The reading from Jeremiah promises fulfillment of all the divine promises. But this passage is explicit about what those promises are. A just ruler is to arise among the people, a "branch from the house of David." This ruler is to maintain law in the land—the divine Law of the Covenant, the true Law that really maintains justice in the nation. Under such a rule the people will live, safe and undisturbed. The implication that is taken for granted here seems to be that where there is not true justice, where the law that is administered is not truly the law of God, there will be no peace and no national security.

As always happens with the letters of the New Testament, the reading from I Thessalonians brings the matter to the immediately concrete, practical level. Paul wishes and prays for this community that their loving concern for one another may grow, overflowing in non-exclusive caring for the needs of others. Paul has passed on the "tradition of the way." It is the way of building up a whole new style of human community from the grassroots—in the face of persecution, indifference, mistakes and failures. Paul writes to keep the hope and the vision alive within the community. His word of encouragement is that the Lord Jesus is coming to meet them. It is not, therefore, as though all depended on them, yet neither is it a matter of the fulfillment of the promises, the just rule and all-embracing peace and well-being, simply dropping out of heaven like a blanket of snow without any real transformation or conversion of human society.

It is to keep this delicate balance between the all-embracing mercy of God and the inescapable divine exigence of human conversion, that we have Scripture passages such as today's reading from Luke. The apocalyptic images that speak of portents in sun and moon and stars and general confusion on earth, are certainly a way of expressing the ultimate confrontation that is bound to come between good and evil, and the ultimate power of God over all creation and all history. But the warning and advice that is interspersed in the apocalyptic passages is focused very clearly on human responsibility and graced human freedom. Because of this focus, it is really important not just to let these passages slide by us, considering them as quaint and out moded expressions of cosmology and the resolution of history. Moreover, because of this focus it is also important not to read the apocalyptic images in a fundamentalist sense, trying to decipher their occurrence in history. These images and warnings are presented to us in the Scriptures because they are always apt— because all of us at all times in history are confronted both with immediate and with ultimate promises, decisions and outcomes.

It has sometimes been suggested that apocalyptic is a style of religious thinking that is adopted when historical hope is lost—a fanciful compensation for a world of human affairs, political, social and economic, which is lost to evil or chaos, and which is not expected to be within the redeeming power of God. This kind of thinking carried the suggestion that there are other gods besides the one God, and that these antagonistic gods fight in the heavens, each maintaining a separate preserve until some post-historical, more or less mythical grand finale in which the one God finally conquers.

But it is possible to understand apocalyptic quite differently, precisely as a commentary on the present historical struggle. These are always in some sense the last times. These are always the days that are coming. Power is always being given to the servants of God to do the divine will in human society in all its structures—but with conflict, with suffering, with patience to do the "do-able" while awaiting the coming Lord, knowing that liberation is always near.

Second Sunday of Advent

READINGS: Bar 5:1-9; Phil 1:3-6, 8-11; Lk 3:1-6.

Prepare a way for the Lord: clear a straight path for him. Every ravine shall be filled in, and every mountain and hill levelled; the corners shall be straightened, and the rugged ways made smooth; and all mankind shall see God's deliverance. Lk 3:4-6.

This message must have been charged with tense longing and expectation for Israel's weary exiles; the straightening and smoothing of the way home appears at least four times in the canonical Scriptures: in Baruch's prophecy, in the second and again in the third Isaian collection, and in Luke's Gospel, not to mention another appearance in the Psalms of Solomon which were not included in the Canon. Even though there have been huge and terrible migrations of conquered refugee populations in our time, for most of us today in the West it is not easy to imagine the weariness and dangers and many sufferings of a long journey by foot over rocky terrain without paved roads, dragging food supplies and household belongings up and down steep slopes, bumping along over the uneven ground. For those who are still culturally close to that experience, the words of the prophetic voice in the wilderness truly speak of salvation, revealing a compassionate and welcoming God.

In the prophecy of Baruch, the promise seems to picture salvation simply in terms of the ingathering of the oppressed and scattered exiles to be once more God's people, living by the covenant. In times of acute suffering people usually see salvation in terms of the ending of that particular suffering. Then, as now, both Jews and their Gentile neighbors and friends were to discover that salvation is more than return to the land, ingathering of the people and political independence. It is not as simple or as one-dimensional as that.

When we meet the promise and the dream of rescue again in the same imagery in the Gospel of Luke, it is applied to the ministry of John the Baptist, who preaches a baptism or rebirth of personal conversion and forgiveness of sins, for the rebuilding of the people. The passage is introduced with great solemnity, locating the preaching of John very formally in the history of the nations, dating it with reference to emperor, governor, princes and high priest, as though this had at one time been intended as the beginning of Luke's Gospel. If so, it begins with a great proclamation of the salvation that is to come, straightening out the problems, making the way smooth. It is a proclamation which encourages all to repentance by an assurance that salvation is imminent.

In the preaching of the Baptist, repentance is not passive nor remote from the practical everyday life. John's idea of repentance is that those who have more than they really need should share with those who do not have the necessities of life, that those who have the advantage in business relations should refrain from making unjust profit at the expense of the poor, and that those who wield military might should refrain from bullying and manipulating the powerless. So Luke's Gospel reports it, though today's selection stops before we discover the concrete content of the conversion that John preached.

Although the imagery of hope is the same as in the reading from Baruch, there is a deeper, more personal, more exigent understanding of what the promises mean and what they ask of the faithful.

The passage from Philippians speaks also of the expectation of the coming salvation, identified here with the Day of Christ that is yet to come. Paul writes from prison, but his letter echoes and magifies the optimism of the other two passages. In spite of persecution and all manner of sufferings—or perhaps even because of these—Paul seems to be convinced that the rough ways have already become noticeably smoother. He writes of his joyful confidence that what has begun in the community is moving towards its completion in the day of the Lord Jesus—love growing richer in knowledge and insight, bringing true discernment. Perhaps it is because Paul had been growing in that discernment himself that he is able to be so optimistic about the transformation of the community, moving towards the fulfillment of the promises.

In our own world and times, as in the three situations of which these three readings tell, it is possible to look at the same set of circumstances in two quite different ways. It is possible to see the flaws and difficulties and tragedies, and to take the world for granted as it is, settling for an uneasy compromise in which one gets the most one can out of it for oneself and one's family, on the plea that the world as a whole is doomed to be forever unjust and tragic. It is also possible to look at the same situation and, drawing one's vision from one's own experience of conversion and transformation, to see the world and its history transparent to the overwhelming power of God's compassion, and therefore to find every strategy for peace and justice worth the attempt, and every labor for the relief of suffering worth the effort. It is possible to be quite practical and realistic about the world of our own time and yet listen to the voice in the wilderness.

Third Sunday of Advent (Gaudete)

READINGS: Zeph 3:14-18; Phil 4:4-7; Lk 3:10-18.

The people asked him "Then what are we to do?" He replied, "The man with two shirts must share with him who has none, and anyone who has food must do the same." Lk 3:10-11.

At first sight there seems to be a curious contradiction between the joyful promises of the other two readings and the harsh demands of this Gospel. When we read the passage of Zephaniah in its original context, however, there is more connection than at first appears. This text is part of a prophecy of consolation, giving assurance that peace and modest prosperity will return to Jerusalem, but the prelude proclaims that the proud and arrogant who have flaunted their pride and self-sufficiency against God shall be removed. It is after their departure when the poor inherit the city that all will begin to go well, and the poor will be confident because their trust will be in God. It is a message which applies in some way to every time and place in human history.

When Paul, in his letter to the Philippians, wishes them all joy in the Lord, and again urges them to be joyful, he urges them as though continuing the same thought, and in the same breath, to be magnanimous towards all, for the Lord is near and they should have no anxiety about anything, but in all things turn confidently to God in prayer with thanksgiving. Both readings seem to make an immediate connection between joy and confidence in God on the one hand and generosity towards other people in various ways on the other. To open one's heart and life to the peace of God which Paul describes as being beyond all understanding, leaves no room for the pettiness about possessions, relationships and status which are the basis of most anxieties and tension between people. Awareness of any great gift usually opens the way for generosity towards others.

This would, however, be easier to assimilate if John's words in Luke's Gospel were not quite so concrete. Most of us, after all, have a lot of shirts, and money in the bank to buy more. It boggles the imagination to think what would happen next if, adding a few more examples, those who have two cars should rush out upon this Sunday to find some poor immigrant family that cannot buy a car and needs one badly to get to a job. One wonders what would happen if those who own a vacation house should quickly inquire after a homeless family who might be installed there. With some flights of the imagination we might picture ourselves turning the clothes out of our closets, the food out of our freezers, furniture and utensils and valuables out of our homes, and finding ourselves surrounded by a very peaceful simplicity. According to the Baptist we would then be ready for the day of the Lord.

It is an interesting fantasy, but it does capture something of the magic of that Christmas that always somehow eludes us. The figure of the Baptist seems to say to us that if the full realization of God's coming to us continues to elude us, it may be because we are too busy defending our possessions, our privileges and our power against the dispossessed. And if the thought of coming judgment is one that inspires fear more than hope, this in itself indicates where our choices lie in relation to God's Reign.

It may be necessary to make some very radical changes and renunciations before we find all our joy in the Lord.

Fourth Sunday of Advent

READINGS: Mic 5:1-4; Heb 10:5-10; Lk 1:39-45.

But you, Bethlehem, in Ephrathah, small as you are to be among Judah's clans, out of you shall come forth a governor for Israel, one whose roots are far back in the past, in days gone by. Mic 5:2.

The day's readings give us three diverse proclamations of the coming savior. The first, in the prophecy of Micah, had of course an original reference quite different from that which Christians see in it. It is part of a poem which promises the restoration of the royal house of David, probably in the near future. It promises a worthy king under whom the exiles will be reunited with their own people. This text is a passage which from earliest times Christians have applied to Jesus as the chosen one of God, chosen to fulfill the promises to the whole people and to the house of David in particular. It speaks of the ruler as one who comes in the strength of the Lord and conducts himself as a shepherd of the people.

The letter to the Hebrews speaks also of the coming of Jesus, but under the imagery of sacrifice and priesthood, in the ultimate simplicity of sacrifice which is complete self-surrender to the will of God in the world. And in that simplicity lies its definitive, once-for-all character. It is a theme that we have met in the readings from Hebrews many times throughout the fall, but its new juxtaposition with the proclamations of the imminent coming of the Lord both them and now give the theme a new relevance. We see that once-for-all coming of Jesus not only as an event in the past, but as an event that is before us to enter into in our own lifetime, in our own present.

The imagery of priesthood and sacrifice should not be seen primarily in terms of a ritual slaughtering, but rather in terms of mediation between God and human persons. This mediation effects a reconciliation, and ushers in an era of peace and well-being, because reconciliation with God is a precondition for peace and justice among peoples.

The third proclamation is a passage, a story, so familiar that there is always the danger that we might not take it seriously. It is all too easy to confuse familiarity with understanding, and acquaintance with assimilation of the message. Certainly, it is a story about the purpose of God in which Mary and Elizabeth represent the new and the ancient covenants, John rising from within the ancient covenant to testify to the coming savior. Indeed, the response attributed here to John is reminiscent of the leaping for joy attributed by the Hebrew Scriptures to the poor when they hear the promise of God's salvation. But it is clear that Bible and liturgy present us with this story that we might place ourselves within it and ask whether we also are ready to leap with joy at the prospect of the Lord's coming to us. The story questions whether our values and hopes are such that we have cause to rejoice beyond measure at the news that he will shortly appear.

The story of Mary and Elizabeth is too easily seen as one about the past. The tradition of Israel had long been without a prophet, like the elderly and barren Elizabeth. The young community and new tradition of the followers of Jesus brings new hope to the old, bringing it to fulfillment, as Mary brings the unborn savior to Elizabeth's house. This certainly bears a message about our relationship as Christians to the traditions of Israel. But it does not stop there. It also suggests that now and always we must be ready to be surprised by the redeeming power of God as it breaks through in unexpected places where for us also Christ shall appear.

Christmas

READINGS: At Midnight: Is 9:1-6; Tit 2:11-14; Lk 2:1-14.
At Dawn: Is 62:11-12; Tit 3:4-7; Lk 2:15-20.

The people who walked in darkness have seen a great light: light has dawned upon them, dwellers in a land as dark as death. Is 9:2.

Although we now have a three year cycle of readings, those for Christmas continue to be the same familiar ones which we heard last year and so many times before. That may be just as well; for many of us who have celebrated the Christmas liturgy for more years than we may care to count, those readings have taken on an aura of connotation and affectivity that is all the more effective because we could not really spell it out. Yet in our distracted times, meditation on the Christmas texts is an urgent demand of a Christian life, especially perhaps for those who do not have many years of celebration behind them to shape their response to the Christmas mystery.

The first Isaian reading sets the tone. It is a poem celebrating the end of a time of terrible suffering. It speaks of darkness and dawn; new light is showing on the horizon, there is reason to hope, a dynamic thrust towards better times, and the newborn crown prince is the token of it. Paul's letter to Titus maintains that we are in a similar situation of dawn and promise, and that Christ who is yet to come in the fullness of his splendor is the token of that hope held out to us. The selection from Luke's Gospel completes the Pauline assertion; the Gospel recites for us the solemn proclamation of the birth of Jesus and the hope that is the outcome of it. Carefully it places the event of the birth of Jesus in the context of the public and secular history of the world, because the light and hope it sheds is for the whole public and secular history of the world.

The readings at dawn echo almost exactly those of the Midnight celebration. The reading from the last Isaian collection expresses dogged hope to a people struggling against discouragement in a difficult time. The passage summarizes a long argument giving reasons for the hope that God will again visit the people as its savior. The corresponding reading from the letter to Titus also summarizes the reason for hope: the dawn of a new age comes not because of our merits but because of the merciful kindness and generosity of God which we have already had cause to know in our lives. How clearly that is so is expressed in the Lukan account of the shepherds' visit to the newborn child. We have here an account of the encounter between the grace of God and the wretched of the earth, for shepherds were no privileged or well-regarded class of people. In fact, while we tend to associate Christmas with a kind of escape from the demands of the everyday world and its problems, the biblical readings combine limitless hope with a ruggedly realistic view of what is going on in the world.

Christmas Day

READINGS: Is 52:7-10; Heb 1:1-6; Jn 1:1-18 (or 1-5, 9-14).

Hark, your watchmen raise their voices and shout together in triumph; for with their own eyes they shall see the Lord returning in pity to Zion.

Is 52:8.

At first sight the readings for the Eucharist celebrated during the day seem to lack the affective import of the midnight and dawn readings, and perhaps those who celebrate the Christmas Eucharist only during the day should really read and reflect upon those earlier readings. Yet the themes of these readings are really the same as those others. The reading from the Second Isaiah is part of a hymn of praise of the pilgrim people finally able to return to the holy city and strongly convinced that God is in their midst on the march. The reading from Hebrews sums up the whole meaning for us of the coming of Jesus Christ into our history and all the confusion of our world with its twisted history of sin and destruction. This reading sets the event of Christ's coming in a grand cosmic perspective, bringing together the creation and the redemption, and showing Jesus as the first-born of all creation, set above the whole realm of spiritual creation, linking the human race directly to God.

John's Prologue also, which has regained its freshness now that we have long ceased to hear it at the end of every Eucharist, is preoccupied with the grand architectonic scheme of redemption. Here the image of dawning light is linked to the notion of eternal light and to that of light as the beginning of the creation. The light which was at the beginning and was the divine light, now returns. Similarly the Word which was at the beginning and which is the divine word, now emerges from the midst of history as God's word returning.

The metaphors of light and word in relation to Jesus have become so commonplace, that most of us seem to need a reminder of their original force, and that is what the Christmas readings and the whole Christmas feast offer. We are in all seriousness, and in the real situations of the real world, invited to listen to what God is saying to us in the person of Jesus because that person really is God's word to us and contains the whole of revelation in its essence. We are seriously, and in the most practical sense, invited to see everyday life and public and secular affairs in the light of Jesus, because that is really the divine light shed on human affairs to make sense of them. And that is Christmas—the mystery of the Lord's returning.

Feast of the Holy Family

READINGS: Sir 3:2-6, 12-14; Col 3:12-21; Lk 2:41-52.

It is the Lord's will that a father should be honored by his children, and a mother's rights recognized by her sons. Respect for a father atones for sins, and to honor your mother is to lay up a fortune. Sir 3:2-3.

The temptation inherent in the feast of the Holy Family is to do a great deal of inappropriate moralizing. The Wisdom of Sirach seems to give an opening for such moralizing, but it also offers something deeper and more valuable. It links some common sense observations on the functioning of human society with the divine pattern of creation and the working of divine providence. We are so constituted that the quality of our lives is expressed and shaped by our relationships. Acknowledgement of dependence and interdependence is a necessary condition for a true and confident self-image and identity, and gratitude and happiness are almost the same thing. Sirach takes traditional human wisdom and links it to divine command, whence it flows originally.

The reading from Colossians expands that understanding to the community of believers in all their relationships with one another, seeing them as called to be interdependent members of a single body. In the community sketched by this text, it is overflowing gratitude to God the Creator and to Jesus Christ as redeemer that makes such relationships possible. In the passage which follows, of which today's liturgy offers us only a small section, existing relationships in society are taken for granted (including even that of slavery), but the message of the text concerns the way in which these social structures can be completely transformed when placed within the covenant of creation and the mystery of redemption, because then gratitude and reverence pervade all relationships.

The Gospel reading is chosen for this day because of the final verses, no doubt. These verses refer to the human maturing of Jesus within the context of his family and tradition. Actually, we know very little about the private life of Jesus and his family; those early writings of the Christian community which purported to tell us much more to satisfy our curiosity were judged unfit for inclusion among the canonical Gospels. That seems to suggest that detailed information about the Holy Family is not useful for salvation. What is useful is the simple fact that God's grace and salvation came to us in the person of Jesus Christ, whose own human identity unfolded within the ordinary patterns of human relationships. Moreover, this reading portrays tension between particular human bonds and the total exigence of divine vocation. It suggests at one and the same time both that the calling of Jesus is unique and that his life and experience is typical of human experience, linking him with all of us by ordinary human bonds.

We are perhaps so much concerned with Church and sacramental worship that it is easy to forget that the redemption is concerned with the whole of life and with the most ordinary of our relationships. Before God and in truth there is no profane sphere of life, but all is originally in God's gracious plan and redemptively called into the new creation. Salvation is effected and expressed in human bonds.

Solemnity of Mary the Mother of God, and Giving of the Name Jesus

READINGS: Num 6:22-27; Gal 4:4-7; Lk 2:16-21.

Eight days later the time came to circumcise him, and he was given the name Jesus, the name given by the angel before he was conceived. Lk 2:21.

In the Hebrew Scriptures the giving of a name often expresses the role that someone is going to play or is expected to play. Jesus, or Yeshua, expresses both the fulfillment of prophecy and a further prophetic promise, in spite of the fact that the name was not uncommon at that time. Because we are expected to pick up all manner of allusions to texts and figures of the Hebrew Scriptures, the account of the naming is a single sentence added to the story of the birth and the shepherd's visit, and out of this text the liturgy of the day draws a second theme, that of the maternity of Mary.

The first reading, from Numbers, prepares us for the importance attached to names by invoking with great reverence and gratitude the name of God, not so that it is spoken, but by the promise that one day Israel will be greatly blessed by the pronouncing of the divine name over the people. Although this is in no way the original meaning of the text, the liturgy clearly invites the Christian imagination to hear that blessed pronouncing of the divine name over the people fulfilled in the name of Jesus. Indeed in the risen Christ the name of Jesus is linked by his early followers with the "name above all names," *kyrios,* Lord, the divine name. It is, perhaps, because this association comes spontaneously and almost unnoticed to Christians, that the liturgy combines the feast of the name, Jesus, with that of Mary, Mother of God, which makes a far larger claim for Jesus than is contained in his given name.

It seems to be the same easy association that leads to the use of this text from Galatians to bind together the themes of Jesus as savior and of Mary as Mother of God, reading back into Paul's argument about Christian freedom from the Mosaic Law, the doctrine of the divinity of Jesus as it was defined centuries later at the Council of Ephesus.

These texts, as the liturgy uses and juxtaposes them, seem to invite us to meditate on the Scriptures with a certain freedom and self-involvement that goes far beyond what a Scripture scholar could determine as the original meaning of the texts, asking not only what they meant then, but also what they mean now, and asking ourselves how the Hebrew sense of the name, Jesus, combines in our Christian vision with the claim that Mary is Mother of God.

Yet in its own simple form, the name of Jesus has long been the basis of prayer—even of mystical prayer in the Eastern tradition where the continual repetition of the name is a pattern of contemplation. In the West it has functioned as an ejaculatory prayer. Today's reading serve to give context and depth to such prayer.

Feast of the Epiphany

READINGS: Is 60:1-6; Eph 3:2-3, 5-6; Mt 2:1-12.

Though darkness covers the earth and dark night the nations, the Lord shall shine upon you and over you shall his glory appear; and the nations shall march towards your light and their kings to your sunrise. Is 60:2-3.

The magnificent poetry of the Isaian promise of future youth and restoration is interpreted by the early Christian community as a foreshadowing of the arrival of Jesus in the world. Matthew's recital of the coming and worshiping of the Magi picks up the imagery of heavenly signs and portents, which must have been deeply ingrained in the memory and imagination of those early Christians who were Jews. The liturgy tries to penetrate our memory and imagination with the same symbolism, that we might recapture the wonder and gratitutde necessary to come into the realization of the promises.

The story of the Magi is so strong in its symbolism that it continues even in our own secularized society to inspire great works of art and to appear frequently on Christmas cards. In these day of more advanced astronomy there are even those who strive by scientific calculation to demonstrate the straightforward historicity of the account. But even without taking a fundamentalist reading of the text, contemporary Christians can readily see that both the Isaian author and Matthew are writing of a continuing present in which we also live and act. The experience of darkness covering the earth and dark night the nations is one that is all too real for many peoples of our time, and one which threatens all of us. But likewise God who created all things and gave us the breath of life, calls in our times with the same purpose to take us, so to speak, by the hand, to form us according to the divine covenant as a beacon light to all nations, as hope for the world.

There is another aspect of the story of the Magi that makes it always our own story, and that is the aspect of pilgrimage or quest, the task of discernment, of interpreting the signs—and all this not without encountering the problem of treacherous friendship and dishonest advice as happened to the Magi. The search for the real Jesus Christ, and indeed the real search for Jesus Christ, in our own lives and times is well represented in the story of the Magi's journey. We too are on a quest which requires divine guidance and continuing discernment.

The reading from Ephesians throws yet another light on the story: the divine epiphany, or manifestation, in Jesus is one that calls all the nations together to their joint inheritance of God's peace. The rising of the star that is Jesus himself calls the nations to come to the light, and their rulers to turn to the sunrise that is yet to come. And year by year, as we celebrate this feast and this whole season, we must ask ourselves whether we have really begun to take the call and the promise seriously, or whether we expect our world to go on in its accustomed way, while we celebrate the liturgical feast in private. We have to ask whether, among the nations, we really expect to see the rising of the star.

The Baptism of the Lord

READINGS: Is 42:1-4, 6-7; Acts 10:34-38; Lk 3:15-16, 21-22.

I have bestowed my spirit upon him, and he will make justice shine upon the nations . . . He will plant justice on earth, while coasts and islands wait for his teaching. Is 42:1, 4.

The terse account which the evangelists give us of the Baptism of Jesus by John leaves much to be supplied from the history of Israel and the symbolism of John's actions. People went to John in the wilderness and were immersed by him in the river Jordan. It is reminiscent of the people's wandering in the desert and their first entrance into the Promised Land. Indeed this ritual of baptism in the Jordan suggests a recapitulation of the vocation of Israel, a new response to God's special election of the people to be a chosen witness people. In the Lucan account read today, we see John redirecting his followers' eager attention to one who is to come who will be the center of God's redemptive action. That is how we are introduced to the statement that as Jesus participated prayerfully in this ritual of re-entrance into the calling of Israel, the divine Spirit (the creative breath of God, the spirit of prophecy) came upon him, and a heavenly voice claimed him as the beloved and favored Son.

In the reading from Acts chosen for this day, Peter, in his sermon at the house of Cornelius, sees this moment in the life of Jesus not only as the beginning of Jesus' own ministry of healing and exorcism, but even as the basis for Peter's understanding that there are no limits of race or nation to God's redemptive purpose. God does not play favorites but welcomes all who will receive the Good News, and Peter knows that he may not discriminate where God does not do so.

By the selection of the particular passage from second Isaiah that is read on this Sunday, the liturgy emphasizes the outward thrust of the account of the Baptism and of the implications that Peter draws from it. The Isaian text speaks of justice for the nations, rooted in the first place in the creation and in the breath of life that God breathes into all human persons, and rooted in the second place in the vocation of God's chosen people—endowed with the spirit of God and chosen precisely to bring justice with a special care for the oppressed (the bruised reed, the smoldering wick).

The celebration of the Baptism of Jesus is in a large and practical sense the celebration of the Spirit that is the Spirit of Jesus in which his followers are called to live. As Jesus comes forth from the water to assume the vocation of God's elect for the salvation of the nations, he undertakes a mission that is ultimately to be fulfilled through the gathering of many witnesses. It is a mission to bring the justice and peace of God to the peoples of the earth.

Ash Wednesday

READINGS: Joel 2:12-18; 2 Cor 5:20-6:2; Mt 6:1-6; 16-18.

Rend your hearts and not your garments; turn back to the Lord your God; for he is gracious and compassionate, long suffering and ever constant, always ready to repent of the threatened evil. Joel 2:13.

Lent is, of course, a season of promise and not of threat. The conviction that human affairs can really change for the better is a very cheerful one, and one that is not widely shared. Rending garments is surely a gesture of despair. Rending hearts is an image that is not similarly self-explanatory. In our use of language today the heart represents the affections and the courage of a person. We might then (incorrectly) assume that rending hearts is a matter of feeling dejected and helpless. For the Hebrews heart meant more; it included consciousness, mind-set, attitudes, goals convictions, self-identity. Rending one's heart in this sense, therefore, means opening new horizons, shedding prejudices, recognizing unpalatable truths about one's own positions and claims, becoming aware of the truths and claims of others. It means breaking through obstinate insistence that nothing can be done about situations of human suffering and oppression in family, work situation, neighborhood, city, country and world. It means therefore, new life and hope—turning back to the Lord in confidence that things can really change for the better.

The reading from 2 Corinthians reminds us how clearly this has become possible for us in Christ, not once only in past history but now in our times, in the continuing present of human history empowered by grace. It is a message both powerful and urgent: "do not let it go for nothing; the redemptive power of God is extended through Christ in us to transform the world." But that redeeming power is extended in our freedom, not in ways that by pass our freedom to accomplish human transformation without really transforming people in their experience, their attitudes, and the relationships and the structures of their society. Paul pleads for reflection and response so that we may not be mouthing unfounded claims of a world made new in the resurrection of Jesus.

This is perhaps another angle of view on the matter of the Gospel reading. Lent brings to sharper focus the three basic disciplines of a Christian life: prayer (or broadly speaking, a life of faith and communion with God); fasting (or broadly speaking, renunciation and self-denial that frees people for a clearer and truer focus in their lives); and alms giving (or broadly speaking, outreach to others' need of whatever kind). The Gospel is certainly concerned that none of these things be done for show, to attract attention. But we might take the implications one step further to say that the reality of the redemption is not in ritualism or legalism; it is possible to go through all the motions of a Christian life, carrying all things to great extremes, and yet missing the fundamental reality. Praying is a waste of time if it does not change the worshipper's attitudes, perceptions and outlook. Fasting is a farce if it does not heighten sensitivity to God's call. Charity which leaves the recipient more dependent and diminished as a person or a people, is no expression of divine love. It is the rending of hearts that is the business of Lent, not the rending of garments.

First Sunday of Lent

READINGS: Deut 26:4-10; Rom 10:8-13; Lk 4:1-13.

The faith that leads to righteousness is in the heart, and the confession that leads to salvation is upon the lips. Rom 10:10.

Today's reading from Romans holds a certain temptation to fundamentalism; it is possible to read this passage in a sense in which Paul clearly did not intend it, namely as though salvation depended on a certain inner experience of being saved along with the profession and proclamation of the right words, independently of any real conversion. What Paul seems to have been concerned about was the simplicity and universality of God's offer of salvation in Jesus—precisely a rejection of ritualism and special privilege in favor of real transformation of everyday life.

This offers a certain complementarity with the message from Deuteronomy. The bringing of the basket of first fruits is the occasion for a confession of the merciful intervention of God who summoned homeless nomads, built them into a nation, rescued them when they were cruelly oppressed, and gave them arable land that made them independent of oppressive alien powers. It is a recognition that there are no claims of special privilege before God; all is divine gift to the needy. God is on the side of the needy.

The liturgy suggests these two readings about the nature of salvation as the background for our reflection on the story of the temptations offered to Jesus. The temptation story is also about the nature of salvation—about the ways in which Jesus might have interpreted the divine promises of salvation and his own task, and about the way we may interpret his messianic role in history. It is a matter of temptation in the sense of trial or testing of what is really at stake.

The story leads us through the discernments that Jesus made. It is not enough that there is material plenty in the world or that technology in our own times can solve the problems of human sustenance, if human hearts are not converted to trust and share and use the wealth of creation constructively. It is not enough to have power to compel by the usual patterns of domination, because it is idolatrous to give unquestioning allegiance to anything less than God. Moreover, salvation is not to be expected by some kind of divine miracle that by passes human conversion.

Taken in their inclusive sense, these temptations have a universal quality that makes them a fitting expression of the meaning of Lent as a time of discernment, a time of testing the spirit, a time to scrutinize our own values and expectations.

Second Sunday of Lent

READINGS: Gen 15:5-12, 17-18; Phil 3:17-4:1 (or 3:20-4:1); Lk 9:28-36.

And while he was praying the appearance of his face changed and his clothes became dazzling white. Suddenly there were two men talking with him; these were Moses and Elijah, who appeared in glory and spoke of his departure, the destiny he was to fulfill in Jerusalem. Lk 9:29-31.

Each of today's readings appears to be concerned with a truly extraordinary event. The temptation, therefore, is to become preoccupied with efforts to recapture the original context of the event in pursuit of a more or less archaeological interest, and fall short of uncovering the universal meaning of the text as it applies to ourselves. This is particularly so in the reading from Genesis, where the covenant custom of laying out halves of slaughtered animals is so strange to us that it intrudes itself into the center of attention—an honor that this quaint custom scarcely deserves.

It is enough to note that here is Israel, perhaps as late as the time of Kind David, retelling the story of the ancestor, Abraham. What becomes clear to a meditative gaze backward in time is that all the secular events of exile and struggle, of wandering and poverty, of loneliness and threat of extinction of the people, come into focus together in a moment of truth when seen in terms of the covenant relationship with God. The flaming torch that passes up and down between the halves is the symbol of the transforming presence of God among us. Could we but give it our attention, doubtless we should see that same fiery presence passing up and down in a ritual drawing together of the covenant meaning of our own lives and our own times.

It is the risk of not discerning this with humility and in relation to the cross and resurrection of Jesus, that seems to motivate Paul's writing to the Philippians in this passage. The Philippians were being offered a legalistic interpretation of their lives and calling by the so-called "judaizers" on the one hand, and an ethereal, dualistic and rather self-centered one by certain gnostics on the other hand. For Paul, the passing fire of God's presence is always the experience of the crucified and risen Christ living in the community as both gift and exigence of unity, mutual service and generosity, of joy and reconciliation and understanding, and of constant unquenchable hope. Paul longs for that moment of truth to dawn for all the followers of Jesus, in which the simple practicality and universality of the covenantal relationship will irradiate everything.

The Gospel reading gives us the concrete story that expresses this. Luke's Gospel, like those of Matthew and Mark, places this story immediately after the realization that Jesus is going towards his death by execution. The symbolism of this story or picture is straightforward. The radiant appearance and dazzling white garments imply a moment of revelation, a vision: Moses and Elijah represent the law and the Prophets respectively; the conversation is about the meaning of Jesus' death; and the companions of Jesus perceive it all, waking as it were out of a deep sleep. It is, of course, our story also—the story of the believer at any time and place. Like Peter, any one of us would prefer to cling to the ecstatic revelatory moment, and resists the transition back into the concrete circumstances of daily life. There is a radiant, buoyant simplicity about the moment of truth that eludes us in the struggle of the everyday.

However, the revelation itself in this story can be understood in two quite different ways. It might be viewed in such a way that the ordinary business of life goes on, the little company trudges along on its journeys, performing its everyday tasks in an obscurity that is both external in the society and internal in their own understanding of what it all means. One day from outside their world, from outside their experience and the realm of their own freedom and responsibility, there is a divine invasion—an invasion of an alien force that overwhelms them, though in a friendly fashion. This is all so extraordinary that they know that they have grounds to believe and trust a special message communicated to them, namely that Jesus is in a unique relationship to the heavenly creator, specially chosen, and is therefore to be heard and followed without reservation. The alien invasion then withdraws, leaving behind the message which it has delivered.

We could also look at the revelation quite differently. While his companions are still going about in a deep sleep, as it were, or in a fog, Jesus lives his life prayerfully, looking to the Law and the Prophets for interpretive categories, living his life in dialogue, so to speak, with Moses and Elijah, with the established tradition and the forward thrust. When this brings him to confront the question of his standing with the elders, chief priests and those learned in the Law, and to anticipate the conflict that can lead to execution, his discernment of his way reaches a dazzling moment of clarity. It is a moment so luminous and transparent that his drowsy and befogged companions are startled wide awake and see him and themselves in their true relationships. It is a moment of divine truth clarifying itself within human experience, not as an alien force, but as intrinsic to the human—an empowerment of the human by grace.

Which way we interpret the revelatory moment in this scene may be quite important in determining the way we dispose ourselves to be open in our own lives in moments of truth.

Third Sunday of Lent

READINGS: Ex 3:1-8, 13-15; I Cor 10:1-6, 10-12; Lk 13:1-9.

All these things that happened to them were symbolic, and were recorded for our benefit as a warning. For upon us the fulfillment of the ages has come. If you feel sure that you are standing firm, beware! You may fall.

I Cor 10:11-12.

With those words Paul warns Christians that Scripture is written in such a way as to shed light on the whole human situation in any time and place, that it is important to reflect on the symbolism in which Scripture interprets our situation, and that much of it is paradoxical, being both promise and warning, both gift and exigence. To be overwhelmed with divine favors within the history of the People of God, is not yet to be saved. This last requires also an appropriate response, in the absence of which Paul looks back and sees "the desert strewn with their corpses."

The story of the call of Moses offers a vivid symbolic picture of divine revelation. In the first place there is a call for reflection in the fact that we have spontaneously and traditionally used the symbol of an unending fire—a fire that burns without consuming—both for God and for damnation, damnation being in its essence God rejected and denied but inescapable because of our own contingency. Rabbinic discourse gives us further insight when it asks what was the bush that burned, and suggests in answer that it was Israel which in all its sufferings was not consumed. That is an important insight because it suggests that we in our time are also standing before the burning bush when we switch on our televisions, read our newspapers or walk in the dark forgotten places in our cities.

The question it raises, of course, is whether we hear ourselves called by name, whether we are able to take our shoes off in reverence knowing that we stand on holy ground because it is the whole world which is the place of God. It raises questions also, in a very practical way, whether we realize that the God we worship is the God of Abraham, the God of Isaac, the God of Jacob, whose promises and demands are quite practical and concrete, concerning all aspects of human lives and human society in all its relationships and structures. Further, the text challenges us concerning our worldview and expectations, whether we really believe that a land flowing with milk and honey, that is to say a state of simple sufficiency, is possible for all God's people. Finally the text anticipates our fundamental question by presenting it as a question of Moses also. What is the nature of the ultimate reality on which our existence and our possibilities depend? "I shall be what I shall be"; the only human relationship to God is trust—not a haphazard trust without foundation, but trust based on the promissory events and experiences of the past. The challenge is to act on that trust creatively and redemptively as we have experienced God acting for and within us.

The passage from Luke's Gospel gives an incisive comment on a situation in which most of us often find ourselves. Our newspapers and neighborhoods are sprinkled with disasters and tragedies—murders and suicides, riots and famines, earthquakes and floods. We look out on them through the windows of our security, our otherness, our distance from them. Jesus challenges us to consider on what that security is based. The victims of wars and tragedies, of human violence and of natural disasters, are not selected because they are in any sense worse than we are. Unless we repent of private and public injustices, of individual and social heartlessness, there is no doubt that disaster will engulf everyone sooner or later. Jesus may well have been thinking quite specifically of Israel under Roman occupation and of the possible outcomes of the responses that those around him were making to that occupation. Yet it is equally applicable to the situations with which we have to deal in our times on a local, national or international level.

The Gospel excerpt does not end on this somber note, however, but on its counterpart. There is still a time of grace, a time of opportunity. The possibilities of a history of redemption are still wide open. There is time to repent, to change direction. There is time for new growth and fruitfulness. The bush is still burning unconsumed.

Fourth Sunday of Lent (Laetare)

READINGS: Josh 5:9-12; 2 Cor 5:17-21; Lk 15:1-3, 11-32.

What I mean is, that God was in Christ reconciling the world to himself, no longer holding men's misdeeds against them, and that he has entrusted us with the message of reconciliation. 2 Cor 5:19.

This mid-Lent Sunday which we know traditionally as Laetare Sunday, might with equal aptness be known as Reconciliation Sunday, for that is the drift of all the readings assigned for the Eucharistic celebration of the day. The Passover celebration described in the excerpt from Joshua is a particularly memorable one, for it is the first in the Promised Land. Moreover it celebrates the renewal and rededication of the nation. In the passage preceding the one read in the liturgy, we are told that all who had left Egypt had died in the 40 years of wandering in the wilderness and that their sons, who had been formed in the desert experience of total reliance on God, had been uncircumcised on the journey. Now all were circumcised in rededication to the covenant of God and in readiness for entering the Promised Land. When they crossed the Jordan river they encamped in the plain of Jericho to celebrate the Passover for the first time with the produce of that land. It had been a long pilgrimage but in the end God had brought them home.

Such a story of wandering far afield in order ultimately to come home to a great reconciliation, is in a sense the human story in the history of the world and in individual histories. It is the story that Jesus tells as his key defense of the company he keeps and of the way he sets about his ministry. The central part of the reading from Luke's Gospel is a moving story. An alienated younger son (a teenager? one wonders) demands the kind of freedom none of us can ever really have—unsituated freedom, freedom without boundaries, freedom without consideration for other people. Against the law of the time, (yet not altogether against the usage of the society in which Jesus lived), the young man asks and receives the legal release of his future share of the farm, converts it into cash and is off to the city to spend it. The prospect of the breaking up of the farm on the father's death could not but be matter of considerable anxiety to the whole family. Times were hard in any case, and the smaller the unit, the more vulnerable it would be economically. The desirable arrangement was for brothers to farm together without breaking up the patrimony. The younger son's departure is an act of rebellion and defiance which has destructive consequences for those he leaves behind. It has terrible consequences for him also, for it is a journey into disaster.

As Jesus views this situation, it is the young man's suffering that shows him his alienation, his disorientation, but it is his confident expectation of the father's welcome that brings him to turn around and retrace his steps. When he does so, the father is interested in one thing only, and that is the return. The elaborate planned confession of the son's misdeeds and his changed status is swept aside as irrelevant to the reconciliation. The return in itself is the reconciliation and cause for great rejoicing and festivities.

But perhaps the most important parts of the reading are the beginning and the end. Respectable and law-abiding, devout citizens took scandal at the company that Jesus kept, many of whom fell into the categories of the undesirable. It did not seem right to them that Jesus should treat these people as his friends, making little distinction between his attitudes to such marginal people and his attitude towards the righteous. The story as a whole responds to this protest. The final part of the story incorporates the protest and interprets it as Jesus sees it, that is as the more subtle alienation of the other brother who, though he does not realize it, also rejects the family and tries to break it up by his judgmental and unforgiving attitude. The father of the story does him no injustice because while the father lives it is he who has the ownership and the right to dispose of the produce of the entire farm, just as the Providence of God is utterly free to offer salvation to all who will turn to accept it, without being tied to the classifications of people that we are inclined to make. The question remains whether we who are the devout in the Christian dispensation, really desire a salvation that is so indiscriminate, that does not follow our own patterns of legalism, that does not give special privilege to the devout and respectable.

The reading from 2 Corinthians approaches this in its own way.

Those who are united with Christ are like a new world, a new creation, as the newly circumcised of Joshua's story were a new people entering the Promised Land. It is in Christ that the world, represented by both brothers of the Lukan story, is reconciled, and the misdeeds of both elder and younger are no longer held against them. Really to know this is to rejoice indeed in the knowledge that our appallingly disoriented and dismembered world can be restored to its familial pattern of unity and cooperation in Christ. But to know it is also to enlist in the ministry of reconciliation at all levels of our own society. And this is not in vain, for in Christ we learn not only the story but the reality of the Father's welcome.

Fifth Sunday of Lent

READINGS: Is 43:16-21; Phil 3:8-14; Jn 8:1-11.

Cease to dwell on days gone by and to brood over past history. Here and now I will do a new thing; this moment it will break from the bud. Can you not perceive it? I will make a way even through the wilderness and paths in the barren desert. Is 43:18-19.

The liturgical readings make this a day of new beginnings. The song or poem from Isaiah speaks of the recreation of the people of God. Set originally in a longer passage which calls rhetorically upon the assembled nations to judge who is true God and whether God is just and faithful, the song of recreation of the people looks back to Exodus as promissory event. But it will not rest there; from the memory of past acts of power and compassion, the attention should move towards the present to discern and interpret the redemptive movement that thrusts towards the yet promised future. The wonderful works of God have not come to an end, though we may feel that we are lost in the wilderness, wandering in a barren desert. In these days of terrible crises in many parts of the world, in which the nuclear threat hangs over all, this song of the new creation and of the wonders of God which have not come to an end in the past, may seem particularly apt.

The passage from Philippians says something similar on a personal and intimate basis. Though part of a longer passage which is a dire warning against the errors of false teachers, this section is like a song of praise and enthusiasm arising out of Paul's personal experience. It is one of the few passages in which we are allowed an intimate glimpse into Paul's own feelings and inner experiences. Paul also writes of taking courage from the wonderful works of God's mercy in the past, but not letting one's gaze remain in the past. Those good memories are grounds for radically hopeful interpretations of the present and the possibilities of the future. From the point of view of his traditional Hebrew outlook, Paul had lost much that was of great value: the privilege of the circumcised; membership of the chosen people by birth; descent from a favored tribe; a Hebrew education; a stance of careful observance, respectable in claims to orthodoxy and faultless legal rectitude. All these things he had lost in the sense that they were no longer a basis for any special claims or any special status; of himself and his own doings he simply had no special claims any more. But he quickly relates that he had found instead the true happiness of union with Christ, a happiness that consisted not so much of grasping anything as of being grasped. It is certainly not that he thinks he has reached perfection, but the promises contained in the memory of past mercies are so plain that he presses ahead with confident enthusiasm towards fullness of life in Christ.

The gospel reading is closely related to these enthusiastic songs of new beginnings. The liturgy seems blissfully unconcerned about the problems in this passage which trouble scholars—the fact that it did not belong in John's Gospel originally, and that we do not know whence it came when it was later inserted in the Gospel. What the liturgy wants us to notice is the simple pattern of the story and its symbolism and implications. It takes place towards the end of Jesus' life, because he was spending his nights out in the garden of olives and his days sitting in the Temple teaching. In front of the eager crowds listening to him, his enemies once again tried to trap him and discredit him in the eyes of the people. Strict observance of the Mosaic law required that those caught in adultery should be put to death, both the man and the woman, and that in the case of a betrothed virgin both should die by stoning. The first thing we notice in this story is that it is only the woman who is brought, and she can hardly have been caught in the act of adultery without a partner. We also notice that her accusers and captors are men (doctors of the Law and Pharisees).

The trap is set by asking Jesus for a legal opinion, as he is after all teaching in the Temple as one having authority. As the question is put, there is no right answer: to stone is unmerciful and totally against the teachings of Jesus, but not to do so is certainly a technical transgression of the Mosaic Law. There are several reasons why Jesus might have been writing on the ground: it might have been a gesture of refusing to give an opinion on a question phrased like that, or it may have been a way of saying that our sins are registered in sand and can be wiped out by forgiveness and repentance. In any case, they persist in asking. As so often in the Gospel, Jesus gives a totally unexpected answer that suggests a totally different way of formulating the question and looking at the situation. He really suggests that instead of looking at the letter of the Law they should look at the real human situation, and most particularly that they should consider the real relationship between the accused and the judges or would-be executioners. Because they press him, he answers them that only the truly innocent could have any claim to initiate the execution. The implications of that for ourselves and our own society are shattering. It is a commentary in life of his constant teaching not to judge others in order to condemn them, because none of us is fit to do that. He writes again on the ground, clearly saying to them by his gesture that this is his whole answer to them. When they have disappeared one by one, and he assures the woman that he will not pass sentence on her either, he seems to be saying again that God does not will the death of the sinner but that such a one be converted and live more fully. This also is the story of the new beginning, the fresh start.

Passion Sunday

READINGS: Procession of Palms: Lk 19:29-40;
Eucharist: Is 50:4-7; Phil 2:6-11; Lk 22:14-23:56,
(or Lk 23:1-49).

Then Jesus gave a loud cry and said, "Father, into thy hands I commit my spirit"; and with these words he died. The centurion saw it all, and gave praise to God. "Beyond all doubt," he said, "this man was innocent."

Lk 23:46-47.

The readings assigned for this Sunday are so long that many celebrants find it better not to preach but to let the texts speak for themselves. Certainly, a commentary on the solemn entry into Jerusalem, followed by an adequate commentary on the Passion narrative would have to be very lengthy. Yet we are so familiar with the text that it can easily pass by without making a deep impression unless it is presented each time from a new angle of vision. As I look at these texts this year, what emerges most strongly is the paradox that runs throughout.

Paradox appears between the two readings: there is the triumphant solemn entry into Jerusalem, but the goal to which it moves is that of a disgraced and fearful death. On his entry into the city, Jesus weeps prophetically over the city and its inhabitants; on his exit from the city to the place of execution, it is the people of the city (or at least the women among them) who lament for Jesus. The reversal of roles in both cases, so deeply and typically human, seems to underscore the solidarity of Jesus with all the tragedy and frailty of the human situation.

The paradox does not end there. In the trial, as Luke tells it, it is his own people, from whom he might have expected support and solidarity, who accuse him, and it is the feared and hated foreign power of Rome, represented by Pilate, that hesitates before the injustice. One cannot but remember prophetic voices of our own times who have said, "it is one thing to suffer *for* the Church, but a more terrible and bitter thing to suffer *from* the church." And yet in the end Pilate also becomes the paradoxical figure who thrice declares the innocence of Jesus and then condemns him to a terrible execution.

Light and shadow also play around the theme of the kingship of Jesus. The triumphal entry of the King, recognized and acknowledged only by his faithful followers, leads to a trial which is a kind of testing of the quality of his kingship. The accusations are crude, the defense carefully chosen. Is it true that he forbids payment of taxes to Caesar because he claims the kingship of the Jewish people for himself? The answer, which in this text is not clear, leaves Pilate inclined to dismiss the case against Jesus. Is he, however, seditious in other ways, stirring up disaffection and rebellion? Pilate can find no evidence, while Herod treats it as a joke, dressing the accused in a royal robe. In the end we are given the sense that he reigns indeed, but that it is from the Cross.

There is another argument going on, and that is about Jesus as Savior. Challenged by Herod to work miracles, Jesus refuses as he did in the story of the temptations in the desert. Challenged to save himself from the Cross, he gives no other answer than to offer paradise to one of those crucified with him. And we are left to reflect on the meaning of the contradictions which the narrative seems to contain, and on that all-inclusive contradiction which our faith seems to contain, grounded as it is in the death of Jesus seen as redemptive.

The other two readings for the day serve, among other purposes, as a reminder that the passion of Jesus is prototypical: it represents the fate of anyone who raises a prophetic voice, of anyone who steps out of line to protest grave injustices. In many places today, and in many situations in contemporary human society, the passion of Jesus continues among many of his courageous followers and among other persons of vision and generosity who would not themselves link their passion with that of Jesus. Perhaps the readings serve to remind us also of the kinds of injustice and cruelty of which we are all capable when we feel ourselves seriously threatened and moved to panic.

Certainly, the Isaian passage, which is taken from the third suffering servant song, is applied by the liturgy to Jesus. But the original context leaves the identity of the suffering servant ambiguous; it might be the prophet himself, or it might be Israel, the people, or yet a faithful remnant of Israel. And because the identity is left undetermined, the passage has a certain universal application.

In the letter to the Philippians, it is quite clear that Paul is indeed referring directly to Jesus, and particularly to his death by execution. But the point of this passage is precisely the voluntary solidarity of Jesus with all human suffering and especially with the depths of human suffering experienced in societal rejection and a torture death. It should not be possible for us to hear this passage read without bringing to mind those who experience these things in our own times, perhaps even because of the policies carried out by our own society in our name.

When the liturgy has passed all these thoughts and images before us, the last word is given to the executioner who has observed it all: "Beyond all doubt this man was innocent."

Easter Sunday

READINGS: *Mass of the Vigil:* Rom 6:3-11; Lk 24:1-12;
            Mass of the Day: Acts 10:34, 37-43; Col 3:1-4; (or
            I Cor 5:6-8); Jn 20:1-9.

Were you not raised to life with Christ? Then aspire to the realm above, where Christ is, seated at the right hand of God, and let your thoughts dwell on that higher realm, not on this earthly life. I repeat, you died; and now your life lies hidden with Christ in God. Col 3:1-3.

There is a common background and a common theme to this bewildering array of readings. The common background is that of the Exodus story which has been read at the Vigil before the first Mass. The common theme is that the Resurrection is our own experience as Christians, one that we share intimately, and not just something we hear about as having happened to someone else long ago. With that background and that unifying theme it is easier to see the coherence of all the readings as commentary on the celebration of the Lord's Resurrection.

The New Testament writers testify that it was Jesus himself who suggested that they should interpret the meaning of his death in terms of the Exodus story, that is to say as a great crossing over into freedom and new peoplehood, an escape from bondage and fear. In the passage from Romans, Paul does not explicitly refer to the Exodus, but he does invoke the theme that the death of Jesus is a great crossing over into freedom and peoplehood both for Jesus and for his followers, who are enabled to leave the old bondage to death and sin behind. The Lucan account of the finding of the empty tomb has its own subtle echoes of the Exodus; we come from the story of the crossing of the Red Sea and the rolling aside of the waters, to the story of the passing through the tribulation of death and the tomb and the rolling away of the great stone that sealed the tomb. God has wonderfully cleared a passage into a new beginning, and into a new and transformed life. It is little wonder that we receive the familiar warning not to look back, because the power of God, the Risen Christ, is here now among the living and not buried in the past with the dead. But anyone reflecting upon them can see that both these readings at the Mass of the Vigil emphasize not only the crossing over into new life, but also that it is *our* crossing over with Christ.

The first reading for the Mass of the Day gives Peter the recital of the events that led up to the Resurrection and of the events that flowed immediately from it, in the speech which the Acts of the Apostles place in the house of Cornelius the Centurion. It is a terse, densely packed account of all that Jesus has been and has meant for his followers in his lifetime. The speech offers witnesses to what Jesus did then and what Jesus is now doing among his followers who have "eaten and drunk with him after he rose from the dead." This reference to eating and drinking brings to mind of course the words of Jesus in Luke's Gospel at the Last Supper, that he would not drink again from the fruit of the vine until the coming of the Kingdom of God. This claim, then, to have eaten and drunk with Jesus after he rose from the dead, is a claim to have crossed over in some sense into the Kingdom of God, to have participated with Jesus in the breakthrough to a new life.

The liturgy gives us a choice whether to read from Colossians 3 or from I Corinthians 5. The passage from Colossians sums up once again the whole meaning of Easter for us, but it is liable to misinterpretation if read without commentary. It would be all too easy to read the admonition of aspiring to the realm above, and dwelling on that higher realm not on this earthly life, as meaning a rejection of responsibilities in the world, and a recommendation to withdraw into inner consciousness away from all that is corporeal. The meaning, as often in Paul's teaching as passed on by his followers, does not intend a distinction between material and spiritual but rather between wordly and sinful ways of living and those which are filled with the spirit of God. Although this passage is expressed in terms of space, it is proclaiming the same message of a new life that is given in the other readings in terms of a time sequence.

The alternate reading, from I Corinthians, takes up the Exodus theme again with the symbolism of the unleavened bread of the Passover celebration. Christians live in the Passover season of Christ, a time of the unleavened bread because the old leaven of sin and corruption has been purged out by the death of Jesus and we become the new bread with him. The old leaven of corruption must by no means be reintroduced. The metaphor may be a little strange to us, but it offers an important link with the theme of Exodus which interprets the death and Resurrection of Jesus.

On this day of the Resurrection it seems particularly apt that the sequence of readings should end with one from the Gospel of John, full of a sense of reverence for mystery. We hear the same story, told with some differences of detail, which was read at the Mass of the Vigil in Luke's version. Modern scholarship, and the empirically oriented contemporary mind, has been tempted to try to decipher these stories to elicit a purely factual account. Because the original authors did not have that in mind, it seems more useful to ask why they recorded these stories for us, and what they meant us to learn and understand from them. The answer to that seems very simple: not to look for an encounter with Jesus in the mists of the past but to seek the encounter with the risen Christ in the living reality of the present, in the community of believers, in the world about us.

Second Sunday of Easter

READINGS: Acts 5:12-16; Rev 1:9-13, 17-19; Jn 20:19-31.

He laid his right hand upon me and said, "Do not be afraid. I am the first and the last, and I am the living one; for I was dead and now I am alive for evermore, and I hold the keys of Death and Death's domain." Rev 1:17-18.

Texts from the Book of Revelation usually need a great deal of commentary to be intelligible to contemporary hearers and readers, but the symbolism of this one is plain enough. It celebrates the Resurrection with all the joy and reassurance and transformation it brings to the persecuted writer and the persecuted communities of Christians to whom the document is addressed. In the guise of a heavenly vision, this text gives the same message that is given in such concrete terms in the Gospel reading of the day. Like the Gospel story it is placed on the Lord's day, the day of the Resurrection, the Sunday, and speaks of being caught up in the Spirit, while the Gospel reading is also concerned with the Spirit which the risen Jesus confers on his disciples. Like the Gospel reading it tells of an encounter between the risen Lord and the disciple, and the message is not only for the disciple in the story but for every disciple throughout all time.

The Gospel story is full of allusive symbolism. It was probably intended as the conclusion and climax of all John's Gospel, though some further stories of Resurrection appearances were later added. It is a climax in a number of ways. It ends the story of the repeated appearance to the gathered disciples with Thomas' confession of faith, "My Lord and my God," returning thereby to the opening theme of the Gospel, the coming of the Divine Word, the Divine Light, into the world. But it also ends the whole passage with an exhortation to faith and an explanation that the "signs" that Jesus did have been recorded so that through faith in Jesus as Son of God and Savior, we might all come to possess life in him.

The story embraces the octave of Easter with the initial appearance to the frightened disciples placed on the evening of the day of the Resurrection, and the later appearance, including Thomas, placed on the following Sunday. In the first, Jesus is there suddenly, inexplicably, within the locked doors, giving them the familiar greeting which will ever after have a new and deeper meaning for them. That he breathed on them saying, "Receive the Holy Spirit," certainly alludes to the Genesis 2 creation account in which God fashioned the human being from the dust of the ground and breathed life into it to become a living person. But it probably also alludes to the saying of John the Baptist who declared that the one to come after him would baptize in the Spirit. The meaning conveyed is that there is a new creation by the outpouring of the Spirit in the Resurrection of Jesus. That outpouring of the Spirit among his followers is also their mission to carry on his testimony and his work in the world—a work of reconciliation. Though their proclamation will be the occasion for forgiveness of sins for those who respond in faith, it will be one of condemnation for those who do not so respond. (It is perhaps stretching a point too far to see the text as the institution of a specific sacrament.)

When one reads and meditates the second half of the story, it becomes clear that the figure of Thomas is very important because it is representative of all of us who were not there to share the first revelatory and ecstatic moments of the Christian faith. We also arrive after it has happened and are confronted with the testimony of the first witnesses who left us word of what it was that so totally changed their lives and perception. Thomas, representing us, says he needs better evidence, empirical evidence. He thereby constitutes himself a curiously apt representative of our own generation which is so inclined to say that the only truth is empirically verifiable truth, and that the Resurrection must have been an empirically verifiable fact if it is to be the foundation of faith. But the whole thrust of the passage is not that Thomas was given this kind of proof because he was able to touch. As a matter of fact we are not told that he did touch, but rather that he made a confession of faith in the redemptive role and divinity of Jesus which was not susceptible of proof by any sort of touching or physical seeing. The thrust of the passage is rather that there need be no wishing that we might have been there, because we who came later are blessed in our faith, and that faith is not the outcome of empirical evidence but the transformation of the Spirit within our personal experience.

One might also say that the final paragraph suggests that the "book of signs" which John presents is given to us to meditate because it interprets for us the continuing reality of grace in which we ourselves live. And that seems to be the point of the passage from the Acts of the Apostles, which describes the power of the Resurrection, the Spirit of the Risen Christ at work in the community of believers in the early days. The text we read on this Sunday follows upon a section in the previous chapter in which the whole community, threatened with persecution, prays passionately that God might stretch out a divine hand in signs and wonders done through the name of Jesus, which would lend persuasion to their preaching. We are told that the building in which they were shook, and that they were filled with the Holy Spirit, empowered to speak the word of God boldly. In that power of the Spirit the faith and enthusiasm of the community goes forth to heal and reconcile and inspire to convert and to console.

Luke, of course, often depicts the life of the early Christian communities very idealistically in the Acts of the Apostles, yet we continue to read and hear these texts in our liturgy, not to wonder at things that happened long ago, but to become alert to the power of the Spirit and the new life of the Resurrection as enabling us to heal and reconcile in works of justice and mercy in our own times, among hostile and intractable forces in our own society.

Third Sunday of Easter

READINGS: Acts 5:27-32, 40-41; Rev 5:11-14; Jn 21:1-19 (or 1-14).

Morning came and there stood Jesus on the beach, but the disciples did not know that it was Jesus ... Jesus said, "Come and have breakfast." Jn 21:4, 12.

The Resurrection accounts are full of belated recognition stories, and Christian hagiography and folklore have taken up the theme with many anecdotes of devout people who waited for an encounter with Jesus and did not recognize him when they met him in other people—in the poor, in lepers, in strangers—and who only realized later that they had indeed encountered Jesus. The stories about those original witnesses of the Resurrection are complemented in the New Testament by that of the conversion of Paul, in which Jesus is identified with his persecuted followers. This story, following on last Sunday's reading about the experiences of Thomas, reinforces the sense that we are included in the story, indeed that it is about our way of experiencing the Resurrection in our own times and in our own society.

As so often happens in the Gospel according to John, the whole passage seems to be woven together out of allusions to themes and persons and symbols that have been used before in sacred Scripture. In this passage, which seems to have been added on as an afterthought in some stage of the editorial history of the Gospel, seven disciples are named as part of the fishing expedition. We know them as being of the Twelve, and we have special stories about five of them in relation to Jesus: Peter the impulsive leader, Thomas the doubter, Nathanael who was without guile, and the passionate sons of Zebedee. Two others who are unnamed are said to have been with them. They are fishing by night, and we remember that other expedition overtaken by the storm; that time also Jesus had not been in the boat, and Peter had attempted to come to him over the water (Jn 6:14-21). The miraculous catch of fish is like an echo of the Lucan story of the calling of the first disciples (Lk 5:1-11). Moreover, there is no doubt that the breakfast of bread and fish on the beach, in which the true identity of Jesus becomes apparent to the disciples, is suggestive of the Eucharist. Indeed, for various reasons the fish became a symbol of Christ for the early Christians.

If there could be any doubt about the meaning of this Resurrection story, it would be dispelled by the verses that follow (included in the longer version of the liturgical reading for the day). Not only is it true that Jesus draws from Peter a triple confession of loyalty and love that balances the triple denial of the Passion narrative. It is also the conclusion of each exchange that love of Christ is appropriately expressed in care for others—for all others inasmuch as Jesus cares for all—and that the call of Christ comes even to those who have previously betrayed him. Resurrection and apostolate are linked in the story, and they are situated within the life of the Church and within the real world with all its ambiguities.

What is presented in such symbolic form in the Gospel reading, is also spelled out quite concretely in the story from the Acts of the Apostles. The experience of the Resurrection implies a vocation to evangelize, to pass on the good experience and the good news, and the Apostles make it plain to the authorities which persecute them, that they have no other option than to put the divine mandate before all human commands and prohibitions, even those that come from the appropriate religious authorities. In their times, as in ours, this is the real world with all its ambiguities; the duly constituted religious authorities may at times be the very ones to persecute the true witnesses of the Resurrection. The apostolic answer to this bewildering state of affairs is worthy of note. The apostles say to the authorities that they, the disciples, are the witnesses, but so is the Holy Spirit given by God to those who are open to it. In the New Testament this seems to be the main "proof" of Resurrection and mandate; the Spirit which has transformed the followers of Jesus, their way of life, their attitudes, the pattern of their relationship with one another, is the witness that confirms the human witnesses, and shows with certainty that this is the work of God.

Such is the assurance of the early followers of Jesus that, in the reading from the Book of Revelation, mission and witness, Resurrection and redemption, are all projected in a grand heavenly tableau. Here all creation is gathered in a mighty chorus of praise and thanksgiving for the reconciliation of all things through the "lamb that was slain," in whom all the mysteries and the tragedies of the "seven seals" are resolved.

We may well wonder what could be the purpose of painting a heavenly scene of ultimate and total reconciliation and presenting it as present reality, when in fact so many tragedies of history and society are yet unresolved—wars and rumor of wars, oppression and injustice, hunger and poverty, prejudices of all types, discrimination against the innocent, and so forth. The purpose is surely not to blind us to the tasks around us by the pretense that all is already solved, but rather to assure us that Christ (the "lamb" of the vision) has the key to the reconciliation of all the world's ills, and that those who align themselves with him in truth and not only in words, may expect persecution indeed, but also the enlightenment and power of the Spirit.

Fourth Sunday of Easter

READINGS: Acts 13:14, 43-52; Rev 7:9, 14-17; Jn 10:27-30.

"I looked saw a vast throng which no one could count, from every nation, of all tribes, peoples and languages, standing in front of the throne and before the Lamb ... *the Lamb who is at the heart of the throne will be their shepherd and will guide them to the springs of the water of life*... Rev 7:9, 17.

The image of the shepherd and the sheep is not the most appealing in our times, but it is a favorite in the Scriptures. The unusually brief Gospel reading is able to convey so much in so few words because the imagery evoked has all the resonance of Psalms and Prophets and Hebrew history. Talk of herds and herders brings to mind the nomadic past which Israel had never forgotten; "my father was a wandering Aramaean" was the recital that accompanied the offering of the first fruits. Abraham, Isaac and Jacob, the great patriarchs, herded flocks. Moses was drawn into the revelation of the Burning

Bush while herding sheep. David, the shepherd boy who became King, was legendary. Amos, the Prophet, was a sheep farmer. It is hardly surprising that Hebrews who knew themselves made in the image of God, should sometimes think of God as the shepherd of Israel who neither slumbered nor slept but was at all times the protector and guide of the people.

The image may seem to us less than flattering, the more so as we think of sheep as some of the less intelligent mammals. But those who lived among them were apparently far more aware of something else—the close relationship between sheep and shepherd, a sense of organic unity, or trust and, one might almost say, of affection. Moreover, there was a general sense that the dedication of a shepherd is total and unconditional, involving perhaps even the risking of the shepherd's life to defend the flock from wild beasts, or to rescue animals stranded in inaccessible places. Even today, anyone who has lived in the Judean wilderness knows that the local shepherds do not need to drive their flocks but can simply lead them, because the flocks have learned that to follow the shepherd means to come to those hard-to-find places where there is fresh grazing and living, that is, running water.

When, in today's Gospel reading, Jesus refers to himself as the shepherd his focus is on the assertion that those who are his own recognize his voice and spontaneously follow him, and he leads them to eternal life, to life-giving waters. Moreover, his dedication is complete and unconditional, and none can snatch his followers from his care. God alone is the true shepherd of Israel, as the listeners know from their Scriptures, but Jesus maintains that they are truly his because he and the Father are one. John's Gospel places this saying in the context of challenge and persecution, but even in its original setting the passage seems to have a double purpose: to present an argument vindicating Jesus, and to offer assurance and consolation to Christians in time of persecution and hardship, offering them confidence that the way they are to follow will be made clear.

The passage from Revelation addresses the situation of persecution directly. A mighty crowd has gathered, made up of people from all parts of the world, and they are those who have passed through a great ordeal. In a sudden shift of metaphors, the Lamb that was slain now appears as the shepherd, who leads this mighty crowd past all suffering to the springs of living water. They have come out of great tribulations but their suffering is to end forever. The author of this text is representing in visionary form an interpretation of history, which is typified in the death and resurrection of Jesus, but is also realized in the experience of his followers. We are presented with an Easter scene for contemplation, not for entertainment but for guidance in interpreting the history in which we also live.

As usual, the reading from Acts suggests a practical and quite concrete way of reading and applying the more poetic and symbolic passages in the other readings. Paul and Barnabas, with some other companions, have gone to Sabbath worship at the synagogue of Antioch in Pisidia, much as any of us might go to church in a strange town while travelling. They have been asked by the officials of the synagogue to address some words of inspiration to the local congregation, but their far-reaching success among Jews and Gentiles alike is not appreciated. The outcome seems to suggest that what is so much resented is the indiscriminate inclusion of Gentiles, making the community of the faithful in the synagogue less special, less elite. The persecution that makes Paul's mission so difficult, comes from the devout, the officially religious. It is the typical pattern of Paul's apostolate, however, that he is drawn to witness to the universality of God's salvific will, to the bursting forth of the saving grace of the Risen Christ into the entire world, among all nations and peoples and tongues. It is the vision of Revelation made concrete, and in the concrete it certainly evokes persecution.

We seem to be involved in this in two ways. On the one hand we are they who have been swept in from the gentile peoples of the earth, so that the promise and the vision and the reassurance are for us. On the other hand, we so easily imagine ourselves the privileged elect, as did the "women of standing" and the "leading men of the city" who supported the synagogue, so that for us also it is not always evident that salvation is for the peoples of the world and not for an elect group. It is a very practical matter of the transformation of all aspects of human life—a call to share and care about all human persons and societies, so that all may come to the inexhaustible springs of living water.

Fifth Sunday of Easter

READINGS: Acts 14:21-27; Rev 21:1-5; Jn 13:31-35.

Now at last God has his dwelling among men . . . there shall be an end to death, and to mourning and crying and pain; for the old order has passed away . . . Behold I am making all things new. Rev 21:3, 4, 5.

Perhaps it was necessary for the seer of the Book of Revelation to write this passage because even the earliest Christians in the first period of enthusiasm and ecstasy had difficulty in seeing the Reign of God coming amid the cruelties, injustices and arrogance of their world. Certainly, in our own times, after nineteen and a half centuries of attempted Christianity, it is quite difficult to see anything in this passage other than wishful thinking, compensatory dreaming, or even the "opium of the people."

Yet there is no doubt that the visions of the book of Revelation intend to offer us an authentic interpretation of the history in which we live. They intend to unveil for us the meaning of history in such a way that we can see human history progressing through colossal struggles toward the ultimate and total rule of God in creation. In particular, it seems originally to have been a strong (though coded) statement against emperor worship. The great powers of the world—military, political, economic, cultural—are not independent forces free to run by norms and standards of their own; they are subject to God and exist for the well-being and happiness of human persons—of all human persons, though the text is particularly concerned with the vindication of the persecuted and apparently quite powerless Christian community of that time.

The import of this text about the end of mourning and crying is a message about the meaning of Easter which it may be too easy to forget, namely, that the real affairs in the real world, in the public sphere as well as in private life, are supposed to be really different because of the death and resurrection of Jesus and the explosion of his Spirit into the world through his followers. We are promised the possibility of ending the unnecessary suffering people inflict on one another because of selfishness, greed for profit and power, and the projection of one's own fears and resentments into an image that makes the other a threat. Perhaps our most serious lack of faith today has little to do with whether we think the tomb was physically empty, but rather concerns whether we think the world is spiritually full of the power of the risen Christ to change things and make all things new. It would seem that lack of faith is not displayed in honest efforts to grapple with contemporary moral issues in sexuality, but far rather in unwillingness to pursue to their logical conclusion in the light of Easter faith those public policy questions of peace and justice that make or destroy the lives of millions of people.

The breathless recital of the passage from city to city that concludes Paul's first missionary journey, seems at first glance to give a quite different sense of Christian faith and presence in the world from that sketched above. Yet the reading from the Acts of the Apostles describes something which we today would call the founding of basic Christian communities—communities which, according to the letters of Paul, are certainly supposed to be changing the structures of society from within, from below, from lowly beginnings. Even the haste, the rapid succession of cities, in today's reading from the Acts, suggests a lively and effective faith in the new life of the resurrection and its power truly to make all things new and remove causes of dissension, distrust, injustice and cruelties. The earliest Christians seem everywhere to have shared in radical transformations of society and its structures at whatever levels of social organization were within their reach.

The Gospel reading puts the matter in the simplest and therefore in the most exigent terms. Though this short passage is set within the narrative of John's Gospel in the great farewell speech before the passion, it is evidently a summary statement of the changed situation after the death and resurrection. The new commandment is the dynamic through which the grace of the resurrection is to be operative in history and throughout human societies. What is new about that commandment is that we now have the completed fact of Christ's love for us as the foundation of the mandate to love as he did, and to build a mutuality in that kind of love. This, evidently, was the leaven that was to raise society at large to new modes of relationship and a radical restructuring of human affairs.

To love as Christ did is to subordinate one's own life and welfare to the common good of the community as a whole. A community of people doing this reciprocally is very powerful in transforming the lives of its members and those of others about them. The expectation of the early missionary journey appears to have been that the formation of many groups of people doing this would release the regenerating power of the resurrection into the world where it would spread and multiply through all aspects of society. The comment that in this reciprocal love the world will know us as disciples of Jesus is significant and also in some measure tragic; it is the one thing necessary, and yet we all know that too often among rigid fidelity to all kind of rules and formulae, it is the one thing missing. Indeed that comment about the essential mark of discipleship suggests to every generation a fresh vision of what it means to be Church—what it means for our relationship within the community and within Church structures, and what it means for our existence as Church in the world.

It is in the new commandment to love as Jesus loved—in that commandment seen in all its structural extension in human society—that the promise is realized to make all things new.

Sixth Sunday of Easter

READINGS: Acts 15:1-2, 22-29; Rev 21:10-14, 22-23; Jn 14:23-29.

I have told you all this while I am still here with you; but your Advocate, the Holy Spirit whom the Father will send in my name, will teach you everything and will call to mind all that I have told you. Jn 14:26.

It is common experience that we seldom understand anything fully and in all its implications when first we hear it. Yet there is always some reluctance to suppose there may be new understanding in matters of faith. The temptation to make everything hard and fast, as though every issue had been adequately dealt with in the past, seems to be one that haunts all human institutions, to which the Church is no exception. It is striking, therefore, that the fourth evangelist, in a summary of the final teachings of Jesus, should be so insistent that Jesus himself expected his followers to live by the enlightenment of the living Spirit after he, Jesus, was no longer bodily among them. But it is a theme that arises in many parts of the New Testament.

In this Johannine text the power and freedom to live by the Spirit, trusting in the continuing self-revelation of God in our lives and our history, is linked to the gift of peace and the overcoming of anxiety and fear. It is a message that seems to be particularly pertinent to Catholic Christians today, when we live in times of rapid cultural and organizational change, and when the Church also has changed in ways that we never expected to see in our lifetimes. It is useless to cling to the past, as though the faith were a matter of learning by rote. To have faith in the living Spirit is also to expect confidently to be guided into deeper and further understanding and clearer vision.

The passage which we read today from the Acts of the Apostles seems to be a particular application of this general advice and observation. Without any explicit teaching of Jesus, so it seems, the young community of his followers is faced quite early with the question concerning Jewish observances and whether these should be required of Gentile converts to faith in Jesus. They make a bold decision which is very interesting: they argue that if there is no compelling reason for imposing such burdens on the Gentile converts, then it should not be done, but they ask the Gentiles to observe, beyond the basic demands of morality, such rules as will make it possible for Jewish followers of Jesus to maintain table fellowship with them and still observe the ritual code in which they have been raised. It seems that they are moved by two important considerations: freedom in the Spirit, and community in the Spirit.

The same kind of confidence is expressed in a very different way in the passage from the Book of Revelation. In elaborately allusive, symbolic language the author tells us that the gift of the new Jerusalem, the heavenly city, the Reign of God, is a radically new and renewing one. It comes down from heaven, because it is so totally the gift of God beyond all human achievements and deserts. It is incomparably precious and has gates enough for all the people to enter, but it has no Temple, no special place of mediation, no external illumination, because the presence of God within it makes all further mediation superfluous. This also is a way of saying that the Spirit will teach.

Ascension Thursday

READINGS: Acts 1:1-11; Eph 1:17-23; Lk 24:46-53.

Then he led them out as far as Bethany and blessed them with uplifted hands, and in the act of blessing he parted from them. Lk 24:50-51.

In these readings we hear the same story twice—once in a very terse form at the conclusion of Luke's Gospel, and once again with more elaboration of symbolic detail at the beginning of the narrative of the Acts of the Apostles. One might almost say that we hear the same story a third time in the account from the letter to the Ephesians.

The first time, in Luke's Gospel, we learn that the risen Jesus, having charged his disciples with the task of witnessing to the Good News, and having promised the power of the Spirit for their task, is last seen by them (parts from them) in the posture of blessing. Their last impression of him is the blessing he leaves with them for their task, and it leaves them returning to Jerusalem exhilarated.

The second time we hear the story, we learn that Jesus lingered among his disciples in a palpable presence for forty days (for a fullness of time, for all the time that was necessary) so that they could not doubt that his living presence and power were among them. We also hear that he then gave them fuller instruction about the Reign of God and let them know that they were not expected to begin their task of witness by their own power or expertise, but were to wait for the power of the Spirit to come upon them. We are even told that at this stage his disciples still misunderstood the nature of the mission and wanted a prediction of future events in the history of Israel, and that Jesus again tries to lift their eyes to larger horizons. But it is in this account also that we have the striking image that has shaped the Christian imagination concerning the passing of the historical event of Jesus; he is lifted up into a cloud (a symbol in the Scriptures for the divine presence) but as he disappears heavenly messengers insist that the disciples direct their gaze earthwards to their task. The Easter morning message was not to look for Jesus down in the tomb among the dead but rather among the living. The Ascension message is not to gaze up to where Jesus was last palpably present but rather out into the world, forward into history.

But there is a third version of the story in the reading from Ephesians, which is now interpreted in more developed theological terms. Here we are told that God who raised Jesus from the dead, enthroned him at the right hand of the Father in the heavenly realms. We are also told that this means that he is placed above all governments and authorities, having all power and dominion placed in his hands, both in the history of the world as we know it and in that transformed world that is yet to come. More particularly he is the head of that body, that assembly that comes together in his name, but this does not exhaust his authority which is over all creation, all human affairs, all governments and all nations.

This understanding was so fraught with consequences that through the ages martyrs died defending the authority of Christ in their lives as one that took precedence over all earthly rulers and their commands. In our own times we tend to assume that such conflicts can no longer happen, at least in our part of the world, but we should from time to time ask ourselves what it means in concrete terms that the authority of Jesus is set above the law of the land and the rulers of the land, above the interests of industry and national wealth and national defense. Perhaps we should ask ourselves also whether we really believe that the Spirit is with us and that we too shall receive power from on high.

Seventh Sunday of Easter

READINGS: Acts 7:55-60; Rev 22:12-14, 16-17, 20; Jn 17:20-26.

I am the Alpha and the Omega, the first and the last, the beginning and the end. Rev 22:13.

These words sum up the meaning of all three readings for this Sunday. Jesus, crucified and risen and alive among us encompasses all history. This final passage of the book of Revelation offers a reprise of a number of biblical themes: the tree of life that was in the midst of the garden at the beginning is again accessible, this time through the twelve gates of the city; the final message of the heavenly messenger sent to the churches is that it is Jesus who fulfills the prophecies to the house of David, and it is he also who is the morning star that heralds the final day; the theme of the bridegroom and of God's espousal with the people reappears; for a final time we meet the prophetic theme of the living water which is a free gift to the thirsty if they will but seek it, recalling the spring bubbling up to water paradise, and recalling the words of Jesus crying in the Temple that out of his own person he offers to all that living water; and to round off the proclamation, Jesus promises, "I am coming" and the faithful repond, "Amen. Come!," naming him Lord.

There are too many themes here to do more than list them, but they offer much matter for meditation and contemplation in expectation of the feast of Pentecost in the following week. Yet, as always, the liturgical selection of readings is rather careful not to leave our reflections in these wonderful and inspiring images without a reminder that they are an interpretation of our real and everyday lives, and that they are a revolutionary interpretation, that is to say one which turns things upside down and calls for action contrary to worldly expectations. Certainly the story of Stephen's death in the Acts of the Apostles forms an important link between the death of Jesus and the life of the community. Stephen is known as the proto-martyr but he is also in some sense the proto-Christian. The author has taken some pains to present Stephen as a follower and imitator of Jesus. Like Jesus, he is accused of blasphemy and condemned to death; like Jesus he is taken outside the city to be executed; like Jesus he prays for forgiveness for his murderers; and, as Jesus commits his spirit to the Father, so Stephen in his final moments commits his spirit to Jesus. The parallels are obviously intended, for the true Christian is the one who in any circumstances is the follower and imitator of Jesus. But Stephen is also the proto-Christian because he sees through the circumstances of history to discern the glory of God and Jesus at the right hand of God, fulfilling the prophecy of Daniel as the one in the form of a Son of Man coming upon the clouds as the great liberator. As the book of Revelation would have it, he sees Jesus as the Omega of history. As the grateful recipient of this vision, Stephen bears witness to it, heedless of the cost to himself.

Most of us, perhaps far too easily, assume that we shall never actually face martyrdom. Certainly the category of martyrdom is not as clear-cut in our times as it appears in retrospect in the early centuries. Yet we have Oscar Romero, the four American women missionaries and countless others whose names are less prominent, who in our own times have borne witness to the Gospel and have been killed for it, often forgiving their persecutors beforehand in expectation of their fate. They were not killed for professing faith in Christ in so many words, but rather for professing their faith in very practical ways by implementing today's Gospel reading without reserve.

What it means that Jesus should be the Alpha and the Omega of our lives and of all human history is spelled out very clearly in the

Gospel reading. Yet the passage is so simple we might miss its import. In the previous passage Jesus has acknowledged that his followers will live with persecution, but has prayed that they may have joy in the midst of it; he has acknowledged that they will be strangers in the world and has prayed that they may find their anchorage or rootedness by being consecrated in the truth. Now he makes it clear that his prayer is not only for his immediate followers but for all of us, and his prayer is one about unity and community, about reconciliation, a oneness that will mirror his relationship with the Father and will at the same time be contained within his relationship with the Father. This is a thought worthy of a long pause for reflection. It invites us to look backward over the Gospel accounts searching for a deeper understanding of the relationship that Jesus had with the Father.

At the end the Gospel returns to the theme we met in the other two readings—the theme of the glory of God which the world at large cannot see, but which is made visible to us in Jesus and which must become visible to others in us. That visibility is linked with the testimony of the reconciled community—the deeply and authentically reconciled community in which all find justice, acceptance and dignity—because this is a testimony that the world can understand.

Pentecost

READINGS: Acts 2:1-11; I Cor 12:3-7, 12-13; Jn 20:19-23.

There are varieties of gifts but the same Spirit. There are varieties of service but the same Lord. There are many forms of work, but all of them, in all men, are the work of the same God. In each of us the Spirit is manifested in one particular way, for some useful purpose. I Cor 12:4-7.

Paul wrote at such length about the variety of gifts, that we can infer that there was a serious problem. His two concerns are the pride of those who claim superiority over others because they enjoy some of the more spectacular gifts of the Spirit, and the bewilderment of those who do not know how to discern what is an authentic gift of the Spirit. These problems are ours as well as theirs. Unfortunately Paul's list of gifts has been omitted from the Sunday reading; it offers examples of complementarity of gifts which are quite apt for our own times. It suggests simplicity and humility on the part of leaders and office-holders in the community when faced with the prophetic, the ecstatic and the unconventional. Moreover, Paul's advice goes beyond this, for it warns against the human inclination to tidy others into our own categories, reduce their works and utterances to our own expectations, edit their living testimony to the Spirit into our preconceived pattersn, and close our eyes and ears to the unexpected. Yet revelation is the unexpected. Grace is the strange and the surprising. The Spirit is odd, whimsical, blowing where it wills.

The Pentecost story has much of this same message for us. We hear the story twice, but in quite different ways, just as we did on the feast of the Ascension. As on that occasion, so now it is the version in the Acts of the Apostles that gives us an elaboration of symbolism and allusions, building a magnificent tableau. The account in John's Gospel is brief and austere. John places the event within the Easter appearance to the assembled disciples. Jesus is there in person, appearing suddenly among them where they cowered behind closed doors, bestowing on them gifts of peace, joy, mission and Spirit. The conventional greeting, *Shalom*!, will never be the same after this; this time it carries reconciliation after their desertion and failure. The sight of him, risen, transformed, fills them with joy, so that they are ready for his next words, commissioning them with the continuation of his own redemptive task. He breathes on them as he says, "Receive the Holy Spirit!," entrusting the task of reconciliation to them, and through them to us.

Because we speak English and not Hebrew, we have to remind ourselves that the Hebrew word for Spirit also means breath and wind. The risen Jesus breathes the Holy Breath into his followers.

It is his breath, his life, the divine breath by which human beings are created (as in the story of Adam), the creative breath of spirit of God that hovers over the waters in Genesis, the divine breath or Spirit that inspires the prophets.

We meet the same allusion in the more elaborate version of the Pentecost story given in the reading from Acts. But this time it is a strong rushing wind that fills the whole house with its noise and its power. This time the event is placed, as the name of Pentecost suggests, fifty days after the Passover feast, the Hebrew feast of the Covenant, which was also the celebration of the first fruits. The author of Acts evidently intends to stress the parallel; this is the new covenant of God with the people, and it is the celebration of the first fruits. As on Sinai, the presence of God is expressed by wind and fire. As on Sinai, the covenant creates a chosen people, entrusted with a mission. But here the immediate effect of the event is the outreach to all peoples, reversing the tower of Babel where the languages were confused. Filled with that wind, that fire, that Spirit, the disciples instantly gain courage, clarity and eloquence to reach across all barriers of language, culture and prejudice with the testimony of the new covenant and of Jesus as the first fruits of the redemption.

No doubt the story is stylized into an ideal representation of the birth of the Church as a community of full-fledged disciples. If we are tempted to mistake it for a magic event (in which people are changed without having to change!), we need but read the rest of the Acts of the Apostles to trace the struggle with which the birth of the Church happened then, and continues to take place now. Yet the ideal representation gives a very clear account of what the Church is called to be—a community of those filled with the Spirit, receiving and discerning the gifts of the Spirit, accepting the complementarity, open to the surprises.

Trinity Sunday

READINGS: Prov 8:22-31; Rom 5:1-5; Jn 16:12-15.

Let us continue at peace with God through our Lord Jesus Christ, through whom we have been allowed to enter the sphere of God's grace, where we now stand ... God's love has flooded our inmost heart through the Holy Spirit he has given us. Jn 16:12-15.

After the cycle of feasts celebrating the events and phases of Christ's life among us, the liturgy moves into "ordinary time." But it passes through two transition Sundays which suggest what ordinary time should mean to us: Trinity Sunday this week, and Corpus Christi next week. Ordinary time means living in "the sphere of God's grace, where we now stand," and it means gathering around the Eucharist to discover our true identity, our relationship to the mystery of redemption and to one another and the world.

However, the Church has more than usual difficulty in finding readings for this Sunday each year of the three year cycle. What is the clearly formulated mystery of the Trinity for the later Church cannot really be found in that form in Scripture, and that lack makes the selection of texts difficult. Yet the very difficulty may be an advantage, because it challenges us to ask what the doctrine of the Trinity means, and particularly what it means for us. What these readings convey is that it means for us a world transformed into a sphere of grace, the guidance of the Spirit of truth, and the providence of God's own wisdom at all times.

That passage about Wisdom in the Book of Proverbs is not only very poetic in its form of expression, but quite practical in its meaning for us. Wisdom is personified here as a maternal figure, and is contrasted to Folly later in the passage (though not in today's excerpt). The text is at pains to tell us that Wisdom is in the very source and pattern of creation, our hostess and God's companion. In other words, the wisdom of God is not withheld from us and offered only to a privileged few. Quite to the contrary, it offers itself to us in lavish hospitality throughout creation. Sometimes in Scripture (Eccls 24), Wisdom is equated with Torah, the Law of God revealed to Israel. Christian meditation has seen Jesus as the wisdom of God, and this links the passage to today's feast: the wisdom that is Jesus is the same that is at the foundation and heart of all creation, accessible to all and at all times—the sphere of God's grace.

The reading from Romans insists, nevertheless, that it is through the mystery of Jesus that we are "justified through faith," brought into the realm of grace in the fullest sense. This must have been something palpable and overwhelming in Paul's experience, for he writes of it often and with passionate conviction. It is not only the hope of future vindication and fulfillment, but the present suffering of persecution and trials, which Paul experiences as solid ground for reassurance. It seems that everything has come into focus for him, and he knows that his hope is not mocked, because of the present experience of the Spirit. The Spirit is known and recognized by divine love radiating from the inmost core of Paul's being.

Most of us would hesitate to say this of ourselves. Perhaps we even hesitate to hope for such an experience for ourselves. Yet this kind of wisdom, and this kind of transforming love, seems to be what Jesus promises to the disciples at large. That seems to be the sense of the farewell speech as we have it in John's Gospel, and of today's excerpt in particular. It is most apt for this transition Sunday of the liturgical year. We have accompanied Jesus through the cycle of mysteries with our prayer and meditation, and are in some ways in a position like that of the first disciples on the evening of the farewell supper. The question is: where do we go now? what do we do now? how are we to find our orientation? And the answer is: the fullness of redemption is to be found in the Spirit. The Spirit completes the mystery of creation and redemption, guiding disciples into "all truth," bringing it all together.

Although the Scriptures do not give us a formulation of Trinitarian doctrine such as we have constructed it subsequently, Scripture does lead us to come to terms with the paradox of God who is so intimately known yet never comprehended, so intimately present yet always transcendent. We are led to reflect that God who is made known in creation by the divine wisdom at play in the world of our experience, has been among us in the most tangible and evident way in our encounters with Jesus in history, and has left us not with memories only but with the living, fruitful Spirit of divine presence and power. We can confidently expect to transform our world in all its structures and possibilities out of oppression into fullness of life and community, because we are in the sphere of God's grace.

Solemnity of Corpus Christi

READINGS: Gen 14:18-20; I Cor 11:23-26; Lk 9:11-17.

The Lord Jesus on the night of his arrest, took bread and, after giving thanks to God, broke it and said: "This is my body, which is for you; do this as a memorial of me." I Cor 11:23-24.

We move from the liturgical calendar that follows the events of the life of Jesus into that section of the year that leaves the Church as the focus of liturgical attention. The Solemnity of Corpus Christi marks the transition, and the combination of readings for the feast gives an important interpretation of what it really means to be Church. The focus is on God's gift to us in Jesus Christ, which becomes our gift to others. It is an interpretation of redemption in terms of hospitality.

Much symbolism has gathered about the mysterious figure of Melchisedech. In the original story, the priest of the local god of pre-Israelite Jerusalem shares bread and wine with Abraham, winner of a recent battle, and Abraham in turn offers the priest a tithe of the spoils of battle. This forms a solemn alliance between Abraham and the people of that shrine. In retrospect Melchisedech becomes priest of God Most High (interpreted as the God of Israel) and the ritual becomes an offering of thanks to God and God's fruitful blessing of Abraham. So important does the figure of Melchisedech become that Psalm 10 has God bestowing the greatest honor in the words, "You are a priest of the order of Melchisedech, and forever." The author of the Letter to the Hebrews sees this fulfilled in the person of Jesus, who holds a unique priesthood like Melchisedech, is king of peace like Melchisedech, and offers bread and wine.

In the context of today's readings what is important about Melchisedech is his likeness to Jesus and his ritual sharing of bread and wine. The symbolism is much enhanced when we recall that the consuming of the bread and wine together forges a solemn alliance, and that the New Testament has carried this symbolism over into our understanding of the Eucharist. Something of this seems to shape Paul's message to the Corinthians. Although today's selection is a very meager account of the tradition that Paul had received about the Lord's Supper, the context within the letter tells much more. Paul has been answering questions and complaints, and establishing some rules and guidelines for Christian community life and worship. He then comes to the matter that most troubles him: the behavior of the Corinthian community in relation to the Eucharist. Factions and class distinctions have been brought into the celebration—a downright contradiction of the meaning of the action. The Eucharist celebrates a solemn covenant; it is a bond of unity with Christ and with all the members, committing all to share the life and death of Jesus which is self-gift to others. The ritual action is a sharing of food, and it is a commitment to live the whole of one's life by this model. Moreover, it is a sharing of food that forges bonds of alliance, of identifying with one another's needs and hopes. Paul's point is especially that it is not in harmony with the Eucharist to exclude the poor, to maintain class distinctions.

The Gospel reading offers us another way of looking at the Eucharist. It is a different image with the same meaning. Jesus is with a large crowd of followers in a desert place, and therefore without food. As the evening draws on and people begin to get hungry, he tells his disciples to share what food they have with the crowd. Their answer is one that most of us might have given: hospitality is all very well when there is something to spare, but, after all, there are only five loaves and two fishes. It may be better to send the people away, to dismiss them from mind and sight, so as not to be involved in the problem of their hunger. Jesus, however, insists that they are our guests, and proceeds to distribute what there is, which turn out wonderfully to be more than enough.

We can, of course, interpret the story at many different levels. We can say that this is a remarkable demonstration that Jesus had superhuman powers. We can say that this is a wonderful work of God which matches the manna in the desert in the time of Israel's dependence upon God. We can say that the passage is presented in Scripture as a foreshadowing of the Eucharist in which Jesus continues to feed thousands and more than thousands. But in all of this we would be keeping ourselves safely out of the picture. We live in a world where thousands and more than thousands go daily unfed, and the question arises whether we say the problem is too great, what we have to share is too little, and that we must send them away to fend for themselves, out of sight and out of mind. And this is a question about the meaning of Church. It is a eucharistic question, a question about the Lord's Table.

Second Sunday of the Year

READINGS: Is 62:1-5; I Cor 12:4-11; Jn 2:1-12.

This deed at Cana in Galilee is the first of the signs by which Jesus revealed his glory and led his disciples to believe in him. Jn 2:11.

John presents his remarkable account of the bridegroom and the wine as the first of the "signs" that Jesus did—the "signs" with which John's whole Gospel is preoccupied. The liturgy, however, presents it on this Sunday as the third manifestation of divine grace and presence. It is, so to speak, the third Sunday of the Epiphany in our liturgical experience, the first being the commemoration of the Magi's pilgrimage two weeks ago, and the second the Baptism in the

Jordan one week ago. It is clear that we are being invited to look at the mystery of Christ's transforming presence in the world from many different angles.

The Cana story itself, however, is not as simple as it first appears; it is a skillfully crafted and many-sided story full of allusions. Here, as elsewhere, John's appears to be not so much a Gospel of proclamation as one of meditative and contemplative assimilation. There is something for everyone and for every stage of reflection and awareness. There is in the first place the story of Jesus, who has just gathered a few disciples about him, accepting an invitation to a local wedding at which his mother is also present, apparently helping the host family with the catering. At this level we have a story about family and neighborliness, about human celebration such as we all know. An embarrassing shortage arises, and through Mary's mediation Jesus comes wonderfully to the rescue. This is a level of the story that appeals to simple Christian piety, and in a rather special way to Catholic piety. The story tells that we may think of our faith as a family affair, turning to Mary's mediation, confident that Jesus cares about ordinary people and their ordinary worries.

This simple interpretation of the story is no less true for the fact that John appears to have had much more in mind. At another level, the incident is placed on the "third day," that is symbolically on the day of deliverance, which must have suggested then as now the day of Resurrection as the day of the great sign. Moreover, in the whole account of the calling of the first disciples, John is at pains to put this event at the end of the first week of the public ministry of Jesus, so that it appears as completing all that went before. Indeed, the story also makes a point that the water jugs that stood there were six in number, which must have suggested to anyone familiar with traditional Jewish symbolism a sense of incompleteness, of waiting for fulfillment, and that sense of incompleteness is connected with purification rituals for which the jugs were used. There is a sense of suspense, as though the empty jugs were waiting for something to happen. Wine is the symbol of joy, and it is joy that happens when Jesus comes to the feast and bestows his blessing on it. At this level, we can hear the story, understanding that all human persons and societies are in quest of true happiness, and that there is always something lacking, something incomplete, for Israel of old, for ourselves, and for all peoples. It is in Jesus that we find the fulfillment of all yearning, the completeness of what seemed always inadequate.

Again, this interpretation in the light of the symbolism of the Hebrew scriptures is not false, in spite of the fact that there is more yet in the story. That it took place at a wedding is very significant. From the beginning, those who read or heard John's Gospel must have been aware that in the synoptic gospels Jesus himself is presented as a bridegroom coming to claim his bride, a bridegroom in whose presence the guests can hardly be expected to mourn and fast—all this echoing the imagery which saw God as the bridegroom or husband of Israel his people. This suggests a new depth to the story. There are, so to speak, two weddings: one which is inadequate to bring true joy and fulfillment but which serves as a figure of joy and fulfillment yet to come; and a second more mysterious, more wonderful one which supplies for the inadequacy of the first in a way far surpassing all hope and expectation. The quest for human joy is met by the overwhelming gift of divine joy, and the search for ordinary life by the ecstatic possibility of the risen life.

John's allusions do not end even here, for the passage is full of hints that should lead us to interpret the story with reference to the sacramental life that we enjoy as Christians. In the story, Jesus the guest becomes the host, and his hospitality is lavish beyond expectation. The wine of the wonderful sign suggests the wine of the Eucharist and the hospitality of the self-gift of Jesus as the cup of joy. Well matched then is the Isaian song that tells of a city made new, justice shining like the sunrise, and deliverance like a blazing torch revealing the divine glory. But Isaiah also implies that the sign of joy is the sign of judgment, that the joy poured out in redemption is not divine permissiveness towards whatever is, but divine transformation into what ought to be.

The reading from I Corinthians, though following its own independent sequence once more, is not inapt for the occasion. The gifts of which Paul writes as the manifold gifts of the spirit are surely themselves wine poured out at the messianic wedding feast in the name of the bridegroom. The challenge to us is the invitation to recognize and appreciate the sign of joy and judgment.

Third Sunday of the Year

READINGS: Neh 8:2-6, 8-10; I Cor 12:12-30 (or 12:12-14, 27); Lk 1:1-4; 4:14-21.

The spirit of the Lord is upon me because he has anointed me; he has sent me to announce good news to the poor, to proclaim release for prisoners and recovery of sight for the blind; to let the broken victims go free, to proclaim the year of the Lord's favor. Lk 4:18-19.

Now that the Christmas season is really over, the liturgy makes another beginning by presenting three readings which seem, each in its different way, to set out a program for action. The reading from Nehemiah is set in the context of a return of exiled Jews to their own ancestral lands at a time of considerable discouragement. They seem to have found the burden of reestablishing life according to the Law of Moses an exhausting one. Ezra the scribe, who is their leader, therefore makes the occasion of the re-learning of the Law into a festival of joyous celebration and of experience of the solidarity and mutual support of the whole people. The thrust of his message is that accepting the burden of God's Law is not intended to be depressing or discouraging but uplifting, because it recreates peoplehood and a sense of identity, dignity and purpose.

This sense of the uplifting and sustaining character of the divine order of things is found also in the passage from I Corinthians. Paul uses a metaphor already well-known in the ancient world but gives it a new urgency and intimacy by reinterpreting it with reference to the unity of believers with one another that is rooted in their relationship with Christ. Paul seems to be concerned with a tragic reluctance of human persons to appreciate and encourage the personal gifts of others while contributing their own gifts in service of the common good. The problem is as common today as it was in Paul's time. Even those of us who are committed followers of Jesus are inclined to see others and their gifts more in terms of competition than of cooperation. The excellence of the other looks more like a threat than a promise. The program for Christian life and action as Paul seems to propose it, is one of learning to accept complementarity—not the broken complementarity of creation disrupted by sin, but the newly created complementarity in the redemptive power of Christ. That is a message apt for any time, and it gives further depth and practical relevance to the passage about Ezra which is the first reading.

What makes any of this practically possible, however, is certainly the impact of Jesus on human history, which is sketched in a powerful image in the Gospel reading. Luke has Jesus embarking on his public ministry with a proclamation that goes out from his hometown synagogue in the context of Sabbath worship. In the power of the Spirit he emerges from the ordinariness of his life among his own relatives and neighbors, with a reading from Isaiah that links his mission to the great traditions of prophecy in Israel. The Isaian passage seems to refer to the Jubilee Year, the year in which according to the strict interpretation of the Mosaic Law social justice and harmony and peace are restored in the economic and social structures of Hebrew life. Ancestral lands are restored to those who have lost or mortgaged them at times of distress, so that all families again own a little parcel of land sufficient to sustain them. Prisoners go free, debts are remitted to those who cannot fulfill their obligations, and slaves are emancipated.

The words that Jesus reads and appropriates to his own ministry in this text are evocative of the long-lost hopes of Israel for a just society ruled by divine wisdom and offering freedom, participation and acceptance to all. They suggest a just sharing of resources and opportunities, and they imply a kind of solidarity of peoplehood that has never yet really been experienced. They may be considered revolutionary words, but in a very profound and far-reaching sense of revolution, not in the sense of a military overthrow of those in power which puts others in their place, but in the sense of a truly radical restructuring of the way people relate to one another.

Luke gives us this "inaugural speech" of Jesus quite stark and unadorned: Jesus has come in the power of the Spirit to make things better for the poor, to set prisoners free, to restore clarity of vision to those blinded in any way, and to rescue "broken victims" of our human society. That is the program that he proclaims for his ministry. When the liturgy confronts us with this text, it is clearly not in order that we might look backward to assess whether the program has been realized. Rather it is that we might look forward with the understanding that this is the program that Jesus proposes to us here and now and in this year. Clearly it is the intent of this text that each time we hear it proclaimed we should realize that it is now, this year, that Jesus addresses us and declares that this is the year of the Lord's favor.

Fourth Sunday of the Year

READINGS: Jer 1:4-5, 17-19; I Cor 12:31-13:13; Lk 4:21-30.

Tell them everything I bid you, do not let your spirit break at sight of them .... I am with you and will keep you safe. This is the very word of the Lord. Jer 1:17, 19.

The theme of the day is that of vocation—the vocation of the prophet which is that of challenge, and the vocation of the faithful which is that of community and of charity. The passage from Jeremiah is clear; summoned by God even from the womb, he is consecrated as a prophet to the nations. But it is a task that will meet with much opposition and will therefore require great strength of purpose and conviction. Jeremiah is not to trust in himself for this, but in God who sends him, who will also make him strong and keep him safe. Jeremiah has become for all time the figure of the persecuted prophet who undergoes great ordeals. But this idea of the persecuted prophet is not something that belongs to ancient times; it applies to those who opposed Hitler in the name of Justice, to those who at various times have taken pacifist positions in the teeth of opposition, those who offered shelter to undocumented alien refugees in the face of the law that excluded them from mercy, those who have preached and demonstrated against unjust and oppressive regimes, and to all the "whistle-blowers" against corruption and injustice. The passage from Luke's Gospel is the counterpart of the Jeremian passage. In the text preceding this, which was read in the previous week, Jesus has entered the synagogue in his home town of Nazareth, and has been asked according to custom to read from the scriptures and to comment if he felt inclined. He had chosen a passage from the prophetic election mentioned in Third Isaiah, in which the prophet is chosen to proclaim a Jubilee year, a time of redemption. And Jesus now declares that this passage applies to him and that his difficulties will lie in his not being accepted by his own people. The passage needs further explanation. If Jesus had literally sat down to teach in the synagogue and immediately told them that he knew he would not be accepted, we could suppose that he was deliberately provoking opposition. But the text probably conflates a series of encounters in the course of which they did indeed reject him because of his familiarity. In that case the story takes on a very different complexion.

It seems that Luke wants to justify the mission of the early followers of Jesus to the Gentiles, by showing that the good news was first offered to those nearest to Jesus and rejected by many of them. But at the same time, having taken the examples of Elijah and Elisha who were sent to take the word of God beyond the boundaries of Israel, Luke also wants to identify Jesus with that long series of prophetic figures who were persecuted and later vindicated by God. Perhaps Luke even wants to console the Christian communities for whom this Gospel is written for the hardships and persecutions which they are enduring.

The Pauline passage is also about vocation, but not about the vocation to outsiders. I stresses that the heart of the Christian calling is concerned with the quality of the life that Christians live together in community. It is not heroic gestures, or extraordinary gifts that constitute the very substance of redemption. In the end there are faith, hope and love, but love is central and most important because it is love that makes everything else possible. This so-called hymn to charity is apt for every community and never outdated.

Fifth Sunday of the Year

READINGS: Is 6:1-8; I Cor 15:1-11, (or I Cor 15:1-8, 11); Lk 5:1-11.

They were calling ceaselessly to one another, "Holy, holy, holy is the Lord of Hosts: the whole earth is full of his glory." . . . *Then I heard the Lord saying, "Whom shall I send? Who will go for me?" And I answered, "Here am I; send me." Is 6:3, 8.*

The Isaian vision may seem far from our contemporary experience. Yet it describes a classic pattern in the divine calling which is ours also. Seraphim, along with other categories of angels, are rather out of fashion these days, but when we realize what they are—messengers of God's glory and God's pervasive presence to us, whose nature and definition is not of interest to the biblical writers—it is clear that we are all visited by angels, if we would but see them.

Isaiah's vision probably referred to the ark of the covenant housed in the Temple, for the throne of God was understood to be above the ark guarded by seraphim, and the smoke seems to be another way of representing the cloud that expresses the glory of the divine presence in the midst of the human community. It suggests, therefore, not really that only on this one occasion did the self-revelation of God flood the Temple, but rather that on this one occasion Isaiah realized it and was overwhelmed. And that is our own situation; the glory of God streams about us in our world and worship, but the moment of special calling is the moment in which we become aware of it and are overwhelmed.

When such a moment happens, then those of us who have been sturdily and doggedly preaching every week, or evangelizing or catechizing in any way, or tapping out homiletic columns, are apt to find ourselves in the same quandary as Isaiah (and indeed as Moses and Jeremiah and Ezekiel and countless others). That is to say, we are apt to find ourselves stunned into silence by the realization of our utter inability to express the glory that has been so graciously and freely shared with us. Isaiah, of course, stands in the Hebrew tradition which warns that an immediate revelation of God's glory is insupportable by human consciousness; one cannot see God and live. It is not surprising that his first response is to cry "woe" rather than "hallelujah." But the next step is classic too: a searing experience of conversion and transformation leaves him focused on message and mission and not on himself.

The liturgy is deliberate in matching this text with the Gospel reading. Simon's experience, though not liturgical but earthy and secular, is remarkably parallel to Isaiah's. The fisherman's perception of the world through the prism of his burdensome work explodes into an experience of the absurdly lavish gift of God in creation. The mediating presence of Jesus has turned his world so dizzyingly upside-down that his first response is to protest that he cannot cope, and to try to dismiss the divine presence from his life. As with Isaiah, his very insight into his own sinfulness and inadequacy is the burning experience that transforms Simon into a bearer of the mission and the message.

The passage from I Corinthians is not deliberately matched with the other two readings, but it speaks of the classic Christian shape of the revelation of God's glory. Like the enthronement of God in the Temple, for the Hebrews, the Resurrection of Jesus is always there for Christians but they do not always see it. Paul reminds Christians in season and out of season that the Glory of God is poured forth all about us in the Resurrection of Jesus. He seems to fear that we might forget that it is good news or that we might not fully realize that it is Good News *for us,* or that it is Good News for us *now.*

The eyes of faith and prayer may see in this selection of readings a certain progression. The revelation of God's glory in creation is gathered for us into a more concentrated experience in our traditions of public worship—in the ritual symbols and sacramental signs, the stories and images in which we cherish our glimpses of God's revelation, celebrating and reliving the moments. This is the privilege of all traditions that seek union with God. The encounter with Jesus of those who lived with him in Galilee and walked with him in the Judean journeys, is a further step. Jesus in person, in today's story about the catch of fish, and elsewhere, challenges the somnolence in which we readily allow the reality of our worship to become alien, unworldly, unreal. The divine revelation to which our tradition has attuned us, bursts forth again in the concrete circumstances of daily life, and Jesus in his person is the bridge that ends the alienation.

But there is a further stage which is the life of the risen Jesus, refocusing human community and human existence and consciousness. There is no longer an opposition, even a difference, between sacred and profane, between the realm of our worship and that of our worldly affairs. The glory bursts forth everywhere, and we may be surprised, overtaken, overwhelmed at any place or moment. We may expect to be stunned into silence by many different kinds of voices that prove to be heavenly messengers of holiness and glory. And we may expect both the sense of inability to respond, and the fiery transformation that enables us to speak after all in words that are not our own wisdom. We may hope for the courage to say, "Here I am. Send me," because of our experience that the earth is full of God's glory.

Sixth Sunday of the Year

READINGS: Jer 17:5-8; I Cor 15:12, 16-20; Lk 6:17, 20-26.

Blessed is the man who trusts in the Lord, and rests his confidence upon him. He shall be like a tree planted by the waterside, that stretches its roots along the stream. Jer 17:7-8.

Jeremiah's imagery of the two trees is very apt as an analogy for human life. To put one's trust in human arrangements or in one's own strength is certainly to rest on very slender resources, like the trees one see in desert land far from reliable water supplies. To be rooted firmly in one's trust in God is to have an unfailing source of strength and vitality. This saying of Jeremiah is part of a collection of such contrasts made in terms of analogies from nature. It may have been a condemnation of renewed nationalism and quest for worldly power in the nation in Jeremiah's time, but the analogy is fitting for human experience at any time and in any context.

The passage from Luke is in the same style and tradition. We may find it rather shocking, because we are more accustomed to hearing the Beatitudes from Matthew's Gospel, which have no Woes attached. Yet the logic of Luke is faultless and very much in tune with the prophetic tradition. If the needy are blessed because the order of things will be reversed and they are to be the fortunate in the Kingdom of God, then it follows that the reversal will also affect those who now are rich and who will lose their privileged advantages in society. If the hungry are to be fully satisfied, there is likely to be a reversal for those who enjoy undue luxury, and if those who weep and suffer in the present order are to have occasion to laugh, then those others whose laughter is provided by an unjust order are likely to mourn the loss of further cause for such laughter. Likewise, the sign of true prophets and false prophets, that is to say persecution in the former case and universal acclaim in the later, will not remain the same when the disorder of the world has been set aright.

By happy coincidence the unmatched passage from 1 Corinthians underscores this theme of contrast and reversal by its insistence on the resurrection of Jesus as indicative of the destiny of the faithful. The Christian hope rests on the most radical reversal of all, namely that those who willingly lose their lives for the sake of God's redeeming word in human history, shall find their lives transformed and enhanced by the power of God. It was the constant message of Paul that this is an experience that we can share now—a gift offered to us with our baptism and our invitation to the Eucharist.

Seventh Sunday of the Year

READINGS: I Sam 26:2, 7-9, 12-13, 22-23; I Cor 15:45-49; Lk 6:27-38.

Love your enemies; do good to those who hate you; bless those who curse you; pray for those who treat you spitefully . . . . if you do good only to those who do good to you, what credit is that to you? Even sinners do as much. Lk 6:28, 33.

The love of enemies has never been a popular commandment. It seems exaggerated, unpractical, more for rosy visions than for real life. David, the legendary hero of many Jewish tales, practices restraint of violence against his enemy the King on rather special grounds. He will not harm Saul because Saul has been anointed in God's name and David fears divine retribution if he touches the anointed one to do him harm. There may even be something of superstition in the attitude expressed by David in this account. Yet it is an heroic feat that he accomplishes and shows great courage and complete trust in God and dependence on God's command.

The teaching of Jesus about forgiveness and goodness to hostile persons goes much further than this. It appeals to the intrinsic logic of redemption, which is a logic of non-violence. If evil is repaid with evil there is an unending series. Even if the hostilities do not escalate, as they are very likely to do, there is no end in sight, until one or both parties are eliminated or exhausted. This has been more or less the continuous history of human societies. As Jesus sees it, violence and destruction arc only brought to an end by those who refuse to participate in it, who will not return evil for evil, but absorb the impact so that it stops at the point. The logic of this is simple and compelling but that does not make it easy to practice, and it has certainly not been the usual behavior of Christians.

Paul's remarks in the passage from I Corinthians, provides an interesting sidelight, as so often happens in spite of the fact that the second reading follows its own separate sequence. In this case the text is about being a new creation in Christ. Adam is the first or natural pattern for human existence; Jesus is the second or spiritual pattern for human existence. If we are remade into the image of Christ we are empowered to do as he did, and our human lives are transformed in redemptive patterns that go beyond anything of which we think we are capable. To live the spiritual life is to enjoy the breath or power of the Spirit acting within us in ways that are redemptive because they are divine. That is not a matter of some obscure or esoteric reality that never impinges on our experience; it is a matter of the way we conduct all our daily affairs, public and private.

Eighth Sunday of the Year

READINGS: Sir 27:4-7; I Cor 15:54-58; Lk 6:39-45.

As the fruit of the tree reveals the skill of its grower, so the expression of a man's thought reveals his character. Sir 27:6.

Some of the teaching that Luke gathers together in the Sermon on the Plain reflects the style and content of the Wisdom literature of the Hebrew Scriptures. Short, pithy sayings suggest insight into human behavior, attitudes and relationships. But although Jesus uses the style and makes many allusions to the existing literature in his imagery, there is a characteristic focus and purpose in his sayings. These are not random bits of advice, nor the expression of a fairly conventional worldly wisdom. They have a logic but it is strictly the logic of Jesus himself, which is the logic of the redemption. Much of the advice contained in his sayings only makes sense if the redemption of the human community from sin and evil is ultimately assured and presently possible.

Thus while Sirach suggests quite rightly that people's character is revealed both in their words and in their work, the purpose of Jesus is always to show the requirements of genuine faith in the coming

Reign of God. In today's excerpt he stresses the need for revelation and for discipleship, the exigence of personal humility and tolerance of the short-comings of others, and the way to discern the dispositions of the heart from the actions that are manifest in the world. This last is a favorite theme of Jesus; it is not the vocabulary that we use or the ritual obligations that we observe which justify us before God, but the ordinary manner and impact of our lives that shows the extent to which we really live by the grace of God.

The second reading of the day interjects a note of hope, and even of optimism into this reflection. It reminds us that the victory over death and all lesser evils is the gift of God in Christ. It insists that the triumph of Jesus over death is also and already our own triumph and that the attitude most appropriate under those circumstances is one of gratitude and of great confidence in God both for our own future and for the outcome of our work. In this Paul assumes that we are as passionately involved in the service of the good news as he himself is. And this is ultimately the characteristic wisdom—and even the characteristic wisdom literature— of Christians.

Ninth Sunday of the Year

READINGS: I Kings 8:41-43; Gal 1:1-2, 6-10; Lk 7:1-10.

Hear in heaven thy dwelling and respond to the call which the foreigner makes to thee, so that like thy people Israel all peoples of the earth may know thy fame and fear thee, and learn that this house which I have built bears thy name.   1 Kgs 8:43.

The mystery of God's dwelling among us is one we do not ever really fathom. The Temple of old, which Solomon was privileged to build, represented and foreshadowed a greater and more elusive mystery of God's presence. But the Temple was, so to speak, sacramental; it effected what it signified because it guided people into the presence of God in prayer. In the present passage, Solomon asks that it may do this not only for Israel but for all the nations. He recognizes the calling of Israel as exemplary—the vocation of a witness people to guide others to the true God—and thus Solomon's prayer becomes truly ecumenical.

The story of the Centurion's faith and humility is a remarkable answer to that kind of prayer in the history of Israel. Even before the event told in this story, the centurion appears to be one who worships with the Jews, adoring the God of Israel, and even providing for the building of a synagogue. He evidently both knows and respects the ritual code of Jews for he tactfully avoids asking Jesus to come into his house or touch anything that would make Jesus ritually unclean by Jewish law. Yet Jesus testifies that the faith of this Gentile professional soldier is greater than any that he has found among the chosen people. The Centurion is confident in his knowledge that all things are under God's authority and that Jesus is sent by God. He knows what authority means in the army, and what a chain of command is, and he perceives the commands of God by analogy with this with a great and admirable simplicity.

It is in such a context, whether among Jews or Gentiles, that the wonderful works of God can be manifest in all their splendor. That is the reason, no doubt, why Paul insists so much on the freedom of the Gentile Christians from the obligations of the ritual law. The Law does not necessarily open people to the divine revelation and mercy. It is the good news of Jesus Christ and the grace that has been given them which must keep them faithful to their calling. If they, the Christians in the local churches of Galatia are to be faithful it must be out of their own experiential grasp of the message and the grace that has been offered to them. They will recognize the true Gospel as always the same message they have received from the beginning. In the last analysis the relationship between God and the faithful followers of Jesus are very simple—as simple as the Centurion's perception of the exercise of God's authority.

Tenth Sunday of the Year

READINGS: 1 Kgs 17:17-24; Gal 1:11-19; Lk 7:11-17.

Deep awe fell upon them all, and they praised God. "A great prophet is risen among us," they said, and again, "God has shown his care for his people." Lk 7:16.

A theme that recurs many times in the Bible is this: the power of God is life-giving, affirmative towards creatures. Yet most of us would probably be very surprised, perhaps skeptical, if we were present at a scene such as Elijah's raising of the widow's son in Zarephath or Jesus' raising of the widow's son at Nain. The central message of revelation, of Christ in death and Resurrection, of the Spirit in the Church, is one of life and hope founded in God whose power is creative, transcending every end and every tragedy. But our response is more often a dull fatalism: there will always be poor and starving populations; there will always be wars and nothing can stop the escalation of weapons; there is no such thing as politics without corruption; and so it goes on.

Today's readings challenge us in a very stark way concerning the reality of our hope. They challenge us particularly to consider whether in our own minds and attitudes we have set severe limits to God's power, whether we have made up our minds that there are things God cannot do because we do not find them reasonable or probable. In the story of Elijah, the widow knows that God can raise her only son to life. Her final comment suggests that she had some doubts but that these were only about Elijah's relationship to the life-giving power of God. What the widow of Nain thought about Jesus we do not learn. We do know something of what Jesus thought about her—he had deep compassion for her. But we read that deep awe fell upon the crowd whose response goes far beyond the widowed mother or the young men raised to life. The crowd is awed because it is a sign to them; a great prophet has arisen and God has shown care for the people.

There are several aspects of the story that our modern minds may miss unless the allusions are pointed out. Elijah raises the child with immense pleading and prayer, arguing the widow's case, and even suggesting that his own credibility as a prophet is at stake. Jesus, however, gives a simple command out of compassion, and the thing is done. There is no doubt that the Gospel writer remembered the other story (as well as a rather similar one about Elisha) and is at pains to show us how much greater our hope can be when it is founded on the mediation of Jesus. But it is also true that a widow with an only son in these stories is reminiscent of Israel and its sole hope of redemption, when it appears again and again as though God had forgotten the people of the covenant. We might even see parallels with the experience of the Church in the course of history. There are times of persecution, times of worldliness and tepidity, times of indecision, when it seems that God has abandoned the covenant people. But the Scriptures recall our attention to the many times that the one who represented the only hope of the bereaved mother, or the bereaved community, was raised even from death—the boy in the Elijah story, the child in the Elisha story, the young man of Nain, Lazarus, Jesus.

The reading from Galatians also seems to address our reluctance to believe good news. Paul finds it necessary to insist once again that he has not invented this good news, that it is no fabrication of the imagination, but that it is indeed the word of God to us through the revelation of Jesus Christ. The people to whom he wrote on this occasion seem to have thought it safer to maintain many observances and to initiate Gentiles into the ritual code of Israel—all to make a little more sure of salvation by going to elaborate lengths to appease God. It is as though they saw God as punitive, disciplinary, oppressive, rather than life-giving, liberating, affirming of human persons.

In this brief recital of Paul's own story we hear of another kind of raising to life, but it is a resurrection that is just as real as a physical one. Paul tells of the dire straits of the young community of believers in face of his own savage persecution of all who followed the way of Jesus. But he tells also of the extraordinary intervention of divine grace in the person of the risen Christ, giving new life and hope to the community. At the same time Paul's story is of himself in a state akin to death because his efforts to attain righteousness were holding the grace of God at bay. He also was brought back, as it were, to life. And so were his converts. That is why the Christian community of the time responded as did the crowds at Nain.

The liturgy invites us to look at these three stories in juxtaposition, and to learn from them to recognize in our own times and in our own lives the signs of God's life-giving, re-creating power—the ways in which God has shown the divine care for the people of the world. The courage of such recognition is a power in the world for peace and survival and justice.

Eleventh Sunday of the Year

READINGS: 2 Sam 12:7-10; Gal 2:16, 19-21; Lk 7:36-8:3 (7:36-50).

Two men were in debt to a money lender: one owed him five hundred silver pieces, the other fifty. As neither had anything to pay with he let them both off. Now, which will love him most? Lk 7:41-42

One cannot read the Gospels without becoming aware that Jesus frequently went out of his way to make contact with disreputable people. Certainly, he did nothing to avoid them. Most of us would probably not have liked the way he behaved, had we been in Simon's place. Jesus is not impressed by the self-righteous and the respectable, and above all he does not accept the way we classify people into good folk and sinners. In this case we know that Simon was a Pharisee, that is someone who took great pains to fulfill all aspects of the Law, including traditional teachings not found in the Pentateuch. But we also know from the reproach that Jesus utters that there was a lack of warmth, even of customary courtesy, in the welcome which Simon extended to his invited guest. About the woman we know that she was considered sinful by pharisaic standards, but we do not learn in what respect. She herself seems to have accepted the judgment that she was sinful in some outstanding way, and Jesus agreed with her judgment about herself.

What makes the attitude of Jesus so different from that of Simon is that for Jesus this acknowledged sinfulness is a special moment of opportunity. Those who know themselves forgiven have discovered a cause for gratitude and love and a source of generosity to others. Those who do not think they have any significant need of forgiveness are more likely to be arrogant towards others, measuring approval and friendship in small doses. It is not accidental that the liturgy matches this text with that from 2 Samuel 12. Any talk of great sin, great repentance and great love, would suggest to a devout Jew the figure of King David, the proverbial passionate penitent. The well-known story of David's sin, in taking Bathsheba and having Uriah killed, had long stood as a reminder that great sinners can become great penitents and lovers.

The part of the story that is read today, however, focuses on the prophet Nathan's response to David. In the first place there is Nathan's strategy. It is the strategy used by novelists and playwrights; they allow us to look from the outside at a human situation. Because it is the situation of another, imaginary person, we are able to look at it with empathy and without defensiveness. But sooner or later we recognize the situation as one in our own lives. Nathan concludes, "You are the man," and the liturgy depends on our remembering the earlier part of the story about the rich man who seized the poor man's only sheep. David grasps the analogy, but all these readings question whether *we* do—whether we recognize ourselves as the sinners who have been forgiven much, who have had the debt of five hundred silver pieces remitted, who are justified not by our own efforts but by the death of Jesus. When Nathan says that the Lord has laid upon another the consequences of David's sin, he means that Bathsheba's infant son will die, but Christian faith sees an allusion to the death of Jesus.

Paul transforms these images and stories into a general theology of justification, not by claims to have observed the Law, but by faith in Jesus Christ crucified and the redeeming grace of God. The paradox of the call to repent and to live lovingly, side by side with the doctrine of universal sinfulness and redemption by the sheer grace of God, has always been a difficult one to accommodate in Christian attitudes and behavior. In our own times particularly, it appears morbid to think of oneself constantly as a sinner and as utterly dependent. We need to search out the meaning and purpose of this paradoxical teaching. Certainly it is not intended as a kind of fatalism, accepting unjust and oppressive situations as inevitable, especially when we do not suffer from them ourselves. Certainly it is not a way of saying that destructive behavior, insensitive attitudes and selfish relationships are inalterable facts of life which God will overlook.

Perhaps the critical aspect to consider is this: to acknowledge onself in the wrong and the recipient of gracious forgiveness, is to leave open possibilities for change, for a new beginning. Moreover, to know the need and the possibility of such new beginnings for oneself opens up a vision and experience offering the expectation of change in others. To experience oneself as a forgiven and repentant sinner tends to dissolve some of the heavy stereotypes we often impose on others. The paradox of justification by faith and grace is not morbid in the light of the question: who will love the most?

Twelfth Sunday of the Year

READINGS: Zech 12:10-11; Gal 3:26-29; Lk 9:18-24.

You have all put on Christ as a garment. There is no such thing as Jew and Greek, slave and freeman, male and female; for you are all one person in Christ Jesus ... the 'issue' of Abraham, and so heirs by promise. Gal 3:27-29.

This text speaks of something that is at the core of the redemption—our recognition of our savior and our salvation in our reconciliation with one another. The passage occurs in the Letter to the Galatians in the midst of Paul's argument that salvation is not by observance of ritual code but by faith in Jesus Christ. At first reading it seems strange that Paul should see such a direct connection between salvation by faith and the breaking down of barriers of discrimination between people. Yet the ritual of Israel was and is certainly intended to mark the separation of Jews from Gentiles. In many ways it also marked out very sharp differentiations of social role and status between men and women.

It is not only the ritual code of Israel but every code of laws that classifies and divides and imposes roles and function on people from outside themselves, independently of their natural gifts and possibilities. That is why Paul is so insistent that law cannot save; it can at best be a tutor that brings people to the point at which authentic freedom begins. When that freedom begins, we shall recognize in and through our union with Christ the essential unity and creative possibilities that we have with one another. Thus for Paul, it is important to recognize the presence and representation of Christ in women as well as in men. It is evidently in conflict with his understanding of the gospel to see a woman as less representative of Christ because of her sex, or a Greek because he is not a Jew, or a slave because of her legal, social and economic status. Privilege or any kind of exclusiveness based on sex, race or socio-economic standing is unworthy of Christ, putting us back under the tutelage of law which cannot save. This message is so radical that it is perhaps not surprising that after two millennia of Christianity we are still inclined to think it must have been intended as hyperbole.

It is a happy coincidence that this particular text should be read on this Sunday, sandwiched between two texts about the recognition of salvation. The text from Zechariah does not give us the original context. It is a text of vindication of Jerusalem by God, of repentance and reconciliation, and of mourning over one who has been "pierced." It is set within a longer passage which is a messianic prophecy full of symbolism. We do not know whether the one who was pierced and is mourned over is God as the Savior of Israel, or Josiah the King of Judah who was slain in battle, or the "good shepherd" mentioned earlier in the prophecy, or some other martyr, or the mysterious "suffering servant." We do know that the Church sees this person as representing Christ. Thus it is an invitation to Christians to recognize the Messiah of our salvation in unlikely places, among the persecuted, the defeated, the oppressed.

When we hear today's Gospel reading after the other two selections, it gains great depth. The story is so familiar that it might otherwise seem quite bland. There are speculations among the crowds as to the identity of Jesus, a question which demands that the disciples take a stand on the matter, Peter's confession of messianic faith, the charge of secrecy, and the explanation of the messianic vocation of suffering and the participating role of the disciple. This sounds like a pattern imposed upon human history and human lives rather arbitrarily from eternity. But the reading from Galatians challenges our understanding by being very practical about the transformation that is the substance of salvation. The suffering spoken about in the Gospel is not at all arbitrary but precisely the kind of persecution and hardship involved in the radical reconciliations sketched concretely by Paul. Moreover, the messianic suffering is such not because it was arbitrarily decreed but, as the text from Zechariah indicates, because out of the defeat and oppression and death comes the liberating and reconciling force that reestablishes God's people.

The final sentence of the Gospel reading sums up the challenge to our understanding and our attitudes. It raises the question: where and how do we seek our safety, our security? In exclusivity and bullying power or in reconciliation and community? In asserting how different we are in order to press privilege and advantage, or in seeking common ground and a common future? In courting universal destruction in order to maintain our superiority and separateness, or in learning to recognize the salvation of the world on the terms on which God gives it?

Thirteenth Sunday of the Year

READINGS: 1 Kgs 19:16, 19–21; Gal 5:1, 13–18; Lk 9:51–62.

No one who sets his hand to the plough and then keeps looking back is fit for the kingdom of God. Lk 9:62.

The different usages of the imagery of ploughing and of the yoke is apt to be confusing in this collection of scripture passages. In the first reading, Elijah, newly emerged from the revelations on Mount Horeb after his forty day walk, passes on his mission to Elisha in the symbolic action of throwing his cloak over him. Elisha leaves his ploughing to run after Elijah, obviously accepting the challenge and the call, but asking leave to say goodbye to his parents. In this story, the senior prophet replies that he has no intention of preventing his disciple and successor from doing this. Elisha therefore returns and burns, not his boats, but the yoke and plough behind him, roasting the slaughtered oxen for a farewell feast. It is a decisive action.

It seems, however, that the intent of the story in Luke's Gospel is to insist on the greater urgency when Jesus calls and the Kingdom of God is at hand. For during his preaching journey through Samaria in the direction of Jerusalem with all its dangers, three separate people come to Jesus with intent to follow him wherever he may go. To the first Jesus gives a warning that this will mean homelessness and hardship. To the second he denies the excuse to wait until after his father's death. And to the third he suggests that there cannot even be a farewell feast (perhaps for fear that the man's friends would persuade him to change his mind). We are not able to fill in the details of what the circumstances were in each of the three cases, but what is clear is that Luke is aware that the call of Jesus to his potential disciples is far more urgent even than the call of Elijah to Elisha at a time of persecution and national crisis.

The passage from Galations also introduces the imagery of the yoke. In this case it is the yoke of slavery to prescriptions of the ritual code. Paul's inistent claim is that Christ has brought freedom from the Law, not for license but for another kind of service, that of love for one another. Paul wants the Galatians, and all his later readers and listeners to be guided by the Spirit. And he sees the Spirit as providing a balance that is neither servitude nor license but the true freedom of redeemed human existence. For him also the call of Christ is absolute, urgent and exigent, but it is nevertheless the entrance into freedom.

The tension between these readings and their varying emphases is the tension that we also meet in daily life. The demands of the gospel of Jesus Christ are very exigent, but embraced wholeheartedly they are liberating.

Fourteenth Sunday of the Year

READINGS: Is 66:10-14; Gal 6:14-18; Lk 10:1-12, 17-20 (or Lk 10:1-9).

God forbid that I should boast of anything but the cross of our Lord Jesus Christ ... the only thing that counts is new creation! Whoever they are who take this principle for their guide, peace and mercy be upon them....
Gal 6:14, 15, 16.

In the powerful poetry of Isaiah 66, God promises to send peace flowing over Jerusalem like a river. It is a message that sounds good in our times, but surely no more so than to the tired remnant of Israel returned from exile under discouraging circumstances. The metaphors change rapidly, from the river of peace to the consolation of the nursing child and the promise of fresh growing things in springtime. They are all images of hope.

The short passage from Galatians also speaks of hope, with a sharp focus on the new creation arising out of the cross of Christ, and issuing in peace. It is not circumcision (the observance of ritual requirements) that matters, nor is it circumcision that hinders. The issue is the question where we place our trust and how we live the implications of that trust. Where the cross of Christ and the new creation form the principle that guides attitudes and actions, there is peace. This was the principle for the original building of the church and it is the principle for reaching out to receive the reign of God into the world of our own times.

The instructions of Jesus to the disciples in this Gospel excerpt suggest very practically and concretely what that means. It means going forth bearing good news in a spirit of utter simplicity and non-violence. The first word of the good news is "peace," and the test of fertile ground for the gospel is whether the peace is reciprocated. When it is, there is a time to bring healing and to declare that the reign of God is close, indeed at hand.

What these three readings have in common is the claim that peace is the manifestation of God's presence. It is the gift of God but it must be received willingly as a gift. When it is welcomed, peace flows over the world like a river. It is clear that this message and this hope are immediately relevant to our own time. We as Christians in today's world are called not only to speak of good news but to *be* good news to others. We are called not only to greet people with words of peace but to be peacemakers in the fullest sense of that word.

In today's reading, the peace that is to flow over the whole earth like a river is also presented as a new creation springing from the cross of Christ. But the newness of redemption in Christ is practical as well as visionary; it is expressed in justice for the poor and the excluded and in structures of society that express community rather than ruthless competition, and harmony rather than cold war tactics. The redemption comes to us as a blessing of peace.

Fifteenth Sunday of the Year

READINGS: Deut 30:10-14; Col 1:15-20; Lk 10:25-37.

Love the Lord your God with all your heart, with all your soul, with all your strength, with all your mind; and your neighbor as yourself . . . do that and you will live. Lk 10:27, 28.

The story of the lawyer's question and its answer in parables is a very familiar one, not only because we hear it often and it is easy to remember, but because we so often find ourselves situated in that story. The lawyer who puts this test question seems to present it in a minimalist way: that are the necessary conditions for salvation. Jesus responds that the law has already covered this question, but asks the lawyer how he interprets the law. He receives a good answer, which goes straight to the heart of the matter, quoting from the *shema* (Deut 6:5) which is the deepest and most frequent expression of Hebrew faith and commitment. Moreover, the lawyer adds to it Lev 19:18 concerning duty to one's neighbor.

It is not surprising that Jesus then responds in effect, "You see yourself how simple it is." That, after all, is also the point being made in the section of Deuteronomy read today: it is not necessary to seek in esoteric sources the meaning of the law of God, for the essence of the law is recited in the people's most common prayers. It comes readily to the lips and is already in their hearts, calling them to observe it. The text was originally part of a movement for the revival of observances after the exile, but its relevance extends to all generations.

It is not difficult to understand the lawyer's next question, because it is a common human gambit. He asks to have it made quite explicit and specific so that he will know exactly how far he must go to observe the law: "who is my neighbor?" The lavish detail and human interest of the story Jesus tells in answer do not conceal but rather reveal the shocking simplicity of the way Jesus himself interprets the law. For Jesus, loving the neighbor as oneself is taken very literally. The neighbor is anyone in need who comes across one's path. To love one's neighbor as oneself is to devote all available time, energy and resources when they are required to succor the needy. No doubt the evangelist wants us to reflect that Jesus himself is the good Samaritan, and that to follow him is to do likewise. Certainly Christian tradition has taken this interpretation as axiomatic.

The passage of Colossians is in tune with this: it is Jesus who is the divine image among us, identified with that very image of God in which all things, but especially human persons, are made. It is the image in which all can be recreated and reconciled. But this is through the blood of the cross— through Jesus' literal interpretation of what it really means to love God with one's whole heart and one's neighbor as oneself.

As Jesus must have told the story it would have had the additional shocking effect of the choice of a Samaritan as hero. The non-observant, or schismatic Samaritans were despised at that time among faithful Jews. The implication of the cast of characters is relevant in our time also. There is an attitude of pious observances that does not aid communion with God but obstructs it. It is that attitude to law-keeping which sets it above the needs of other people. One meets God truly when one cares for people in need.

Sixteenth Sunday of the Year

READINGS: Gen 18:1-10; Col 1:24-28; Lk 10:38-42.

The secret is this: Christ in you, the hope of a glory to come.   Col 1:27.

The passage from Genesis and the one from Luke both tell of entertaining God's representatives. In the Genesis story Abraham and Sarah showered lavish attentions on their guests and were rewarded with the promise of a child. God is hospitable too. This story, in its setting in Genesis, contrasts with the account in the following chapter of the inhospitality of the people of Sodom. The contrast seems straight forward and proper, yet the story of Luke suggests that we should think quite differently about being hospitable to a divine visitation.

If we were to take the story of Martha and Mary quite literally it would be a rather cruel story, because Martha provides the traditional hospitality that would be expected and, instead of being thanked, is brushed off with what seems to be a contemptuous remark. But the story suggests a meaning beyond the literal. The behavior of the two sisters as it is described is very like the behavior of two traditions in Israel. Martha suggests the pharisaic tradition of being very busy observing the law. We do not need to look back to ancient Israel for examples of that attitude; we are very familiar with it in Catholic circles. It is the anxiety of living a devoutly religious life by the sheer multiplicity and literal thoroughness of the obeying of rules and prescriptions. It is genuinely a way of welcoming the divine presence in our lives, and Jesus does not condemn it. But he does say that there is a better way.

Mary's attitude and behavior in the story suggests another way. It is the way associated with the tradition of the *anawim,* simple in their faith and trust, recognizing their poverty before God, not attempting to be justified by their own efforts. Jesus says it is a better way. Not only that, but Jesus himself follows this way in his lifestyle and preoccupations; the letter of the law never takes precedence with him over simple communion with the Father and direct response to human need. It implies a willingness to be led, a willingness to forego the security of having everything predictable and under one's own control. It implies unselfconscious spontaneity and a willingness to take risks, to be vulnerable.

It is noteworthy that the context of the story is a dinner party, a festive meal. In Martha's view the success of the party depends on the special character of what she can provide. In Mary's view the success of the party depends on what Jesus provides. Martha sees herself as the giver; Mary sees herself as receiver.

It is this sense of the teaching of Jesus that lies behind the attitude that the apostle Paul constantly displays—his sense of liberation from the tutorship of a burdensome law into the freedom of Christ. No doubt that is why he describes his divinely assigned task as one of announcing a divine secret now revealed: "Christ in you, the hope of a glory to come."

Seventeenth Sunday of the Year

READINGS: Gen 18:20-32; Col 2:12-14; Lk 11:1-13.

Is there a father among you who will offer his son a snake when he asks for fish, or a scorpion when he asks for an egg? . . . how much more will the heavenly Father give the Holy Spirit to those who ask him. Lk 11:11-12.

Some of the most moving passages of the New Testament are surely those in which Jesus shares his own experiences of prayer and his own convictions about prayer with his disciples. Something about him while he was at prayer impressed them so profoundly that they were moved to ask him to teach them to pray. In this passage Jesus gives a two-fold answer: he sketches the appropriate content for prayer, and describes the appropriate attitude.

The content of the Lord's prayer is so familiar that we might miss the significance of Jesus' answer. God is to be addressed in familial fashion, and at the same time glorified, so that prayer begins with praise. There can only be one main petition, for the coming of the Reign of God, for the fullness of redemption. But then there is room to present to God our basic human needs in the meantime, and to seek reconciliation, knowing the demands that makes on us to forgive and be reconciled with one another, and asking not to be put to the ultimate test.

It is perhaps because this is the content that Jesus sees as appropriate for prayer, that he can recommend such dogged and confident persistence. To plead for the conversion and redemption of the world is to ask for something God cannot refuse. Jesus does not say that God will give anything whatever that we might ask for, but that God will surely give what we need.

Abraham pleading that the city be spared for the sake of ten just men is well matched in the liturgy with Jesus pleading for the salvation of the world. The prayer of Abraham anticipates much in the teaching of Jesus about the coming Reign of God—the wheat and weeds growing together until the harvest, the edible and inedible fish drawn into the net, and so forth. And this prayer of Abraham also describes life as we experience it; while there is any goodness, any move towards repentance, there is also hope for the world. And when Jesus speaks of the friend begging for bread during the night, he is describing himself and also all those who keep clinging to hope against overwhelming evidence of the corruption and irresponsiveness of the world.

The excerpt from Colossians underscores that hope by recalling the reason. In Christ we have seen our own passage from death to life. Therefore we know in the depth of our own being that when we persevere in asking, we shall receive.

Eighteenth Sunday of the Year

READINGS: Eccles 1:2, 2:21-23; Col 3:1-5, 9-11; Lk 12:13-21.

Be on your guard against greed of every kind, for even when a man has more than enough, his wealth does not give him life. Lk 12:15.

The story of the rich man who hoards and hoards and then dies a sudden death is to be found as easily in the morning newspaper as in the Gospel for today's celebration. Accumulation of capital resources, personal wealth or good insurance is no guarantee against heart attacks, cancer or traffic accidents. Yet we are rightly cautioned by this gospel reading, for it is characteristic of our culture that we accumulate property as though it were our security. The only real security is to use one's wealth for the needy and to set one's heart on God. The only persons to whom death does not come as a thief, to rob and despoil, are those whose being is an act of overflowing gratitude for the goodness of God.

There is perhaps a peculiar irony in the reading of this Gospel story in the American context, because it is a matter of storing grain reserves in a hungry world. But the story is common enough that even Ecclesiastes is concerned with it. The preoccupation with the accumulation of wealth is sheer vanity, sheer emptiness, for it must be left behind at death to someone other than the toiler. The anxiety lavished upon it is useless because the wealth is gathered for oneself and that self can only really enjoy a very limited amount of it. The rest is frustration.

Paul offers the positive aspect of the same admonition. In the passage from Colossians his thesis is that having been raised with Christ to new life, we are truly enabled to raise our desires to heavenly matters. It is a time to cast aside whatever is not authentic and truthful and to accept a new beginning in the image of the creator for whom there cannot be specious divisions making some rich and powerful while others are excluded. It is a time to recognize where the true treasure is, because the perennial truth of our human lives has become radiantly clear in the Risen Christ. The only true and lasting treasure is the personal happiness and peace of mind that comes from deep communion with God and genuine, self-surrendering community with fellow human beings. It is simply not possible to pursue these and also commit one's best energies to profit and accumulation. That is why a clear-sighted and sometimes ruthless decision is needed to appreciate and pursue the true treasure.

Nineteenth Sunday of the Year

READINGS: Wis 18:6-9; Heb 11:1-2, 8-19 (or 1-2, 8-12); Lk 12:32-48 (or 35-40).

And what is faith? Faith gives substance to our hopes, and makes us certain of realities we do not see. Heb 11:1.

The letter to the Hebrews offers many examples of faith, but the one that has had most appeal for Christians since the beginning is that of Abraham. In this passage Abraham is admired particularly for the risks he took and for his great detachment and singleness of purpose in pursuit of what he understood to be God's call. It is these characteristics—singleness of purpose, detachment, and willingness to take risks—that make Abraham a singularly apt model for our turbulent times, and indeed for any time.

The Gospel reading suggests something similar, for it speaks of being ready for action, alert and watchful at all times, totally singleminded. But the parable of the servants and their behavior in the master's absence also takes on a rather grim tone when speaking of the responsibility of the more gifted, of those on more intimate terms with the master. The worst warnings are reserved for those who, being in charge, take advantage of it by bullying fellow servants while living comfortably themselves. But if the end is grim in the longer form of this reading, the beginning has a coaxing quality to it. It coaxes the community of the Messiah, the little flock, to go forth beyond fear and in faith, to take great risks, to be singleminded, to trust and to have great hope for the restored reign of God in their midst. That also seems an apt message for our times, in which it often seems more realistic to fear the worst and live defensively in public and private life, rather than to have great hopes and risk all.

While the Gospel parable says that the thief, the master, the savior, may come at any time, on any night, the first reading dwells on the recollection of such a night—the Passover night. It was a night in which those who were watching, and who trusted in God and risked all, were vindicated. Those, on the other hand, who had taken advantage of their position to bully the poor and powerless were mightily punished. So impressed is this author with the wonder of the occasion, that he even imagines that on that first night of the great liberation the Hebrew ancestors were already celebrating the full Passover Seder, including the prescribed hallel psalms of a much later pattern of observance.

As Passover has been for Israel the reason for hope and for risks, so the Resurrection offers Christians the faith that gives substance to our hopes. Moreover, Passover continues to be present in the experience of succeeding generations who experience liberation of various kinds by the merciful power of God. And the Resurrection likewise continues to be present in the community of the followers of Jesus who experience newness of life and hope where it might least be expected.

Twentieth Sunday of the Year

READINGS: Jer 38:4-6, 8-10; Heb 12:1-4; Lk 12:49-53.

I have come to set fire to the earth, and how I wish it were already kindled! I have a baptism to undergo, and what constraint I am under until the ordeal is over! Lk 12:49-50.

It is startling at first to read that Jesus does not expect to bring immediate peace to the earth but rather division, even to the heart of the family. Somehow, in spite of all that we know of sin and redemption, we are still inclined to think that the life of the Church and the process of Redemption should be non-conflictual. We are reluctant to acknowledge that it cannot possibly be so. Charity to individual victims seems good but challenge to oppressive structures which create victims seems dangerous to the life of the Church. But Jesus himself insists that redemption from sin involves conflict and challenge. When he speaks of the baptism which he is to undergo, he refers to his own execution for the challenge he poses to the oppressive and sinful structures of his society. That he yearns for this can only mean that he has come to see that his death is the necessary outcome of the great conflict of values and expectations.

The passage from Jeremiah is clearly chosen because it offers a parallel. The fate of Jesus at the hands of the powerful of his time is not something so unique as to be quite different from the life story of any other courageous and outspoken person who judges what goes on by the word of God. It is a story that repeats itself around us all the time—in our own country at this time not as spectacularly as among those of Central America, for instance. But the story is universal. Many a Jeremiah is thrown into the pit of mud in our own times in the hope that such an inconvenient witness will simply disappear. But the message of Jeremiah's own story, like the gospel of the death and resurrection of Jesus, is not one of hopelessness. On the contrary, it is a message of redemptive grace and of the divine vindication of those who are faithful in their witness.

The reading from Hebrews speaks of a cloud of witnesses to faith, who form a kind of aura of encouragement around the central figure of Jesus. History has indeed offered us such witnesses of faith and hope and courage at all times. The contemplation of these witnesses offers unfailing encouragement, no matter how overwhelming the struggle against evil in the world may be. It is surely in this sense that Jesus intends to bring fire to the earth, and to wait again and again for it to be kindled in various situation and circumstances.

Twenty-first Sunday of the Year

READINGS: Is 66:18-21; Heb 12:5-7, 11-13; Lk 13:22-30.

From east and west people will come, from north and south, for the feast in the kingdom of God. Yes, and some who are now last will be first, and some who are first will be last. Lk 13:29-30.

All three readings today are concerned with our difficulty in understanding God's ways which always transcend what we are able to project or imagine. If the passage from Isaiah seems comfortably familiar and acceptable to us, that is because we have no difficulty with the proclamation that the Gentiles shall come into the inheritance of the Jews. We only have difficulties when we follow the principle further and realize that many are called to the Kingdom who are not members of our churches, who are not devout, who are not respectable. It is hard to take quite seriously the proposition that many who are now last in our own society and in our own esteem will be first, and that many who now are first in reputation and achievement will not fare so well.

Although Luke draws together into a single narrative and discourse sentences which are scattered utterances in Matthew's gospel, there is a clear design in this. Placing them in the context of the final journey to Jerusalem, Luke gathers together sayings of Jesus which challenge our too easy assumptions. How many are to be saved is not really our business to know in advance, but we must know that it is a struggle like going through a very narrow door. Familiarity with tradition and worship is no guarantee of admission to the Kingdom. Some will come from far away and will be more readily welcomed.

We know from other texts why this is. Salvation is by charity not by glib recitation of formulae nor even by assiduous performance of religious duties. Again and again we find to our amazement, and perhaps to our chagrin, that the more disreputable and irreligious among us are those who are moved more profoundly by charity. Moreover, such movements of charity are often so spontaneous that it does not occur to such non-religious people to credit themselves with any virtue on account of compassionate and hospitable actions. This realization does indeed suggest a reversal of first and last.

The excerpt from Hebrews deals with a different but related puzzlement among the devout. Why should good people suffer? Why does God allow persecution of the faithful? The analogies of family and athletic discipline suggest more intimate involvement in God's purpose. Yet we cannot always understand God's ways of inviting us to the Kingdom. Here also Christian tradition has expressed hope and trust in God by appealing to radical reversal for those who suffer innocently. The whole teaching of Jesus has led us to think in paradoxes about the invitation to the Kingdom.

Twenty-second Sunday of the Year

READINGS: Sir 3:17-18, 20, 28-29; Heb 12:18-19, 22-24; Lk 14:1, 7-14.

You stand before ... the full concourse and assembly of the first-born citizens of heaven, and God the judge of all, and the spirits of good men made perfect, and Jesus the mediator of a new covenant. Heb 12:22-24.

To remember where we stand, to be aware of the mystery that surrounds us is in itself a gift of grace. It means a clearer vision of reality, a steadier sense of purpose, a deeper and more humble sense of gratitude. The contrasts which the author of Hebrews draws are significant. Sinai provides the model for understanding our covenant relationship with God, but where Sinai suggests majestic distance, the Christian covenant mediated by Jesus suggests intimacy. Where Sinai suggests awe, the assembly in which Jesus mediates suggests confident hope.

In this context of remembering where we stand, the other two readings become far more persuasive. The Wisdom of Sirach points out that the approach to true wisdom is in a humble and unassuming attitude, not in pretentiousness. To study the commandments, to seek to live by the Law and guidance of God, to be first and foremost receptive to the divine self-revelation, is worthy of our calling to wisdom. Great subtleties and shows of erudition are more likely to impair judgment than to aid further progress towards the real goal. This is a message that is as fresh and pertinent today as it has ever been, for there is much temptation today to bury some very simple human and moral questions under a great avalanche of sophisticated technical argumentation until the real issues disappear.

This discourse of Jesus is also about modesty, but takes the matter one step further. To the guest at the banquet Jesus is also saying, in a sense, "remember where you stand, and in whose presence," and for Christian readers this bears reference to our position in the heavenly banquet. But to the host Jesus addresses the question: what is your motivation in entertaining? Is your hospitality a benefaction or a bargain? Do you extend hospitality to the poor and abandoned who need it, or to those who are useful to you? In our world today, in which so much dire human need comes daily to our attention, that is a hard question but a real one. It is a question that invites us in no uncertain terms to remember where we stand and before whom.

Twenty-third Sunday of the Year

READINGS: Wis 9:13-18; Phlm 9-10, 12-17; Lk 14:25-33.

None of you can be a disciple of mine without parting with all his possessions. Lk 14:33.

We are used to hearing some hard and radical sayings from Jesus as Luke's Gospel portrays him, but this saying goes further than others. The context seems to be important, for Jesus is speaking in response to a wave of immense popularity. It is almost as though it were the latest fashion to accompany Jesus on his preaching journeys. As Luke's Gospel portrays this period, people followed Jesus in crowds as in a long festivity.

It is in this context that Jesus is at pains to point out the cost of discipleship. Allowing for the extremes of contrast statements in Hebraic idiom, we hear Jesus saying that one must be prepared to renounce even one's immediate family or one's life if necessary in order to be a true disciple. One must be prepared to face criminal execution if necessary. One must stand ready to renounce everything. That is not the way we usually think about the Christian commitment in our own time, yet the message is clearly for us also, because for us also being Christian is more or less the acceptable thing to do in most of the circles in which we move. We are inclined to say that it cannot really be as difficult as is portrayed in this Gospel reading. But the two analogies Jesus offers are instructive. Someone who sets out to build must reckon the construction costs at the outset. Someone who goes forth to battle must realistically consider what forces will be required. The question is not how things look at the outset, but what will be necessary to meet the test situations, the critical moments, the difficult times.

It is well that this reading is preceded by one from the book of Wisdom which acknowledges human weakness and inadequacy but also acknowledges and affirms the willingness of God to share the divine wisdom and bestow the holy spirit which makes all things possible. The humble and realistic confidence of the author provides good matter for meditation.

The reading from the letter to Philemon gives an interesting example of the kind of renunciation called forth by the gospel. In spite of Paul's cautious way of putting it, the appeal really shows that ownership of others as slaves is incompatible with faith in Jesus. But we may not immediately realize that the way Paul puts it is a criticism of any use whatever of others simply as instruments to one's own purpose—whether they be domestic servants, migrant farm workers, populations of countries strategically important to us, or people in any relationship in which they are easily bullied. This reading gives some substance to the cost of discipleship as we meet it in everyday life in our own times and our own society. This is important because it is all too easy to see the difficult and heroic times of Christianity as far behind us, and our own times as a state of normalcy in which no great effort is required to be a Christian.

Twenty-fourth Sunday of the Year

READINGS: Ex 32:7-11, 13-14; I Tim 1:12-17; Lk 15:1-32.

There will be more joy in heaven over one sinner who repents than over ninety-nine righteous people who do not need to repent. Lk 15:7.

We live in a history not of righteousness but of redemption from sin and from the manifold consequences of sin that distort values, relationships and structures of society. The passage from Exodus stresses this in the prayer of Moses on behalf of the people of Israel. Moses, finding the people dancing about the Golden Calf, was shocked himself we are told, but when the idea of God's rejection of the chosen people occurs to him as a possible outcome of this event, he reacts vehemently against it, remembering in prayer that the whole character of the relationship was redemptive and that this should not change even after the incident of the Golden Calf.

The second reading calls attention to the pattern of Paul's apostolic vocation as one that follows this principle. Paul was a persecutor of the followers of Jesus who, instead of being cast off and left to his own devices, was urgently called to radical conversion and to an important mission to Gentile cities and the founding of churches. In all of this Paul is exemplary because God does not wish the death of the sinner but that person's radical conversion to personal holiness and apostolic involvement.

This is the thrust of the three parables which Luke groups into Chapter 15, and which are read in their entirety today. There is a very persuasive progression in the sequence. No one is likely to question the outlook of the shepherd of the hundred sheep who takes great risks to reclaim one lost sheep, and who cannot forbear to share his delight with his friends when he eventually finds it. In the same way there is little doubt that a housewife who loses one of ten silver coins will search frantically until she finds it, and will share the news with her neighbors with great enthusiasm and amid congratulations. It is when we come to the parable of the lost son that the meaning of it for our own dealings with God and with one another begins to become plain from the analogies that have led up to it. It is at this point that we might begin to sense some hesitation. The ways of the father in this story are not the ways of God as we have projected them onto God from our own ways of behaving, and the reaction of the older son is one that most of us can recognize all too easily. The insistence on merit and on our own measure of fairness, which discriminates always against the less fortunate and the less successful, is something that most of us do not give up easily. But everything on this Sunday tells us that God's ways are not our ways.

Twenty-fifth Sunday of the Year

READINGS: Amos 8:4-7; I Tim 2:1-8; Lk 16:1-13 (or Lk 16:10-13).

No servant can be the slave of two masters; for either he will hate the first and love the second, or he will be devoted to the first and think nothing of the second. You cannot serve God and money. Lk 16:13.

The Hebrew Scriptures are replete with warning against the seductive power of wealth. The sabbath is seen as a brake applied to the runaway pursuit of material accumulation. So are the sabbatical year and the jubilee year. Prophets, such as Amos in the passage read today, constantly proclaim the concern of God to vindicate the despoiled and oppressed who are the victims of others' accumulation of wealth. The prophets are keenly aware that accumulated wealth gives its owners a degree of coercive power over others not intended in the order of God's creation. It is not a question of making a living for one's family, but of accumulating enough to gain power to oppress others.

In the Gospel reading Jesus sums this up bluntly: a life in the service of money, of accumulation of wealth, simply cannot at the same time be a life in the service of God. Money is properly a means to an end, to be valued only in proportion to the end that is sought, and to be judged according to the degree to which the end sought is in keeping with the divine order of things. To provide adequately for one's family, for instance, is clearly good in the divine order; to provide them with luxury by driving others into destitution cannot be seen as good before God. To invest surplus to produce what is genuinely for the common good is necessary and praiseworthy, but investment for the highest profit without scrutiny of the human effect of the investment effectively puts money above God in the order of values.

Commentators of our own times have remained greatly puzzled by the parable that Jesus told in support of his saying about God and money. Perhaps the simplest interpretation is that the dishonest steward represents the single-mindedness of those whose concern is worldly advantage, compared with the compromises and vacillations of those whose concern is with the reign of God. Among the former, decisions are clear and appropriate. Among the latter, decisions are often reluctant and hedged about with reservations.

The passage from I Timothy is also concerned with single-mindedness in the service of God, and links faith in Jesus Christ with a concern for universal salvation—a concern incompatible with unjust profit at others' expense. This advice to Timothy is concerned with reshaping the awareness and sense of identity of the Christian worshippers. Before God they are called to express their inter-dependence, their common dependence on the hospitality of God, and their oneness in destiny. That call to realize our oneness in destiny is particularly apt in our own times on a worldwide basis, where it is often a choice between God and money.

Twenty-sixth Sunday of the Year

READINGS: Amos 6:1, 4-7; I Tim 6:11-16; Lk 16:19-31.

Pursue justice, piety, fidelity, love, fortitude, and gentleness. Run the great race of faith and take hold of eternal life. For to this you were called. I Tim 6:11-12.

This Sunday's readings pursue the same theme as last week's. It is a matter of our attitudes to people and to things, a question of the hierarchy of values that is really effective in our lives. More particularly, this Sunday's theme is that of reversal of roles in God's vindication of the oppressed. This theme in Scripture challenges our too easy customary assumption that material wealth and well-being can be taken, without qualification or further examination, as the sign of God's approval. It is true that Scripture elsewhere maintains that a good life brings God's blessing in practical and temporal ways, but that thesis cannot be simply reversed in the assumption that wealth is God's stamp of approval on a good life. This is a difficult truth to assimilate because the world flatters the rich and powerful.

The passage from Amos warns those who live in luxury, unconcerned with the sufferings and critical situation of the nation. They are not accused of specific injustices, only of a degree of self-interest and self-indulgence that is oblivious to the common danger and the distress of the society. It is a situation repeated in every generation including our own.

The parable of Jesus depicts this dramatically in the form of two individuals in sharply contrasting circumstances. The only misbehavior attributed to the rich man is his preoccupation with his own pleasure and wealth to such a degree that he appears to be quite unaware of the utter misery at his gate. The only thing told about Lazarus is his desperate plight; he is not presented as the deserving poor man, nor are we told that he is in any way particularly virtuous. When both die, and their fate is reversed, it is hard to avoid the conclusion that God vindicates the poor, the oppressed, the excluded of our human society without reference to any special virtue in them.

The excerpt from I Timothy follows on an exhortation to avoid the love of money as the root of all evil, and rather to place all one's hopes and desires in God, expecting the appearance of Jesus in triumph in our world. Such hope and expectation demands a commensurate life style, one that rewrites the story of the rich man and Lazarus, and one particularly called for in our own times and in our wealthy western society. Indeed, much of the Bible, both in the Hebrew Scriptures and in the New Testament, tries to change our ways of seeing rich and poor.

Twenty-seventh Sunday of the Year

READINGS: Hab 1:2-3, 2:2-4; 2 Tim 1:6-8, 13-14; Lk 17:5-10.

Keep before you an outline of the sound teaching which you have heard from me, living by the faith and love which are ours in Christ Jesus. 2 Tim 1:13.

The readings for this Sunday give us three texts which link faith, fidelity and security, ideas which are bound together by a common root in Hebrew. In the excerpt from Habakkuk, the prophet cries out in protest against God's tolerance of the violence and cruelty of the Chaldean conquerors of his time. In response to this perennial human complaint, God offers a vision that interprets the historical developments differently. God's own reckoning is coming, and in face of this the reckless will experience their insecurity while the righteous live by being faithful.

There is a suggestion here that in the eyes of God and to the eye of faith no situation is hopeless and nothing escapes the justice of God in the long term. The saying of Jesus about faith, which introduces today's Gospel reading, is concerned with this same conviction: there are no impossible tasks or situations with God. Faced with a challenge as ludicrous as the double impossibility of uprooting the deeprooted sycamore and planting it in the ocean, we should not underestimate God's power. The concern, of course, is not with forestry but with human situations which appear hopeless.

At first glance there seems to be little continuity of thought and meaning in the placing of the servant parable after the saying about faith. It is the inseparability of faith, fidelity and security that makes the continuity. If we have faith as it is understood in the Scriptures, we see our own relationship to God in a new light. There is no room for the conventional idea of religion—the prescribed and calculated service of worship which earns protection from the deity. Although the analogy of the slave is not one we find comfortable, it is apt. Slavery is a total commitment, so the notion of credit for overtime work does not arise. No matter how much work the slave does, he does not acquire a corresponding claim to a higher status. The slave is totally dependent on the good graces of her mistress or master.

Unflattering as the comparison may be, it carries a crucial message about our relationship to God. It is not a bargain or contract, and we do not earn our way to a better position by good works. It is a covenant whose initiative is entirely that of God—an alliance which calls us to total dedication so that there is no room for calculating merit or checking off overtime. No matter what we may do, it leaves us just as dependent upon God. The intent of Jesus, in telling the parable, seems to be to show that a life which is really lived by faith is a life of utmost fidelity and of deep-rooted security. It is a life of faithfulness in both senses that that word has in our language. It is also a life in which the power of God is at work explosively, realigning the whole landscape of human possibilities.

It is this understanding of our relationship with God which brings into harmony the conviction that all is grace with the conviction that the Christian life demands great effort and dedication. The excerpt from 2 Timothy expresses this harmony in the exhortation to stir into flame the gift of God that has been bestowed by the laying on of hands. The text insists that that gift is not a spirit of fear or diffident passivity, but a spirit of courage, energy and action. The reference to keeping the sound teaching before one's eyes offers a certain parallel to Habakkuk's vision which he was to share with his fellow citizens that they might see it clearly. The vision contained in the sound teaching is a vision that one needs to keep in view in order to live by the faith and love that are offered in Jesus Christ. The fidelity follows from the faith, and the security is discovered in the fidelity. We can begin to experience the invincible fidelity of God when it is reflected or echoed in our own fidelity.

These New Testament passages deepen the sense of the prophetic passage from Habakkuk. It is truly by faithfulness that we live—God's faithfulness first as the precondition, and our own faithfulness as the response that lets itself be carried on the wave of the divine initiative. It is because of our total dependence on God's grace that we can and should respond energetically and perseveringly in all circumstances. We live not only by faith as an inner attitude but also by faithfulness as its outward expression.

Twenty-eighth Sunday of the Year

READINGS: 2 Kgs 5:14-17; 2 Tim 2:8-13; Lk 17:11-19.

One of them, finding himself cured, turned back praising God aloud. He threw himself down at Jesus' feet and thanked him. And he was a Samaritan. Lk 17:15-16.

The story of Naaman the Syrian, cured of leprosy by bathing seven times in the Jordan at Elisha's bidding, is so familiar that the liturgy gives us only the end of the story. The story is deceptively simple, as is the one about the ten lepers cured by Jesus; there is depth of meaning in both stories, and there are allusions and further implications.

In both stories it is emphasized that it is a stranger, one outside the chosen and long-prepared people of God, who is deeply moved by the gratuitous cure and loudly, publicly thanks God. Yet Naaman was certainly not like this in the beginning of the story. He came with credentials and recommendations from his king, provided with an enormous fortune in coin (for the rich often think they can buy anything), and presented his credentials to Elisha surrounded by an extravagant retinue. Nor was Naaman pleased when the prophet, instead of coming out with equal pomp and ceremony to perform a solemn ritual of healing, sent out a messenger suggesting the ridiculously simple remedy of washing seven times in the Jordan river.

Yet the cure effected a change of heart. Naaman is not only thankful to God and to the prophet, but he is converted to the worship of Israel's God alone, turning away from idolatry. Luke's story about Jesus and the ten lepers seems to allude to this when it ends with the wonderment of Jesus that only the stranger, the Samaritan, returned to give thanks. In this story it is the healing brought by Jesus, not the long training in the Law according to the Mosaic covenant, that truly converts the leper to gratitude, humility and reverence before God. Ten were cured, but the other nine seem to have been too busy fulfilling the prescriptions of the Law to sense a residuary need to express gratitude to God and to Jesus through whose mediation the cure had been wrought.

As with many passages of the Scriptures, it is much too easy for us to read these as interesting stories about the past. If we place ourselves within the picture it is more likely to be as the Gentile outsiders whose attitude is praised, than as the self-satisfied insiders who tend to take salvation for granted and see little need to express intense gratitude. Yet the truth of the matter may be rather the reverse.

There was a persistent tendency in biblical times, as indeed sometimes since then, to see leprosy as punishment for sin. Therefore the stories about cures from leprosy always have overtones of redemption from sin and the consequence of sin. Those cures implied readmission to full participation in the life of the community, freedom of social intercourse, and the ritual purity required to participate in public worship. Without stretching the point too far, it may be pertinent to apply the story to our own attitudes towards our baptism into the Christian community, and even to our attitude to the reconciliation rituals of the Church. These seem often to be occasions of far greater gratitude to adult converts to the Church, than to those of us who have grown up and grown old in the community.

Between these two stories we are presented with a text from 2 Timothy which suggests that our gratitude for having been included in the mystery of the Resurrection should be such as to motivate great fidelity in the face of any kind of hardship. Paul's example of this is held before us. He values the gift of the great redemptive reconciliation in Christ so highly that he will endure anything for the sake of sharing that gift with others. The words, the promise, which Paul considers trustworthy are that dying with Christ means also living with him, suffering with Christ means also reigning with him, and that in the end in spite of our infidelities, Christ is utterly faithful because that is his nature and character.

There is in this message so often expressed by Paul in the New Testament, that same attitude of the overwhelming gratitude of the outsider who is left amazed at the utter gratuity of the gift of healing and restoration. Again and again, Paul tries to cajole or surprise us into that attitude of delighted and astonished gratitude. But the question remains whether in the practice of our lives we take our place with the insiders or with the grateful outsider among the ten lepers.

Twenty-ninth Sunday of the Year

READINGS: Ex 17:8-13; 2 Tim 3:14-4:2; Lk 18:1-8.

He spoke to them in a parable to show that they should keep on praying and never lose heart. Lk 18:1.

Some of the comparisons Jesus draws or suggests are startling, even shocking. If anyone else had dared to compare God with an unjust judge swayed ultimately by the nuisance value of the plaintiff, we should be inclined to consider it blasphemous and irresponsible. And yet, in times of persecution, disaster, oppression and widespread injustices in society, God may appear to the victims as just that—an unjust judge. While the violent and the greedy continue to enrich themselves, the poor suffer. The wickedness of the powerful against the powerless seems to go unchecked in the affairs of the world.

No one could have realized better than Jesus that it frequently looks as though God is asleep or simply does not care. Certainly the circumstances in which he himself lived and died could well have been interpreted in that way. The response that Jesus urges is to believe, trust and pray against all the appearance of divine indifference. But the question which the whole passage prompts is whether, when the Son of Man comes, he will indeed find that sort of faith among his followers.

The widow in the parable is of course, more than anyone else, Jesus himself. Yet he stresses that the only claim she has upon the judge is her powerlessness, her need, and the injustice that has been done to her. And this, Jesus suggests, is the claim that the elect, God's chosen, have against the all-powerful compassion of God, whether the elect be the people of Israel, or the friends of Jesus, or simply the powerless poor who enjoy God's predilection.

Certainly the parable is applicable to the story from Exodus which forms the first reading in the liturgical setting. The preceding sections of Exodus not only suggest that Israel's resources to fight the ebb. Entirely dependent for sustenance on the heavenly manna, barely calmed of their riotous panic by a miraculous flow of water to slake their thirst, they are attacked in their precarious existence by the forces of Amalek. Here it is in the first place Moses who is the poor widow of the parable. Sustained in his dramatic gesture of prayer hour after hour, through discouraging weariness and powerless exhaustion, by the support of Aaron and Hur, Moses is surely the one who pleads without ceasing, in the dogged faith that God will vindicate the elect.

The excerpt from 2 Timothy is also about patient perseverance in the confident expectation of final vindication. But it is concerned not so much with prayer as with perseverance in the way of life that has been shown to the followers of Jesus, and particularly with perseverance in the pastoral ministry that has been entrusted to Timothy. The context of the passage tells us that this advice also is given in the expectation of persecution of the "godly" while the wicked and the deceitful move unchecked from bad to worse. There is more than a suggestion here that the credibility of the Christian faith may be strained to the utmost, and that steadfastness in the Christian life and ministry will not come spontaneously. It will be necessary to seek wisdom and discernment in the Scriptures, and to take constant care to lead a disciplined life.

It is only in the confident expectation of the coming of Jesus in judgment and in victory, that the courage and perseverance can be found to continue the ministry of the gospel in season and out of season by every means available. So the text proclaims, and so it has in fact been, then and ever since the apostolic foundations. But the implication of this passage is not only that great confidence in God is required, but also that the life and ministry of the gospel requires great confidence in the possibility of human conversion. It is clear here that the expected vindication is not so much the punishment of the ungodly, as the conversion even of the most unlikely, even under the least promising circumstances. The attitude of ceaseless pleading in the face of seeming indifference is appropriate not only in prayer when God does not appear to answer, but also in action for faith and justice in a world that does not seem to respond.

Reflection on all three readings suggests that the shocking comparison of the parable of Jesus penetrates to the core of our own situation as Christians in the world of our own times, with its unchecked cruelties and oppressions, its heedlessness of the threat of total global annihilation, its increasing gap between rich and poor, its money-hungry compromises with poisons, addictive drugs and disease. Ours is a time for the poor widow to plead in the face of a seemingly hostile silence in the indomitable hope that God will still vindicate.

Thirtieth Sunday of the Year

READINGS: Sir 35:12-14, 16-18; 2 Tim 4:6-8, 16-18; Lk 18:9-14.

Do not offer him a bribe, for he will not accept it . . . for the Lord, is a judge who knows no partiality. He has no favorites at the poor man's expense, but listens to his prayer when he is wronged. The prayer of the humble pierces the clouds. Sir 35:12, 13, 17.

It is truly a remarkable admonition which bids us remember that God cannot be bribed. It implies that we might be tempted to try it, and it begs the question as to how one might set about bribing God. The reading from Sirach refers to dishonest sacrifices, and implies that it is a certain easy self-righteousness, combined with social and personal injustices, which makes worship dishonest. It is the prayer of the humble which pierces the clouds to reach God's throne, but in this context the humble are simply those of humble station. No particular virtue is attributed to them; they are defined by their powerlessness and their desperate persistence in pleading for justice. We are assured that God sees justice done in the end, and the text assumes that that will usually mean the vindication of the poor and powerless.

In the Gospel reading we meet the same theme in a story form. Following last Sunday's reading, which counseled perseverance in prayer with the image of the poor widow before the reluctant judge, today's parable is concerned with the character of those who pray. We are presented with a Pharisee and a publican—an intensely devout person and a disreputable one. The parable of Jesus is intended to turn our habitual expectations upside-down, to challenge our easy assumptions. The effect is usually lost, however, because we persist in thinking of the Pharisee as basically an evil person, an enemy of Christ, a consistent hypocrite. Our long-standing anti-Semitic prejudices prevent our understanding of the parable which Jesus told. The Pharisees were not more hypocritical than other people; they were simply much, much more devout in their religious observances. According to our customary values and expectations, therefore, we might suppose the prayer of such persons to have swift access to the ear of God, compared with those whose attitude to religious rules is casual or ambivalent.

But it is at this point that the question of bribing God recurs. Is God to give us a preferential hearing because we are the devout, because we have paid for the divine favor with abundant devotional practices? Is God to favor us against the poor nations of the world and against the Communist countries because these are pagan or atheist in their leadership? Is God to attend more to the church-goers than the homeless? To be more concerned for those in seminaries than those in jails? For those at the Sunday morning coffee hour in the church hall than for the starving?

The answer of Jesus reaffirms the answer of Sirach: God is a just judge who does not favor the privileged but rights the wrongs of the poor and the oppressed. God responds to our need; we do not merit God's favor by our piety. Our piety is worthless, dishonest, just like a bribe in a court of law, if it is a substitute for efforts to bring about justice and community in a world full of injustices and exclusions. Rightly understood, this parable of Jesus is rather shocking. There are times and circumstances when it might be summarized; why trouble to attend church; of what use is it until the realities of the world are being dealt with according to God's will? And the answer is: it is only useful if we know that we are there as the publican, the ambivalently and marginally committed, not as the devout.

It may be something of a relief to turn from these reflections to the reading from 2 Timothy which presents Paul's last farewell. We see Paul, perhaps as depicted by another hand, placing the consummation and judgment of his life and work confidently into the scrutiny of the all-just judge. Paul does not always appear as humble, according to our expectations, in his verbal expression, but there can be no doubt that he is at this time one of humble estate, a powerless prisoner facing the death sentence. Indeed, he has been powerless in a worldly sense ever since his conversion to Christ. He stands in the tradition of the poor who expect the vindication of the true justice of God. Almost in spite of himself his cry is the prayer of the humble.

These readings confront us with a dire warning but also with a far reaching promise. God hears the prayer of the humble, that is of the powerless.

Thirty-first Sunday of the Year

READINGS: Wis 11:22-12:2; 2 Thess 1:11-2:2; Lk 19:1-10.

In thy sight the whole world is like a grain that just tips the scale or a drop of dew alighting on the ground at dawn . . . all existing things are dear to thee and thou hatest nothing that thou has created—why else wouldst thou have made it? Wis 11:22, 24.

The theme of this Sunday's reading seems to be that nothing is too insignificant to be precious to God. The text from Wisdom emphasizes the sheer power and grandeur of God, and sees all creation as dwarfed by it. On the other hand the writer is deeply convinced that God creates all things out of love and rejects none of them. That is why God looks patiently to the conversion of the sinner and not to destruction. The theme is constant in Scripture but here it has a certain serenity and inevitability to it.

The second reading shares that same serenity about the fulfillment of God's purpose in the unfolding of the plan of redemption for the Thessalonians. The author prays that they may continue their

Christian life and calling without being alarmed by any talk of sudden and catastrophic divine interventions. The author inclines heavily against the expectation of anything spectacular or extraordinary. Quiet hope and perseverance in the way of Jesus seems to be more appropriate in the lives of Christian communities.

Bringing to a climax the theme of God's concern for the apparently insignificant, and God's patience in seeking the conversion of the sinner, is the story of Zachaeus, the small man, the tax collector, the disreputable in religious circles of his time and society. The story is so simple that it can all too easily slip by us. Zachaeus was the kind of person whom the devout avoided because his class of people (the tax collectors) had the reputation of being "shady" in their dealings and breaking the Law of Moses. Seeing his efforts to catch a glimpse, Jesus calls to him and asks for hospitality, as though he were quite unaware of what the devout would think about it. But the action of Jesus is not casual; it exactly expresses the attitude of God as envisaged in the other two readings. Jesus sees his task as bringing salvation wherever it is needed and is welcome.

The serenity of these readings about the continuing project of the redemption of the world seems a very good point for reflection and remembrance in a world where so much seems desperate or insoluble.

Thirty-second Sunday of the Year

READINGS: 2 Macc 7:1-2, 9-14; 2 Thess 2:16-3:5;
Lk 20:27-38.

May our Lord Jesus Christ himself and God our Father, who has shown us such love, and in his grace has given us such unfailing encouragement and such bright hopes, still encourage and fortify you in every good deed and word. 2 Thess 2:16-17.

In these words the Thessalonians are being exhorted to be steadfast in their hope and in the action appropriate to that hope. And yet the content of main point is that the Lord is to be trusted at all times and in all circumstances, but what is to be the outcome of that trust is not nearly so clear.

That, no doubt, is why the language of resurrection came to be current in the several centuries immediately before the time of Jesus and the apostolic generation. Just how things would be set right for those who suffered cruelly under the persecution of the conquerors, no one would really see. But that God was not less faithful than those who put their trust in the divine promise was a matter of faith that was basic to the whole tradition. God would indeed vindicate all who suffered for their fidelity, but that vindication was evidently beyond contemporary power to observe. So the language of resurrection arose as a poetic way of expressing absolute confidence in God.

The story about the terrible tortures of the Maccabean brothers is probably a literary device, though actual persecution of real people was going on and was full of physical cruelties. But the point of the story in this case was to assert the power and will of God to redeem even from the jaws of death. In the Gospel text of the day, Jesus defends the language and doctrine of resurrection but warns against interpreting it too literally. His explanation is that there is a break-through to a quite radically new kind of existence.

We know that this desire to have an exact definition, or even an exact description, of the resurrected life haunted some Christian communities from the beginning and crops up among us from time to time. Yet it is in the very nature of death that we cannot see beyond it. It is the nature of death that it demands a complete surrender into the hands of God—a complete letting-go of control over our own destiny. It is precisely this which makes it possible to enter definitively into salvation by radical acceptance of the Reign of God without any of those compromises which we can maintain through the course of our lives without even being aware of it. Hope in the resurrection is a way of expressing ultimate trust in God.

Thirty-third Sunday of the Year

READINGS: Mal 3:19-20; 2 Thess 3:7-12; Lk 21:5-19.

*The day comes, glowing like a furnace; all the arrogant and the evil-doers
shall be chaff, and that day when it comes shall set them ablaze, says the
Lord of Hosts, it shall leave them neither root nor branch. But for you who
fear my name, the sun of righteousness shall rise with healing in his wings.*
                                                                 Mal 3:19-20.

That "day" of the great revelation and vindication that is to come
is a frequent theme in the Scriptures. The Hebrew prophets picture
the coming "day of the Lord" in vivid cosmic imagery. It is a day of
clouds and fire, recalling that past wonderful intervention of God in
which the divine presence went before Israel as a pillar of cloud by
day and a pillar of fire by night. It is a time of upheaval in the heavens
when the earth trembles. People are terrified, but it is a time of
purification and the preparation for the end; God is doing battle for
the chosen people, and all who have placed their faith in God can be
full of confidence in the midst of apparent confusion and disaster,
because God has not lost control of the world, but is guiding all of
history to its fulfillment. There is a certain ambiguity in the
prophetic texts that deal with the day of the Lord, for sometimes
they refer to a particular deliverance within history and at other
times they refer to the final deliverance or resolution of history.

In the New Testament the day of the Lord, which is the moment
of God's judging and saving intervention, becomes also the day of
Jesus Christ. Again there is an ambiguity, because the term "day of
the Lord" refers to the final vindication *of* Jesus by God and also to
the vindication of the faithful *by* Jesus. It is presented as a moment of
revelation and therefore also as a time of judgment and of the end of
oppression and injustice. This day of the Lord Jesus in the New
Testament pictures Jesus transfigured, manifest in his true splendor
and power, coming as a judge, suddenly and swiftly, or as a
triumphant warrior completing his victory to the accompaniment of
cosmic portents and wonders. But all this is generally envisaged as
concluding a period of heightened sufferings, persecutions and

disasters making a kind of final paroxysm of the world's struggle in the grip of evil.

The Scriptures make it clear that these images are not proposed as idle entertainment. They express the exigence which the coming day of the Lord places on our present historical situation. The texts have a meaning for our present which is quite practical and concrete in its implications. The way we live our lives now, and the dispositions we make of our society and its resources and opportunities in the economic and political spheres, have clear consequences for the unfolding of the events that make up the day of the Lord both within history and in the resolution of history. By seeing the world and its affairs in the light of God's judgment, that is in the light of Jesus Christ as the criterion by which everything in our affairs both public and private is to be evaluated, we are invited to reconsider our attitudes and expectations.

The first reading, from the prophecy of Malachi, declares in images of fire and sunshine that there is no escape from the coming judgment of God. But what is destruction for the evil and the arrogant is at the same time comfort and healing for those whose trust is in God. The Gospel reading takes up the same theme at considerably more length. Because it speaks not only in cosmic imagery but also in sketches of social and political situations, there is a certain recurring temptation for devout Christians to try to decipher those sketches as references to specific political events of our time. There is a temptation, for instance, to try to predict the "end of the world" by identifying references to certain political events. But this is not the intent of the passage. If the evangelist had specific events in mind at all, they were related to the siege and fall of Jerusalem and to the persecution of the early Christians. They were not intended as predictions of events in later history.

Yet there is a sense in which comments about conflicts and persecutions do refer to our own times. All such events at any time in history are to be seen as part of the great struggle against evil in the world, and as such are the prelude to the definitive judgment of God that is represented by the "day of the Lord." This suggests an attitude that is spelled out in the reading from 2 Thessalonians. Christians should live useful lives that are helpful to others, earning their living in constructive ways, building up a good society and helping to maintain order and peace and justice for all. That is what is meant by living in expectation of the final judgment of God over history. Idle, irresponsible and uncommitted behavior motivated by speculations about the nearness of the end-time is not at all appropriate to Christians. A way of life which does not accept responsibility for the long-term structures and policies of the society, on the pretext of spiritual preoccupations or other-worldly interests is soberly condemned in this scripture reading.

The message of this Sunday at the end of the Church's year is that we must live our lives in full realization that the day of the Lord is coming.

The Last Sunday of the Year: The Feast of Christ the King

READINGS: 2 Sam 5:1-3; Col 1:11-20; Lk 23:35-43.

He rescued us from the domain of darkness and brought us away into the kingdom of his dear Son, in whom our release is secured and our sins forgiven. He is the image of the invisible God; his is the primacy over all created things. Col 1:13-15.

The liturgy of this day is rather ruthless in confronting us with the character of Christ's Kingship. Both the New Testament passages link celebration of the Kingship of Christ directly to his death by crucifixion. However, the first reading also throws a special light upon it. According to this passage from 2 Samuel, David enters into a covenant of kingship with the people of Israel in the presence of God. It is a kingship modeled on God's own relationship to the people as their "shepherd." It is, therefore, a ministry to their needs. But there is one more aspect of this brief passage which is important: David has already been anointed King of Judah, so that his anointing as King of the separated northern Kingdom of Israel effects a reconciliation in his person between the two halves of God's people.

The passage from Colossians also speaks of a reconciliation. It is here a reconciliation in the person of Jesus between God and the human community, not (as elsewhere in the Pauline letters) between Jew and Gentile. Yet the hymn which is quoted does link the kingship and primacy of Jesus through his reconciling death with his role in the plan of creation in which all things are integrated or held together by their relationship to him. As image of the invisible God and first born of the dead, he has the fullness of divinity dwelling in him. That is to say that in him are now reflected all the divine attributes which are otherwise reflected only severally and in scattered fashion in various spiritual beings. As seen in the Pauline literature, the whole universe suffers from its estrangement from God and from its consequent disintegration, until in his death and resurrection Christ draws it all back into proper focus. It is this which constitutes the kingship of Jesus, exercised more intimately in his body the church, but also universally in creation.

The Lukan passage, full of allusions to Psalms 22 and 69, presents the kingship in a contrast between mockery and deep reverence. Psalm 22 has the just one surrounded by those who mock him in his distress, but the lament ends in a confident expectation that God will come to the rescue. Psalm 69 speaks of similar ridicule and persecution and again insists that God vindicates the chosen faithful. Given these allusions, the scene in Luke seems to be a kind of debate whether Jesus is indeed the chosen, the messiah, the anointed King of Israel. The argument on the side of those who mock is that one who cannot even save himself from an ignominious and terrible death is scarcely to be respected as a savior-king for others. The argument on the other side, in the mouth of the second criminal, seems to rest on nothing more than the sheer innocence of Jesus, but expresses confidence in his coming into his royal power (possibly in a far-off resurrection.) The evangelist ends the exchange with the promise of Jesus that the other is to enter Paradise immediately in company with Jesus. That sentence says more than at first appears to modern readers and listeners. A non-biblical tradition had it that the priestly messiah would open the sealed gates of the enclosed garden which was God's promise to the faithful. This paradise or enclosed garden was a complement to the garden of Eden, to be found at the end of the redemptive history.

This argument is really not so different from the one that goes on constantly in our own times and continues throughout history. On the one hand are those who mock, discreetly or blatantly, pointing out that the crucified is hardly a key to the conduct of affairs in the "real world," though quite nice as an object of private devotion—a king of hymnody and Sunday ceremonies rather than a king of those affairs that really shape people's lives in everyday terms of food, dignity, freedom and peace. On the other hand there are those who are convinced that because of his innocent death Jesus comes into the royal power to open the gates of the walled garden, and that this happens not in some remote future but now, not in some ethereal realm of the pious imagination but in the solid substance of human affairs at every level of complexity and risk. That is the kingship of Christ, and it is a different kind of kingship a different mode of government from that to which we are accustomed. It is the messianic rule of a savior-king who truly has the power to change oppressive structures.